THE PERSIAN CARPET

A TEHRĀN CARPET IN AN INTERESTING DESIGN WOVEN *c.* 1930

Frontispiece

THE
PERSIAN CARPET

A SURVEY OF THE CARPET-WEAVING INDUSTRY OF PERSIA

BY

A. CECIL EDWARDS

DUCKWORTH

First published 1953
Reprinted 1960, 1967, 1975

All rights reserved

Printed in Great Britain

FOREWORD

It is a practice among writers of technical books to present their credentials early to their readers. This may be accomplished by printing on the title page, after the author's name, a series of letters; or a list of learned societies—foreign or domestic—which may have conferred upon him the honour of membership. The writer of these pages is unable, unhappily, to avail himself of either technique. His qualifications—such as they are—were acquired in the hard, but lively, school of trade. For nearly fifty years he was engaged in the Persian carpet business; and of those years thirteen were spent in Persia. His work during that period required him to visit, at frequent intervals, every weaving centre of importance in the country.

At the end of 1947 he retired from business. He then resolved to occupy his leisure with a task which had long been in his mind: to produce a survey of the admirable carpet industry of Persia.

Many books have been written, in many languages, about Persian carpets; but with few exceptions their authors have written of the past achievements of the weaver's craft rather than of its present activities. Furthermore, writers have been, for the most part, unfamiliar with the vast land where these carpets are woven; with the language and the way of life of the ingenious people who produce them; and especially with the craft itself—so skilled, so curious and so varied. Assumption, therefore, has too often served for research; and errors have been repeated, with melancholy persistence, in successive works.

The volume which I envisaged would be a record —as full and as accurate as I could make it—of the weaving industry as it exists today. It should contain—in addition to a detailed survey of the weaver's craft—maps of the weaving areas, photographs of the localities where the carpets are made and of the processes employed in making them. Above all, it should include a collection of Persian carpet and rug designs. Clearly, such a record could only be produced in Persia itself; for at every moment questions of fact would arise—as the location of a weaving village, the habitat of a tribe, the origin of a pattern, the source and usage of a dyestuff—which could only be determined by enquiry on the spot. And only in Persia could the maps be prepared, the photographs taken and the designs collected. I resolved, therefore, to return once more to Persia and to spend another year there, visiting again those remote, exotic but friendly towns and villages where Persian carpets are produced; and recording, day by day, my observations of the weaver's craft.

Thus, in April 1948, my wife and I set out once more for Persia. We had previously arranged for a station wagon to be shipped for us to Khurramshar, at the head of the Persian Gulf, where we planned to enter the country. There began a pilgrimage which was to last nearly a year and cover 8,500 miles.

Let me say, before proceeding further, that throughout this book I propose to use the older words "Persia" and "Persian", rather than "Irān" and "Iranian"—the more recent usage. I trust my Persian friends will not be displeased that I have chosen the more venerable forms. I have done so because to me, at least, the word "Iranian"—particularly when applied to the products of the weaver's art—does not suggest the antiquity, the elegance or the renown which the word "Persian" awakens in my mind.

May I also explain the sense in which the words "carpet" and "rug" have been used; because these words do not mean quite the same thing on both sides of the Atlantic. In Britain, the distinction between them is a matter of size: a rug is a textile floor-covering which measures from about 10 to 40 square feet. If it measures more than that, it has reached (in Britain) the status of a carpet. In America, on the other hand, the distinction is a matter not of size but of unity: if the floor-covering is in a single piece it is a rug, no matter what it measures. A carpet, on the other hand, in the American idiom, is a textile floor-covering woven in a strip—either plain or in a repeating pattern—which is cut into lengths, matched and sewn together. Hence, in the American sense, no carpet could ever have come out of Persia.

Between the American and the English usage a choice had to be made. For no other reason than that I happened to have been born a subject of Queen Victoria, I chose the English.

In the spelling of Persian place-names I have followed, wherever possible, the recommendations of *The List of Names in Persia*, issued by the

Permanent Committee of Geographical Names of the Royal Geographical Society. When a place-name does not appear on their lists, I have used a transliteration of my own.

During the reign of Shah Riza Pahlavi Persia was divided, for administrative purposes, into ten "Ustans" or provinces, which were known only by numbers. The system is artificial and is hardly likely to endure. I have therefore retained the older and more familiar divisions.

Writers on technical subjects are generally expected to present a bibliography. I have refrained from doing so. Firstly, because there are so few works on Persian carpets which can with honesty be recommended; and secondly, because two useful bibliographies already exist: (1) *A Short Bibliography for the Student of Oriental and Western Hand-Knotted Rugs and Carpets*, by Rudolf M. Riefstahl (New York University Bookstore); and (2) A bibliography by Kurt Erdmann in the introductory chapters of *Old Oriental Carpets*, vol. II, mentioned below.

The surest guides to the great period carpets of Persia are: (1) *Old Oriental Carpets*, 2 vols., translated by A. F. Kendrick, Vienna, 1926–8. The first volume contains reproductions, mostly in colour, of the carpets in the Austrian National Museum; the second of carpets from other museums and collections. Scholarly monographs by Friedrich Sarre and Herman Trenckwald were specially written for this, the latest edition of the "Vienna Book". The introductory material of the earlier editions of 1892 and 1908 is of little value.

(2) The six chapters devoted to carpets (with the sumptuous plates which accompany them) in the *Survey of Persian Art*. Although I have ventured to disagree with Mr. A. Upham Pope on some of his assumptions, I am deeply in his debt. No one who is interested in the subject can fail to be illumined by his knowledge, or stimulated by his industry and enthusiasm. His chapters, however, are mainly concerned with the past of carpet weaving; whereas the subject of this survey is the Persian carpet of today.

The reader will find—if he adventures far enough into this book—that a considerable number of pages have been allotted to the history and topography of each important weaving centre. These digressions may, I fear, be regarded as foreign to the subject. I can only say, in defence, that the Persian carpet is a peculiarly localised product; that each piece is unique in itself and is created in a particular town or village, or by a particular nomadic tribe. A person who possesses such a piece, and is sufficiently interested in the weaver's craft to read about it, may perhaps wish to learn something of the history and topography of the remote locality where his carpet was made.

The reader may further object that in a book which purports to be a serious survey of the carpet industry of Persia, a number of trivial tales or sketches have been included—under the sometimes misleading designation of "Conversation Pieces". I confess that I find such inconsequential behaviour difficult to defend. I can only vaguely indite the words "background" and "atmosphere"; and add that perhaps the reader may benefit from a few moments of relief from the perusal of so many cheerless pages on the technique of carpet weaving. In any case, the sections of the book which treat of these irrelevant matters are clearly indicated, and the critical reader may, if he chooses, omit them.

It has been my misfortune to carry out this survey of the Persian carpet industry at a time when design and colour, craftsmanship and output were at their lowest level for nearly a generation. Having watched the development of the industry during the best part of a lifetime, it would have been a happy task to praise its present state; instead of which I have too often been compelled to assume the thankless rôle of monitor and critic. The student of Persian affairs, however, cannot fail to be impressed by the persistence and resilience of the Persian peoples; and I, for one, refuse to believe that an industry which for many generations has been a part of them, is now on the way to permanent decline.

I cannot mention by name the scores of persons whose kindness and hospitality added so much to the ease and pleasure of our journey. Nor can I hope to do justice to all those whose counsel was invaluable to me in the preparation of this survey—especially to those colleagues and other friends who helped me to assemble the collection of Persian carpet designs. Whatever value this book may possess lies there. If few names are mentioned, the many are not out of mind:

John and Irene Campbell, and Nasrollah Mustaufi of Ahwāz; A. Homayoun, Golam Reza Sarafraz, Robert P. Simmons and Mary Zoeckler of Hamadān; Prince Malak Mansūr Kajar of Shirishabād (Hamadān); Abdul Ali Sanandaji of Senneh; Hallil Zīaī of Bijār; Abdol Hosain Zardūsht of Arāk; Abdol Hosain Fershji of Malayer; Livingstone and Florence Bentley and Barur Harutiunian of Tabrīz; Morteza

Kazvini and M. Karimi of Tehrān; Joseph and Bernice Cockran, Nizami Shahidi, A. Marandi, and A. N. Shakiba of Meshed; Mohammed Riza Seperi of Birjānd; A. Rahmani of Tabas; J. Timoyannakis and Mūstafa Kemāl of Kermān; G. Gulbenkian of Shirāz; and the late Sayyid Hosain Tabatabai of Kashān.

I am particularly beholden to my friend Professor V. Minorsky—whose authority on the history and topography of Persia is unrivalled. Whenever I needed counsel and assistance on some historical, topographical, tribal or linguistic question, he gave it to me—out of his vast store of learning—with open hands. I have on many occasions referred to his valuable contributions to the Encyclopædia of Islam.

Above all, my thanks are due to Bryan Huffner who accompanied us on our long journey and who combined in his cheerful and efficient person the offices of secretary, photographer, chauffeur—and friend.

A friend of mine recently translated a book from the Dutch and sent me a copy. It was a treatise on the Classification of Archives—a subject on which I do not possess, and never expect to possess, any opinions. But I was enchanted with the opening phrases. I read: "This is a meticulous and tiresome book; the reader has been warned."

A. CECIL EDWARDS

It has been a matter of great regret that the author, though he corrected the text proofs, did not live to see publication of the volume on which he had lavished so much loving care; and the publishers acknowledge with thanks the help given by Mr. Bryan Huffner of O.C.M. (London) Ltd., in seeing the book through the press.

A DETAIL FROM THE SIXTEENTH/SEVENTEENTH CENTURY
ROSE-GROUND CARPET ILLUSTRATED ON PAGE 16.

CONTENTS

CHAPTER		PAGE
	Foreword	v
I.	Retrospect	1
II.	Carpets of the Great Period	7
III.	The Weaver's Craft	22
IV.	The Craft of the Dyer	29
V.	Some Notes on Design	35
VI.	Tabrīz; the Herīz Weaving Area; and the so-called Zenjān Rugs	52
VII.	Hamadān and its Environs; with a Note on Malayer	87
VIII.	The Kurdish Weaves: Senneh, Bijār and the Kurdish Tribal Rugs	119
IX.	Arāk (Sultānabād) and its Environs; with a Note on Seraband	135
X.	The Turkoman Rugs of the Persian Steppe	155
XI.	Meshed, the Qaināt and Turshīz (Kashmar)	160
XII.	The Balūchi Tribal Rugs of Khŭrasān	185
XIII.	Kermān and its Environs; the Afshāri Rugs; and a Note on Yezd	197
XIV.	The Tribal and Village Rugs of Fārs	281
XV.	Isfahān and the so-called Bakhtiari Weaves; Jōshaqān; and a Note on Naīn	303
XVI.	Kashān and Qūm	333
XVII.	The Future of the Industry	362
	Appendix I: A Chronology of the Persian Carpet	369
	Appendix II: Carpet Exports from Persia	373
	Appendix III: Persian Measures and their Equivalents	374
	Index of Places, Tribes and Persons	375
	General Index	381

COLOUR PLATES

I. Tehrān Carpet, c. 1930 — *Frontispiece*

II. Modern Tabrīz Carpet — *facing page* 52

III. Meshed Carpet, c. 1910 — 160

IV. Isfahān Carpet, c. 1920 — 308

MAPS

I. The Weaving Areas of Persia — *page* 6

II. The Herīz Weaving Area — 62

III. The Hamadān Weaving Area — 90

IV. The Arāk Weaving Area — 138

V. The Turkoman Weaving Area — 158

VI. Eastern Persia — 165

VII. The Kermān Weaving Area — 209

VIII. Summer Quarters of the Principal Weaving Tribes of Fārs — 291

IX. The Chahār Mahāl Weaving Area — 309

LIST OF ILLUSTRATIONS

	PAGE
1. The Ardebil Carpet	9
2. Hunting Carpet	12
3. The Chelsea Carpet	14
4. All-over Animal and Floral Carpet	15
5. Rose-ground Vase Carpet	16
6. Medallion, Animal and Floral Carpet	19
7. Inscribed Medallion Carpet	20
8. Medallion, Animal and Tree Carpet	21
9. Horizontal-type Loom	22
10. Tabrīz-type Loom	23
11. Roller-beam-type Loom	24
12. Hook used by Tabrīz Weavers	24
13. Comb-beaters, old and later type	25
14. The two basic types of Knot	26
15. Preparing the Warp, Arāk	28
16. Dye-house, near Kermān	29
17. The Herātī Design (Type 1)	37
18. The Herātī Design (Type 2)	37
19. The Herātī Design (Rectilinear)	37
20. The Boteh Miri Pattern	38
21. The Leaf Pattern: various forms	39
22. The Leaf Pattern: various forms	40
23. Fifteenth-century Book-cover Design (outline drawing)	41
24. Fifteenth-century Book-cover Design (outline drawing)	41
25. Detail of Antique Carpet from the Qaināt in the Mina Khanī Design	42
26. Shah Abbasī Motives	43
27. Shah Abbasī Motives	44
28. Shah Abbasī Motives	45
29. Shah Abbasī Motives	46
30. Shah Abbasī Motives	47
31. Classic Motive	48
32. Bid Majnūn Design: weeping willow pattern	48
33. Saūjbulāgh Kellegi in the Crab Design	49
34. Gol Henaī Pattern	50
35. Tabrīz Carpet in Jōshaqānī Design	50
36. View of Tabrīz	54
37. Caravanserai, Tabrīz	55
38. Arrangement of Pieces in the Home	56
39. Interior of Tabrīz Carpet Factory	59
40. Karaja Village, Herīz area	63
41. Medallion and Corner, Tabrīz Design	64
42. Herīz interpretation of above design	64
43. Pattern from the Herīz area	65

	PAGE
44. The same Pattern reproduced as a Herīz Weaver would interpret it	65
45. Bakshaīsh Village, Herīz area	66
46. Herīz Weaving Instruments	66
47. Group of Villagers, Herīz area	66
48. Tabrīz Carpet of unusual design (c. 1910)	68
49. Tabrīz interpretation of the sixteenth-century Vase Design (c. 1913)	69
50. Tabrīz Carpet Design (c. 1923)	70
51. Detail of Tabrīz Carpet (c. 1935)	70
52. Design for Tabrīz Carpet (c. 1945)	71
53. Tabrīz Carpet (c. 1930)	71
54. Tabrīz Carpet (c. 1930)	72
55. Tabrīz Carpet (c. 1930)	73
56. Bazaar Tabrīz Carpet (c. 1935)	74
57. Bazaar Tabrīz Carpet (c. 1935)	75
58. Tabrīz Carpet (c. 1935)	76
59. Medallion Design for Tabrīz Carpet (c. 1940)	77
60. Design for Tabrīz Carpet, classic design (c. 1945)	78
61. Design for Hunting Carpet	79
62. Tabrīz Carpet, designed by Ibrahim Rizai (c. 1945)	80
63. Tabrīz Carpet, designed by Ibrahim Rizai (c. 1945)	81
64. Tabrīz Carpet, designed by Ibrahim Rizai (c. 1945)	82
65. Tabrīz Hunting Carpet (c. 1930)	83
66. Karajā Rug (c. 1946)	84
67. Sarāb Runners (c. 1935)	84
68. Typical Carpets of Herīz area	85
69. Herīz Village Carpet (c. 1925)	86
70. Hamadān and the Alvānd range	88
71. The Gombad-i-Alivian, Hamadān	89
72. A Beauty shows her face, Hamadān	97
73. Sorting Colours from White Wool, Hamadān	97
74. Washing Carpets, Hamadān	98
75. Weaver's Cottage, Nenej Village, Malayer	100
76. "Mian Farsh"—Bubukabād (c. 1910)	101
77. Tafrish Rug, Zil-i-Soltan Design	101
78. Bozchelū Rug (c. 1940)	102
79. Bozchelū Rug (c. 1940)	102
80. Tuisarkhān Rug (c. 1940)	103
81. Bergendeh Rug, Tuisarkhān district (c. 1940)	103

	PAGE		PAGE
82. Rug from Gombād Village (c. 1945)	104	122. Bijār Carpet (c. 1890)	129
83. Mehribān Rug, showing Kurdish influence (c. 1945)	104	123. Early Bijār Rug	129
84. Mehribān Rug, showing Kurdish influence (c. 1945)	104	124. Bijār Carpet in Anchor Design (c. 1930)	130
85. Jechaneh Rug, Tuisarkhān district (c. 1940)	105	125. Tekentepeh Rug in Bid Majnūn Design (c. 1935)	131
86. Tuisarkhān Rug (c. 1940)	105	126. Detail of Carpet from Helvai Village (c. 1935)	131
87. Joraghān Rug with Bird Motive (c. 1940)	105	127. Senjabi (Kurdish) Rug (c. 1935)	132
88. Tuisarkhān Rug (c. 1940)	106	128. Qulyahi (Kurdish) Rug (c. 1925)	132
89. Detail of Strip from Sard Rūd (c. 1936)	106	129. Shirishabād (Kurdish) Rug (c. 1940)	133
90. Kerdār Rug from Zarānd district (c. 1935)	107	130. Qulyahi Rug (c. 1940)	133
91. Zarānd Rug from Shrine Collection, Meshed (c. 1920)	107	131. Shirishabād Rug in Anchor Design (c. 1940)	134
92. Khamseh District Rug (c. 1945)	108	132. Street in Arāk (Sultānabād)	135
93. Kalajūk Rug (c. 1940)	108	133. Weavers' Instruments, Arāk Village	137
94. Khamseh District Rug (c. 1940)	109	134. Spring in an Arāk Village	138
95. Khamseh District Rug (c. 1945)	109	135. Weaving a Sarūk Carpet	140
96. Bahār Rug (c. 1945)	110	136. Lilihān	143
97. Rug from Shrine Collection, Meshed (c. 1925)	110	137. Early Repeating Design by Ziegler & Co. (c. 1885)	146
98. "Mian Farsh" (Middle Carpet) (c. 1910)	111	138. Classic Design for Mūshkabād Carpet (c. 1945)	146
99. Hamadān Town (Alvānd) Carpet (c. 1935)	112	139. Design for Mahāl Carpet (c. 1912)	147
100. Medallion and Corner Design for a Hamadān Town Carpet (c. 1933)	113	140. Design for Mahāl Carpet (c. 1910)	147
101. Design for a Hamadān Town Carpet (c. 1935)	113	141. Early Sarūk Carpet (c. 1905)	148
102. Hamadān Town (Alvānd) Carpet (c. 1935)	114	142. Sarūk Carpet (c. 1910)	148
103. Hamadān Town (Alvānd) Carpet (c. 1935)	114	143. Design for Sarūk Carpet (c. 1920)	148
104. Rug from Malayer Village in Grape-vine Design (c. 1900)	115	144. Working Drawing for Sarūk Carpet (c. 1948)	149
105. Malayer Carpet, Biqāsh Village (c. 1900)	115	145. Design for Sarūk Carpet (c. 1923)	149
106. Jozān Rug (c. 1935)	116	146. Sarūk Carpet (c. 1935)	150
107. Malayer Rug (c. 1905)	116	147. Sarūk Carpet (c. 1935)	150
108. Malayer Rug (c. 1935)	117	148. Design for Sarūk Carpet (c. 1910)	151
109. Design for Camel-ground Hamadān Village Carpet	118	149. Lilihān and Reihān Designs	152
110. Repeating Design for Hamadān Village Carpet (c. 1945)	118	150. Traditional style Sarūk Carpet (c. 1915)	153
111. Senneh (Sanandaj)	120	151. Sarūk Carpet (c. 1948)	153
112. Weaving a Senneh Rug (1948)	121	152. Sarūk Carpet (c. 1935)	154
113. Gentleman's House, Senneh	121	153. Seraband Carpet (c. 1948)	154
114. Bijār	123	154. Turkoman "Yurt"	156
115. Doorway, Bijār	124	155. Tekkeh Weaver	157
116. Kurdish Woman Spinning, Bijār	124	156. Yomūt Rug: Old Style	159
117. Kurdish Village	126	157. Yomūt Rug: New Style	159
118. Detail of Senneh Carpet in Gol-i-Bolbol Design (c. 1890)	127	158. Meshed Courtyard before the Tomb Chamber of Ali Riza	162
119. Senneh Rug (c. 1890)	127	159. Meshed Portico leading to the Tomb Chamber of Ali Riza	163
120. Detail of Senneh Rug in Vekilli Design (c. 1905)	128	160. Birjānd	172
121. Detail of Senneh Carpet (c. 1910)	128	161. Design for Meshed Carpet, Islimi style (c. 1910)	174
		162. Design for Meshed Carpet, Islimi style (c. 1900)	175

LIST OF ILLUSTRATIONS

	PAGE
163. Meshed Carpet in Islimi style (*c.* 1910)	176
164. Meshed Carpet woven by Emogli (*c.* 1924)	177
165. Meshed Carpet (*c.* 1925)	178
166. Birjānd Carpet (*c.* 1935)	179
167. Meshed Carpet (*c.* 1935)	180
168. Design for Meshed Carpet in classic Persian style (*c.* 1945)	181
169. Design for Meshed Carpet (*c.* 1945)	182
170. Design for Meshed Carpet in the Islimi (serpent) style (*c.* 1945)	183
171. Meshed Carpet (*c.* 1945)	183
172. Meshed Carpet (*c.* 1945)	184
173. Weavers at Ayask	188
174. Tabas	188
175. Balūch Rugs from the Tūrbat-i-Haidarī area	191
176. Balūch Rugs from the Tūrbat-i-Shaikh-jām area	192
177. Balūch Rugs from the Turshīz (Kashmār) area	192
178. Brahuī Balūch Rug from the Tūrbat-i-Haidarī area	192
179. Balūch Rug woven by Kurds	192
180. Balūch Rugs from Nishapūr area	193
181. Seistān Balūch Prayer Rugs	194
182. Balūch Rugs from the Sarākhs area	195
183. Arab Rugs from Firdaus	196
184. Kermān, outskirts of city	197
185. Kermān: Design for border of Hunting Carpet	198
186. Mausoleum of Shah Nimatūllāh	199
187. Caravanserai of Ganj Ali Khan	199
188. Wind Towers, Kermān	199
189. Gate of the Unbelievers, Kermān	200
190. Doorway, Kermān	200
191. House of carpet contractor, Kermān	204
192. Washing Wool, Kermān	204
193. Spinning Yarn, Kermān	205
194. Winding Yarn on Bobbins, Kermān	205
195. Clipping the Finished Carpet	205
196. Hassan Khan	207
197. Gentleman's House, Kermān	211
198. Weaving an Afshāri Rug, Saadatabād	213
199. Ravār Carpet (*c.* 1890)	216
200. Detail of Ravār Carpet (*c.* 1900)	216
201. Ravār Carpet, Classic Period (*c.* 1914)	217
202. Detail of Design for Kermān Carpet in style of Shawl Period	218
203. Design for Kermān Rug, Shawl Period	218
204. Kermān Rug, Shawl Period (*c.* 1900)	219
205. Kermān Rug, Shawl Period (*c.* 1910)	219

	PAGE
206. Kermān Carpet, Shawl Pattern (*c.* 1900)	220
207. Kermān Carpet, Shawl Pattern (*c.* 1925)	221
208. Kermān Rug, Shawl Period (*c.* 1915)	222
209. Design for Kermān Rug (*c.* 1921)	222
210. Designs for Kermān Runners (*c.* 1912)	223
211. Design for Kermān Carpet, Classic Period (*c.* 1915)	224
212. Design for Kermān Carpet, Classic Period (*c.* 1915)	225
213. Design for Kermān Carpet, Classic Period (*c.* 1919)	226
214. Design for Kermān Carpet, Classic Period (*c.* 1922)	227
215. Design for Kermān Carpet, Classic Period (*c.* 1927)	228
216. Design for Kermān Carpet, Classic Period (*c.* 1925)	228
217. Design for Kermān Carpet, Classic Period (*c.* 1925)	229
218. Kermān Carpet, Classic Period (*c.* 1925)	230
219. Design for Kermān Carpet, Classic Period (*c.* 1925)	231
220. Classic Period, Kermān adaptation of Persian Garden Design (*c.* 1928)	232
221. Classic Period, Design for Kermān Rug (*c.* 1927)	233
222. Classic Period, Detail of Kermān Carpet (*c.* 1927)	234
223. Classic Period, Kermān Carpet (*c.* 1927)	235
224. Classic Period, Kermān Carpet (*c.* 1927)	236
225. Classic Period, Kermān Carpet (*c.* 1928)	237
226. Classic Period, Design for Kermān Carpet (*c.* 1928)	238
227. Classic Period, Panel Design for Kermān Carpet (*c.* 1928)	239
228. Classic Period, Detail of Kermān Carpet (*c.* 1928)	240
229. Design for a Kermān Rug (*c.* 1912)	240
230. Classic Period, Panel Design Kermān Carpet (*c.* 1928)	241
231. Classic Period, Panel Design Kermān Carpet (*c.* 1928)	242
232. Classic Period, Kermān Carpet (*c.* 1928)	243
233. Classic Period, Medallion and Corner Design, Kermān Carpet (*c.* 1929)	243
234. Classic Period, Medallion and Corner Design, Kermān Carpet (*c.* 1929)	244
235. Classic Period, Kermān Carpet (*c.* 1929)	245
236. Classic Period, Kermān Carpet (*c.* 1929)	246
237. Classic Period, Design for Field of Kermān Carpet (*c.* 1929)	247

	PAGE		PAGE
238. Classic Period, Animal and Tree Design for Kermān Carpet (*c.* 1929)	248	265. Floral Period, Kermān Carpet (*c.* 1946)	270
239. Classic Period, Panel Design for Kermān Carpet (*c.* 1929)	249	266. French Floral Period, Design for Kermān Carpet (*c.* 1946)	271
240. Classic Period, Design for Kermān Carpet (*c.* 1931)	250	267. French Floral Period, Design for Kermān Carpet (*c.* 1948)	272
241. Classic Period, Design for Kermān Carpet	251	268. French Floral Period, Kermān Carpet (*c.* 1944)	272
242. Classic Period, Design for Kermān Carpet	252	269. French Floral Period, Kermān Carpet (*c.* 1948)	273
243. Classic Period, Sixteenth-century Vase Design for Kermān Carpet	253	270. Kermān Carpet (*c.* 1947)	274
		271. Kermān Carpet (*c.* 1947)	275
244. Classic Period, Design for Kermān Carpet	254	272. Kermān Carpet (*c.* 1947)	276
245. Period of Covered Grounds, Design for Kermān Carpet (*c.* 1931)	255	273. Detail of Afshārī (Balvardi) Rug (*c.* 1935)	277
		274. Afshārī (Kutlū) Rug (*c.* 1935)	277
246. Period of Covered Grounds, Design for Kermān Carpet (*c.* 1929)	255	275. Afshārī (Kutlū) Rug (*c.* 1935)	277
		276. Afshārī (Dashtab) Rug (*c.* 1935)	277
247. Period of Covered Grounds, Detail of an Arabesque and Floral Design for Kermān Carpet (*c.* 1935)	256	277. Afshārī (Deh Shotorān) Rug (*c.* 1938)	278
		278. Afshārī (Saarabad) Rug (*c.* 1940)	278
		279. Afshārī (Al-Saadi) Rug (*c.* 1940)	278
248. Period of Covered Grounds, Floral Design for Kermān Carpet (*c.* 1929)	256	280. Afshārī (Parizi) Rug (*c.* 1945)	278
		281. Mohammedabād (*c.* 1940)	279
249. Period of Covered Grounds, Kermān Carpet (*c.* 1930)	257	282. Afshārī (Deh Shotorān) Rug (*c.* 1940)	279
		283. Afshārī (Dehāj) Rug (*c.* 1940)	279
250. Period of Covered Grounds, Kermān Carpet (*c.* 1930)	258	284. Afshārī (Beilleri) Rug (*c.* 1940)	279
		285. Kermān Carpet (*c.* 1948)	280
251. Period of Covered Grounds, Kermān Carpet in Mosaic Pattern (*c.* 1932)	259	286. Yezd Carpet	280
		287. Garden of Orange Trees and Cypresses	282
252. Period of Covered Grounds, Kermān Carpet (*c.* 1934)	260	288. Tomb of Ahmed Ibn Musa	283
		289. Tomb of Mir Mohammed	283
253. Period of Covered Grounds, Kermān Carpet (*c.* 1935)	261	290. Tomb of Sa'adi	283
		291. A Qashqaī Tent	285
254. Period of Covered Grounds, Kermān Carpet (*c.* 1934)	261	292. Qashqaī Weavers	285
		293. Shish-Būlūkī Saddle-bags	292
255. Period of Covered Grounds, Kermān Carpet (*c.* 1935)	262	294. Antique Qashqaī Rug	292
		295. Fragment of Antique Qashqūlī Rug	293
256. Period of Covered Grounds, Kermān Carpet (*c.* 1937)	263	296. Basirī Kolomec Rug	293
		297. Gondashtli Rug	293
257. Period of Covered Grounds, Kermān Carpet (*c.* 1935)	264	298. Safi Khanī Rug	293
		299. Shish-Būlūkī Rug	294
258. Floral Period, Design for Kermān Carpet (*c.* 1944)	265	300. Shish-Būlūkī Rug	294
		301. Arab Ghani Rug	295
259. Floral Period, Design for Kermān Carpet (*c.* 1943)	265	302. Pir Islami Rug	295
		303. Gishni Chahār-rā Rug	295
260. Floral Period, Kermān Carpet (*c.* 1944)	266	304. Arab-Farsi Rug	295
		305. Basirī Rug	296
261. Floral Period, Kermān Carpet (*c.* 1945)	267	306. Basirī Saddle-bag	296
262. Floral Period, Kermān Carpet (*c.* 1945)	268	307. Antique Lab-u-Mahdī Rug	297
263. Floral Period, Kermān Carpet (*c.* 1946)	268	308. New Lab-u-Mahdī Rug	297
264. Floral Period, Kermān Carpet (*c.* 1945)	269	309. Laverdāni Rug	297
		310. Derazi Rug	298
		311. Kurshul Rug	298

	PAGE		PAGE
312. Arabi Shirī Rug	299	360. Bakhtiari Rug (Shahr Kūrd Village) (*c.* 1945)	327
313. Arabi Ghanī Rug	299	361. Bakhtiari Rug from Shrine Collection, Meshed	327
314. Mazidi Rug	299	362. Bakhtiari Carpet (Beīn Village) (*c.* 1945)	328
315. Gishni Chahār-rā Rug	299	363. Bakhtiari Carpet (Destgird Village) (*c.* 1940)	328
316. Lūri Rug	300	364. Bakhtiari Carpet from Qefarūkh Village (*c.* 1945)	329
317. Kevelli Village Rug	300	365. Jōshaqān Carpet (*c.* 1920)	330
318. Abadeh Village Rug	300	366. Jōshaqān Carpet from Shrine Collection, Meshed	336
319. Abadeh Village Rug	300	367. Fragment of Jōshaqān Carpet in the Victoria and Albert Museum	330
320. Shuleh Sarūkh Village Rug	301	368. Naīn Carpet (*c.* 1946)	331
321. Goshnaqūn Village Rug	301	369. Tehrān Rug, Portico Design (*c.* 1915)	331
322. Deh Bīd Village Rug	301	370. Tehrān Carpet, Panel Design (*c.* 1920)	332
323. Maligandeh Village Rug	301	371. Kashān	333
324. Nerīz Village Rug	302	372. Kashān Dwelling-houses	333
325. Nerīz Village Rug	302	373. Kashān, Women Sorting Wool	335
326. Sirānd Village Rug	302	374. Weaving Village of Nūshabād	335
327. Karftar Village Rug	302	375. Headman's House, Nūshabād Village	335
328. View of Isfahān	304	376. Mosque at Qūm	338
329. Bridge of Hassan Beg, Isfahān	304	377. Kashān Carpet (*c.* 1900)	341
330. Bridge of Allah Verdi Khan, Isfahān	304	378. Kashān Carpet (*c.* 1905)	341
331. Masjid-i-Shah, Isfahān	305	379. Kashān Carpet (*c.* 1910)	342
332. Detail of Tilework, Masjid-i-Shah	305	380. Kashān Silk Rug (*c.* 1910)	342
333. The Ali Kapū, Isfahān	306	381. Kashān Carpet (*c.* 1915)	343
334. The Chehel Sitūn, Isfahān	306	382. Kashān Carpet (*c.* 1915)	343
335. Dome of the Medresseh Mader-i-Shah	307	383. Silk Kashān Carpet (*c.* 1915)	344
336. Jōshaqān Village	313	384. Kashān Carpet (*c.* 1915)	345
337. Isfahān Carpet (*c.* 1925)	315	385. Kashān Rug (*c.* 1920)	346
338. Isfahān Rug (*c.* 1925)	315	386. Kashān Carpet (*c.* 1920)	346
339. Isfahān Rug (*c.* 1935)	316	387. Kashān Carpet (*c.* 1925)	347
340. Isfahān Rug (*c.* 1935)	316	388. Detail of Kashān Carpet (*c.* 1935)	347
341. Design for Isfahān Rug (*c.* 1935)	316	389. A typical modern Kashān Carpet	347
342. Isfahān Carpet (*c.* 1935)	317	390. Floral and Arabesque Design for Kashān Carpet (*c.* 1945)	348
343. Isfahān Carpet (*c.* 1935)	317	391. Floral and Animal Design for Kashān Carpet (*c.* 1945)	348
344. Isfahān Rug (*c.* 1940)	318	392. Medallion and Corner Design for Kashān Carpet (*c.* 1945)	349
345. Isfahān Carpet (*c.* 1940)	318	393. Arabesque Design for Border of Kashān Carpet (*c.* 1945)	349
346. Isfahān Carpet (*c.* 1945)	319	394. Arabesque Repeating Design for Kashān Carpet (*c.* 1945)	349
347. Isfahān Rug (*c.* 1945)	319		
348. Isfahān Carpet (*c.* 1945)	320		
349. Design for Isfahān Carpet (*c.* 1945)	321		
350. Design for Isfahān Carpet (*c.* 1945)	322	395. Medallion Design with Arabesques for Kashān Carpet (*c.* 1946)	350
351. Design for Isfahān Carpet (*c.* 1945)	323		
352. Design for Isfahān Carpet (*c.* 1945)	324	396. Design for Kashān Carpet (*c.* 1946)	350
353. Design for Isfahān Carpet (*c.* 1945)	325		
354. Bakhtiari Rug (Boldaji Village) (*c.* 1940)	326		
355. Bakhtiari Rug (Hajiabād Village) (*c.* 1940)	326		
356. Bakhtiari Rug (Shalamzār Village) (*c.* 1940)	326		
357. Bakhtiari Rug (Beīn Village) (*c.* 1935)	326		
358. Bakhtiari Rug (Chahār Shotūr Village) (*c.* 1945)	327		
359. Bakhtiari Rug (Chahār Shotūr Village) (*c.* 1945)	327	397. Repeating Medallion Design for Kashān Carpet (*c.* 1946)	351

	PAGE		PAGE
398. Detail of Design for Kashān Carpet (c. 1946)	351	406. Kashān Rug (c. 1948)	356
399. Tree Design for Field of Kashān Rug (c. 1946)	352	407. Kashān Carpet (c. 1948)	356
		408. Natanz Rug (c. 1946)	357
400. Detail of Design for Kashān Carpet (c. 1946)	352	409. Detail of Qūm Carpet	357
		410. Detail of Qūm Carpet (c. 1940)	358
401. Design for Field of Kashān Rug (c. 1947)	353	411. Qūm Rug (c. 1942)	358
402. Detail of Design for Kashān Carpet (c. 1946)	353	412. Detail of Qūm Carpet (c. 1945)	358
		413. Qūm Rug (c. 1945)	358
403. Detail of a Kashān Medallion Carpet (c. 1948)	354	414. Detail of Qūm Carpet (c. 1945)	359
		415. Detail of Qūm Carpet (c. 1945)	359
404. Design for Kashān Carpet (c. 1948)	355	416. Design for Qūm Carpet (c. 1945)	359
405. Medallion and Corner Design for Kashān Carpet (c. 1948)	355	417. Qūm Rug (c. 1945)	359
		418. Qūm Carpet (c. 1946)	360
		419. Qūm Carpet (c. 1948)	361

CHAPTER I
RETROSPECT

The Plan of the Book

I purpose in the following pages to attempt a survey of the craft of carpet weaving as it is carried on in Persia today. Such a survey would, however, be incomplete—if not, indeed, incomprehensible—without a brief enquiry into the history of the industry: (1) its origin; (2) its sudden leap into full fruition in the sixteenth century; (3) its decline during the two centuries thereafter; (4) its resurgence in our own time; and (5) its present disabilities.

The first three of these headings will be discussed very briefly in this and the following chapter of the book. The subsequent chapters will deal with the real subject—which is the resurgence of the industry within the memory of men still living; and its present state.

Origins

The pile carpet is a comparatively modern amenity in the West. It was almost unknown in the seventeenth century. Except for rare importations from France and the Low Countries, and some still rarer from the East, it was equally unknown in our elegant eighteenth-century drawing-rooms. Not until the power loom had become thoroughly established in the early nineteenth century was the pile carpet regarded, by poor and rich alike, as a necessity in the household.

But in Persia it has been in common use for many centuries—for how many no one knows and no one will ever know. For "the termless antiquity of the Persian carpet" is an accepted rather than a proven theory. The phrase is Sir George Birdwood's. That famous orientalist and classic scholar delved, with characteristic zeal, into the ancient writers for proofs of the existence of pile carpets in the time of Cyrus —who died in 529 B.C. He quoted in support of his thesis from the Bible and from a score of classic writers. It might be expected that from such a galaxy of authors he would produce convincing proofs. But what do we find? There are references in plenty to vestments, hangings, draperies, brocades, tapestries and embroidered cloths; but there is no reference which can be construed as establishing that the pile carpet was derived, fully fledged, from the older civilisations of Egypt, Nineveh or Babylon; or even that it was in use in Achaemenian times.[1] We do not know, and it is unlikely that we shall ever know, if the floors of the palace of Darius at Persepolis were covered with pile carpets.

Birdwood, in his anxiety to prove his thesis, pleaded that the hangings—so frequently mentioned by the ancient writers—were actually rugs; adding that to this day the Persians hang them on their walls. Unhappily for the argument, the Persians— certainly when Birdwood wrote—rarely did so. Their furnishings were of an extreme austerity: one or more carpets covered the floor; a pair of oil lamps stood, in studied symmetry, in niches in the walls; the windows (in the wealthier mansions) were pranked with coloured glass, and the walls embossed with white plaster. That—with a small table and a few straight chairs—was all. There were no *objets d'art*, no vases of flowers, no pictures—and rarely, very rarely, a hanging rug.

Nevertheless, although the antiquity of the Persian carpet is unproven, it may be fairly deduced. For Persia is a very cold country in winter, where some form of covering for the ground under the tents of the nomads must have been in use from earliest times. The Persian people are by nature skilled and artistic craftsmen. Such a people would not for long remain content to cover their tent floors—like Eskimos or Red Indians—with the skins of beasts. The urge to fashion something closer to the need, more varied and above all more colourful, was there. The materials, too, were there—for the sheep is an indigenous animal in Persia. Thus, the hand-knotted carpet may well have been evolved by art out of the sheepskin rug—the primal floor-covering of the pastoral nomads of the plateau.

Is it not more probable, therefore, that the true ancestors of the great carpets of Persia were not the sumptuous hangings, brocades and embroideries of Egypt, Babylon and Nineveh, but the humble tribal rugs of her nomadic shepherds?

---

[1] The two well-known references in Xenophon are not very convincing. In the *Anabasis* (VII, 3) he refers to "a carpet worth ten minae". Was it a flat weave, a hanging, an embroidery or tapestry—or a pile carpet? We do not know. Again in the *Cyropaedia* (IV, 8) he writes that the Persians placed rugs under their bedding for softness. These might have been thick, embroidered felts, such as the Persians make to this day.

Gradually some of the nomads settled in villages; and—when the villages had expanded into towns and the houses had grown in importance—larger pieces became a necessity. The accepted urban method of floor construction was—and still is—to lay mud over poplar beams, criss-crossed with poplar branches. Without a stout floor-covering to protect it from wall to wall the dust would become intolerable. The earth floor would quickly wear away. Thus, it became the custom in Persia—and still is—to cover the floors, from wall to wall, with carpets.

To this need and to the need for warmth in the bitter cold of their uplands, the Persian people applied a flair for the production of textile fabrics and an unrivalled sense of colour and design; and thus they became, for the delectation of mankind, the supreme masters of the craft of carpet weaving.

Other writers, however, have suggested that the craft did not originate in Nineveh or Babylon or in Persia itself, but that it was introduced by Turkish or Mongol invaders from Central Asia. Some of the discoveries of Lecoq, Kozlor and Sir Aurel Stein in those regions seemed to lend support to this theory. But on historic grounds it can hardly be sustained.

The earliest Mongols to enter Persia were the White Huns who invaded Khūrasān in the fifth century A.D. But they got no farther, and they were destroyed a century later. Furthermore, the Mongol tribes never brought their women with them on their campaigns;[1] and rug weaving was practised by the women, not the warriors.

The next Mongol or Turkish invaders were the Seljūks who established their dominion over Persia in the eleventh century. But in the geography called *Hudūd-al-'Alam*,[2] written in the ninth century, the author states that rugs were woven at that time in distant Fārs; and this was confirmed in the tenth century by the geographers Istahri and Mukaddasi. The latter further states that the highlands of the Qaināt (which he visited) were already famous for their carpets and prayer rugs.

It may, I think, be safely affirmed therefore that carpet weaving in the Persian manner existed in the country long before the Seljūk or Mongol invasions, and that it was an invention of the Persians themselves.

Carpets before the Arab Conquest

If we regard 650 B.C. as the approximate date of the establishment of a truly Persian kingdom, the history of Persia—to the present day—covers twenty-six centuries. That long duration is divided into two almost exactly equal periods by the most important event in Persian history—the defeat of the last Sassanian king by the Arabs at Nehavand in A.D. 641. This defeat was followed by the Arab conquest of Persia—which altered the religion, the laws, the language, the script, the administrative system and in many respects the way of life of the Persian people.

We know very little about carpet weaving in Persia before that crucial date. There are no Persian records of the craft during the rule of the Achaemenian (553–330 B.C.), Seleucid (312–129 B.C.) and Parthian (c. 170 B.C.–A.D. 226) kings. The two vague references of Xenophon (400 B.C.) have already been mentioned (see note on p. 1).

There are more references—however vague and unsatisfying—during the three centuries of Sassanian rule (A.D. 224–641). They indicate that some at least of the Sassanian carpets appear to have been in the nature of embroideries embellished with gold and precious stones—unsuitable materials, we would think, for floor-coverings. The immense Garden Carpet of Khosrō I, which covered the floor of the great hall of the palace of Ctesiphon, was thus bedizened. It was probably not a pile carpet at all; because pile fabrics are unsuited to the hot climate of Mesopotamia and are ill-adapted to jewel ornamentation. Furthermore, a pile carpet of such dimensions (it is said to have measured 90 × 90 feet) would have weighed over two tons. It could not, in any case, have been woven in one piece; for there is no tree in Persia tall enough or straight enough or strong enough out of which a loom beam could have been fashioned to carry such a carpet.

Nevertheless, pile rugs—as distinguished from large, sumptuary carpets—woven by the tribes or in the villages for their own use or for barter against commodities which they could not themselves produce—probably existed. They may, indeed, have been in common use in Sassanian times.

Testimony of the Arab Geographers

After the Arab conquest of Persia in the seventh century, however (which put an end to the Sassanian dynasty), the veil is lifted. For in the succeeding centuries some twenty Arab geographers and historians visited the country; and in the writings of some of them we find, for the first time, unmistakable references to the use of carpets on the floors.

---

[1] Professor V. Minorsky.
[2] *Hudūd-al-'Alam, The Regions of the World*, translated and explained by V. Minorsky, E. J. W. Gibb Memorial (Luzac and Co., 1937).

Thus (as we have seen) in the geography called *Hudūd-al-'Alam*, written in 892, the author states that rugs were being woven in Fārs; and Mukaddasi, a century later, refers to carpets in the Qaināt. Yakūt (A.D. 1179–1229), too, assures us that carpet weaving existed in Azerbaijān in the thirteenth century. A hundred years later, Ibn Batūta (A.D. 1304–1378)—that informed and observant traveller who was on his way from Khor Mūsa on the Persian Gulf to Isfahān—mentions that when he visited Idhej,[1] a town in the Bakhtiari country, a green rug was spread before him.

These passing references by Arab geographers indicate that the carpet weaving which existed in Persia under the Caliphate was a tribal or rural industry. As such it supplied the needs of the population for a warm, pleasing and durable floor-covering at a reasonable cost. It is likely that the designs in vogue were repeating rectilinear patterns —such as are woven in most of the villages today. They were probably traditional in each locality—as they are today—and they were woven without the aid of designers and draftsmen.[2] This does not exclude the possibility that, here and there, a prince or a member of the landed aristocracy may have possessed a loom or two in his house in charge of a master-weaver; where the lord indulged his sensibility for the arts by producing something superior to the rugs of the village weavers. This, too, is still a common practice in Persia.

Neglect of the Industry by the Seljūk Sultans and the Mongol Conquerors

It is probable that the great Seljūk sultans who ruled Persia in the eleventh and twelfth centuries— and who were great builders and patrons of the arts of painting and calligraphy—failed to perceive the possibilities in the weaver's craft. For there are few references to it in contemporary writings. Doubtless it prospered during that enlightened period—but only as a rural or tribal industry. In the thirteenth century, the devastations of the half-savage Mongol conquerors, Jenghiz Khan and Hulagū, must have brought production to a standstill.[3]

The later Mongol Il-Khanis, however, were men of culture. Ghazān Khan at the end of the thirteenth century, built (as we shall see) a new and splendid capital at Shām on the outskirts of Tabrīz and covered the floors with rugs from Fārs (which, presumably, he would not have done if large carpets from Tabrīz itself had been available). Timūr (Tamerlane) was probably too busy with his campaigns to pay much attention to the weaver's craft; but there are indications that during the reign of his illustrious son Shah Rūkh it attained a certain notability, and that sumptuary carpets were produced— for they are depicted in fifteenth-century miniatures. Their designs, however, are mostly rectilinear— which indicates that the craft had not yet reached an advanced stage of mastery.

We know that at least one other Mongol prince besides Shah Rūkh—the enlightened Uzūn Hassān of the White Sheep dynasty (1469–1478)—possessed sumptuary pieces in his palace. We know it from the report of the Venetian, Barbaro, who was Ambassador of the Republic to his court in Tabrīz. The Venetian describes his visit in great detail and mentions more than once the splendid carpets which he saw at the palace. Some of them, he wrote, were of silk.

Of these early Persian weaves no vestiges remain. This is not surprising, because (and the fact is sometimes overlooked) Persian carpets are made of two highly perishable materials, wool and cotton. The former wears away under the constant friction of the human foot; and it is of course attacked by grubs and insects. Both materials are rapidly destroyed by damp and are slowly oxidised by exposure to the atmosphere. Thus, although it has been the practice among the Persians for many centuries—except among the poorer peasants—to carpet all their rooms from wall to wall, no pieces have survived of the many thousands which were woven before A.D. 1500.

The Great Period

The first of that company of master-weavers and designers to practise the technique of curvilinear weaving—a technique more elaborate than the earlier and more primitive system of weaving in straight lines and one which demanded (before a knot was tied) full-sized cartoons of their carpets—probably appeared in the late fifteenth century. But it was not until the establishment of the Sefavi dynasty early in the sixteenth century that the craft received the recognition and the royal patronage which it merited.

---

[1] From A.D. 1155 to 1424 a strong Moslem dynasty, the Fasluyeh, ruled the Bakhtiari country from Isfahān to Shushter under the title of Atabegs. The centre of Atabeg power was the mountain of Mungāsht and their winter quarters were at Idhej, the present Izeh.

[2] This question is examined in detail on pp. 35–51.

[3] This invariably happens in Persia: in periods of security weaving goes on in the villages; in times of war and tumult the villagers conceal their possessions and output falls or ceases altogether.

In 1499, after seven centuries of alien rule, a new dynasty arose in Persia. Although Ismail, its founder, claimed descent from the Prophet himself (an Arab) and was a kinsman of Uzūn Hassān (a Mongol) and of his wife Despina (a Christian princess of the house of the Comneni) he is regarded by the Persians as the first national sovereign to occupy the throne of Cyrus and Shahpūr since the Arab conquest in A.D. 641. He was a fanatical Shi'a and established the Shi'a faith as the national religion. To the Persians he is the Restorer, the Liberator, the saintly founder of a famous national dynasty.

The first three monarchs[1] of the new dynasty were men of vision and ability. There are, indeed, few instances in history where three rulers in the direct line have equalled in the kingly virtues of their time the three Sefavi monarchs—Shah Ismail, Shah Tahmasp and Shah Abbas.

We have seen that with the possible exception of Shah Rūkh and Uzūn Hassān, the predecessors of the Sefavi kings were alien monarchs who were oblivious of the possibilities which lay in this purely Persian village craft. But the first Persian princes to reign after 800 years of alien rule might well have sought to acquire merit in the eyes of their subjects by becoming patrons of an industry so peculiarly Persian and so receptive of the inspiration of art. Whether they were moved by policy or virtuosity, or both, it is to the high credit of these princes—particularly of the last two—that they perceived the possibilities of the craft. They endowed it with their interest and patronage, so that in a short time it rose from the level of a cottage *métier* to the dignity of a fine art.

For the production of their carpets both princes enlisted the talents of the first painters and master-weavers of the age. The painters were peculiarly fitted for this task because their work was circumscribed by convention, diminutive in scale and usually in two dimensions. Indeed, many of the miniatures and illustrations of the period partake more of the nature of designs than paintings; so much so that in recent years some of the master-weavers of Kermān and Tabrīz have used them—with hardly any alteration—as carpet designs.

The carpets which were woven under the aegis of these princes were of necessity urban, not rural, productions; for they demanded equipment and craftsmanship far beyond that which the tribes and villages possessed. They were made in elaborate curvilinear patterns; with floral, animal and other decorative motives—Persian, Arabic and Chinese. The most famous of the carpets which today adorn our museums and collections—carpets which have placed the Persians in the premier position as designers and as weavers of floor-coverings, and which have been copied and recopied in countless fabrics the world over—were almost certainly produced during the long reigns of Shah Tahmasp and Shah Abbas. Under the former the movement reached its highest development; under the latter it gained its greatest renown.

There are no indications that Shah Ismail established a court factory in Tabrīz, his capital. He was probably too busy consolidating his régime and fighting the Turks and Uzbegs. Shah Tahmasp, however, may have done so. The question will be referred to later (Chapter II) when the heritage of the Sefavi carpets is examined.

We do know something, however, about Shah Tahmasp's interest in carpets. He is said, indeed, to have designed a few himself. We know, too, that he wrote to Sultan Suleiman the Magnificent offering to send him carpets for the mosque—now known as the Suleimaniyé Jami—which the great Sinan was building for him in Istanbul. (Tahmasp very properly importuned his royal brother not to forget to send him a list of the sizes.) The carpets were in due course woven and despatched. The Hungarian ambassador (who reported the matter) said that there were some silk pieces among them made in Hamadān and Dergezin (Deryazin). I suspect the accuracy of the ambassador's story. So far as I am aware, silk carpets have never been woven in Hamadān or Deryazin. Indeed, it is doubtful if carpets of any kind were woven in the town of Hamadān before 1912. As for Deryazin,[2] it is a fertile agricultural area some forty miles north-east of Hamadān, where carpets and especially small, inexpensive rugs have been woven for many centuries and are still woven. It may well be that Tahmasp sent Suleiman a carpet which had been woven there, but it is highly improbable that the carpet was silk.

The Hungarian ambassador's report is valuable, too, for another reason: it throws light on the vexed

---

[1] There was a confused period of ten years between the death of Shah Tahmasp and the accession of Shah Abbas, during which three rival princes struggled for power.

[2] Upham Pope's statement (*A Survey of Persian Art*, p. 2335) that "no carpets have been woven within memory in Dergezin" is incorrect.

problem of the origins of the great carpets which were woven during the reign of Shah Tahmasp; because it indicates that a court factory could hardly have existed at the time. For had the Shah possessed such a factory, the carpets which he sent to his royal brother would almost certainly have been produced there, and not in Hamadān or Dergezin.

Happily, there is no doubt at all that Shah Abbas —the most famous of the Sefavi kings—established a court factory in his new capital, Isfahān. For there are a number of contemporary references to it. We know from two Frenchmen, Tavernier and Chardin, from Sir Robert Sherley, from a Polish Jesuit, and particularly from the Shah's secretary—who wrote a long and detailed chronicle of his reign—that it was situated near the palace, between the Chehel Sitūn and the Great Maidān. As both landmarks exist today, it can be placed quite accurately. Tavernier says that carpets were being constantly woven there for the royal court. This we can well believe: for Shah Abbas was building his new capital with great rapidity, and there must have been a constant demand for carpets for the palaces, for the offices of state, for the houses of the courtiers' and high officials, and for presentation to foreign potentates and their envoys. We have seen a similar activity recently, during the reign of Shah Riza Pahlavi.

The century between the death of Shah Abbas and the Afghan invasions was for Persia a period of decay, turmoil and defeat. The four last Sefavi monarchs possessed few of the kingly virtues of their predecessors of the dynasty. They devoted the greater part of their lives to the pleasures of the harem and the table and to planning political murders. On every front the Persian armies suffered defeat. Baghdad, Tabrīz and Hamadān were captured.

The Period of Decline

It has been truly said that every movement in art carries within itself the seed of its own degeneration; and that without the perennial stimulus of patronage, praise, and a congenial atmosphere, genius will wilt and fail to flower.

The successors of Shah Tahmasp and Shah Abbas failed to maintain their interest in the art of carpet weaving. The royal patronage was withheld from the designers and master-weavers who had worked for Shah Abbas. They were soon scattered, or died and were not replaced. Although their designs endured, craftsmanship degenerated. It became slovenly, inexpert. Finally, in 1722 Shah Sultan Hosain, the last of his line, surrendered his capital and throne to the Afghan invaders, and the great period came to an inglorious end.

The short but bloody rule of the Afghan chiefs almost extinguished what was left of the art of carpet weaving.

This, one of the darkest periods of Persian history, was followed by twenty years of uninterrupted conflict. One Nadir Qūli, a tough but capable military commander—who had previously been a successful leader of a robber band—drove out the Afghans, recaptured Tabrīz, Hamadān, Derbend, Bakū and the Caspian provinces, and was elected to the vacant throne. During the turbulent reign of that rough soldier, scant attention was given to the weaver's craft.

Neither does evidence exist of a revival of the craft during the regency of the kindly but illiterate Kerim Khan Zand (1750–1779), who made Shirāz his capital. Indeed, Sir John Malcolm, who wrote a detailed history of the period and devoted a whole chapter to the products, manufactures, commerce and arts of Persia at the end of the eighteenth century, had no word to say about its carpets. That such a meticulous observer should have made no reference to the craft is an indication of the low level to which it had sunk.

Revival

Carpet weaving, however, had not disappeared: it had shrunk once more into an insignificant but useful handicraft. The establishment and consolidation of the Qajar dynasty, which followed soon after the death of Kerim Khan, provided Persia with a long period of order and comparative peace and gave the industry the opportunity of revival.

The three important Qajar monarchs—Fath-Ali Shah, Nasir-ud-Din Shah and Muzaffar-ud-Din Shah—pursued with success the ancient traditions of the Persian monarchy. These traditions tended, no doubt, to prevent Persia from acquiring the uncertain benefits of western reform. But they endowed her instead with other benefactions of inestimable worth—stability and a large measure of security. After the Qajar monarchs had provided for themselves—and had permitted their subordinates to provide for themselves—a proper and traditional measure of self-compensation, these princes allowed their people freedom to pursue their lawful occasions: to plough, to sow, to reap, to traffic —and to weave. Whereas early in the nineteenth century the careful Malcolm had omitted carpet

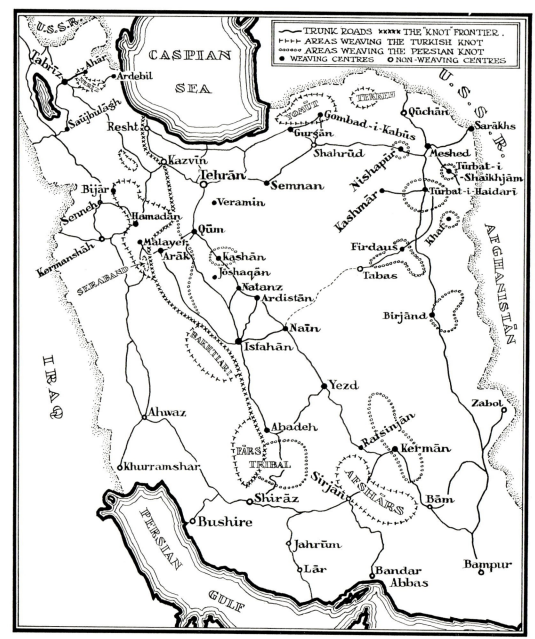

Map I. The Weaving Areas of Persia

weaving from the industries of Persia, travellers in the succeeding fifty years testified to its interest and importance.

This long period of stability, security and peace gave to the industry the climate which it needed for revival. The opportunity called for leadership; it was taken by the merchants of Tabrīz. They became the founders of the modern industry of carpet weaving in Persia.

This modern revival—which began about 1885[1]—brings us to the end of this short, historical sketch. Before proceeding to survey the industry as it exists today, I propose to devote one chapter to the great period from which it derived.

[1] E. Stebbing, referring to the condition of the industry in 1877, mentions that "in place of the 4–5 designs to which the industry was [then] entirely confined [sic] there are now [1892] some twenty or more of the designs of the finest of the old carpets being produced, with skill and fidelity.... The revival has begun" (E. Stebbing, *The Holy Carpet of the Mosque at Ardebil* (London, 1892)). Stebbing is, I fear, a dubious authority. He was not himself in touch with Persia, but obtained his information from his suppliers, Ziegler and Co. *Their* designs, no doubt, numbered only four to five when they started operations in Sultānabād, but to say this about a whole industry was absurd. Nevertheless, the statement indicates that the industry had reached a turning-point. The revival, as he says, had begun.

CHAPTER II

CARPETS OF THE GREAT PERIOD

The Heritage

Our heritage of Persian carpets of the sixteenth and seventeenth centuries has been estimated at 1,500–2,000 pieces, including fragments. By no means all of them are worthy of note. Many are weak in design and faulty in execution. Of these it may be said that if age be a merit, they have no other. There are, however, at least 200 pieces of renown among them, and many more of excellence.

Before attempting to appraise the quality of this legacy which the designers and master-weavers of the great period have bequeathed to us, I propose briefly to examine some of the problems which the legacy presents. They are problems which have puzzled experts for two generations, and will puzzle their successors for generations to come.

Problems Presented by the Carpets of the Sefavi Period

Although these great carpets were woven some four centuries ago (which, measured by the time-scale of the antiquarian, is not long) we know surprisingly little about them. How is it that the art came—as it were at a bound—into full fruition? When were these carpets made? Where were they made? And why, after a few generations of splendour, did the art decline?

A reply to the first of these questions has already been suggested: the sudden rise of a village craft to the dignity of a fine art coincided with the establishment of a new, national and dynamic dynasty in Persia. It coincided also with that puissant, fructifying wind which was blowing through the whole world in the sixteenth century.

The second question is: how do we know that the great carpets which have come down to us were produced (as we declare with such assurance that they were) during the reigns of Shah Tahmasp or Shah Abbas? It must be admitted that incontrovertible proofs for most of them do not exist. Indeed, until comparatively recent years, the dating of antique carpets was a haphazard business. The authorities of a generation ago, like Martin and Bode, made some sad guesses. They propounded dates and origins with a temerity which is surprising in persons of such eminence. How much more satisfying was the caution of Tattersall and Kendrick of the Victoria and Albert Museum. To them a carpet was "Persian" or "north-west Persian", and its date "probably sixteenth century". Their reserve was not the fruit of indolence or dullness, but of devotion and integrity.

During the last two decades, however, the matter has been studied further. Much circumstantial evidence has been collected and a technique has been devised which has enabled authorities to attach approximate dates to many of the great carpets; and these dates generally fall within the period indicated.

The technique consists of establishing the dates of certain carpets about which we possess positive information; and grouping round them other carpets, similar in style, about which we possess no clues. The phrase "similar in style" is here used to denote a family resemblance—an affinity in design, materials, colour and weave.

The "positive information" which enables us to date a carpet—which can be used as the nucleus of a group—is the following:

(a) The date may be woven into the carpet itself.
(b) The carpet may be identifiable historically.
(c) The design of the carpet may be traceable to an illustrated or illuminated manuscript, to a painting or book cover, the date of which is known.

The first of these methods would be, of course, the most valuable of all—if only the master-craftsmen of those days had possessed the foresight to weave the dates into a few more of their productions.[1] Unhappily, they omitted to do so. Of the many hundreds of carpets and fragments which have come down to us from Sefavi times only a few were dated. Still, the dated pieces include the Ardebil carpet—the pride of the Victoria and Albert Museum—and a fine hunting carpet in the Museo Poldi Pezzoli, Milan. It has been possible to use these two dated pieces—and others of less renown—as starting points for the formation of groups of carpets similar in style.

---

[1] For the benefit of future amateurs or historians, may I urge the master-weavers of Persia—or those who may be in a position to influence them—to weave the date into their best productions.

The second method—that of basing a group on a carpet which can be identified historically—has also proved of value. The most notable instance of historical identification is that of five pieces in the Residenz Museum of Munich. In 1601 Sigismund III Vasa, King of Poland, sent an Armenian merchant by the name of Muratovitz to Persia with instructions to order a number of carpets for the royal palaces. Muratovitz travelled by sea to Trebizond and thence—via Erzerūm, Kars, Tabrīz and Kazvīn—to Kashān. There, as he himself declares, he placed his orders and superintended the weaving of the carpets, two of which bore the royal coat of arms. Only one of the five pieces is a knotted carpet; the others are tapestries.[1]

The carpets of Sigismund Vasa are, so far as I know, the only period carpets still extant of which the actual weaving was recorded. They have enabled us, with some assurance, not only to date a group of pieces similar in style, but to affirm that they were woven in Kashān.

The third method—from the design alone—is fruitful in results; but only if we are prepared to agree that a design which appears in a carpet—as well as in a dated manuscript, book cover or painting—must have been drawn by one and the same hand.

There are good grounds for accepting this premise. For an intelligent and ardent monarch—anxious that carpets should be produced during his reign which would be superior to the best products of previous ages—would be likely to call upon the first painters and illuminators of his court to co-operate with his most renowned master-weavers in their production.

The task of fixing the place where each of these great carpets was made is even more perplexing than that of determining their approximate dates. For there is no positive evidence of their origin. Each piece, indeed, might have been woven in one of half a dozen localities. The perplexity of the problem can best be indicated by examining a few of the more outstanding pieces. For it is outside the province of this book—which is primarily concerned with the weaver's craft of today—to describe (much less to illustrate) a large collection of antique carpets. This has been admirably done already by the compilers of the last edition of *Old Oriental Carpets* and in the monumental *Survey of Persian Art*.[2]

Nevertheless, it would be improper to leave the great period of the Persian carpet without an account of some, at least, of its noblest achievements. I have, therefore, dared to choose from about two hundred carpets of renown, eight pieces which—to me, at least—are among the best carpets in the world. I have not eschewed fragments or pieces imperfectly preserved, if they manifest supremacy in design, colour and craftsmanship. These eight carpets are shown on Plates 1–8. No attempt has been made to arrange them in order of merit, date or place of origin. For—as I have explained above—the dating of ancient carpets is a precarious adventure; and—as I shall now attempt to show—the task of determining their place of origin is no less uncertain.

Plate 1. The Ardebil Carpet; Victoria and Albert Museum, London

This renowned carpet is so called because it came from the mosque in Ardebil where Shah Ismail and Sheikh Sefi-ud-Din, his ancestor (after whom the Sefavi dynasty was named), are buried. The carpet was acquired (on the advice of William Morris) from Messrs. Vincent Robinson and Co. in 1893, who had purchased it from Messrs. Ziegler and Co. of Tabrīz.[3] It bears the following inscription which is taken from the beginning of an ode by Hafiz:

I have no refuge in the world other than thy threshold,
There is no protection for my head other than this door.

    The work of the slave of the threshold
    Maqsūd of Kashān, in the year 946.

The Ardebil carpet is—by reason of its design and craftsmanship—one of the great carpets of the world. It is also a historical document of first importance, because it bears a signature and date. Thus, it has become the nucleus of a group of splendid medallion carpets, similar in style, which can be ascribed with assurance to the middle of the sixteenth century; for the carpet was woven in the year A.D. 1539 (A.H. 946), the thirteenth year of the long reign of fifty-two years of Shah Tahmasp.

The warps and wefts of the carpet are of silk. The knot is Persian. There are approximately 17 × 19 knots to the inch—which is about equal to the best quality Kashān carpets of about thirty years ago.

---

[1] "Some Documents from Polish Sources Relating to Carpet Making in the Time of Shah Abbas I," Tadeusz Mankowski, *A Survey of Persian Art*, Oxford University Press, 1939.

[2] *A Survey of Persian Art*, vols. III and VI. Although, to the cautious-minded, some of Mr. Pope's conclusions indicate a certain temerity, I gladly add my humble tribute of respect to the compiler of this prodigious work.

[3] Another carpet in the Ardebil design was removed from the mosque at the same time as its more famous counterpart and is now in America. A portion of it—notably part of the border—was used to repair the carpet now in the Victoria and Albert Museum.

1. THE ARDEBIL CARPET
Victoria and Albert Museum, London

Unlike many of the famous carpets of the period, the Ardebil is tranquil in design and free from disturbing images of animals and figures. For it was woven to lie in a holy place, where representations of animals or human forms were banned by the Qūrān.

The drawing and execution are admirable. The sixteen ogival panels, radiating and equidistant from an almost round sixteen-pointed medallion, suggest that the design was intended to indicate a circular dome, from which the two golden lamps were suspended. As usual, a quarter of the centre design is repeated in the four corners—a harmonious and satisfying convention.

The cartouche border with its twin guards, in which the cloud-band motive has been cleverly introduced, is justly famous. It has become the prototype of this style of border in every country where carpets are made.

All authorities agree that a carpet of such outstanding design and craftsmanship could not have been produced except by a combination of the first designers and craftsmen of the age—such as might be found, most probably, in a court factory. And because, during part of the reign of Shah Tahmasp, his capital was Tabrīz, it has been asserted that the carpet was woven there—in a royal factory established by that prince. Furthermore, these authorities have maintained that the splendid group of sixteenth-century medallion carpets—which undoubtedly possess a strong family affinity with the Ardebil —must therefore have been woven in Tabrīz as well.

But how could this be? The Ardebil is dated A.H. 946 (A.D. 1539); but long before that date Tahmasp—realising that Tabrīz (owing to its exposed position) was in danger of attack from his enemies the Turks—had moved his capital to Kazvīn. His caution was well founded. For in 1533—six years before the Ardebil was completed—Tabrīz was captured by the Turks. During the succeeding twenty years it was abandoned and reoccupied no less than four times. Are we to believe that when Tahmasp removed his seat of government for safety to Kazvīn he left his factory behind; and that the carpets which he ordered for the mosque at Ardebil were woven in Tabrīz during the Turkish occupation? Had he done so, the chances are that the Ardebil carpet would be hanging today in one of the museums of Istanbul instead of in the Victoria and Albert Museum.

Tabrīz may be dismissed as the birthplace of the Ardebil on technical grounds as well. For the carpet was woven with the Persian knot, whereas the people of Tabrīz were Turks and undoubtedly wove the Turkish knot—as they do to this day. It is possible, of course (but very unlikely), that Maqsūd who made it[1] may have been ordered by the Shah to come north to Tabrīz with several hundred weavers and to set up a court factory there; and that the factory with the weavers was transferred to Kazvīn when Tahmasp moved his capital. In that case the Ardebil—and probably most of the other carpets of that group—were woven in Kazvīn. If that were so, however, we would expect that some record, some vestige or some tradition would remain in Kazvīn of this important undertaking. Yet nothing remains; and it has never been suggested by the Persians that any of the Sefavi carpets were woven there.

If then the claims of Tabrīz and Kazvīn appear too shadowy, where could the Ardebil and its companions have been woven?

The towns of South Persia (Kermān and Shirāz) and of east Persia (Herāt and Meshed) may be excluded on technical grounds. Sultānabād did not exist, for it was founded in the nineteenth century. In Hamadān the Turkish knot was used; and there is no evidence that fine carpets were woven there. Isfahān should also, I think, be excluded, because it did not become a centre of fine weaving until Tahmasp's grandson, Shah Abbas, made it his capital and established his court factory. There remain Ardebil itself and Kashān, the birthplace of Maqsūd, who produced the carpet.

Ardebil is a remote possibility. Maqsūd might have been instructed to bring his weavers and set up his looms there—perhaps in the precincts of the mosque where the carpets were to be laid. Indeed, the inscription on the carpet itself may have been intended to convey that it was woven on hallowed ground. But again we are met by the total absence in Ardebil of any tradition that this took place. It is hardly conceivable that a tradition would not have existed in the mosque itself if, besides the two carpets, all the other pieces of the group had been woven within its precincts, or in the neighbourhood.

Finally, the Ardebil may have been woven in Kashān. This does not follow, however, from the fact that Maqsūd's cognomen was Kashāni. For in a country where surnames did not exist, the birthplace following the given name was merely an added

---

[1] Herr Sebastian Beck has stated (*Old Oriental Carpets*, notes on Plate 18) that the word *amel-i* may mean "ordered by" and not "made by". He is mistaken. The word means "the work of", and in carpet making it always refers to the master-weaver. The word *fermaish-i*, i.e. "made to the order of", is used for carpets which have been specially ordered.

means of identification. It did not necessarily indicate that Maqsūd lived and pursued his craft in Kashān. Yet Kashān undoubtedly possesses a claim —as against Tabrīz, Kazvīn or Ardebil—to be the birthplace of the famous carpet. It is now, and has been for centuries, a centre of fine craftsmanship. M. le Chevalier Chardin, writing in the sixteenth century, observes: "Cachan . . . il ne se fait en aucun lieu de la Perse plus de satin, de velour, de taffetas, de tabis,[1] de brocard uni et a fleurs de soie et de soie melee d'or et d'argent qu'il s'en fait en cette ville et aux environs."[2] Sir Anthony Sherley says much the same thing about Kashān and specifically mentions "Persian Carpets of a wonderful fineness".[3] So did the Carmelites Father Paul Simon of Jesus and Mary and Father Peter of St. Andrew, who visited Kashān in 1607-1608. And, of course, the Kashānis use, and have always used, the Persian knot.

Here, then, we must let the matter rest, with the hope that the reader has not been wearied by the vain pursuit. The object of the short enquiry has been to indicate the danger—if, indeed, a stronger term should not be used—of making positive assertions as to the birthplace of any of the Sefavi carpets. The Ardebil was chosen for the enquiry because it is one of the very few carpets which is dated and signed. Yet, in spite of these precious indications, we are unable to trace its origin. How then dare we postulate about the origins of those pieces which do not possess even these important clues?

We do not know, and it is doubtful if we shall ever know, where these carpets were woven. All that we can do is to indicate some of the more likely localities and to register their claims. The reader, if he is sufficiently interested, may inwardly record his preference.

Plate 2. Hunting Carpet; Austrian Museum for Art and Industry, Vienna

This carpet is in the first rank of the great carpets of the world. Some authorities, indeed, have declared it to be the finest carpet ever woven. It is the only carpet listed here in which warp, weft and pile are of silk. Parts of the figures are brocaded in silver or silver gilt. It counts 27 × 29 knots to the inch, which is far closer in weave than any other of the Sefavi carpets.

The hunt is a catch-as-catch-can affair. The huntsmen are mounted and armed with spears, swords and bows. They are attacking—with considerable élan, but apparently without much method—a concentration of lions, leopards, wolves, bears, antelopes, wild asses, jackals and hares. This is strictly in the Persian tradition. For with the Persians—as, indeed, with us—the hunt is often prepared for the huntsman, so that he may be spared unnecessary fatigue. The eight-pointed green medallion is embellished with golden dragons and phoenixes, in the Chinese manner. Again, as is common in Persian design, the corners repeat a quarter of the medallion.

The border is an outstanding feature of this magnificent carpet. Its ground colour is a deep crimson. The design consists of a succession of winged figures receiving offerings of bowls of fruit from other winged figures. These are beautifully drawn and evenly spaced upon a background pattern of birds, cloud-bands and flowers.

The carpet was almost certainly designed by a court painter; perhaps—as Dr. F. R. Martin and others have suggested—by Sultān Mohammed, the celebrated court painter of Shah Tahmasp. It has all the animation, movement and the superb pictorial skill of that admirable master. If, indeed, it was designed by him, it was probably woven about the middle of the sixteenth century; for Sultān Mohammed died about A.D. 1555.

The carpet has been attributed to Kashān, on the grounds that the Kashānis were accustomed to weave silken fabrics and that some silk carpets were undoubtedly woven there in the sixteenth century. But this proves nothing. A silk carpet can be woven in any factory if the competent craftsmen are there. Still, Kashān probably possesses as good a claim as any other town to the distinction of having produced perhaps the finest silk carpet ever woven.

In the opinion of some authorities the weak point of the carpet is the ground colour, which is salmon pink. The colour was probably very rich and lovely when the carpet was first woven.

Plate 3. The Chelsea Carpet; Victoria and Albert Museum, London

This famous carpet was acquired by the Museum over fifty years ago from a dealer in the King's Road, Chelsea; and it has been known as the "Chelsea Carpet" ever since.

Some authorities have claimed that it is earlier than the Ardebil. It may be; but there appears to

---

[1] *tabis* is not a misspelling of *tapis*; it is *tabby*, or watered silk. [2] *Voyages de M. le Chevalier Chardin* (Amsterdam, 1711).
[3] *Brief and True Report of Sir Anthony Sherlie, his journey into Persia, etc.* (London, 1600).

2. HUNTING CARPET
Austrian Museum for Art and Industry, Vienna

be no special reason for this assertion. The carpet possesses an undoubted kinship with the Ardebil and probably belongs to the same group.

It is without doubt one of the great carpets of the world. Kendrick and Tattersall (in whose care it was) declared that it almost challenged the Ardebil to the first place in the Victoria and Albert collection. Bode declared that it occupied "the first place among all carpets". We cannot but agree with these authorities. The carpet is indeed a triumph of imaginative and elaborate design combined with perfect execution. It possesses all the nobility and tranquillity of the Ardebil, with the added interest of beautifully drawn animal figures. Its colour is a sober combination of deep carmine red with bold medallions and ogees in dark blue. Like the Ardebil its warp and weft are of silk. It counts 21 × 22 knots to the inch, which means that it has about 50 per cent more knots per square inch than the Ardebil. It is in excellent state of preservation.

Where was the Chelsea carpet woven? I can only refer the reader back to the previous discussion of this question; adding that the Chelsea and the Ardebil were probably woven in the same place—wherever that was.

Plate 4. All-over Animal and Floral Carpet; Austrian Museum for Art and Industry, Vienna

This is one of the finest examples extant of the all-over animal and floral group of carpets, of which a number have come down to us. As such it has an undoubted claim to a high place among the great carpets of the world. Like the Ardebil, the Austrian Hunting carpet and the Chelsea, its warp and weft are of silk. It counts 17 × 19 knots to the inch—about the same as the Ardebil. The whole design (with the exception of the twin large green flowers in the middle of the upper and lower halves) is admirably drawn and executed. The distortion of the two flowers is probably due to faulty execution, because they are woven on the bias—a difficult operation.

The border displays a superb treatment of the cloud-band motive with entwined arabesques. The inner guards are made up of cartouches of equal length—each filled with an inscription—and there is nothing more decorative than an inscription guard or border. The ground of the carpet is rich red; the border dark green; the inner guards yellow.

Where were the carpets of this group woven? They have been attributed—on what appears to be rather flimsy grounds—to east Persia; which means Herāt or Meshed. They may have been made in one of those places. But to the writer at least they appear nearer in fabric to the carpets of the west. But again we do not know.[1]

When were they made? Authorities are generally agreed that they were woven at the end of the sixteenth century. They probably were.

Plate 5. Rose-ground Vase Carpet; Victoria and Albert Museum, London

The eight best among the great carpets must include a representative of the Vase design and its various modifications. For one thing, many more carpets in this design have come down to us from the Sefavi period than in any other. And no wonder. For it is, by and large, one of the best designs for a floor-covering that has ever been devised. It has determined and defined for all time a large number of classical Persian forms and motives which have been copied and recopied for four hundred years. It has been woven in almost every textile floor-covering that exists, and it has been used by printers of furnishing materials the world over.

Including fragments, there must be more than fifty pieces in the Vase design in the museums and private collections of the world. Most of the important collections possess examples. It was not a simple matter to select the carpet out of the best half-dozen which expresses most completely the designer's plan. For if ever a design was elegantly planned, this was.

The choice finally lay between a carpet in the National Museum, Berlin, and one in the Victoria and Albert Museum (which formerly belonged to William Morris). The London carpet is more refined and more graceful; the Berlin piece bolder and more striking. The motives in the London carpet are smaller than those in the Berlin carpet, so that more of the ground is shown. Thus, the plan of the design is more in evidence. In the Berlin carpet much of the surface is taken up by the large motives, so that the plan is almost lost. Both pieces are fine examples of the genre; although the borders of both are weak—as indeed the borders of most of the Vase carpets are. The final choice was the London carpet.

Where were the Vase carpets made and when?

The reader must not be wearied with another hopeless quest. But I cannot refrain from registering a mild protest against Mr. Upham Pope's surprising

[1] This question is examined in greater detail on p. 163.

3. THE CHELSEA CARPET
Victoria and Albert Museum, London

4. ALL-OVER ANIMAL AND FLORAL CARPET
Austrian Museum for Art and Industry, Vienna

5. ROSE-GROUND VASE CARPET
Victoria and Albert Museum, London

and personal *ukase* that they were woven in the small mountain village of Jōshaqān.

That village enjoys a just but limited renown in Persia. For it is the only locality which has continued to produce the same style of carpet—in weave, dyes and design—for at least 200 years, and (for aught we know) for much longer. Except for the absence of wear, and of the bloom and patina of age, some of the Jōshaqān carpets of today might have been woven two centuries ago.

But these carpets, old and new, possess one peculiarity which must have escaped Mr. Pope—otherwise he would surely have refrained from his strange attribution. *They are all woven in straight lines.* No Jōshaqān of the last 200 years possesses a single curvilinear motive or flower; yet Mr. Pope asserts that the Vase carpets—those masterpieces of curvilinear design—were woven in this village.

I was recently given the opportunity of examining, side by side, on the floor of the Victoria and Albert Museum, two pieces from their collection: a large fragment of an eighteenth-century Jōshaqān carpet (Plate 367) and the famous rose-ground Vase carpet of Plate 5. I attempted—with all the objectivity which I could muster—to trace some similarity in design, colour or construction, some hint of parentage between the two pieces which might account for Mr. Pope's strange whim. I failed to find them.

It is almost unnecessary to add that carpets of such fine quality and intricate design as the Vase carpets call for the associated efforts of skilled dyers, of creative designers, of planners and draftsmen, and of master-weavers—all of whom must have been trained for long years in their craft. Such persons are not to be found in small mountain villages in Persia. There is no scope for their activities among the poor and ignorant peasantry. They can only work in the more civilised atmosphere of the towns.

The monumental *Survey of Persian Art* contains no less than 152 plates of Persian carpets. Of these Mr. Pope has definitely attributed no less than thirty-six to this small village, with four more possibles! But to Isfahān itself, where we know—beyond a doubt—that Shah Abbas had established a court factory close to his palace (so that this curious and indefatigable prince might watch from day to day the progress of his carpets) Mr. Pope attributes only *one* piece, with eight possibles! Where, then, are all the carpets which were produced in the court factory during the reign of the great king? The writer suggests that the Vase carpets were woven in that factory.[1]

We know that a considerable number of carpets in the Vase design were made. Would it not be in the nature of things for Shah Abbas to select a fine design from among those submitted, and to order from it a number of carpets to be made in his factory in various sizes and ground colours—rose, red, dark blue, medium blue, cream and tan—like the Vase carpets which have come down to us? If this suggestion appears reasonable we can plead, with some assurance, that the carpets of this group were woven in Isfahān during the reign of Shah Abbas; that is, in the late sixteenth or early seventeenth century. Most authorities are at least agreed upon the date.

Plate 6. Medallion, Animal and Floral Carpet with Inscription Guard; Museo Poldi Pezzoli, Milan

This splendid carpet appears to bear a family resemblance to the Chelsea carpet. Its weave is similar; it has the same tranquillity, deriving from its low tones of red and dark blue. Like its relative in London, its warps and wefts are of silk. It counts 18×20 knots to the inch—not as fine as the Chelsea carpet, but somewhat finer than the Ardebil. Unlike those two carpets, however, some of the figures in the Milan carpet are brocaded with silver gilt.

The design possesses some unusual features. Light, realistic trees—very different from the conventionalised tree patterns which usually appear in Persian carpets—have been introduced into the field. Though skilfully drawn and perfectly executed, they may appear (to some eyes at least) out of harmony with the staid formalism of the rest of the design. Again, the head of the medallion is separated from the medallion itself—a breach of an accepted convention which may be disturbing to the devotees of tradition.

The animal and floral figures in the field, the stately medallion, the broad inscription guard and the graceful flowering border are superbly drawn and carried out.

Authorities are generally agreed that it was woven—like its relatives the Ardebil and Chelsea carpets—in the middle of the sixteenth century, during the long reign of Shah Tahmasp. As to its birthplace, the reader is referred to the discussion on p. 10.

---

[1] Kendrick suggests that they were woven in Kermān. They may have been. Kermān is, in any case, a better guess than Jōshaqān.

Plate 7. Inscribed Medallion Carpet with Animal and Flowers and Inscription Border; Metropolitan Museum of Art, New York

A number of carpets similar to this in design and style have come down to us from Sefavi times; but this is admittedly the best of the group. Its warp and weft are of silk. In quality it is among the finest of the woollen pile Sefavi carpets; for it counts 23 × 24 knots to the inch, which is finer than the Chelsea carpet and is only surpassed by the silk Hunting carpet of the Austrian Museum.

The design is more austere, less elaborate, than that of most of the great carpets. But it is no less admirable for that. Apparently the artist who conceived it did not aim to compel admiration or wonder; he sought rather to appeal to a deeper, stiller emotion. The round medallion with its strange cruciform panels in green enclosed by an inscription on black, the large medallion heads (with their suggestion of Islamic headstones), the magnificent inscription border—again with silver lettering on black—give to this carpet a ritualistic, an ecclesiastical air.

It was probably woven in the sixteenth century during the reign of Shah Tahmasp. Where, we do not know.

Plate 8. Medallion, Animal and Tree Carpet; Musée des Arts Décoratifs, Paris

This is only a fragment—another fragment of it is in the cathedral at Cracow—but it cannot be excluded from the list because of that. For it possesses nearly all the hallmarks of renown. The design has interest, grace and proportion; the drawing is perfect; the colouring is lively, yet harmonious. Although it was woven 400 years ago, it does not date: it has been reproduced, down the centuries, in many fabrics and in many climes; and—as far as we can judge—it will continue to be reproduced as long as pile carpets continue to be made.

Nevertheless, the fastidious critic may contend that the border lacks distinction—that its primary motives are drawn on too small a scale.

This carpet, too, probably belongs to the large group of beautifully balanced medallion carpets which includes, among many others, the Ardebil, the carpet in the Museo Poldi Pezzoli and perhaps the Chelsea. If this surmise is correct, it, too, dates from the middle of the sixteenth century.

The Imprint of the Great Period

We have seen (p. 5) that the Afghan invasions (1722) finally extinguished an art which had been declining since the death of Shah Abbas a century earlier. During that century carpet weaving sank once more to its former status of a small but useful handicraft.

The handicraft had, however, undergone a fundamental change. The great period had left its imprint upon it—an imprint which has endured for four centuries and which will seemingly endure as long as carpets continue to be woven in Persia.

The technique employed in the preparation of the materials and in the weaving process remained the same. The imprint was in design. For the influence of the designers whom the Sefavi princes had gathered about them was profound and permanent. They had copied, invented, adapted and fixed for good a large and varied series of lovely floral and animal forms—Chinese, Arab and Persian—which appear, time and again, in a thousand permutations in the designs of their successors. Every Persian designer of today can draw them with his eyes shut. Any suggestion that one of them could be altered or improved would be received with polite but unmistakable disfavour.

These motives are the foundation of Persian classical design. Their influence has spread far beyond the confines of Persia. They have been used the world over by designers of floor-coverings, tapestries, printed fabrics, wallpapers and every other form of artistic decoration. I shall have something more to say about them in Chapter V, entitled "Some Notes on Design".

6. MEDALLION, ANIMAL AND FLORAL CARPET, WITH INSCRIPTION GUARD
Museo Poldi Pezzoli, Milan

7. Inscribed Medallion Carpet with Animal and Flowers and Inscription Border
Metropolitan Museum of Art, New York

8. MEDALLION, ANIMAL AND TREE CARPET
Musée des Arts Décoratifs, Paris

CHAPTER III

THE WEAVER'S CRAFT

I purpose in this chapter to describe the technique of the carpet weaver as it has been carried on in Persia, with unimportant variations, for many centuries. To do so, it will be necessary to designate the types of loom, the tools and accessories which are in use today; to specify the materials of which the fabric is normally constructed; to differentiate between the two basic types of knot (and their variations); and, finally, to endeavour to explain the complicated technique of weaving.

The Loom

Four different types of loom are used in Persia:
(1) The ground (or horizontal) loom.
(2) The upright loom:
    (a) village type,
    (b) Tabrīz type,
    (c) roller beam type.

I have suggested in Chapter I that the hand-knotted carpet of Persia was an invention of her nomadic shepherds; for it would seem to be in the natural course of things that a people who possessed a disposition for form and colour would not for long be satisfied to cover their tent floors with the skins of animals. The urge to decorate would have stimulated them (I suggested) to devise something warm and comfortable; but gayer, more amusing and more colourful than a sheepskin rug. Such a fabric must consist of two main elements: a woollen pile—to give thickness and warmth, and to embody the colour and the pattern; and a solid back or foundation to which the tufts of wool could be attached. Inevitably, the tribal rug would be evolved. Indeed, I have myself seen Kurdish rugs so rough and crude that they suggested the kind of fabric which must have been produced by those early shepherds.

The loom on which those shepherds wove their rugs was the forerunner of the horizontal ground loom of today. Indeed the ground loom which is in constant use by the nomadic and most of the semi-nomadic tribes is itself so primitive that it cannot be far removed from its early forerunner. Although many of the settled tribes have abandoned it, there are many villages—particularly in Fārs and Kermān provinces—where it is still in use.

Its chief merit (for the nomad) lies in its lightness and portability. For the two loom beams are not supported (as in the upright loom) by strong side-pieces which would add considerably to its weight. Instead, the two beams are kept apart by stakes which are driven into the ground. The tension of the warp is maintained by driving wedges between the ends of the loom beams and the stakes.

When the order to march is given the stakes are taken up, the unfinished rug is rolled on its two beams and hoisted on to the back of a transport animal. At the next camping ground it is unrolled, the stakes are driven into the ground once more and the loom is ready for weaving. Plates 9 and 198 show tribal or village weavers working at looms of this type.

The rugs of nomadic tribes are generally small, i.e. under 4 feet wide, because a loom beam over 5 feet in length is too awkward and too heavy for transport. The largest tribal pieces are the so-called

9. A LOOM, HORIZONTAL TYPE
Qashqaī tribal weavers at work outside their tent.

Shirāz carpets, which are woven in Fārs; but even these are now mostly woven by settled tribes or villagers.

Loom beams in Persia are invariably made of poplar, because the poplar is the only tree on the plateau which is fairly straight and inexpensive. In the villages, the beams are often crooked—which accounts (in part) for the high proportion of crooked rugs and carpets woven in the rural centres.

Of the three upright types, the village type is—as might be expected—the simplest and crudest. It consists of a fixed upper beam (or warp beam) and a lower (or cloth beam), the ends of which fit into slots in the side-pieces. The lower ends of the warp are usually laced to a rope which is wrapped round the cloth beam. The loose upper ends are twisted together into half a dozen bunches and tied to the upper beam. Tension is obtained by driving wedges into the slots of the side-pieces.

The village weaver sits on a plank, the ends of which rest on the bottom rungs of two ladders. As the work proceeds the plank is raised, so that in time the weaver may be working 4 or 5 feet above the floor level. When that height is reached the wedges are withdrawn and the upper ends of the warp are loosened. The carpet is then free. The woven part is then lowered and sewn along its whole length to the rope wrapped round the cloth beam; the loose ends of the warp are again bunched and tied along the upper beam; tension is restored by driving the wedges into the side slots; the weaver's seat is lowered to the first rung of the ladder; and the work of weaving begins again.

The Tabrīz type of upright loom (Plate 10) is so called because it seems to have been invented in Tabrīz. No other type is used there. It is simple, easy to operate and inexpensive. It is now in use in most of the urban weaving centres of north-west and central Persia. It possesses many advantages over the village type, described above. The tiresome operation of bunching and tying the loose upper ends of the warp, and of periodically sewing the woven portion of the carpet to the cloth beam, are obviated. When the time comes to lower the carpet, the warp can be quickly loosened by withdrawing the four wedges from the slots in the side-pieces. The carpet is then lowered and the woven part slides up behind, where it can be easily inspected.

The roller beam type of loom is more developed, mechanically, than either of the two types already described. In it both beams revolve in sockets. A

10. A LOOM, TABRĪZ TYPE

The weavers are waiting for the factory attendant to remove the wedges and loosen the carpet so that it may be lowered and the work resumed.

rod, sometimes of iron, is passed through the ends of the warp, and is then lashed or otherwise fixed to the lower beam. The upper end of the warp is then fixed to the upper beam in the same way, and the beam is revolved with levers until the warp strings are taut. As the weaving proceeds the woven carpet is rolled round the lower beam and the warp is unrolled, *pari passu*, from the upper.

The roller beam type (Plate 11) possesses certain advantages over the Tabrīz type: (*a*) it can carry a carpet of any length—while the Tabrīz loom cannot carry one which measures more than twice the distance between its upper and lower beams; (*b*) a greater and more even tension can be obtained with revolving beams and levers than by driving wedges into slots; and (*c*) the roller type produces straighter carpets than any other.

Every loom—horizontal or upright—possesses a

11. A LOOM, ROLLER-BEAM TYPE
The interior of a carpet factory, Kermān.

simple mechanism which enables the weaver to separate the alternate warp strings into two sets or *leaves*; and by so doing to create a channel or *shed* between the leaves into which the weaver can slip her left hand to draw the warp through. The essentials of the mechanism are the same in all the four types of loom. The weaver crosses the two leaves after each weft has been passed, before passing the next.

The Weaver's Instruments

Besides the loom on which the carpet is woven, the weaver must possess a few simple instruments which are essential to his craft. They are: a knife for cutting off the yarn after the knot is made; an instrument like a comb for beating in the wefts; and a pair of shears for trimming off the ends of the yarn after each row of knots is finished. These are the essential tools. They vary somewhat in size and design, and in some areas they are supplemented by other tools. An important variation in the knife has been introduced in Tabrīz. There, a combined blade and hook has been devised. The hook, which is like a button hook, projects from the end of the blade and is used for knotting (instead of knotting with the fingers); and the blade is for cutting off the yarn when the knot is tied. It is claimed that a weaver can tie the knot more rapidly with the hook than with the fingers. After watching the Tabrīz weavers at work I can well believe it (Plate 12).

Two very different types of comb-beater are used in Persia: the old type (*A*)—which is used mainly by the tribes and in the villages—has a heavy

12. THE TABRĪZ WEAVERS TIE THE KNOT WITH A HOOK INSTEAD OF WITH THE FINGERS ONLY
The surface of the woven part is rough because the carpet is usually clipped after it is finished.

wooden body with an upstanding handle and projecting iron teeth. These pass through the warp strings to beat in the wefts. A later and more sophisticated type (*B*) is used by the urban weavers. It is made of a dozen thin strips of iron $\frac{3}{4}$ inch wide and 9 inches long, riveted together for half their length (to form the handle) and splayed out for the other half to form the beater (Plate 13).

The Kermān weavers use two instruments for beating in the wefts: Type *A* or *B* is used first, and afterwards a second beater, like a short, blunt sabre, is introduced sideways into the "shed"; with it the weaver hammers the weft again along its whole length. Thus the wefts are packed thoroughly into the fabric.

In Bijār, type *A* is used; but it is supplemented by a second beater like a heavy nail, with which the

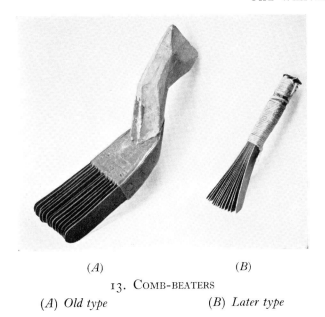

13. COMB-BEATERS
(A) Old type   (B) Later type

thick woollen weft is laboriously hammered in a second time.

The shears, too—which are used for trimming off the ends of yarn after each row of knots is finished—differ with the area and the fabric. Some are a foot long and curved; others shorter and straight, like a tailor's shears. In Kermān and Tabrīz the ends of yarn are usually left untrimmed until the carpet is finished. Then the whole surface is "clipped" in one operation (Plate 195).

When a row of knots is finished, and before the ends of yarn are trimmed, the careful weaver takes hold of them between finger and thumb and pulls them towards her to tighten the knots. This operation is sometimes performed (notably in Kermān and Arāk) with a small steel comb which tightens the knots and at the same time combs out the strands of yarn—thus producing greater definition in the design of the carpet (Plate 133).

The Materials of the Weaver's Craft

There are only three of importance: silk, wool and cotton. Goat's hair is used by the Balūchi tribes for the selvedges of some of their rugs. Camel's hair is hardly ever encountered. Some commentators appear to have taken it for granted that the characteristic brown Hamadān rugs were woven with camel-hair yarn. Actually, it was very rarely used in the past; and it is never used today. Jute, which is commonly used in India for wefts, is never used in Persia.

Of the three standard materials, silk is the least important. It was used in a number of the Sefavi carpets which have come down to us (the Hunting Carpet in the Vienna Museum—sometimes regarded as the best carpet ever woven—was made entirely of silk); and some of the finest of the woollen carpets of the great period have warps of silk. This may be because the short staple Persian cotton did not produce a thin yarn strong enough to withstand the tension on the loom or to carry the weight of the carpet when finished.

Silk (produced and spun in Persia) is still used, mainly in Kashān. But the output of silk rugs is small. The material, indeed, is cold and hard and unsuitable for a floor-covering. Rugs made with it are sumptuary products appropriate for wall decoration, table covers and suchlike. By and large, cotton and wool are the materials from which Persian carpets are made.

Cotton is produced in many districts of Persia; indeed, there is hardly a province which does not grow it. The principal producing areas are Isfahān, Kashān, Kazvīn, Yezd, Meshed and Kermān. Although American strains have been introduced from time to time, the quality has not greatly improved. It is still short in staple.

Cotton has proved itself (not only in Persia) to be on the whole the best fibre for the warps and wefts of hand-knotted carpets. Wool has been used for centuries by the tribes for this purpose—because it is a pastoral product which they raise themselves; whereas cotton is not. But it is inferior to cotton as a foundation: it is too elastic; it is liable to shrink unevenly; and it produces a spongy fabric which is inclined to slip on a hardwood floor. A cotton foundation, on the other hand, produces a firm and solid fabric which shrinks evenly and holds the floor well.

Handspun cotton is used, almost exclusively, for the warps and wefts of the cheaper grades of rugs and carpets—most of which are woven in the villages. It is also used for the thick wefts on the finer urban and semi-urban qualities. For this purpose it is preferred to millspun, because it is cheaper and packs better.

Millspun cotton was formerly imported from India; but during the last twenty years cotton mills have been built in Isfahān, Yezd, Kashān, Tabrīz, Kazvīn and Mazanderān; so that today the Persian carpet industry is supplied by home-grown and homespun cotton. The yarn is not so good as that which was formerly imported; but it is good enough. The industry is heavily protected. Millspun cotton is used for the warps and the thin wefts of the finer urban (and semi-urban) qualities. "Twenties" is the count in common use. The warps are usually nine ply; the thin wefts two or three ply.

I do not propose to say anything here about the wools and woollen yarns of Persia. The types used in each centre will be described in Chapters VI to XVI.

The Two Basic Knots

In all hand-knotted carpets from the East the knots are made by tying pieces of coloured yarn to two (or four) strings of the warp. In Persia the pieces of yarn are tied in one of two different ways, depending on whether the weaver is of Turkish or Persian race. This rule is almost invariable, and the few exceptions can always be traced to an extraneous influence.

The two types of knot may be applied differently in different localities, or even in the same locality; but basically there are two, and only two, knots used in Persia. They are illustrated—together with their variations—opposite.

The two basic types are commonly known as the Ghiordes knot and the Senneh knot. By whom this erroneous and misleading nomenclature was first devised, I do not know; but it has been repeated, times without number, by writers and rug fanciers alike. The little town of Ghiordes in western Anatolia possesses an ancient and honourable record as a weaving centre; but that is hardly a sufficient reason for naming after it a technique which is common to all the peoples of Turkish race. Among the famous weaves which are woven with the Turkish knot are the Ushāk and Ghiordes carpets; the many types of Anatolian rugs; the Shirvāns, Kubās, Kazāks, Genjehs and Karabāghs of the Caucasus; the carpets of Tabrīz and of the Herīz area; the rich variety of the Hamadān weaves; the multifarious tribal rugs of Merv and Kashgar; the Kizil Ayāks, the Beshīrs, Yamūts and Kara-Kalpāks; and many others, equally meritorious, if less renowned. All these weaves are produced by peoples of Turkish race and speech. Surely—if things are to be called by their proper names—the knot which they weave should be called the Turkī or the Turkish knot.

But the choice of the name Senneh for the second basic type is stranger still. The person who first named it after the small town of Senneh in Persian Kurdistān (of all places) perhaps presumed that the thin and supple rugs woven there must have necessarily been woven with the knot of the second basic

14. THE TWO BASIC TYPES OF KNOT USED IN PERSIA

1. TURKĪ (TURKISH) KNOT
used by weavers of Turkish or Kurdish race

2. FARSĪ (PERSIAN) KNOT
used by weavers of Persian race

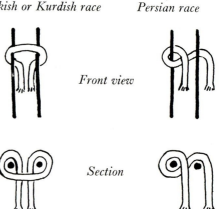

Front view

Section

Three fraudulent variations of the above two basic types woven on four warp strings instead of two:

1a. TURKĪ (TURKISH) KNOT   2a. FARSĪ (PERSIAN) KNOT

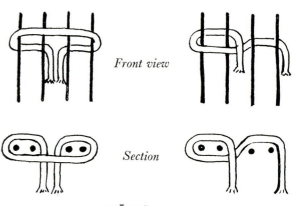

Front view

Section

KHŪRASĀN TYPE

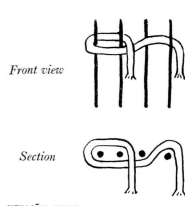

Front view

Section

KERMĀN TYPE

type. For this knot does, indeed, produce a fabric somewhat more supple and more delicate than the Turkish knot. But that incautious pioneer—whoever he was—was deceived by appearance and failed to check his sources. For the rugs of Senneh (like all the Kurdish weaves) are woven with the Turkish knot. The term Senneh is therefore a complete misnomer for the knot of the second type.

This is the type which is used by weavers of Persian race and speech—the weavers of Arāk, Meshed, Birjānd, Kermān, Isfahān, Naīn, Kashān and Qūm—but not of Senneh. It must be called, then, by its proper name—the Farsī or Persian knot.

How came it to pass that both basic types—the Turkish and Persian—are used in Persia today? Not, as might be expected, side by side in the same town or village; but only in separate and distinct sections of the country. The explanation must be sought in history.

In the tenth century A.D. some important tribes of Turks—later known as Seljūks after the founder of their famous dynasty—which, with their wives and families had been moving westwards from Central Asia, reached the borders of Khūrasān. During the eleventh century they wrested the whole of Persia from the empire of the Arab Caliph of Baghdad. Although they established their authority throughout the country, it was only in the provinces Azerbaijān, Hamadān (and perhaps in Seraband and Chahār Mahāl) that they settled down and supplanted the Persian inhabitants. Many of these fled southward before the invaders. The womenfolk of both the incoming Turks and of the Persians whom they supplanted or expelled were carpet weavers—but they knotted their rugs in a different manner. Thus, a racial and linguistic frontier line was established across Persia—on one side of which the population speaks mainly Turkish and weaves the Turkish knot; and on the other side it speaks mainly Persian and weaves the Persian knot (see Map on p. 6).

In the distant provinces of Kermān and Fārs there are important areas inhabited by Turkish tribes—Afshārs and Qashqaīs—who in past centuries were transplanted there from motives of discipline or policy by the reigning monarch. There they continue to dwell as Turkish enclaves, and to weave their tribal rugs; still Turkish in design and colour, and still woven with the Turkish knot which they brought with them centuries ago. For further details about these tribes, see Chapters XIII and XIV.

It was mentioned above that some local variations have appeared in the basic two types of knot—the Turkī (or Turkish) and the Farsī (or Persian). The two types, with their variations, are illustrated on p. 26. I have not reckoned as variation (as some have done) the tying of the knots from left to right or vice versa. This appears to me to be an over-refinement in classification. It makes no difference, in effect, whether the weaver ties her knots left to right or right to left: the knot is the same.

It will be noticed from the illustrations that the so-called variations in the two basic types are not, in fact, variations at all. The method of tying is the same. Only, instead of the knots being tied to two strings of the warp—as they should be—they are tied to four.

I shall have a good deal to say in the course of this survey about this method of weaving. For it is a fraudulent device: a device whereby the weaver ties one knot in place of two, and so doubles output to the detriment of quality. In a closely woven fabric the fraud is difficult to detect before the weft is passed; and almost impossible to detect afterwards. Only the feel of the carpet betrays it. Because, of course, a fabric in which a large proportion of the knots are tied on four strings of the warp instead of two must lack density, and without density a carpet will not give good service.

This type of knot is known in Persia as *jūftī* or *jūft ilmeh*, i.e. the double knot. Twenty-five years ago it was little used, except in northern Khūrasān. But it has spread with alarming rapidity—particularly during the last decade. Unless the malady is arrested the renown of the Persian carpet will be imperilled. The question of what can be done to arrest it will be discussed in the last chapter on "The Future of the Industry".

The Technique of Weaving

As may have been gathered from this and the preceding chapters, there are two classes of weavers in Persia: the rural (of which the tribal weavers form a part) and the urban or semi-urban. Among the latter must be included the weavers of those villages which are situated in the vicinity of an urban centre and who produce rugs and carpets similar to the urban products. They are generally under the direction of an urban merchant.

The technique of weaving practised by both rural and urban weavers is essentially the same. The first operation is to lay the warp. It may be laid directly on the loom; or it may be first prepared (as shown in Plate 15) and then placed in position. It is

15. Preparing the Warp, Arāk (Sultānabād)

customary to divide the loom beams into units of measurement and to lay the proper number of warp strings in each division. Thus a proper and equal number of lateral knots is obtained per unit.

The weaving operation consists in tying a piece of coloured yarn to each pair of warp strings along the whole width of the carpet, in accordance with a prescribed pattern; in passing, above each row of knots, one, two or three wefts in and out of each warp string (taking care to cross the warps after each weft has been passed); in beating the weft into place with a comb beater; and in trimming off the ends of the yarn along the width of the carpet with a pair of shears. This operation is repeated, time after time, until the carpet is complete.

Up to this point the techniques of rural and urban weaver are parallel; beyond it—in the task of building up the pattern—they diverge. For the rural weaver either builds according to a pattern which she learnt in childhood from her mother (who learnt it in the same way from hers); or she builds out of her own fancy—utilising forms peculiar to her village or tribe. The urban or semi-urban weaver, however, knows nothing of all this. He (for the weaver may well be a man or boy) is given a section of a drawing on scale paper to work from.

Scale-paper designs are usually drawn full size—or nearly full size—so that (in the case of a non-repeating design) it may be as large as a room. When the line drawing of the design has been made on the scale paper the position of each knot is indicated by dotting the little squares where the lines of the drawing pass. The design is then coloured, cut into horizontal sections, mounted and varnished. From this the head-weaver works, while calling the pattern to his assistants. Or he may crouch between a pair of looms set back to back, and call the pattern to the weavers sitting at both looms; watching as he does so the backs of the carpets for mistakes. (This is why carpets are so often woven in pairs in Persia: one design and one head-weaver can thus serve for both pieces.)

Why, it may be asked, was this urban technique —seemingly so artificial—ever introduced? The question will be dealt with more fully in Chapter V, "Some Notes on Design"; but meanwhile it may be stated that there is no alternative: complicated curvilinear designs cannot be executed except from scale-paper drawings; and such drawings can only be prepared by skilled designers and draftsmen, working in urban *ateliers*. In some parts of India the technique is stranger still: there the whole carpet is written out, knot by knot, like a book, by the "*talim writer*"; and it is called to the weavers by a "reader". Neither "reader" nor weavers have any notion of what the design may turn out to be. There are whole libraries of *talims*.

Carpets are finished off at both ends by the *gilim*, which is a strip of cloth formed by passing the wefts back and forth clothwise through the warps. Beyond the *gilims* the warp ends are trimmed and knotted, to form fringes.

The selvedges of the carpet are formed by passing an extra woollen weft (in place of the knots) in and out of the last few warp strings on either side.

CHAPTER IV

THE CRAFT OF THE DYER

The master-dyers of Persia are regarded with respect by their fellow-citizens; for theirs is an ancient and honourable craft. It is a craft, moreover, which is commonly believed to embrace secret processes; and this in itself entitles its professors to the consideration of ordinary persons.

Yet the accepted notion that hidden skills and formulas are in the possession of the guilds—which have been handed down to them by bygone generations of dead dyers—is fabulous, however picturesque. For their skills and formulas are known. Indeed, a second-year student of dyeing in any Western college possesses wider and clearer notions of the matter than the most noted member of any of the guilds of dyers.

Nevertheless, the fact that the west possesses techniques far in advance of those practised by the Persians does not in the least imply that western methods should be adopted in the Persian carpet industry. That would be, indeed, deplorable; not only because (as I shall endeavour to explain) western dyes are unsuited for the purpose, but also because Persian dyestuffs, together with the ancient skills employed in their use, are an integral part of the make-up of the Persian carpet—as much a part of it as the wools, the weave and the design—and to discard one of these fundamental elements is to upset the balance of the whole.

Unhappily the use of western dyes is increasing rapidly in Persia. It is proper, therefore, to state here what they are and why their adoption would be a disaster for the industry.

Imported dyestuffs[1] may be conveniently divided into two categories, which differ widely in merit and in methods of application: (*a*) the cheap acid or basic dyes, which are known in Persia under the generic (though not strictly scientific) term "anilines"; and (*b*) the much superior synthetic dyes, which are generally mordanted with potassium bichromate, and are known under the generic term "chrome dyes". The former are cheap, easy to use—and fugitive. The shades to which they fade on exposure to light are generally villainous. When washed with alkalis some of them almost disappear. Chrome dyes, on

16. DYE-HOUSE, NEAR KERMĀN

the other hand, are expensive and considerable technical skill is required for their correct application. If properly applied, they are extremely fast.

The So-called Aniline Dyes

The disastrous effect upon the carpet industry of the introduction of cheap foreign dyes has occupied the attention of the Persian authorities for many years. As far back as the nineties of last century Nasir-ud-din Shah, who was, in his way, a patron of the arts—took steps to prevent it. His decree was repeated, with further elaborations, by his successor, Muzaffar-ud-din Shah in 1900. These decrees went so far as to order the destruction of all "aniline" dyestuffs and the confiscation of all carpets made with aniline-dyed yarns. The first of the two penalties was carried out for a time; and still continues, at least nominally, in force. The second remained a dead letter. Some twenty-five years ago the decree was modified: in place of confiscation, all carpets proved to contain aniline were subjected to an export tax of 3 per cent. The revenue which accrued was to be employed in research connected with the dyeing processes. Unfortunately, however, the Ministry of Finance discovered in the decree a new, convenient and lucrative source of revenue. The export tax was raised from 3 to 9 per cent, and later to 12 per cent; and research was forgotten.

---

[1] In referring, throughout this survey, to imported—in contradistinction to Persian—dyes, I exclude indigo and cochineal. Both of these dyestuffs are imported; but they are in a class apart, and they have been in use in Persia for centuries.

In spite of these restrictive ordinances the importation of cheap European dyes continued on an ascending scale. This is hardly surprising in view of the profitable nature of the trade and the length and remoteness of the Persian frontier. No doubt the Persian customs officials of those days allowed themselves to benefit from the hopelessness of their task—on the legitimate grounds that the stuff would come into the country anyway.

These dyewares are, indeed, an ideal commodity for contraband operations; for a little goes a very long way. They are used in strengths of only $\frac{1}{2}$ to 1 per cent of the weight of yarn. Thus 200 lb. of anilines is sufficient to dye over 20,000 lb. of yarn, which is enough to weave two hundred and fifty 12 × 9 feet carpets—providing all the yarn in the carpet is aniline dyed. As, however, it is unusual for more than 10 per cent of the yarn in a Persian carpet to be dyed with anilines,[1] the 200 lb. of dyestuff would be enough for 2,500 carpets! Thus the bazaar merchants (who are mostly Jews) are able to sell their dyes in small quantities to the villagers, and to make a very good thing out of the traffic.[2]

The principal shades for which anilines are used are the reds, because madder—the traditional dyestuff of the Persian dyers for red shades—is a tricky and expensive dyestuff, and is sometimes difficult to obtain. Furthermore, the task of dyeing with it is usually assigned to the local dyer—who has to be paid; whereas the cottager can boil a little aniline red himself and dye his yarn in his own pot over his own fire.

For their browns and yellows, on the other hand, the Persian weavers employ their own dyestuffs—walnut husks, oak bark, pomegranate rind, straw, vine leaves and weld—instead of anilines; because many of these dyestuffs can be had for nothing or for very little. There is no inducement, therefore, to use anilines instead.

The inconsequence with which some villagers abandon their native dyes for anilines may appear surprising. For they know very well that these dyes are condemned by their customers in the bazaar. They use them because they are cheap. Fortunately for the carpet industry they have remained generally faithful, for their blues, to indigo—because acid blues are among the worst of the cheap dyestuffs. Had acid blues been adopted in place of indigo on anything like the scale in which acid reds have replaced madder, the knell of the carpet industry in Persia would have sounded. Since World War II there has indeed, been a tendency in a few areas to use an imported acid black in place of dark blue (indigo); and in a few other areas the range of aniline colours in common use has widened. The problem is thus becoming more serious and less tractable.

This may be due—at least in some measure—to the fact that cheap imported dyes are needed in the production of textile fabrics, which Persia is beginning to produce. Permission was given to her industrialists and merchants to import these dyes under special licence; but once this was done the whole protective system broke down. A new approach to the problem of the use of anilines in carpets is therefore called for. It will be discussed in the final chapter of this survey on "The Future of the Industry".

Synthetic Chrome Dyes

The second of the two main categories of imported dyestuffs is the synthetic dyes, usually mordanted with potassium bichromate, and thus commonly known as "chrome dyes". They are generally fast to light and to washing with alkalis. The more important dye manufacturers have submitted samples of their products to the Persian Government for testing. Following these tests, many of their dyestuffs are admitted into the country.

If fastness were the sole criterion of excellence a case might be made out for the use of imported synthetic chrome dyestuffs in Persian carpets. But there is such a thing as a dyestuff which is too fast. The great merit of the native dyes of Persia and of the technique of the Persian dyers is that together they produce shades which lose something of their intensity by the action of light and by oxidation. Thus, either by the slow passage of time or the swifter agency of alkalis, the colours are softened and blended. It is this slight fugitiveness which produces the mellow tones in old Persian carpets. The virtue, indeed, of the Persian system of dyeing lies in its imperfection.

---

[1] In India and Turkey, on the other hand, anilines, when used at all, are generally used in the whole carpet.

[2] The prevalence of these dyes in the period before World War I may be judged by the following figures for the year 1913-1914 which was regarded as a normal year:

	Batmans
Exports of carpets containing aniline	563,037
Exports of carpets not containing aniline	404,592

One *batman* = $6\frac{1}{2}$ lb. The customs statistics at that period were fairly reliable, so that the figures may be taken as approximately correct. Since World War II the proportion of aniline-dyed carpets is certainly higher, but the post-war customs statistics are misleading, so they are not given.

In 1947 an exhibition of French tapestry was held in London, which will not be easily forgotten by those who saw it. Nothing could be more enchanting than the shades of rose, the blues, the buffs and the old golds of the earlier pieces. The French Government had sent some weavers to London with their looms to show the public that the ancient craft was still pursued. The yarns which these men were using were extremely crude in colour. Yet they assured me that the dyestuffs and the technique employed to dye the yarn were the same as those which had produced the enchanting colours in "The Lady and the Unicorn". "We weave," they said, "not for today but for posterity."

I do not suggest that we should wait 500 years for the fruition of our efforts. I do suggest, however, that we are not seeking a technique which will produce permanent colours; but one that will give shades which may fade slightly but which will produce in the carpet depth, harmony and a natural glow. The Persians possess such a technique. It has been in operation for many centuries. Its results are plain for everyone to see. To allow another system to supplant it on the grounds of cheapness or ease of manipulation would be short-sighted, irrational and dull.

For chrome dyes in Persian carpets are hardly ever satisfying. In a new carpet the colours have a hard, metallic look; in an old one, they are dull and dead. Age—which imparts a glow, a depth, a richness to the simple dyes of Persia—degrades the products of the Western chemists.

Why, I asked myself, should the synthetic madder of the West—which is no mere *ersatz* imitation of the natural product, but is chemically identical with its tinctorial element—produce a different result from that produced by the Persian dyers from natural madder? As the two dyes were chemically the same (natural madder, however, contains small quantities of two other dyestuffs which are not present in the synthetic product) the reason must lie in the modes of their application. And here there is an essential difference: the Persians use alum as a mordant; the western dyers, bichromate. A series of trials was therefore made in which the synthetic madder of the West (alizarine red) was mordanted with alum, the mordant of the East. The result opened up an interesting field of enquiry: it suggested that the time-honoured Persian processes might be usefully applied to a number of western synthetic dyestuffs; and that the resultant shades might be comparable to those obtained with natural Persian dyes. If, therefore (as some persons believe), synthetic dyes are bound, in the end, to displace the natural dyestuffs of Persia, perhaps a marriage of convenience could be arranged between them. Thus the constancy and the ease of manipulation of the western dyes would be combined with the ancient technique of the eastern dyers.

We are not, however, concerned with the processes which may be employed with synthetic dyes; but with the technique of the Persian dyer—which he still practises in the steamy half-light of his vaulted dye-house. It is proper, therefore, that some of the more common Persian dyewares should be specified, and the methods employed in their use briefly described.[1]

The Natural Dyestuffs of Persia

The most important of these is madder (Pers. *rūnas*); for it was, until recent years, almost the only dyestuff in use in north-west Persia for dyeing all the shades of red and rose.

Madder has been used as a dyestuff in the countries of the Near East as far back as written history goes. It grows wild in many parts of Persia—particularly in the Yezd, Kermān and Mazanderān provinces—where it is also cultivated. The principal market for it is Yezd.

The madder plant (*Rubia tinctorium*) is a perennial which grows to a height of several feet. It has a yellow-green flower and a thick, pulpy root which sometimes reaches a depth of 6 feet. The root is saturated with a liquid which possesses the property of absorbing oxygen and converting it into a red dyestuff. The dye is found in the root only.

The root has little tinctorial value before its third year. From that time on it increases in strength until the seventh year. After the ninth year it has no further commercial use. The roots are pulled up in October or November; then dried, beaten with a flail and ground to a coarse powder. Users, however, prefer to grind the roots themselves, because powdered madder can be easily adulterated.

The dyeing process commonly used in Persia is as follows:

The yarn is first scoured in hot water for half an hour; if it is greasy 3 per cent of carbonate of soda with a little soap is added.

It is then steeped for 12 hours in an alum bath, cold (1 lb. of yarn to $\frac{1}{4}$ lb. of alum, by weight). A second alum bath is then prepared, and the operation is repeated; or, the second 12 hours steeping may

[1] I am indebted for some of this information to the Department of Economics of the Banque Melli, Tehrān.

be replaced by boiling for 1 hour in the alum bath.[1]

The madder vat is prepared by boiling finely sifted madder—of equal weight with the yarn to be dyed—in a small quantity of water, until the colouring matter is dissolved out of the root. The scum is then removed from the liquor and water is added, according to the depth of the shade required. The mordanted yarn is then placed in the vat, which is again brought to the boil. After boiling for 30 minutes a small quantity of the juice of sour grapes is added. The yarn is then boiled for another hour (making 1½ hours in all). It is then allowed to steep in the cooling liquor for 12 hours. Finally it is thoroughly rinsed, preferably in a running stream.

The Mehribān (Hamadān) villagers have a peculiar method of dyeing with madder which they share with their neighbours in Bijār. The yarn is first steeped for 3 days (in the sunlight) in a bath of *dūgh* (whey) and alum. It is then washed thoroughly and afterwards boiled in the madder pot. When the dyestuff has been absorbed, the yarn is withdrawn. Water and cow's urine is then added to the liquor, and the yarn is replaced for about 15 minutes. It is then scoured and hung in the sun to dry.

The well-known *Dūghi* rose of Arāk (Sultānabād) is dyed in the following manner: After mordanting with alum the yarn is steeped for 2 days in a bath of finely ground madder and whey (*dūgh*). When it emerges from the bath it is orange in colour. It is then scoured for 24 to 48 hours in running water. This gives the rose a characteristic bluish tinge which is probably produced by the precipitation on the yarn of a calcium salt of madder.[2]

Another method in use in Arāk consists in steeping the yarn for 5 days (after mordanting with alum) in a bath of madder and whey, and afterwards exposing it to the sunlight for some hours. This induces a fermentation which fixes the dyestuff. Both these processes are more picturesque than effective, as the rose which they produce is fugitive to alkalis (see p. 142).

Weld (*Reseda lutuola*—Pers. *Isparak*) is a thin, delicate plant which grows wild in many parts of Persia and is cultivated in Khūrasān. Its stalks, leaves and flowers yield a yellow dye which is used alone and in combination with other dyestuffs for dyeing carpet yarns. A variety of beautiful greens are obtained by dyeing the yarns first with weld and afterwards with indigo.

The dyeing process is as follows. The yarn is mordanted by boiling for an hour in an alum bath (1 lb. of yarn to 1¼ lb. of alum). The weld (which is broken up into small pieces) is first boiled for an hour, and the liquor is then poured slowly into the vat containing the mordanted yarn, and is brought almost to the boil. The vat is kept at about this temperature for an hour. The yarn is then allowed to steep in the cooling liquor for 12 hours. The quantity of weld used varies from 5 to 40 per cent of the weight of yarn, in accordance with the depth of colour required.

Vine leaves (Pers. *Balg-i-mō*) are also used extensively in Persia for dyeing yellow—they produce a brighter, less delicate shade than weld. The dyeing process is the same.

Pomegranate rind (Pers. *Pūst-i-Anār*) is another dyestuff which is much used for yellows, etc., as it is plentiful and cheap. It is fast, but produces a rather muddy yellow—less attractive than either weld or vine leaves. The same method of dyeing is used as with the other two.

Walnut husks (Pers. *Pūst-i-gerdū*) are unrivalled for producing beautiful shades of camel and brown. The dyers are, unfortunately, in the habit of steeping the yarn for two or three days in lime water before mordanting—a wholly unnecessary proceeding if the yarn is properly scoured. After the lime treatment the yarn is washed in running water. It is then mordanted with alum, as described above for weld and vine leaves. The mordanted yarn is then boiled for 1½ hours in a vat containing from one-quarter to one-third its weight of walnut husks.

A great variety of beautiful shades are produced by combining walnut husks with madder, weld and other dyestuffs.

Oak bark (Pers. *Jāft*) comes from Lūristān and is used in the Hamadān area and in Kurdistān for dyeing browns. Its use for this purpose is not as widespread as walnut husks. It is mordanted with alum in the same way as other Persian dyestuffs.

Indigo and Cochineal

Neither indigo nor cochineal are strictly products of Persia, but both dyewares have been identified for many centuries with Persian carpet weaving and they are still among the most important resources of the Persian dyer. It is proper, therefore, that they should be considered here.

---

[1] Pers. *Zāgh sefīd*, natural alum; it is mined near Zenjān.
[2] Or possibly the lime in the water combines with the alum to form a calcium–aluminium mordant; or again it may be that the lime neutralises the lactic acid in the whey, producing slight alkalinity in the yarn.

Indigo was once cultivated in the Kermān province and is still produced, in a small way, in Khūzistān. But the product which is used by the carpet dyers is all imported from abroad. Until thirty years ago natural indigo from India was used; but it has been almost entirely superseded by the synthetic product. This was first imported from Germany only; it now comes from Switzerland and the United States as well.

The ancient method of dyeing with indigo in a fermentation vat was the only method employed in Persia until thirty years ago. But the introduction of the synthetic product brought with it the simpler and more rapid method of dyeing with sodium hydrosulphite. The latter technique need not detain us here, as it may be found in any modern handbook on dyeing. The former, which is still practised in many dye-houses throughout the country, is worthy of record.

The methods employed are not everywhere the same, as local products are generally used to induce fermentation, and they differ from place to place. But the principle is the same throughout. I propose to describe a technique which is employed in a number of localities in Persia.

The vats are large earthenware vases, wider at the top than at the bottom and about 5 feet high. The dye liquor is prepared as follows: 13 lb. of ordinary red potter's clay are mixed with water to the consistency of syrup in a copper vessel. Half the quantity is then emptied into the vat; to the remainder are added $\frac{1}{2}$ lb. of finely ground Bengal indigo, $1\frac{1}{2}$ lb. of finely ground potash (obtained by burning plants), $2\frac{1}{2}$ lb. of grape sugar and $\frac{3}{4}$ lb. of slaked lime. This mixture is boiled until it is reduced to three-quarters of its volume; it is then poured into the vat containing the remainder of the clay and water, and stirred. The vat is then covered with a wooden top and thick cloths, and left alone for 3 days, care being taken to keep the temperature above 15°C. After 3 days, $\frac{1}{4}$ lb. of ground indigo is added each day for 12 days, the liquor being stirred for several minutes each time. Finally, $\frac{3}{4}$ lb. more lime is added and the liquor stirred for 5 minutes.

When the operation is complete the liquor should be tested with a small quantity of white yarn. If the vat is ready the yarn, which is yellow-green on withdrawal, should slowly turn blue on exposure to the air. When in use the vat can be fortified by the addition of more indigo. The liquor from the vat may be used to induce fermentation in other indigo vats.

There has been a good deal of controversy on the question as to whether synthetic indigo produces as fine a range of blues as the natural product. Supporters of natural indigo point to the deep, lustrous blues of the old Persian carpets and roundly declare that the synthetic product could never have produced such colours. Actually, however (as I have suggested in the case of natural v. synthetic madder), the real difference does not lie in the dyestuff itself but in the method of its application; because natural and the synthetic indigo are chemically the same. If, therefore, synthetic indigo is used in the fermentation vat instead of with sodium hydrosulphite, the result would be the same as that obtained with the natural product. Unfortunately, the hydrosulphite method is so much more simple and speedy than the ancient fermentation vat, that there is no prospect of its being abandoned by the Persian dyers who have once used it.

Cochineal, like indigo, is an imported dyestuff which has been used in Persia for many centuries—particularly in the eastern provinces. How has it come about that the dyestuff has been for so long in use in Khūrasān and Kermān and hardly at all in the West? Here is an explanation, which at least complies with the facts:

Dr. Malcolm Burr, D.Sc., F.R.Ent.S., in his fascinating book *The Insect Legion* describes a dyestuff which is produced in India and which closely resembles Mexican or Canary Island cochineal. He writes that the young larvae of *Tachardia lacca*, one of the Scale Insects, puncture the barks of certain trees in India—particularly of the genus *Ficus*—suck up the sap and then exude a resinous secretion which forms a hard, resinous covering, enveloping a whole twig. Within this covering the females—which form the greater part of the insect population—are prisoners for life. The twigs, encrusted with these indurated females, are melted and strained. The resulting product is known in India as "lac" or "laq" (meaning hundreds of thousands) which suggests the vast numbers of the little creatures which produce it. The lac consists of 70–90 per cent of resin (shellac) and 2–10 per cent of red dye. The dye is recovered and is sold in the form of small cakes.

This red dyestuff was formerly exported from India by the land route into nearby Khūrasān and Kermān; indeed, to this day, the name by which the dark cochineal red colour is known in east Persia is "laq". Thus the use of the dyestuff became firmly established; so that when the kindred, but superior, cochineal from Mexico and the Canary Islands[1] made its appearance in Persia, it was accepted as a matter of course in the eastern provinces. Neither the Indian "lac" nor the true cochineal became popular in west and north-west Persia, because in those areas the madder plant grows wild and the inhabitants had been long acquainted with its virtues.

Cochineal dye is used in Meshed as follows: before the dyeing operation begins the yarn is steeped in lime for 24 hours. (This is a pernicious practice and is partly responsible for the poor wearing quality of the Meshed carpet, see p. 167. The dyers declare that it produces a more brilliant shade of red. But I was unable to detect any difference between the carpets produced by one of the factories in Meshed which did not follow this practice and those of another which did.) After steeping in lime the yarn is washed; and it is then boiled in alum to which a small quantity of madder has been added. This produces a light salmon-pink shade. The yarn is then re-washed and dried; and is afterwards boiled a second time in cochineal, acidulated with citric acid or barberry—which grows in Birjānd. It is then finally washed and dried.

---

[1] The Cochineal Scale insect is a native of Mexico, where it feeds on various kinds of cactus. Cortez found it in use by the Aztecs, and it was introduced into Europe in 1525; but it was not until 1703 that van Leeuwen proved it to be not a seed but an insect.

While Mexico was still a Spanish colony the cochineal industry was an important source of wealth, and was protected by a law which inflicted the death penalty upon anyone who took the female insect out of the country.

At the beginning of the nineteenth century the cochineal insect itself was introduced into Europe, and attempts were made to establish it in Spain and Italy. It did not flourish in Europe, but in 1810 some living specimens from Cadiz were placed on prickly pears in the Botanic Gardens at Orotava in the Canaries. It is curious that the energetic attempts made by the authorities failed to induce the Canary Islanders to take up the cultivation of the insect. They even made efforts to exterminate it, as they found it was destroying the prickly pear, whose fruit they prized.

A few, however, were more intelligent, and began to cultivate both cactus and insect, and the result was startling. When the vineyards were wiped out by Phylloxera in the middle of the nineteenth century, the cochineal industry came to the rescue and burst into a prosperity that astonished the natives. In 1831 8½ lb. of cochineal were exported; in 1850, 842,827 lb. The insect had not only saved the Canaries from starvation but brought them wealth. The wheel of fortune revolved again. Aniline dyes were discovered, and the Cochineal Scale lost its industrial value and was reduced to the humble role of decorating cakes.

Malcolm Burr, D.Sc., F.R.Ent.S., etc., *The Insect Legion.*

CHAPTER V
SOME NOTES ON DESIGN

Persia, the Home of Carpet Design

I purpose, in this chapter, to consider the subject of design in Persian carpets, but only in a general sense. A more detailed examination of the subject —as exemplified in specimen carpets from the principal areas—will be attempted in subsequent chapters in which the products of the different areas will be under review.

Persia has been described as the home of carpet design. There is more truth in this generalisation than there is in most; for design—particularly carpet design—is a form of art for which the Persians possess peculiar gifts and understanding. Their instinct, indeed, is to formalise any subject or conception, to make of it a design or a planned pattern in accordance with accepted conventions. They regard these conventions not as impeditive shackles but as diverting precepts which they have inherited from bygone generations and which they delight to observe. Only their greatest artists have dared to ignore them.

Persia has, of course, a far longer experience than the West in the art of carpet design. For carpets in the West (as we have seen) are a comparatively modern refinement—they were not in general use in England before the nineteenth century—whereas in Persia their beginnings are lost in the half-light of antiquity.

The Two Orders of Persian Carpet Design

Persian carpet design falls naturally into two orders or styles, which are distinct and instantly recognisable. They are (1) the rectilinear; and (2) the curvilinear.

The designs of the first category are built up out of three straight lines: the horizontal, which consists of a row of knots tied side by side; the vertical, which consists of a row of knots tied one above the other on a single pair of warp strings; and the diagonal, which consists of a row of knots tied successively one-up and one-along to form an angle of about 45 degrees. A "square" fabric—i.e. one in which the number of knots per inch, horizontally and vertically, is the same—would produce a diagonal of exactly 45 degrees; whereas a fabric in which the number of vertical knots per inch outnumbered the horizontal would produce a diagonal of less than 45 degrees; and vice versa.

Designs of the second, or curvilinear, order are made up of curved lines—though straight lines are generally introduced to mark off the borders.

These two basic orders of design coincide in the main with the two basic types of Persian weaving: the tribal or village weaves, which are usually rectilinear, and the town or factory weaves, which are curvilinear.

The discrepancy between the two orders did not arise from chance; it is due to simple and inevitable causes: a tribal or village rug is almost invariably woven in straight lines because a design of this character can be woven *direct*, and does not necessarily demand a high standard of craftsmanship; nor does it require to be previously drawn full size by an experienced draftsman on scale paper—which, of course, the tribe or village cannot provide. The weaver of a curvilinear design, on the other hand, must be provided with a cartoon on which the design has been carefully and accurately plotted. Such cartoons can only be produced in town factories by skilled designers assisted by qualified draftsmen and colourists; and the weaving of designs of this character calls for skilled weavers and for close control by skilled technicians.

I am aware, of course, that weaving in the villages around Arāk (Sultānabād) and Kermān is largely curvilinear; but the productions of these villagers partake of the character of urban weaves; because (*a*) they are not spontaneous, but have spread outwards from the towns; and (*b*) the carpets are woven from cartoons drawn and coloured in the towns. Though woven in villages, they are really urban carpets.

The rectilinear is, of course, much the more ancient of the two orders of design. The second, or curvilinear, order was probably not evolved before the end of the fifteenth century. Up to that time rugs, runners and *kellegis* had been produced by nomadic tribes and villagers, either for their own use or for barter or sale in the bazaar; and it is doubtful if, for many generations, there had been any appreciable advance in craftsmanship. When, therefore, enlightened princes like Shah Rūkh of Herāt (and perhaps his remarkable wife Jawar Shādh) or Uzūn

Hassān of Tabrīz commissioned the painters of their courts to draw intricate floral and animal designs for large carpets, it is most unlikely that any of those villagers could be found to weave them. It became necessary, therefore, to devise a new technique for their production. The technique evolved consisted in drawing a cartoon of the design, enlarged full size, on squared paper—each square representing a knot. At first the position of each knot was marked by a pinhole; but before long the pinholes were replaced by dots in ink or pencil.

Sheets of paper, ready printed in squares, did not exist in those days. I have no doubt that the cartoons were prepared then (as they were in Kermān twenty years ago) by first drawing the design full size on plain sheets, and afterwards ruling in the squares by hand. When I first visited Kermān twenty-five years ago I met a gentleman of over eighty whose profession it was to draw parallel lines with a ruler on these cartoons. Since his youth he had been ruling lines—14 to the inch—for ten hours a day; and at the age of eighty he was doing it still with speed and accuracy. The work appeared to agree with him, for he was in fine fettle.

Convention in Persian Carpet Design

In spite of the influence of western decorators and stylists, convention has happily maintained most of its sway over Persian carpet design. We are so accustomed, for instance, to see borders in Persian carpets that we overlook the tenacity and immutability of the border convention. Yet carpets are produced in many countries, both of the East and West, without borders (as in China). But no man has yet seen a Persian carpet without a border. For the Persians regard the border as a necessary framework to set off the ground pattern. Their designers would maintain that without it the attention is distracted from a steady contemplation of the main design. The border, furthermore, must consist of a middle band, which is the border proper, with one, two, or three narrow bands (or guards) on each side.

The pattern of the middle band—floral, arabesque, or both, or broken up into cartouches, as the case may be—should be a bold repeat, and on a fairly large scale. In contrast, the pattern of the guards should be short, insignificant repeats, not to detract from the importance of the middle band, which is the border proper.

The design of the field, which is the area enclosed within the framework of the border, is equally bound by convention. The first and most important is *balance*: the left and right halves of the carpet must be identical.[1] And in the majority of carpets the top half and the bottom half must also be the same. These conventions enable the spectator to appreciate the design of the carpet from either end, or even from either side. The last, however, is not a rigid rule, as "drop" or one-way designs (like the Vase carpet, Plate 5) are not uncommon.

The force of convention in the designs of the field is manifested by the persistence, down the centuries, of a number of designs which are common to almost every weaving area. Although local peculiarities may affect their presentation, the designs are recognised and accepted by every Persian as a part of his daily life. Indeed, it is unusual to find a household in Persia without at least one carpet, rug or strip, in one or another of these designs, on the floor. There are nine of them. Some are more common than others. I append a list with their Persian names and their English equivalents. They are arranged in an approximate order of their prevalence:

Plates 17–19. Herātī: of Herāt.
Plates 20–22. Boteh: (lit. a bush or cluster of leaves); the so-called pine or palm patterns.
Plate 33. Harshang: the crab.
Plate 34. Gol Henaī: the Garden Balsam; or the Henna flower.
Plates 23–24. Lechek Torūnj: medallion and corner.
Plate 25. Mina Khanī: said to have been named after a certain Mina Khan of Tabrīz.
Plates 26–31. Shah Abbasī: of Shah Abbas.
Plate 32. Bid Majnūn: the Weeping Willow.
Plate 35. Jōshaqānī: of Jōshaqān.

The Herātī Pattern

Of these, the most renowned and the most widespread is the Herātī. (Known also as the Mahi or Fish pattern.)

The fame of this design is well deserved. When woven in a good quality fabric on a dark blue or cream ground, it is among the most refined and elegant of the small repeating patterns of Persia— those patterns which so cunningly yet so artlessly express the restraint and delicacy of Persian taste. A well-woven Herātī has been described as the gentleman's carpet, and so it is. Although many hundred years old, it never dates. The oldest examples of it which we possess undoubtedly came from eastern

[1] The so-called picture carpets (see Plates 54, 55) are merely interesting freaks.

Persia; so that we may, with confidence, accept the name Herātī as an indication of its east Persian origin. This does not necessarily imply, however, that these carpets were woven in the city of Herāt (which until 1857 was a Persian city and had been for a long period the capital of Khūrasān). For in Persia the name of a province is frequently confounded with the name of its chief city. Thus the term Herātī may have meant from Herāt (province) and not from Herāt (city). This question will be examined in greater detail on p. 163.

The Persians weave the Herātī pattern in two different ways, as shown on Plates 17 and 18. The former—which is the type more common in west Persia—contains a well-defined diamond-shaped figure around which the four "fish" are arranged; the latter—which is encountered more frequently in Khūrasān—does not.

In Arāk, where the design is most prevalent, it appears in thousands of medium-priced carpets. It was in this province that the famous dark-blue Ferahān carpets were woven in this pattern in

18. THE HERĀTĪ DESIGN (TYPE 2)

Detail of a Ferahān carpet. This type of Herātī (with the "lozenge") is common throughout Persia.

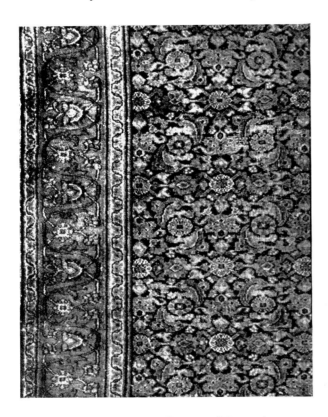

17. THE HERĀTĪ DESIGN (TYPE 1)

Detail of a Qaīn carpet from the Shrine Collection, Meshed. This type of Herātī (without the "lozenge") is found only in Khūrasān.

19. THE HERĀTĪ DESIGN (RECTILINEAR)

As woven in Bakshaīsh, Herīz area; c. 1890. Note the serrations on the diamond, an uncommon feature.

the second half of last century (see also p. 139). The design is hardly less prevalent in the Hamadān villages; and three-quarters of the output of Senneh is in the same pattern. It is also common in Tabrīz, Meshed, the Qaināt, Yezd, Bijār and the Herīz area; and it is found even in the tribal rugs of the Balūchis and of Fārs. It has long since crossed the borders of Persia to be reproduced in almost every country where pile carpets are made.

By an immemorial convention the Herātī pattern is invariably combined with the so-called Tosbagheh or Turtle border (see Plate 18). Although the figure which gives the border its name certainly suggests a turtle, the inhabitants of the semi-arid plateau of Persia could hardly have been familiar with this aquatic reptile; so that the origin of the figure may not be a turtle at all. In Tabrīz the border is known as the Samovar—which, indeed, its principal motive closely resembles. The reader may take his choice of origins.

The so-called Pine Pattern and its Variations

The origin of the famous Persian Pine pattern has been for many years a subject of discussion among amateurs of the Persian carpet. It has been related to the Sacred Flame of Zoroaster; to the pine, to the palm, to the almond and to the pear; also to a leather purse and to the imprint of a closed fist upon a mud or plaster surface (which, indeed, it closely resembles); and even to the loop made by the river Jumna on its way from the vale of Kashmir to the Indian plain! All these attributions appear to me to be remote, and some fantastic. The explanation is, I think, much simpler. It is to be found in the name which the Persians give to the design. They call it the *boteh*—which is their word for a cluster of leaves. It is, in fact, the Leaf design; and in its simplest form it closely resembles a serrated leaf. The Persians—with their passion for inventing intricate and artistic variations on a central theme—have produce a multiplicity of forms of the *boteh*, many of which have special names; as: Boteh Mirī (Plate 20)—small pine: Boteh Termeī—medium-sized pine: Boteh Kharqaī—large pine: Boteh Bademī—almond-shaped pine: Boteh Jeqaī—large pine with a small pine protruding from it.

There is no pattern (except perhaps the Herātī) which—with its variations—is so widespread. In the Seraband area they weave nothing else, and it is common in the Hamadān villages. Occasional carpets are produced in Tabrīz and in Kashān. A larger variation—the Boteh Kharqaī—is woven in areas

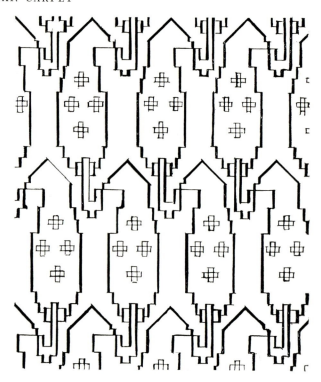

20. DRAWING OF THE BOTEH MIRI
The most typical of the Persian leaf patterns. It was copied from an old Seraband carpet, c. 1890.

as far apart as Senneh and the Qaināt. In Sarāb (Herīz area) it is uncommon, but I possess an example (Plate 22). During recent years the Qūm designers have created some new and interesting variations of it (Plates 21 and 22). Finally, Kermān (as might be expected) has produced the most graceful and ornamental of them all, derived, no doubt, from an earlier shawl pattern (Plate 21).

The commonest type is the Boteh Mirī. This is the small pine pattern of the old Mir carpets (see p. 144) and of the modern Serabands. Like the Herātī, it has been copied in every country where carpets are produced—whether by hand or machine; and like the Herātī it does not date. Thirty years ago a well-known British firm of carpet manufacturers produced a perfect copy of an old Mir carpet in their mills. It is still selling.

The simpler types of the Boteh designs appear easy to produce. They are, in fact, among the most tricky of the commoner Persian patterns. An error in a single shade, a change in the position of a knot will throw the pattern out of gear and rob the carpet of its gentility.

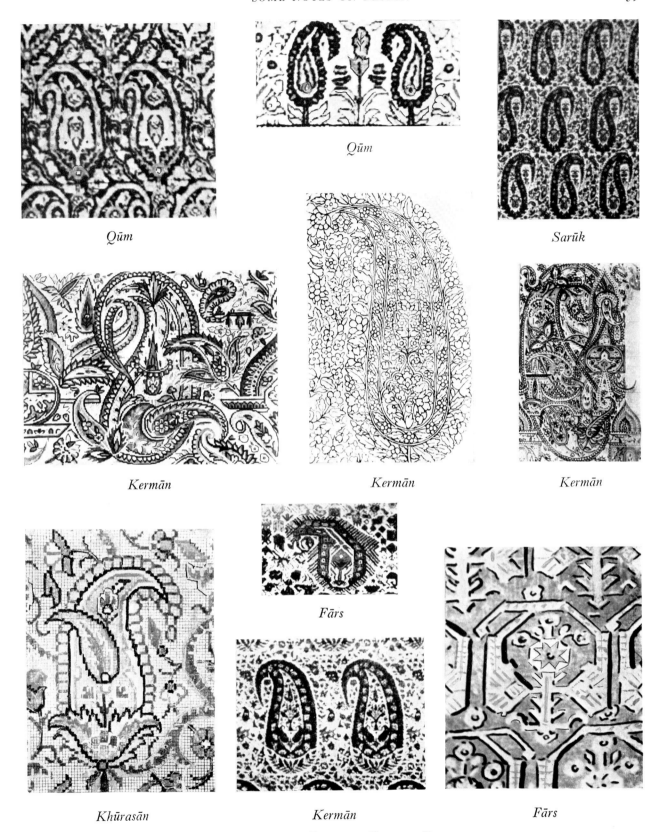

21. THE LEAF PATTERN: VARIOUS FORMS

22. THE LEAF PATTERN: VARIOUS FORMS

SOME NOTES ON DESIGN

The Lechek Torūnj Design

The medallion-and-corner design is typically Persian in its elegance and refinement. It was first used in the fifteenth century as a design for embossed leather book-covers (Plates 23 and 24). In the sixteenth century the design was adapted for carpet weaving, and it has remained one of the standard types of Persian carpet design ever since.

There are many hundreds of different examples of it. Many of them display the extraordinary invention and high artistry of the best Persian designers. It might appear improper, therefore, to include among the ten more common Persian designs one which lends itself to such wide variations. It must be borne in mind, however, that thousands of carpets have been produced during the last fifty years in the less complicated forms of this design—as, for instance, in the commoner types of Tabrīz and Meshed carpets; and in the carpets of the Herīz area—where it was converted from the curvilinear to the rectilinear style (see p. 64) and has become the best known and most popular of the Herīz or Georavān designs (see Plate 68).

In view of these considerations, we are, I think, justified in including the medallion-and-corner design—at least in its simple forms—as one of the nine common and generally recognised types of Persian design.

There are no prescribed proportions for the usual type of this design. Nevertheless, the Persians possess certain rules for it which they like to apply whenever possible; because they know that these

23. OUTLINE DRAWING OF A FIFTEENTH-CENTURY BOOK-COVER

The medallion-and-corner design was probably adapted by the master-weavers of Tabrīz from these early book covers.

24. OUTLINE DRAWING OF A FIFTEENTH-CENTURY BOOK-COVER

prescriptions, if followed, will produce a well-proportioned carpet. (The rules could not, of course, be applied to carpets of unusual shape, such as square or long-and-narrow pieces.) There are three rules, viz.:

(1) The length of the *torūnj* or oval part of the medallion (i.e. minus its two heads and necks) should equal one-third of the length of the whole carpet.

(2) The width of the border should equal one-sixth of the width of the carpet.

(3) The sum of the widths of the guards (i.e. small borders) should equal the width of the middle or large border.

The Mina Khanī Pattern

This design is said to have been named after a certain Mina Khan, a Tabrīzi, who originated and popularised it. I fear that this explanation must be accepted with reserve; because the design is older than the third quarter of the nineteenth century, when the Tabrīzis began to influence design in Persia. The design is, I think, more likely to be of Kurdish origin, as it is frequently found in old carpets from Saūjbulāgh and Bijār.

The design, though monotonous, is effective; and because it possesses a comparatively small repeat, it is easy to weave. It has therefore become popular in many parts of Persia. Before the war it was the only design known to the weavers of Veramin—a fertile agricultural area south of Tehrān. The villagers wove so many pieces in it—all alike—that they had difficulty in disposing of them. So they discarded the pattern for another—which does not appear to have brought them any better luck than the first.

The Mina Khanī design is one of the standard patterns used by the weavers of the so-called Mūshkabād carpets (see p. 139) of Arāk. The master-weavers of Tabrīz occasionally use it, too; and it

25. DETAIL OF AN ANTIQUE CARPET FROM THE QAINĀT IN THE MINA KHANĪ DESIGN
Victoria and Albert Museum, London

appears from time to time in carpets from the Herīz, Hamadān and Chahār Mahāl areas.

The Shah Abbasī Designs

The term Shah Abbasī is applied by the Persians to a type of all-over design composed of classical motives of the middle Sefavi period. These motives —the various types of palmettes, cloud-bands, halberds, vases, etc.—were fixed for all time in the so-called "Vase" carpets which (it is generally agreed) were woven during the reign of Shah Abbas. They appear in the field of the carpet, isolated from each other, evenly spaced and invariably combined and interconnected into a pattern by some form of stalk or trellis.

They are woven in every part of Persia. The designers of Kermān, Kashān, Tabrīz, Isfahān and Meshed love to draw their elaborate and varied beauties. In the villages, too, many of the weavers are familiar with the commoner palmettes and vases, and often introduce them in simple, rectilinear form into their rugs and carpets.

I am fortunate in being able to reproduce a series of perfect scale drawings of most of the so-called Shah Abbasī motives of the great period of Persian classical design (Plates 26 to 31). They were drawn by Tahir Zadeh Bihzad of the Tehrān School of Art. Their outstanding merit is their accuracy. At a time when traditional forms of beauty are being cast aside, it is well that accurate models of these motives should be preserved. For however much they may be neglected now, they will surely come into their own again.

The Bid Majnūn Design

This is the Weeping Willow design (Plate 32), one of the most famous and attractive of the old Persian patterns. It is a fact in combination of the weeping willow, cypress, poplar and fruit trees; and it is so full of interest and character that it has been copied in every country where carpets are made. Its origin is obscure; but, like the Mina Khanī, it is probably Kurdish, as the earliest examples which we possess of it are from the Bijār area.

26. SHAH ABBASĪ MOTIVES OF THE GREAT PERIOD OF PERSIAN CLASSICAL DESIGN
Drawn by Tahir Zadeh Bihzad (Tehrān School of Art)

27. Shah Abbasi Motives

28. Shah Abbasī Motives

29. Shah Abbasī Motives

30. SHAH ABBASĪ MOTIVES

31. A Classic Motive drawn by Tahir Zadeh Bihzad (*c.* 1945)

32. The Bid Majnūn Design: Weeping Willow Pattern

The fact that the design is entirely rectilinear indicates that it is of tribal or village origin. Its prototype was never produced—like the designs of the great Sefavi carpets—by a designer at a drawing board. It was surely devised by a dusky village matron, looking intently, as she sat before her loom, at the willows, the cypresses and the poplars in her garden while she wove them into a pattern for her carpet. The design was formerly widespread in north-west Persia—in Bijār, and in the Hamadān, Arāk and Malayer villages.[1] It is less so now. The Tabrīzis, however (those arch copyists), still weave it. It is rarely seen today in any of the Arāk weaves.

A rectilinear pattern is unsuited for a fine quality fabric: the design comes out too rigid, too stiff. Hence the Bid Majnūn design is unknown in Kermān, Isfahān, Kāshān, Qūm—and even in Meshed. It is, however, eminently suited to a medium or coarse fabric. Thus, in the days when the Ushāk (Turkey) carpet was enjoying a deserved popularity, many thousands of carpets were produced in this pattern in Ushāk.

The Harshang or Crab Design

The design (Plate 33) takes its name from its principal motive, which suggests a crab. Here again we have a repeating pattern which is as widespread as the Mina Khanī and the Bid Majnūn designs. Yet we have no positive knowledge of its origin. My guess is that it is Turkish; because it is common among the rugs of Karabagh, an area north-east of Tabrīz on the Russian side of the border; and again among the Shirvān weaves of the south Caucasus. It is common, too, among the Turkish villages of the Herīz area and of Hamadān. The large oval motives, however, bear a certain resemblance to some of the palmettes of the Sefavi period, and the claws of the "crab" may be conventionalised arabesques. Perhaps its prototype was a curvilinear pattern drawn by one of the great Sefavi designers which the Turkish village weavers of Karabagh, of the south Caucasus and of Bakshaīsh attempted to reproduce —breaking up the curves into straight lines in the process—as they always did.

Like the Bid Majnūn the Crab Design is a simple, well-balanced, rectilinear pattern, easy to weave and full of character.

The Gol Henaī Pattern

Commentators have frequently stated that this small repeating pattern is named after the Henna

33. A SAŪJBULĀGH (KURDISTĀN) KELLEGI IN THE "CRAB" DESIGN

Probably middle nineteenth century

plant, which it does not much resemble. *Gol henaī* is, however, also used to denote the Garden Balsam, which the pattern does suggest (Plate 34). Although it is a well-known pattern in Persia, it is not widespread. It appears to have originated in Arāk (Sultānabād) and it is still one of the most common patterns used by the weavers of the Mūshkabād and Mahāl qualities. In the West the design is frequently called the chestnut pattern, because it recalls the blossom of the horse-chestnut.

The Jōshaqānī Design

Two classic Jōshaqānī designs have been woven for at least two centuries (and probably for much longer) in the village of that name, and are

---

[1] Mr. Upham Pope has attributed a carpet, reproduced in the *Survey of Persian Art*, vol. VI, Plate 1241 B, to Jōshaqān; but the design is foreign to that village. The carpet in question is certainly a Bijār. To this day the Bid Majnūn design is a favourite in the Bijār area.

34. GOL HENAĪ PATTERN

still woven there. They are depicted on Plates 365–6. There are several variations: sometimes the medallion is omitted, sometimes the corners, and sometimes both. But the essential motives and the border have remained unchanged for many generations. Sometimes the design takes the form of a repetition of the corner lozenges (Plate 367) over the whole of the field, sometimes with and sometimes without the dividing lines.

It is a favourite design among the Persians. One meets it in the most unexpected places. In 1915 I spent a month in Kashān and I found a masterweaver there who was so married to it that he would weave nothing else. A simplified version of it has been woven for generations in Reihān, a village in the Kemereh area (Map IV); and a still more simplified version is woven in the Mahāl and Mūshkabād qualities of Arāk. The design is also woven in Tabrīz, in Hamadān and occasionally in the Herīz

35. A TABRĪZ CARPET IN THE JŌSHAQĀNĪ DESIGN

area. It is practically unknown in Khūrasān, Kermān and Fārs.

Symbolism in Persian Design

Students of Oriental art have often drawn attention to what is known as symbolism in carpet design. The term is used to describe the practice of introducing motives or figures in a carpet to represent an idea or some form of life or being.

I suggest that in respect of urban carpets this notion should be taken with more than a grain of salt. For the Persians are an artistic people who regard design as an end in itself. For them a tree design, if well and truly drawn, is important and, in itself, sufficient. To call it a Tree of Life design is—for them—to give it a bogus significance.

The motives in Persian design are traceable either to concrete models—as a tree, a leaf, a flower or cluster of flowers, a bird, an animal, a vase, etc.—or to models which have been appropriated from foreign sources, mainly Chinese or Arab. With these the Persian designers have combined geometric or curvilinear forms to build their patterns. The fact that cloud-bands and birds of paradise sometimes appear does not mean that the Persian designers, who appropriated these motives, accepted the mystical significance which they possessed in the country of their origin. The Persians took them because they liked them. The end which they had in view was delight through symmetry and beauty; but no more. During the years which I spent in Persia I never heard any reference to symbolism in carpet design.

Some writers, however, have insisted on the mystical significance of certain motives which appear in tribal rugs. Many of these geometric, ornamental forms, no doubt, possessed meanings when they were first devised, many centuries ago. But it is doubtful if there was any *mystique* attached to them. It is more probable, I think, that they were intended to represent some common animal, bird, plant or object; and that by reason of countless repetition down the centuries they have degenerated beyond recognition. The rugs of Fārs are particularly rich in forms of this kind. When I was in Shirāz I tried to find out if any significance was now attached to some of the more interesting of them. I failed.

My friend Professor V. Minorsky furnished me with a list of the tribal marks of the twenty-four Ghūzz (Turkish) tribes, some of which overran Persia in the eleventh century; and I was hopeful that I would be able to discover some of these marks on rugs of the Afshār, Qashqaī and other Turkish tribes. Again, I am sorry to say, I failed.

I suggest, therefore, that caution is indicated in our approach to these matters. A tribal weaver, as she crouches over her horizontal loom, is more likely, I think, to seek inspiration from what she sees than from what she thinks—if, indeed, she thinks at all.

CHAPTER VI

TABRĪZ; THE HERĪZ WEAVING AREA; AND THE SO-CALLED ZENJĀN RUGS

TABRĪZ

The Importance of Tabrīz

A survey of the carpet-weaving centres of Persia must allot pride of place to Tabrīz.[1] Not because the best carpets are woven there—for better carpets are produced in other localities—but because of the long and honourable association of that city with the craft; and especially because the revival of the industry itself—in the second half of the nineteenth century—was due in a large measure to the skill, the enterprise and the vision of the men of Tabrīz.

Historical Note on the City of Tabrīz

Tabrīz—like most of Persia's more important cities—lies at the intersection of a number of caravan routes. But it is much more than a mere focus of communications, for it lies at the centre of the large and fertile province of Azerbaijān; and it is also the guardian of one of the gates of Persia. As such it stands in an exposed and dangerous position—which is rendered more precarious because its people are not Persians, but are a mixed race, mainly Turkish; and indistinguishable from their kinsmen across the border. Thus, throughout its history, Tabrīz has been involved in irredentist or liberating movements—engineered first by the Ottoman, and afterwards by the Russian, power; while it has incurred, at the same time, the distrust of the rest of the empire, which is mainly Persian in race and language.

Little is known of Tabrīz before the Arab conquest of Persia in A.D. 641. But after that date the city was mentioned repeatedly by Arab travellers and geographers, to whose curiosity and indefatigation we owe practically all of our knowledge of Persia under Arab rule. It was described by one of the early geographers as a noble city, the most prosperous in Azerbaijān, with a strong wall, surrounded by woods and gardens. In A.D. 791 it was rebuilt by that remarkable woman Zobeida, wife of Harūn-al-Rashīd—who must have had a bent for building cities, for she built Kashān as well.

Perhaps the most momentous event in its history was in the eleventh century when Persia was conquered by the Seljūk Turks; for the Seljūks settled permanently in the provinces of Azerbaijān and Hamadān. Before long Turkish replaced old Persian and Arabic as the language of these two provinces, and Tabrīz became a Turkish-speaking city. It has remained so to this day.

In A.D. 1220, a band of marauding Mongols appeared before Tabrīz for the first time. They were bought off; but they soon returned and within ten years they had ravaged and subjugated the whole of the Azerbaijān province. Fifty years later Tabrīz became the official capital of the Mongol Empire, which stretched from the Oxus to Egypt; and it was during the reign of the Mongol Ghazān Khan (the first Il-Khani to be converted to Islam) that the city attained its greatest splendour. In the village of Shām, to the west of the city, he built a new town which became the seat of government of the empire. It contained a palace for the Il-Khani, an administrative building, a magnificent mausoleum (described as the highest building in the world), a mosque, religious schools, a hospital, a hostel, an observatory, a library, baths and caravanserais. The town itself was at the same time enlarged and beautified. Of the splendours of Shām nothing remains today.

In 1392 Tabrīz was sacked by Timūr (Tamerlane). But it soon recovered under the rule of the Mongol Il Khanis Jahān Shah[2] (who built the Blue Mosque) and his successful rival Uzūn Hassān of the White Sheep tribe. Uzūn Hassān proved to be a peaceful and enlightened prince. He revived the splendours of Tabrīz, which have been described for us in detail by Giosafa Barbaro, an envoy of the Venetian Republic.

Twenty years of confusion and anarchy followed the death of Uzūn Hassān (A.D. 1477); until, in 1499, his grandson, Ismail I, warrior and saint, having

---

[1] Of the derivation of the name, nothing positive is known. The popular explanation that it means "making fever disappear", from *tab*, fever, and *rikhtan*, to dispel, is too remote and fanciful; although V. Minorsky suggests that it may mean "that which makes the heat disappear". The same authority mentions a possible Armenian or pre-Sassanian derivation.

[2] Timūr's (Tamerlane) fourth son and the first of the Timurīd sovereigns, A.D. 1377–1447.

A Modern Tabrīz Carpet of outstanding quality both in weave and design

overcome his rivals, was proclaimed the first "Shah" of Persia, from his capital Tabrīz (see p. 54).

The advent to the throne of Persia of a fanatic Shi'a prince was the beginning of a long series of wars with the Sūnni Ottoman Empire which lasted for 200 years. Tabrīz, only a few miles from the frontier, was continually threatened and attacked; until Shah Tahmasp (who had succeeded his father Ismail at the age of ten, in 1524) decided to move the capital to Kazvīn. He appears to have moved it back again after signing peace with the sultan in 1555. But his grandson, Shah Abbas, wisely decided to establish the seat of government in Isfahān, a more central and more secure locality.

Thus, at the end of the sixteenth century, Tabrīz ceased, perhaps for ever, to be a capital city. It had suffered grievously during the Turkish invasions; yet it was so favourably placed for trade and agriculture, its merchants were so enterprising and its cultivators so industrious, that it soon recovered. Chardin, in 1673, declared that it was a large and important town with a population of over half a million.[1]

In spite of its remoteness from the scene of the Afghan invasions (A.D. 1722), Tabrīz did not escape from the repercussions which arose out of this disaster; for the Turks, taking advantage of Persia's affliction, invaded the country once again. The conquest, however, was short-lived, for in the meantime Persia had thrown up a military leader, Nadir Qūli, who quickly drove out the Afghans and Turks and ascended the throne.

The gradual decline of the Turkish power during the eighteenth century relieved Tabrīz from the threat of invasion from the West. But no sooner was that threat removed, than another—more formidable and more relentless—developed from the North.

In 1796 Persia had lost her Transcaucasian provinces to Russia. Georgia was annexed in 1801. The threat to the Persian homeland became very real and the Persian Government began to give serious attention to its defence. An important British military mission was sent to Tabrīz, the gateway of Persia. Arsenals, cannon foundries and workshops were established there and it became, once again, a centre of activity. Adversity, indeed, seemed powerless to paralyse or destroy this phoenix among cities.

These preparations proved, however, to be of little value against the Russian power. Tabrīz was occupied in 1827, and in the following year by the treaty of Turkman-Chai,[2] Persia lost all her provinces north of the Araxes.

After the signature of this treaty, Tabrīz enjoyed, for nearly a hundred years, an era of comparative peace. Under the Qajār dynasty it became the largest and wealthiest city in the empire. Its merchants and bankers trafficked in every bazaar of Persia, and most of Persia's foreign trade was in their hands. Its population—which at the end of the period of turmoil which followed the Afghan invasion had fallen to 30,000—rose under the somnolent Qajārs to nearly ten times that number.

As the town grew in wealth, its leading citizens began to look with disfavour upon the capital. They regarded it as the seat of a corrupt and inefficient administration, and of a reactionary court. Thus, in 1904, Tabrīz became the centre of a nationalistic and revolutionary movement. The movement was suppressed. But Russian troops crossed the frontier (for the first time since 1827) to protect the consulates and foreign subjects. There they remained, in spite of Persian protests, until the outbreak of the Soviet revolution.

In 1921, the Qajār dynasty came to an inglorious end; and that dynamic personality, Riza Shah Pahlavi, a soldier who had risen from the ranks, ascended the throne of Persia. He was not a monarch to tolerate in any part of his dominion the existence of a centre of power which might challenge his own; and he counted the merchants of Tabrīz among his most recalcitrant subjects. He therefore made plans to destroy their authority and strength. This he accomplished by driving a road round the Kaflan Kūh pass—which for the first time brought the city within two days' journey from the capital; and by building up Tehrān as the administrative, financial, commercial and cultural centre of Persia. Within a very few years no person of consequence—whether merchant, banker or landowner—could conduct his affairs without an office or seat in the capital. And as Tehrān waxed in importance, Tabrīz, from the proud position of a successful rival, sank into the semi-obscurity of a provincial town.

In 1944 Tabrīz emerged once more into the limelight. A separatist movement, under the aegis of Russia, was started there and an insurgent government—the Democratic Government of Azerbaijan—was established. It collapsed in 1946, when the

---

[1] Professor V. Minorsky very properly thinks the figure is exaggerated.
[2] A village on the road to Kazvīn, 60 miles south of Tabrīz.

36. A View of Tabrīz

Persian Government forces marched into the province. The Russians appear to have been taken by surprise and did not interfere.

The City of Tabrīz

Tabrīz, which before World War I was the largest and most prosperous city in the kingdom, is today unfortunate and unblessed. A large part of Persia's profitable trade with Czarist Russia was formerly centred there; so, too, was the trade with the West by way of Trebizond and Istanbul. Today the commerce with Russia has dwindled, and the transit trade with Istanbul has disappeared. With them have gone the merchant princes of Tabrīz. The population, which was formerly estimated at over 300,000, has shrunk by a third.

Nevertheless the city is no longer the huddle of mean and dirty streets which it was when I first knew it thirty-five years ago. Like most of the larger Persian towns, it boasts today of a number of broad asphalted avenues and pleasant public gardens. Its vaulted bazaar is still one of the largest in Persia. The stately caravanserais which lead off from it are bereft of much of their activity; yet they still stand —quiet and dignified—attending, as it were, with patience, the revival of their fortunes.

Although nothing remains of the splendours of Shām but dismal mounds in the suburb of Karamalek, Tabrīz still possesses a few buildings which are worthy of note. The most prominent (though not the most picturesque) is the Ark—a huge, rectilinear block of masonry 120 feet high, which dominates the city. It must have been a *donjon* or inner fortress of some kind. A portion of it is said to date from the fourteenth century; the rest was built in 1809.

The most noteworthy building in the city is the so-called Blue Mosque, which was built by Jahān Shah in the fifteenth century. There is not much left of it but the facade—magnificently tiled in turquoise blue, ultramarine, black and yellow. Though nothing but a splendid ruin, it is still an outstanding example of Mongol architecture, rivalling the colleges and mausoleums of Samarkand itself.

The Revival of the Carpet Industry

It was stated at the end of Chapter I that the bloody Afghan invasions, followed by the turbulent reign of Nadir Shah, brought the carpet industry of Persia near to extinction. The consolidation of the Qajār dynasty, however, and with it a long period of comparative order and peace, gave the industry an opportunity of revival. Much of the credit for this revival must be accounted to the enterprising merchants of Tabrīz.

37. TABRĪZ: A CARAVANSERAI WHERE THE CARPET MERCHANTS CONGREGATE

The Persian Carpet becomes an Article of Commerce

For many centuries, but in a small way, Persian carpets had been articles of foreign commerce. As far back as the fifteenth century they were known and valued in the West. They appear in ancient inventories and in a few Italian and Flemish Renaissance paintings.[1]

It was not until the middle of the nineteenth century, however, that Persian carpets began to find their way into the West in appreciable quantities. The trade was in the hands of Tabrīzi merchants—men of credit and renown. They had branch offices in Istanbul, where their principal business was to buy the manufactures of the West and ship them home via Trebizond. They had their agents, too, in the important towns of Persia, who collected carpets from the houses and in the bazaars. Most of these pieces had been long in service; for there were no banks in Persia in those days, and the custom was (as, indeed, it is today) for people to invest their savings in carpets, which could, at need, be reconverted into cash. These pieces invariably realised a higher price after ten to forty years of service than their owners had paid for them in the first instance; because the West was willing to pay more for an old carpet than for a new one. Thus, there issued from the houses, into every bazaar in Persia, a constant stream of antique or semi-antique pieces.

These rugs and carpets had been produced for the home market. They had not been woven in factories: they were tribal or village pieces; and they were usually in small repeating patterns. The sizes were usually long and narrow—and to our way of thinking, awkward. There was the *Mian Farsh*, or middle carpet, which usually measured 16–20 feet long by 6–8 feet wide; the *Kellegi*, or head piece, usually 10–12 feet long by 5–6 feet wide; and a pair of *Kenarehs*, or side-pieces, 16–20 feet long by 3 feet 4 inches (1 *zar*) wide. These four pieces were laid

[1] Most of the carpets which were thus depicted were, however, Caucasian or Turkish weaves.

as shown in the diagram below. If the owner should have the misfortune to move into a house with smaller rooms than his former residence, there was no need for him to scrap his carpets—as we should have to do. The four pieces could be laid in the same manner as before, but with slight overlaps—a simple and practical solution of the problem.[1]

38. THE ARRANGEMENT OF THE PIECES IN THE HOME

The agents of the Tabrīzi merchants collected as many of these old carpets as they could find in the houses and bazaars of the more important towns, and sent them by caravan to Tabrīz. There they were sorted, baled and despatched upon their long overland journey—via Bayazid and Erzerūm—to the Turkish port of Trebizond. At Trebizond the bales were loaded (probably on a trim steamer of the Cie Paquet, or in one of the ancient, portly bottoms of the Cie des Messageries Maritimes; or maybe of the old Austrian Lloyd) to Constantinople—which became the world's market for carpets. Buyers from Britain, from the United States and from France (the demand from Germany came later) visited the Turkish capital in increasing numbers. The demand continued to grow; but as it grew the supply of old carpets steadily diminished.

What was to be done? The enterprising merchants of Tabrīz were faced with the danger of the extinction of their profitable trade. They resolved to meet the crisis by producing new carpets, to be specially woven for export, in sizes and colours which they believed would appeal to Western taste.

Thus, about the year 1880, the weaving industry of Persia—which since the Afghan invasion had dwindled into an insignificant village craft—received from the merchants of Tabrīz a stimulus which has placed it today in the forefront of Persia's commercial activities.

The basic character of the craft was, of necessity, changed. The Persian carpet, from being an article produced to meet a restricted domestic need, became essentially an article of export, with a demand as wide as the world itself. From that time on, out of every hundred pieces woven on the handlooms of Persia, probably ninety saw service for the first time upon Western floors.

The Tabrīzi merchants were not content merely to place orders with the village weavers and leave it at that. They soon established small factories of a few looms in the towns, where the weaving process could be more easily and more properly controlled. The movement began in Tabrīz itself; but they extended it before long to Meshed, Kermān and Kashān. In each locality the moving spirit was the Tabrīzi merchant.[2] Besides the work in the towns, they began to organise the manufacture in a few village areas as well—in the Herīz district, east of Tabrīz itself, and among the hundreds of villages east of Sultānabād.

The Technique of Carpet Washing is Born

I well remember those Tabrīz, Meshed and Kermān carpets of the new era. They were few in number and they aroused a warranted curiosity. Unlike the old-time, mellow pieces which we had been accustomed to receive from Persia, these carpets had never before seen service. They were new,

---

[1] Carpet sizes (such as Persia is producing today in great quantities for export) were uncommon until the end of last century. It became, no doubt, the established practice in Persia to cover the floors with small or long and narrow pieces because the tribal and village looms were small and their owners were disinclined to change them. I know from experience how difficult it is to induce villagers to scrap their looms for wider ones, to carry carpets. The change involves household and economic adjustments which they dislike.

[2] I am happy to be able to record some of the names of those noted families of traders—some of whose descendants are traders still: Sadaqiani, Ipekji, Mamaghāni, Mahmedoff, Urdubatli, Dilmaghāni, Tehrānji, Salmāsi, Antikaji and Ehrabi.

and to our unaccustomed eyes extravagantly crude in colour. Their sale presented a formidable problem; but the ingenious merchants of Tabrīz attacked it with sagacity. Before long, the roofs of the Hans in old Istanbul where they traded were covered with carpets of price, exposed to the fierce rays of the Turkish summer sun. And in the early morning, men with watering-cans roamed among them—like gardeners watering their flowers; for it was found that watering the carpets before the sun was up tended to speed the fading process.

Other methods, too, were tried. The carpets were placed face upwards on the ground in the bazaar, where traffic was thickest, and left for many weeks to be trodden on by man and beast. Then the accumulated filth was washed off with wood ash or a native cleaning root. The result was passable. But it was soon discovered that the reduction in the colour had been produced, not by trampling the rugs in the dust, or by cleaning them with root, but by the wood ash. And so the covered ways of the bazaar ceased to be garnished with carpets. Washing with wood ash alone became the accepted technique. Thus, by a long process of trial and error—by persons ignorant of the existence or properties of oxidising or reducing agents—the technique of carpet washing was born.

Change in the Character of the Industry

The development of the export trade changed the character of the craft; but was it changed for the better? The answer must be, I think, in the affirmative. It can hardly be disputed that the carpets produced in Persia between 1700 and 1900 cannot compare in variety, in excellence of design or craftsmanship with the best products of the Kermān and Kashān weavers of the early twentieth century; nor with the weaves of Qūm and Naīn of more recent years. A glance at the plates shown in the chapters XIII and XVI will confirm this. Nor can it be doubted that this incontestable advance was largely due to the stimulus which reached the Persian weavers from the West.

Although the effect of this sudden change in objective was profound, it had little effect on the technique of carpet weaving. That, indeed, had hardly varied down the centuries. And the essentials of design—modified as they have been in recent years to meet the public taste of the West—have persisted, with surprising constancy, from generation to generation. The calls of fashion, the demand of the stylist and the interior decorator have their day and are forgotten. But the motives of the great designers of the sixteenth century still stand. They continue to appear in a thousand combinations, to proclaim the continuity of a great tradition.

Tabrīz as a Carpet Centre

When I visited Tabrīz once more in August 1948, the city had recently emerged from a distressful period. These latter-day misfortunes began in 1941, when it was occupied by Russian troops. The Russian occupation, though orderly, was dour; and was not accompanied by that orgy of spending which followed the entry of American and British troops into Persia. Thus Tabrīz suffered the trials of occupation without the compensating advantages which accrued to many towns in the southern and central areas of the country.

The Russian occupation was followed by the establishment of an insurgent "democratic" government in Azerbaijān. The carpet merchants of Tabrīz fled to the capital with their goods, and production from the city looms came almost to a standstill. After the re-establishment of the authority of the Central Government at the end of 1946, the merchants returned, the factories were reopened, and production—howbeit on a smaller scale—was resumed. At first the merchants encountered serious difficulties in attempting to satisfy the accumulated demand: labour was undisciplined; materials were scarce; some dyestuffs were unobtainable. This period of disorganisation left its mark on the quality of the goods that were then produced.

By the time I reached Tabrīz most of these troubles had been overcome, but not all. The industry was trying hard to get back into its stride; but was still halting. Perhaps, on the whole, it was as well: for the European markets—on which Tabrīz depended—were almost out of business. And the American market—which had kept Kermān, Arāk and Hamadān alive in the post-war period—was not interested in the Tabrīz carpet. Production, therefore, on anything like the pre-war scale, would inevitably have resulted in a slump.

It would be unfair not to make full allowance in this survey for these adversities. For I am persuaded that unless the future of Azerbaijān is thrown once more into the melting-pot (as may well happen) the merchants of Tabrīz will overcome their difficulties, as they have overcome them, time and again, in their long history.

The weaving area of Tabrīz produces five main categories of goods: (1) the Tabrīz carpet, which is woven exclusively in the city itself and its immediate suburbs; (2) the so-called Herīz or Georavān carpet, which is woven in some thirty villages situated in an area about 40 miles east of Tabrīz, on the south-west side of the Savalān massif; (3) the single-wefted, closely woven Karajā rugs and strips; (4) the rugs and strips of the Sarāb villages—directly south of the Savalān massif; and (5) the so-called Zenjān rugs which are woven in the rich agricultural district which lies immediately west of the Zenjān–Kazvīn road. The rugs and strips of Karajā and Sarāb have been included under the section devoted to the Herīz area, because both places are very close to it.

The Tabrīz Carpet

The Tabrīz carpet is a double-wefted fabric, woven (as in all Turkish-speaking localities) with the Turkish knot. It is produced exclusively in the town and suburbs of Tabrīz.

Most of the yarns which are used in Tabrīz are spun from wools from the Makū district—a strip of mountainous country which lies in the extreme north-west of Persia, between Turkey and the Soviet Republic of Nakhichevan. Rizaieh, on the far side of Lake Urmieh, Khoy and Salmas supply smaller quantities of wool.

The Makū wools are good, but they are somewhat harsher and more kempy than the Kurdish wools of Kermanshāh or the wools of northern Khūrasān. It is these characteristics which impart a harsh surface to the Tabrīz carpet.

The sheep in the Makū area are clipped twice in the year—once in the early summer and again in the early autumn. The latter clip—mixed with the wool from the lambs born in the previous March—is known as *Kuzem*, or lamb's wool. It is used in carpets of fine quality only.

Both clip and skin wools (i.e. wools pulled from the sheepskins in the tanneries) are used in Tabrīz. The use of yarns spun from skin wool is general in the lower grades of carpet—which constitute the largest part of the Tabrīz production. Factory owners declare that they do not use it in the better grades, because, they say, it does not take the dye sufficiently well. *Si non e vero....*

The wools are carded by power-driven carding machines, of which there are several in Tabrīz. Although there is a spinning factory in the city and another in Kazvīn, millspun yarn is happily not used in carpet manufacture. The Tabrīz carpet is mechanical enough in appearance, and the use of millspun yarn would accentuate this defect.

Most of the weaving in Tabrīz is carried on in factories of from 10 to 100 looms. There are about twenty of these factories in the town, containing in all about 700 looms. The factories are owned or controlled by master-weavers who either produce carpets for their own account and sell them in the bazaar, or weave under contract with other merchants or exporters. In addition to the 700 factory looms there are about 300 more in the houses or cottages. These are operated by the householder, who invariably weaves a low-grade carpet for sale in the bazaar.

The best of the Tabrīz carpet factories are the most up-to-date in Persia—clean, light, well ventilated and not overcrowded. Even the less modern ones compare favourably with those of other localities. On the threshold of one of the more advanced establishments I was startled by the raucous blare of a loudspeaker vociferating words of welcome. No sooner was this alarming speech concluded than the voice was raised in song—the kind of song, I suppose, which the Azeri composers have evolved out of the reveries of western crooners. I trust that the weavers were comforted by this exhibition of modernity and that it helped to shorten for them the long and dreary day.

The type of loom on which the carpet is woven was devised in Tabrīz itself. Being practical, simple in construction and cheap, it has been adopted in Hamadān and other localities as well (see p. 23).

The following qualities are woven in Tabrīz: 25×25; 30×30; 35×35; 40×40; 50×50; and 60×60 knots per *punzeh* of 7 centimetres.[1]

The first of these is a low-grade carpet woven for sale in the bazaar. Most of the 300 household or cottage looms and some of the factories produce it; but it is an ill-woven fabric and it has brought the Tabrīz fabric into disrepute. The 30×30 grade is the average bazaar quality of Tabrīz carpet. The 35×35 is the quality usually ordered by European firms, who prefer a carpet made to their own designs in a quality superior to the bazaar grade. The

---

[1] The approximate equivalents of these qualities per square inch are:

25×25 per 7 centimetres $= 9 \times 9$ per inch
30×30 ,, ,, $= 11 \times 11$,, ,,
35×35 ,, ,, $= 12\frac{1}{2} \times 12\frac{1}{2}$,, ,,
40×40 ,, ,, $= 14\frac{1}{2} \times 14\frac{1}{2}$,, ,,
50×50 ,, ,, $= 18 \times 18$,, ,,
60×60 ,, ,, $= 22 \times 22$,, ,,

demand for the three finer qualities is small on account of their high cost.

The knots per *punzeh*, mentioned above, are theoretical, rather than actual, standards. Thus, when the seller indicates that his wares are of the 30×30 quality, the buyer knows that the merchandise will not count over 27 (or at best 28) each way; and the seller knows that he knows. On this fictional and pleasant basis the deal goes forward and everybody is happy.

It was said of the British soap manufacturers (of a bygone generation) that they had succeeded in making a bar of water stand on end. In like manner it might be said of the manufacturers of Tabrīz carpets that they had succeeded in producing a hand-woven floor-covering with the expenditure of a minutiae of materials. For the factory owners of Tabrīz are among the most skilled technicians in Persia and what they do not know about economising in materials is not worth knowing. The weight of yarn which a Hamadān or Sarūk weaver puts into a yard of carpet would scandalise them. They would aver that with an equal poundage they could produce two yards. And so they could. But whereas the Hamadān or Sarūk carpet will last for two or even three generations, the expectation of life of the average Tabrīz is (at best) uncertain and (at worst) brief.

This saving in materials is accomplished by the use of thin yarns and by shortening the pile—because a short pile enables the weaver to cut the woollen strands close to the warp before clipping. In a 35×35 quality (12½×12½ knots to the square inch) or over, thin yarn and a short pile are not serious defects: because the closeness of the weave gives the carpet sufficient density. Unhappily, however, during the last twenty years large numbers of carpets have been woven in Tabrīz in a much lower quality. There would be no harm in that if yarn of the proper thickness were used. But the Tabrīz weavers too often use the same thin yarn for an 8×8 or 9×9 quality as they quite properly use for a quality of 12½×12½ or over. The resulting fabric lacks density and so wears out in a few years—a consequence which has given the Tabrīz carpet an unfortunate reputation. This reputation (I hasten to add) belongs only to the coarser grades; those counting 11×11 knots to the inch and over give good service. I have had one in my possession for thirty years, and it shows no sign of wear; it looks, indeed, as though it were good for another thirty.

The Weavers of Tabrīz

The weavers of Tabrīz are the fastest in Persia. I was amazed and fascinated with the speed and accuracy with which they worked. For tying the knot they use a knife with a projection like a button-hook on the end (Plate 12). Unerringly, this hook picked out the correct warp string (out of, it seemed to me, a hundred possibles) and with a flick of the wrist a knot was tied. We timed one of the weavers. He was tying the knots at the rate of one a second; 8,000 knots a day is a common performance; the best weavers can tie 15,000.[1]

39. INTERIOR OF A TABRĪZ CARPET FACTORY

I have already referred (p. 17) and shall have occasion later in this survey to refer to the spread throughout Persia of a fraudulent method of weaving which is rapidly impairing the reputation of the Persian carpet. This pernicious practice consists in tying each knot on four strings of the warp instead of the proper two, so that the finished carpet contains only half the proper number of knots. Tabrīz is one of the few weaving centres of Persia where the disease has failed to penetrate. The reason for its immunity is not because the Tabrīz weavers are

[1] It must be borne in mind that at least a third of the weaving time is taken up by operations other than knotting; i.e. passing the wefts, clipping, weaving the selvedges and the *gilims*, lowering the carpet, etc.

less guileful than their colleagues of Meshed, Kermān and other localities. It is because they tie the knot with the hook instead of with the fingers; and the fraudulent knot cannot be tied with the hook. The effect of this immunity is bound, in the long run, to militate in favour of the Tabrīz carpet, provided that the Tabrīz weavers correct their own misdemeanours—which are, happily, less grave.

I was surprised to see in Tabrīz—that stronghold of the Moslem faith—men and women working side by side at the same loom. A few years ago such a thing would have been unthinkable. The recrudescence of the influence of the priesthood has succeeded in re-introducing the veil into Persia; will it succeed in eliminating women from the Tabrīz carpet factories? The general opinion seemed to be that economics will prevail over the church.

Wages in the Tabrīz carpet industry have been steadily rising during recent years. In August 1948 the rate varied with the different factories between 21 and 23 rials per *Kabal* of 14,000 knots. Four weavers working at a loom would be expected to weave a minimum of two *Kabals* or 28,000 knots per day. In that case the head-weaver of the four would receive a minimum of 42 to 46 rials, out of which he would pay his three *shagirds* or assistants. The wages of the *shagirds* varied between 6 and 10 rials.[1]

Design in Tabrīz

The designers of Tabrīz are excellent draftsmen and good adaptors; but they are not—like the designers of Kermān—creators of new and exciting forms of beauty. They borrow what they conceive to be good or saleable—whether it be from the classic designs of the sixteenth century or from some modern western print. Some of the finest pieces of weaving which I encountered were in sad taste. I have in mind a carpet of supreme workmanship which depicted a muscular gentleman carrying over his shoulder a lady with her hair streaming in the wind (both figures hurried and incomplete in their dress) the whole enclosed in a classic sixteenth-century border.

There is, however, one type of design for which the world has, I think, to thank Tabrīz: the so-called medallion-and-corner design. It was certainly derived from the tooled leather book-covers of the fifteenth century (see Plates 23, 24). No doubt the early Tabrīzi carpet designers—with that facility for borrowing which has always distinguished them—realised its fitness for carpet design and adopted it. It has stood the test of centuries and has been copied by floor-covering designers of every country the world over.

Dyeing in Tabrīz

The more important factory owners of Tabrīz have small dyehouses on their premises where they dye their own yarns. There are, in addition, about ten independent dye-houses in the town which dye for the smaller factories and for the 300 individual weavers.

Tabrīz is the only weaving centre of Persia where the use of western dyestuffs has become firmly established. The new dyes have, indeed, driven out the old. They were introduced for the first time on an important scale by a German firm of carpet importers which made Tabrīz its headquarters before World War I. The firm was compelled to close down in Persia; but the Persian dyers whom they had trained soon established themselves in the bazaar and have continued ever since to use dyes of German, and later of Swiss, manufacture. The ease, swiftness and cheapness of the dyeing process—compared with the slow and costly Persian technique—appealed to the hard-headed, practical master-weavers of Tabrīz.

Both chrome[2] and acid dyes (anilines) are used in Tabrīz. The master-weavers declare that the latter are employed only in the lower grades of carpets—those counting 25 × 25 knots to the *punzeh* or under. The truth or falseness of this statement will appear only after the carpet has been in use for some time—and then it will be too late.

The use of European dyes in the Persian carpet industry is discussed on p. 365.

Characteristics of the Tabrīz Carpet

Most of the weaves of Persia possess a dominating colour which appears in most of the carpets of the area and helps to give them their distinctive character. In Hamadān, Seraband and the Herīz area it is madder red; in Arāk, *dughi* rose (see p. 32); in Kermān, cream; in Meshed and Birjānd, cochineal red; in Qūm and Naīn, white; in the tribal rugs of Fārs and northern Khūrasān, dark blue. Tabrīz carpets alone among the important weaves possess no distinctive shade. The master-weavers of the city are a practical fraternity, who produce carpets in the

---

[1] See p. 99 for a note on the value of the rial in foreign currency.
[2] Synthetic dyes of foreign manufacture, mordanted with potassium bichromate (see p. 30).

colours which happen to be in demand at the time.

Among the positive characteristics which distinguish the Tabrīz carpet from other Persian weaves are: (a) The knot: every Tabrīz carpet (freaks excepted) is woven with the Turkish knot; and any carpet which is not woven with the Turkish knot (again freaks excepted) cannot be a Tabrīz carpet. (b) The Tabrīz fabric is double wefted, and it is usually shorter in the pile, thinner and lighter in weight than most of the non-tribal Persian weaves. (c) The drawing of the design is so perfect and its execution so accurate that the carpet is invariably too set, too regular; so much so that many Tabrīz carpets have a machine-made appearance. This mechanical accuracy is accentuated by the shortness of the pile. (d) The wool of the Makū area, and especially the skin wool from the Tabrīz tanneries is harsher than that of other carpet wools of Persia. Consequently the carpets of Tabrīz lack the velvety feel of the Meshed, Kermān and other weaves. (e) The colours employed in the Tabrīz carpets are often hard and crude.

It is, indeed, this combination of shortness of pile, mechanical accuracy, harshness to the touch and crudeness of colour which has given to the Tabrīz carpet its distinctive character, and has placed it among the less attractive of the Persian weaves. To these characteristics there must, I fear, be added a deterioration in the quality of the fabric.

For this last demerit the weavers of Tabrīz are in no wise to blame. They are more skilled and more industrious than their rivals in other weaving centres. One has only to watch them to realise that. The responsibility lies with the master-weavers. They possess all the technical knowledge and experience which would enable them—with the expert labour which they command—to produce some of the finest carpets in Persia. But they are—I regret to say—a cheese-paring lot. They are content to produce a fabric which, they well know, will not give proper service, and which is often poor in design and crudely coloured. Unless they mend their ways, the reputation of the Tabrīz carpet will continue to decline.

These strictures do not, happily, apply to all the factories of Tabrīz. There are at least three which are producing worthy carpets. And in some of the others one may encounter a few carpets of good quality—an indication of what might be produced on every loom in the city.

It must be stated in the defence of the master-weavers of Tabrīz that since the outbreak of World War II, their principal market—western Europe—has been all but lost to them. In the interval a new demand arose from Irāq, Syria, Palestine and Egypt for cheap carpets in bright colours. They met the demand by lowering their quality and using cheap yarns and aniline dyes. If and when western Europe recovers, the demand for better grade Tabrīz carpets will revive and the master-weavers of Tabrīz will, no doubt, once again produce carpets worthy of their skill and of the renown of their city as a weaving centre.

Conversation Piece

Overheard in the bazaar:

"Hassan, bring the yard-stick."[1]

"Which yard-stick, sir; the one for buying or the one for selling?"

THE HERĪZ AREA

Forty miles due east of Tabrīz as the crow flies, and about 50 miles by road, lies one of the most interesting—because one of the most untouched—of the weaving areas of Persia. I have called it—for want of a better name—the Herīz area; but it might be named, with almost equal propriety, the Georavān,[2] the Mehribān or the Bakshaīsh area. Carpets bearing the names of these and other villages are daily trafficked for in the Tabrīz bazaar; and some of these names are in common use in the West as well. Herīz is, however, the largest and most important of the thirty villages which comprise the district, and it possesses the further distinction of being the village in which the best carpets are woven. Its claim to the leadership of the area is, therefore, substantial.

The district—which measures about 35 × 35 miles—lies west and south of the great Savalān massif. The population is exclusively Turkish; and, like all weavers of the Turkish race, they weave the Turkish knot. Agriculturally, the area is not particularly important. It exports no wheat. But the prosperous carpet-weaving industry has brought considerable wealth to some of its villages. For it is this area which produces those remarkable carpets—so hardy, so full of character, yet so inexpensive—which the world has known for half a century as Georavāns or Herīz.

[1] Actually the *nim-zar*, an iron measuring rod.
[2] The name "Yoraghān", which is sometimes applied to this village, is incorrect. For a time the name "Serape" (Sarāb) was used in America; but it appears to have been dropped.

Weaving has been carried on in the Herīz area certainly since the beginning of the nineteenth century, and possibly before that date; though I am not aware of any pieces which may be ascribed, with assurance, to a period before 1800.[1]

Bakshaīsh is the village where weaving has been going on the longest. One may still occasionally encounter an old Bakshaīsh *kellegi*—invariably in the Herātī design, and invariably woven in lovely tones of blue, buff and mauve. If the buffs are closely examined they will probably prove to have been originally dyed red, which has oxidised with the passage of time.

The existence of so few old pieces from the Herīz area indicates quite clearly that the extensive weaving industry of today—with its output of some 10,000 carpets a year, plus as many rugs and strips—is a comparatively modern development. It is, indeed, a little over half a century old. Before that period, the unique and unmistakable style of carpet which we call Herīz or Georavān did not exist. There are no antique carpets of this type to be found anywhere.

The Herīz area may be conveniently divided into three parts: (1) the Karajā district; (2) the Herīz area proper; and (3) the Sarāb district.

(1) *The Karajā District*. In the north-west of the area there is a group of half a dozen villages of which the pretty and prosperous village of Karajā (Plate 40) is the most renowned. Karajā is situated on the Tabrīz–Ahār road about 35 miles from the city. As in Bakshaīsh, weaving has been carried on there for a century, or probably more.

The village has given its name to a type of rug and strip which is unique, well known and unmistakable. The fabric is single wefted, closely woven and well finished. All the villages of the group weave the same design (Plate 66). The grounds of the rugs and strips are usually madder red and the borders dark blue. Two of the three medallions are invariably cream or green and the centre one dark blue. The output of the Karajā area is probably in the neighbourhood of 800 pieces a year, almost all of which are rugs and strips.

(2) *The Herīz Area Proper*. Five miles beyond Karajā, on the Tabrīz–Ahār road, is the small village of Khūrmalī, whence a track leads from the main highway into the Herīz area proper. It goes by way of Bilverdī, Kildīr, Mina, Parām, Turkeīsh and Būrazī to Herīz itself. As far as Herīz, the track—

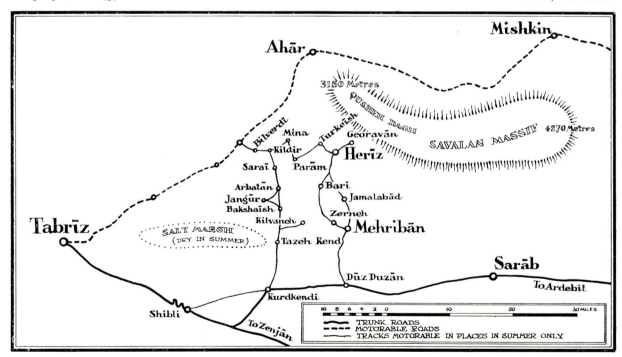

MAP II. THE HERĪZ WEAVING AREA

[1] Mr. A. Upham Pope has attributed two antique carpets—one in the Pennsylvania Museum (Williams Collection) and the other the property of the late Edith Rockefeller McCormick—to "Bakshaīsh, a town south of Ardebil". Bakshaīsh is actually a small village situated 130 miles due west of Ardebil; and there is no evidence that carpets in any but simple, rectilinear designs were ever woven there.

40. Karajā Village, Herīz Area

though rough in places and intersected by watercourses—is passable by car in the dry season. If, however, the traveller should wish to cross the area from north to south, he would be well advised to hire a guide in Herīz and half a dozen men with spades and pickaxes, to see him through as far as Zerneh. Beyond that village there is a serviceable track through Mehribān to Dūz Duzān, on the main Tabrīz–Ardebil road.

The first village in the Herīz area proper is Bilverdī. The carpets which are woven there are not particularly good; but Bilverdī is worth mention because it is the only village in the area which weaves the regular Herīz medallion design in a single-wefted fabric. All the other villages make double-wefted carpets. Perhaps Bilverdī was once a member of the nearby Karajā group and wove the Karajā design; but was later attracted into the orbit of Herīz and began weaving carpet sizes in the Herīz pattern, retaining, nevertheless, its single-wefted fabric. Thus the garment was changed but the body remained the same.

I have already described how, during the last quarter of the nineteenth century, the Tabrīz merchants, finding that the supply of antique carpets was coming to an end, began to place orders for new carpets for export. The nearby district of Herīz —where a tradition of weaving had long existed— was an obvious field for development. We can, I think, reconstruct with some assurance the story of what took place.

The Tabrīz merchants knew that the West was at that time demanding carpet sizes in medallion designs, in place of the long and narrow pieces in small repeating patterns which the village weavers had hitherto been producing. It was in the course of things, therefore, that one of those enterprising traders should send to Georavān (at that time a large and important village) or to Bakshaīsh or Herīz an ordinary, curvilinear medallion-and-corner Tabrīz design—to see what the village weavers would make of it. And then, of course, the inevitable happened: the weavers of the area (as incapable then as they are today of weaving curves) broke up the design into straight lines—the vertical, the horizontal and the diagonal of 45 degrees; and thus, unwittingly, produced the Herīz or Georavān design (see p. 64).

That, I am persuaded, was the origin of this famous pattern; in which, during the last fifty years, probably half a million carpets have been woven.

A sketch is appended (Plates 41 and 42) which shows, side by side, an early medallion-and-corner Tabrīz design, and the same design broken up into straight lines—as the Herīz weavers would have then interpreted it, and as they would interpret it today.

This propensity of the weavers of the area to break up curves into straight lines may be seen in operation any day in any of their villages. One has only to ask a weaver to show her design. A piece of white cloth will be produced, measuring about 9×6 inches, of which the pattern of one-quarter of the carpet has been drawn and roughly coloured. The pattern is always curvilinear—yet the design of the carpet which is being woven from it is always in straight lines (Plates 43 and 44).

The weavers of the area possess another skill which, so far as I am aware, is possessed by the weavers of only one other centre in the East—Ushāk, in Turkey. In both places they scoff at scale paper designs, or at the sing-song of the master-weaver calling out the pattern. They merely pin a piece of cloth—like the one described above—upon the wall; and glancing at it from time to time, they can weave any sized carpet from it that you may wish to order—an astonishing feat of instinctive, intuitive planning.

Some years ago while I was visiting one of the villages of the Herīz area I noticed on a loom a carpet of unusual and interesting design. I asked the weaver to show me her pattern. Shyly, she produced from a box in the corner a square handkerchief of the kind which is printed in Manchester for the Eastern trade. It had a floral border, a round floral medallion and corner pieces; and it was printed in two colours—red and white. From this unpropitious pattern she was weaving an admirable carpet in a dozen colours, complete with border, elongated medallion and corner pieces—all correctly spaced and all in broken straight lines!

Carpet weaving is carried on in practically all of the thirty villages of the area. The principal villages are Herīz, with about 800 looms; Mehribān, with about 600; Bakshaīsh, with about 500; Asleh, with about 150; Saraī and Sainsaraī (loc. Sinsireh), with about 100 each. The best carpets are woven in Herīz, with Mehribān a good second. Unhappily, a few years ago the Mehribān weavers (in response to the demand for all-over patterns) adopted a rather

41. Medallion-and-Corner, Tabrīz Design   42. Herīz interpretation of the same design

43. PATTERN FROM THE HERĪZ AREA
It is drawn on white cloth and roughly coloured. The pattern is always curvilinear; yet the design of the carpet which is woven from it is always in straight lines.

44. THE SAME PATTERN REPRODUCED AS A HERĪZ WEAVER WOULD INTERPRET IT

poor design of this type (Plate 44). It has spread throughout the area and has already ousted the familiar medallion pattern from many of the villages. Before the war a number of good all-over patterns were being woven, but they have been lost and forgotten.

Until recent years the weavers of the Herīz area procured their wools or spun yarn from the neighbouring Shahseven tribes. That admirable practice is, unhappily, fast disappearing. Today the villagers buy their yarn ready spun in the bazaars of Tabrīz or Ardebil. Most of it is spun from skin wool and is a very different material from the yarn which they formerly procured from the nomad tribesmen. The former was long in the fibre, lustrous and lofty; and when dyed it gave a clear, bright shade. The latter is short in the fibre, dull and springless; and when dyed the shades are often flat or muddy.

The system of dyeing, too, has sadly deteriorated. Until the last decade the yarns were dyed in the villages; the blue, red and green by the village dyers; the other shades by the weaver herself in her own pots over her own fire. Both used the excellent, time-honoured technique of their ancestors. Now, alas, the village dyer has disappeared from many of the villages and will soon, I fear, disappear from them all. The blue, red and green are now dyed in Tabrīz by the town dyers, with synthetic dyes. The use of natural madder—which for fifty years was the outstanding colour in the carpets from the Herīz area—is disappearing.

It is proverbially difficult to induce a dyer—especially a Persian dyer—to reveal his secrets. Many of them still believe (though in recent years this belief has been somewhat shaken) that their

45. IN BAKSHAÏSH VILLAGE, HERĪZ AREA

47. A GROUP OF VILLAGERS, HERĪZ AREA

ancient formulas are of inestimable value. I realised, therefore, that it would not be an easy matter to discover from the Tabrīz dyers what method they were using in dyeing the yarn for the Herīz weavers. Happily, I met an old friend—one Amir Ali—who was employed by one of the Tabrīz factories. As a member of the guild of dyers he had the *entrée* to the town dye-houses; to him I explained my dilemma and he agreed to show me round. Before we set out he bade me use my eyes, hold my tongue and listen.

I soon discovered that in place of natural madder the Tabrīz dyers were using a synthetic alizarine dye of Swiss manufacture. This is the dye which produces the dark, browny-red which I had seen everywhere in the Herīz area. Indeed, the grounds

46. WEAVING INSTRUMENTS USED BY THE HERĪZ WEAVERS

of half the carpets were in this murky, sombre shade. The dyestuff, if properly employed, is fast to light and alkalis. But the shade which it produces is very different from the lighter, warmer red which the village dyers formerly obtained with natural madder.

Unhappily, however, the dyestuff is not always properly used. The lighter red, which is employed in the motives (but not as a ground colour), is often dyed without the use of a mordant. The shade is, therefore, fugitive to light and alkalis.

This information was imparted with disarming frankness by one Ostad Mohammed, a Tabrīz dyer. "It is like this," said he to my friend Amir Ali. "When a villager asks me to dye this colour" —and he pointed to a hank of lightish red yarn— "I inform him that if he wants a colour that will not fade, the price is 8 tomans a *batman*; but if he is content with a colour which may perhaps fade a little, the price is 4 tomans. These avaricious villagers appear always to prefer the cheaper method."

"I presume," suggested my friend Amir Ali, "that in order to meet the inadequate price offered by the parsimonious villagers you have been compelled to readjust your methods—perhaps by omitting the first boiling in alum."

"It is obvious," replied Ostad Mohammed Ali, "that no dyer could be expected to provide two boilings, one with alum and the second with the dye (to say nothing of a scouring between the two processes), for the miserable price of 4 tomans a *batman*."

"That would, indeed, be impossible," agreed my friend Amir Ali.

It must, therefore (I fear), be accepted that the Tabrīz dyers are in the habit of omitting the mordant from some of the secondary colours which they dye for the weavers from the Herīz area.

(3) *The Sarāb District.* The small market town of Sarāb is situated on the main Tabrīz–Ardebil road, 56 miles from Ardebil itself. It is an ancient township. Le Strange[1] quotes references to it by Ibn Hawkal (A.D. 978), Yakūt (A.D. 1225) and Mustaufi (A.D. 1340). Yakūt states that it was destroyed by the Mongols in A.D. 1220 and its inhabitants put to the sword; but it had recovered when Mustaufi wrote a century later. During the Middle Ages it was certainly a large and prosperous town. It still remains a centre of a fairly rich agricultural area.

The weaving district of Sarāb consists of some twenty villages which lie on both sides of the Ardebil road. Until quite recently the district was remarkable for its production of strips or runners of all lengths, from 8 to 25 feet. The shorter and cheaper grades were mostly produced in the eastern part of the area and were generally marketed in Ardebil. Hence they became known in Tabrīz as Ardebil strips. The better grades were woven in Sarāb itself and in the nearby villages, and are called in Tabrīz after the town of Sarāb. The best woven and the most prized among them have grounds of a lovely shade of camel, with copper-red lozenge-shaped medallions (Plate 67). Before the war the area also produced important quantities of rugs and mats, mostly with madder-red grounds and blue or cream geometrical medallions.

In referring to the rugs of this area I have been constrained to use the past tense; because production, when I visited it in 1948, had sunk to such a low level that the industry appeared to be almost extinct. In Sarāb itself—which before the war had been a busy weaving centre—there was not a single loom in operation. That was a sombre fact enough; but to make matters worse, I found that the weavers had recently left the place and migrated to Arāk (Sultānabād) where no doubt they are busy weaving Sarūks for the American market. Conditions in the neighbouring villages were hardly any better. Everywhere production was at a very low level, or had ceased altogether.

The reason for this is, I think, quite plain: runners of all lengths were the principal product of the area; and these goods are among the least expensive of any which are produced in Persia. Thus a Herīz carpet of good quality sells in the Tabrīz bazaar for 80–90 tomans a square metre; whereas a Sarāb strip—closer in stitch than a Herīz, well dyed and perfectly woven—sells for half that price. With wool at the highest figure that it has ever touched in Persia, there is no profit for the weaver in producing a strip for which he can only get between about 30 and 40 tomans a metre. It is more profitable to sell his wool (if he has any) rather than to weave; and if he has no wool and has to buy it, the finished strip may cost him more than he is likely to get for it in the bazaar.

Why, then, did not the Sarāb weavers take up the weaving of carpet sizes instead of emigrating to Arāk? The answer probably is that their looms were not wide enough to carry carpets and that they were unfamiliar with the technique of carpet weaving. In Arāk they work under the direction of a master-weaver: all they have to do is to tie the knots.

Will the industry in the Sarāb area ever recover? If and when there is a fall in the price of wool, or a rise in the price of rugs and strips, or both—I think it will. Weaving has come to a standstill there (as it has in other localities in Persia) because it is no longer profitable. But it is an ancient cottage industry and there is nothing in the villages to replace it. The probabilities are, therefore, that weaving will revive—though perhaps on a smaller scale than before.

THE SO-CALLED ZENJĀN RUGS

The so-called Zenjān rugs are included in this chapter out of courtesy; because—since Tabrīz ceased to be a point of shipment to the West (via Tiflis and Batūm)—Tehrān has become the principal market for the small quantity of these goods which is now being produced. If and when shipments via Russia are resumed, the Zenjān rugs will no doubt again find their way to the European markets via Tabrīz.

These rugs are not produced in Zenjān itself—as their name might imply—but in some twenty villages which lie, strung out one beyond the other, in a highly fertile valley west of the Kazvīn–Zenjān road. The area begins in the neighbourhood of Abhār and continues north-westward beyond Sultaniyeh.

The rugs produced in these villages are among the least attractive of the village rugs of Persia. They are generally coarse in weave; ordinary in design; and the reds are invariably dyed with aniline. From the traders' point of view, they have one merit—they are cheap. The output, which used to be 3,000–5,000 pieces a year, is today insignificant.

---

[1] *The Lands of the Eastern Caliphate*, p. 163 (Cambridge University Press, 1930).

48. A Tabrīz Carpet of Unusual Design (c. 1910)

49. A Useful Interpretation by a Tabrīz Designer of the Sixteenth-century Vase Design (*c.* 1913)

70 THE PERSIAN CARPET

51. Detail of a Tabrīz Carpet
Note the ingenious way in which the repeat is arranged to avoid rigidity in a rectilinear design (c. 1935).

50. Design for a Tabrīz Carpet (*c.* 1923)

52. Design for a Tabrīz Carpet, with Arabesques, Palmettes and Lotuses
School of Art, Tehrān, c. 1945

53. A Tabrīz Carpet with Medallions and Animals (*c.* 1930)
The medallions are taken from Arāk. The Tabrīz designers are skilful copyists and adapters; they rarely originate a design.

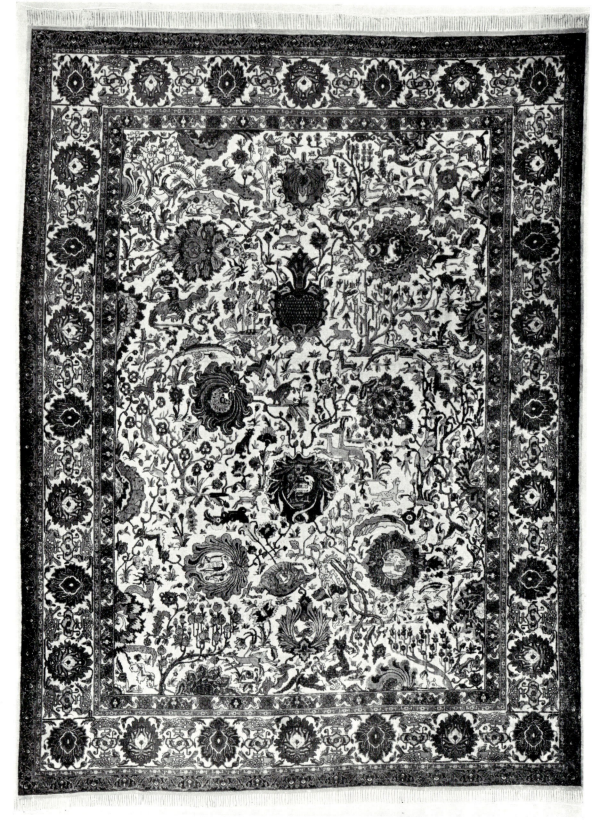

54. A Tabrīz Carpet (c. 1930)
An ingenious design which produces an effect of balance without uniformity.

55. A TABRĪZ CARPET (*c.* 1930)

An ingenious design in which Persian and Chinese motives have been cleverly combined. The two halves of the design are almost identical, but they have been reversed; the upper right hand corner coincides with the lower right hand corner, etc.

56. A "Bazaar" Tabrīz Carpet (c. 1935)
The weeping willow is successfully introduced in the ground.

57. A "Bazaar" Tabrīz Carpet (c. 1935)

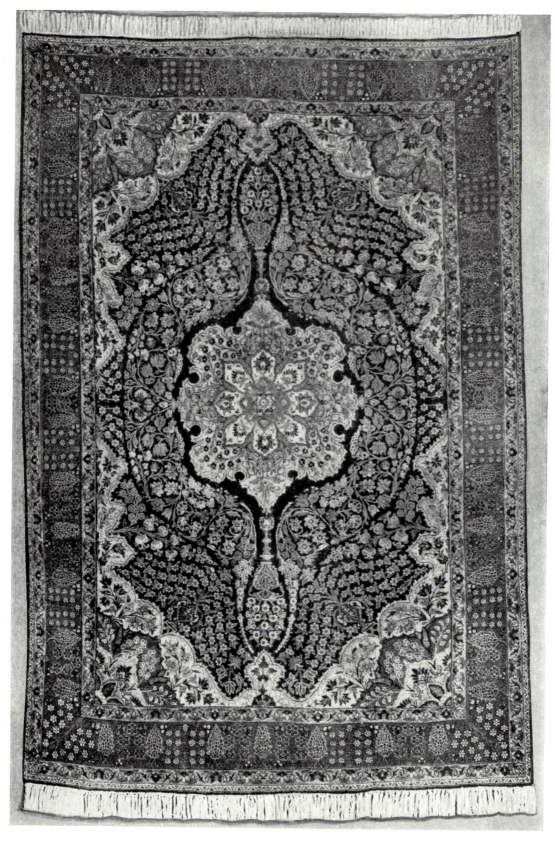

58. A Tabrīz Carpet (*c.* 1935)

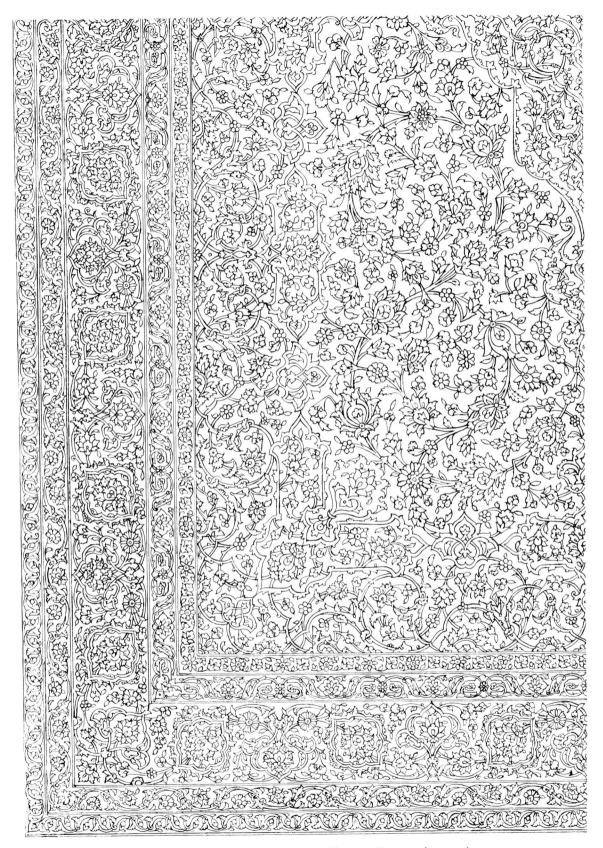

59. Medallion Design for a Tabrīz Carpet (c. 1940)
Drawn by Tahir Zadeh Bihzad, School of Art, Tehrān

78 THE PERSIAN CARPET

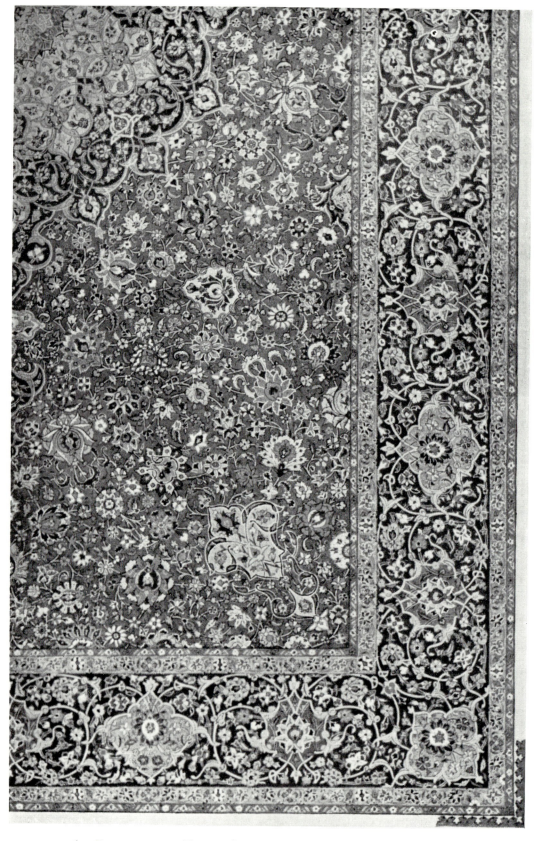

60. Design for a Tabrīz Carpet in the Classic Style (*c.* 1945)
School of Art, Tehrān

61. Design for a Hunting Carpet
School of Art, Tehrān

62. A Tabrīz Carpet, Designed by Ibrahim Rizai (*c.* 1945)

63. A Tabrīz Carpet, Designed by Ibrahim Rizai (c. 1945)

64. A Tabrīz Carpet, Designed by Ibrahim Rizai (c. 1945)

65. A Tabrīz Hunting Carpet (c. 1930)

84 THE PERSIAN CARPET

66. A Karajā Rug (*c.* 1946)

67. Sarāb Runners (*c.* 1935)
They are generally closely woven and on camel grounds.

68. Typical Carpets of the Herīz Area. *Above:* Medallion Design. *Below:* All-Over Design
During the last fifty years, upwards of half of a million carpets of these types have been woven in the villages of the area.

69. A Carpet from the Village of Herīz (c. 1925)

CHAPTER VII

HAMADĀN AND ITS ENVIRONS; WITH A NOTE ON MALAYER

HAMADĀN AND ITS ENVIRONS

Of the Town of Hamadān[1]

Hamadān—the seat of government of the province of the same name—is a town of some 70,000 people, situated on the foothills of Mount Alvānd (11,641 feet). Its situation, like that of many Persian towns, was determined by the position of a pass—in this case the pass of Assadabad—which lies on the historic highway between Mesopotamia and Persia.

It is one of the most attractive of the larger Persian towns. Its climate is healthy. Its altitude—6,000 feet above sea-level—renders it cooler and pleasanter in summer than its sister towns of north-west Persia. In winter the temperature falls many degrees below freezing; but its harshness is mitigated by frequent sunshine and the general stillness of the atmosphere.

The melting snows from Mount Alvānd, supplemented by many irrigation tunnels, minister to the fertile soil. Vineyards and orchards cover the foothills and the pleasant valleys above the town. Before it, for 60 miles, stretches a level plain dotted with prosperous villages. The area is noted for the excellent quality of its cereals and fruits.

Hamadān is a town of great antiquity but of limited historical importance. Perhaps its finest hours were when it was the capital of the great Median kingdom (675–553 B.C.) which overthrew the Assyrian power in 606 B.C. But the supremacy of the Medes was short-lived. Fifty years later Cyrus of Persis (Fārs) revolted against his Median overlord and established the Achaemenian dynasty. Hamadān, nevertheless, retained its importance; for the Achaemenian kings—to escape the intolerable Babylonian heat—made it their summer residence. That proud period ended in 331 B.C. In that year it was taken and sacked by Alexander (who seized great treasure there) after he had defeated Darius III, the last Achaemenian king, at Nineveh, and had captured Babylon, Sūsa and Persepolis. On his return from India, Alexander halted there again. And it was there that his friend and general, Hephaestion, died.

Then, for a thousand years, the town remained in comparatively safe obscurity. It emerged once again in A.D. 641, after the fatal battle of Nehavānd. The battlefield was only 40 miles away and Hamadān was the first important town to be captured by the Arabs after their victory.

The most momentous event in the somewhat uneventful history of Hamadān was the incursion of the Seljūk Turks at the beginning of the eleventh century. They first subjugated Azerbaijān, which in time became entirely Turkish-speaking. The province of Hamadān was also overrun; but being nearer the limits of the Turkish flood, it was less affected. Nevertheless, the villagers in the area still speak Turkish; though in the town itself Persian is the current speech. Racially the people are a mixture of Persian, Arab, Turkish and Mongol strains—like their neighbours of Azerbaijān.

In the thirteenth century Hamadān, like almost every important town of north-west Persia, experienced the terror of the Mongol invasions. This second incursion by Turkish tribes[2] fixed for good the Turkish character of the province. In 1252 Hulagū Khan, a younger brother of the Great Khan of the Mongols, was granted the fief of Persia and was ordered to destroy the Caliphate of Baghdad. Some of the descendants of the Seljūk Khans of Hamadān—notably a prominent chieftain, Suleiman Shah—appear to have sided with the Caliph against him. But to no purpose. Hulagū occupied Hamadān, advanced slowly along the highway into Mesopotamia and finally captured and sacked Baghdad (A.D. 1258). Nearly a million of its inhabitants were said to have perished in that awful holocaust. The destruction of the priceless books and artistic treasures of the Caliphate was a disaster hardly less deplorable.

During the two hundred years' war with Turkey (which persisted, with periodic interruptions, throughout the sixteenth and seventeenth centuries) Hamadān was captured by the Ottoman Turks and its inhabitants put to the sword.

After that it enjoyed a long period of tranquillity

---

[1] Hagmatāna, in old Persian inscriptions; Achmetha, in the book of Ezra; Agbatāna in Herodotus and Ekbatāna in the classical authors.
[2] Most authorities agree that the Turks and Mongols possess a common ancestry.

70. HAMADĀN AND THE ALVĀND RANGE FROM THE MUSALLA HILL

until it was again destroyed in 1789 by Aga Mohammed Shah, the first Qajar monarch.[1] Since then the town has been allowed to pursue, undisturbed, its provincial devices.

In the movement for the industrialisation of Persia which was set in train by Riza Shah Pahlavi, Hamadān was passed by; so that the population is not agitated by the sound of the factory whistle or the harangues of the party leader. In this the Hamadānis are fortunate; for they are a simple, clannish people who mistrust the dangerous notions which emanate from the capital. For many generations their destinies have been directed by one of the great land-owning families (with its manifold ramifications)—a family which traces its descent from the period of the Mongol invasions. It is said that every flat loaf which is baked in the town contains flour from the wheat of their villages. The family is so old and has lived in Hamadān so long that it has become, as it were, an institution. The Hamadānis regard its members with respect and view their peccadillos with tolerance.

Architectural and Archaeological Remains

Hamadān has little to boast of in the way of archaeological remains; for it was a summer residence rather than a seat of government of the Achaemenian kings. The citadel of seven concentric walls painted (or more probably tiled) in white, black, purple, blue, orange and silver/gold (which Herodotus describes) may have been sited on the Musalla Hill, on the southern outskirts of the town. But if anything remained of that gay circumvallation it was destroyed by Aga Mohammed Shah. Thirty years ago a French archaeological expedition excavated in the Musalla area and other likely sites, but with meagre results. This is not surprising. For Hamadān is today, and has always been, a town built of mud or sun-dried bricks; and the wall of the citadel was certainly constructed of those inexpugnable but impermanent materials. Though it might have withstood the batterings of an enemy, it would, if neglected, have succumbed to the perennial infiltrations of rain and snow—to subside, at last, into the formless mound of the Musalla Hill.

The city contains three buildings of interest: the tomb of Esther and Mordechai—a domed structure in the middle of the bazaar; the tomb of one of the fathers of medicine, Abu Ali Bin Sina (Avicenna) —which has been recently (but not too tastefully) repaired; and a handsome mausoleum situated in the Boni Bazaar quarter of Arab workmanship known as the Gombad-i-Alivian.

Conversation Piece

The square in front of the Gombad-i-Alivian.

I: How fortunate that this Gombad has been repaired at last! It is the most elegant monument in Hamadān, and it was falling to pieces. In a few more years there would have been nothing left of it.

---

[1] I wonder how serious were those periodic destructions of Persian towns. For it is no easy matter to destroy a town of narrow streets, flanked by windowless one-storey houses, built of sun-dried bricks. Such a town is indestructible by fire or the light weapons which a conqueror might bring to bear upon it. Destruction probably meant squeezing the rich, looting the bazaar, and killing a certain number of inoffensive citizens—a misfortune rather than a disaster. However this may be, the damage was invariably repaired, the city pursued its primitive economy under a new master, and life went on very much as before. If, as in some cases, the city never recovered, the reason must be sought elsewhere.

71. THE GOMBAD-I-ALIVIAN, HAMADĀN,
LATE TWELFTH CENTURY

The Caretaker: Thanks be to God, the work is finished! As you see, the front has been restored and the chamber behind, with its dome, has been entirely rebuilt. A million rials has been expended.

I: I have never been able to find out who is buried here. Can you, perhaps, enlighten me?

The Caretaker: How could you expect to learn about such a matter from these ignorant Hamadānis? All they think about is buying and selling. Listen: this is the tomb of Zaid-ibn-Ali, the Peace of God be upon him! He was a holy man who suffered martyrdom at the hands of the Mongols—those sons of dogs. They cut off his head with the stroke of a sword. But when they had done this, the Saint (who had remained standing) stooped down and lifting his head from the ground, placed it under his arm and departed. The cursed Mongols were so overcome by this unaccustomed experience that many of them swooned; and when they recovered, they accepted Islām. Thus are the designs of God accomplished!

Hamadān as a Weaving Centre

Hamadān is one of the foremost weaving centres of Persia. Its importance arises from the fact that the output of cheap and medium-priced rugs is greater from this area than from any other in the East. It is, indeed, the headquarters of the inexpensive rug. In the early years of the present century the output of rugs of this class from the north-eastern Caucasus—Shirvān, Kubā and Derbend—was greater than that from Hamadān. But production has declined in those areas since the Soviet revolution; so that today the pre-eminence of Hamadān for the supply of rugs in the lower price levels is undisputed.

No one can say for how long the craft has been pursued in the province. We have already seen that it existed in Dergezin (Deryazin)—a district on the Hamadān plain—in the sixteenth century; for we are told that Shah Tahmasp presented a Dergezin carpet to his brother of Istanbul, Suleiman the Magnificent. It would appear, therefore, that 400 years ago the craftsmen of the province had already achieved renown.

There is no evidence, however, that any of the outstanding carpets of the Sefavi period were produced in the province. The indications, indeed, point to the contrary. In the first place no local tradition exists to support such a theory; and in Persia the absence of a tradition in a matter of this kind is significant. Moreover, the great carpets were woven with the Persian knot; whereas the carpets from the Hamadān area have been woven—down the centuries and probably without exception—with the Turkish knot. The great Sefavi carpets are, indeed, so foreign in construction, design and colour from pieces whose Hamadān origin is not in dispute that no relationship can be perceived between them.

The limits of the Hamadān weaving area extend beyond the administrative borders of the province. Thus most of the rugs and carpets of Malayer, Senneh, Bijār and the Kurdish tribal rugs—all of which are produced outside the Hamadān province—find their way into the Hamadān bazaar. A note on nearby Malayer is included in the present chapter; but the interesting Kurdish weaves of Senneh and Bijār, together with the tribal rugs of Persian Kurdistān, deserve a chapter to themselves.

Village Weaving and Town Weaving

The Hamadān weaving industry—as in most of Persia's weaving centres—falls naturally into two main divisions: a cottage industry—which has existed for centuries in the villages of the Hamadān area; and a factory industry—which is a recent foundation and is carried on in the town itself. Although there are affinities of weight and texture between the products of the town and country looms, they differ widely in other respects, and they will be considered separately here. The village industry, being by far the more important, will be first considered.

The Hamadān Village Industry

If we climb to the summit of Mount Alvānd (an easy ascent, which can be made in a day from Hamadān) we would see, stretching before us to the east, a level plain which extends in a vast semicircle, from Tuisarkhān and the hills of Malayer on the right to the foot of the Assadabad Pass on the left. This is the plain of Hamadān, and it is here that the majority of the weaving villages lie.

The records of the local Department of Finance indicate that there are about 600 villages in the Hamadān plain; but because (as mentioned above) most of the rugs which are woven in nearby Kurdistān, Saveh and Malayer find their way into the Hamadān bazaar, the whole Hamadān weaving area probably includes twice as many. There are looms in most of them. The larger villages may contain as many as a hundred, the smaller as few as half a dozen. A census of the number of looms in the area has never been made but they probably number in the region of 30,000. The total output of the area has been estimated at about 100,000 pieces a year; of which over 90 per cent are small rugs.

It rarely happens that all or even the majority of the looms are in operation at any one time. For rug weaving is a sideline in the villages; and its pursuit depends upon a variety of circumstances. The bazaar, in the first place, must be "sweet"—which means favourable to the seller; if not, the price which the rug will fetch may leave the family nothing after the outgoings have been paid for. Also (before weaving begins) there must be money in hand to buy cotton for the warp and weft and wool for the yarn, with some left over for the village dyer who dyes the indigo and madder. And money is scarce in the villages. Above all, there must be time to weave—time between bearing and rearing a dozen children, performing the daily round of household chores, and helping the men in the fields at harvest time.

Nevertheless, every woman will contrive to finish

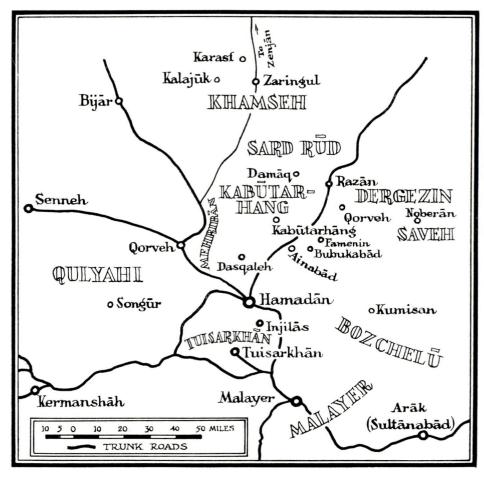

MAP III. THE HAMADĀN WEAVING AREA

at least one or two rugs before the feast of the New Year, which is at the Vernal Equinox: for its sale will bring in a few *tomans* to the household at a time when each member of the family must have something new to wear. This is the season which gladdens the heart of the trader; for the rugs come pouring in from the villages and he can quickly fill his stores with the wares of his choice.

In the West the products of these village looms are known by a variety of names which have more to do with their sizes than with their places of origin.[1] They were once commonly called Mosūls —after the town of Mosūl in northern Irāq—which has as much to do with Hamadān as it has with Hoboken. How this name came to be applied to the rugs woven in the Hamadān villages is a mystery. I surmise that at the end of the last century the then Turkish town of Mosūl was an assembling point for the rugs of nearby Kurdistān; and that the Kurdish rugs were despatched from there to the Constantinople market. Perhaps the merchants who received them (and who, in those days, may have been a little hazy in their geography) used the name Mosūl as a handy designation for all the inexpensive rugs which were despatched to them from that busy town— whether the rugs came from Kurdistān or from points farther to the east.

In the bazaar, however, a rug is named either after the village where it was woven—for the rugs of every village possess distinctive characteristics of design, colour or workmanship; or (if it be a distant village) after the district—for the rugs of a district or group of neighbouring villages possess a similarity of style. Every *dellal*[2] or trader who is worth his salt can recognise at once the group—if not, indeed, the village—where a rug was woven. This is an impressive but not (to the initiated) a mysterious accomplishment.

The Hamadān weaving area comprises about twenty of these well-defined districts or groups of villages. Some of them are administrative areas with names of their own—as Sard Rūd, Dergezin or Khamseh. Others are merely groups of villages. The latter may be conveniently named after the principal village of the group—as Injilās, Kabūtarhāng, etc. Some of these groups consist of only half a dozen villages; yet they may be none the less renowed for that. There are districts, on the other hand, which can boast of as many as fifty or sixty villages.

The products of the various groups or districts differ widely in excellence. In general the best rugs are produced by those weavers who spin the wool from their own sheep or from wool which they buy from the tribesmen in the vicinity; and the worst ones by those who buy their yarn in the bazaar. For the yarn of the bazaar is invariably poor in quality —for most of it is spun from skin wool from the local tanneries.

The position of each district or group with its more important weaving villages is shown on the map of the Hamadān weaving area (p. 90). To attempt a survey of the diversified products of all these groups would be neither practicable nor useful; but some account of the more important or more renowned among them is necessary—if we are to obtain a balanced view of the carpet industry of Hamadān. I have therefore selected ten of the twenty groups for special notice.

The most important weaving district in the Hamadān area is Dergezin. It is also the only district which is said to have been producing carpets for four centuries (see p. 89). It comprises about sixty villages and it is thus one of the largest and probably the wealthiest of the Hamadān weaving areas. It takes its name from the ancient country town of Deryazin which is today a village. The market centre of the area is at Qorveh—a rich village of about a thousand houses. The administrative centre of the area is at Razān situated on the Hamadān–Kazvīn trunk road.

The weavers of Dergezin are among the best of the Hamadān area and their rugs command the highest prices in the bazaar. They use wool from their own sheep, supplemented by purchases from the neighbouring Shahseven tribesmen. The wool is thoroughly scoured, tidily carded with the comb and evenly spun. As in most of the weaving areas, the indigo blues and greens (dark, medium and light) and the madder reds and pinks, are dyed by the local professional dyers—because these shades call for special skill. Their colours are clear and bright—an indication that the Dergezin dyers take pride in their work. The rest of the shades which are used—the creams, the yellows, the camels and the browns—are dyed by the weavers themselves in their own pans over their own fires. Unhappily, in recent years, the villagers have taken to using a villainous imported crimson in place of madder, which has sadly impaired the beauty of their rugs.

It is a melancholy reflection on the state of the rug industry in Persia that this ancient and experienced area which, during many centuries, has produced rugs in great variety in its own designs

---

[1] Such names as *do-zar*, *zar-o-nim*, *zar-o-cherek*, *pushti*, etc., are merely indications of size. [2] i.e a broker or dealer.

and colours and in its own way should have been lured during the last decade from the free exercise of its gracious craft. For today the whole area is weaving rugs for the New York rug importers; and the rugs which are being produced are no longer true Dergezins. They are not the type of rug which the Persian weaver would, of herself, have created. They are bastard productions, foreign in design and colouring, with a pile half an inch thick. A hundred of them are as alike as a hundred peas.

Kabūtarhāng is a village of over a thousand cottages—the largest village in the Hamadān plain. It belongs to Emir Nizām, a wealthy member of the ancient Karageuzlū family which has been a power in Hamadān affairs for many generations.

Kabūtarhāng—together with Daghadaghabād, Khanabād, Dastajīrd, Amirabād and a few other nearby villages—form an important group, because they are the only villages in the Hamadān plain which habitually weave carpet sizes. Carpets are occasionally woven in some of the other districts, but the great majority of the village looms cannot carry a piece over $4\frac{1}{2}$ feet wide.

Carpets have been woven in the Kabūtarhāng area for many generations. There are at least three antique pieces in existence which were probably woven in a village near by: one of them is in the Philadelphia Museum (Williams Collection), another in the McIlhenny Collection, and a third was formerly in the Lamm Collection. They are attributed to "north-west Persia" and dated "early seventeenth century". The design of these antique carpets is well known in Hamadān under the name of "Elliyeh". Several late nineteenth-century pieces passed through my hands between 1911 and 1923. The *dellals* of the bazaar will tell you that the design has been woven in the village of Famenin for many generations; and indeed, the knot, the construction and the general style of these carpets suggest that they were made there. I think, therefore, that they may be safely attributed to the village of Famenin. The dating of the three antique carpets above mentioned is largely guesswork; but I should hesitate to place them earlier than the beginning of the nineteenth century.[1]

Unhappily, we do not possess an example of a Kabūtarhāng carpet of the same period as these three carpets. But Kabūtarhāng is only 10 miles from Famenin; so that carpet weaving may well have been going on in both places 150 years ago or more. It is in any case certain that carpets were being woven in Kabūtarhāng at the end of last century; and (if we are to accept the testimony of the Hamadān *dellals*) they were being woven there a good many years before that.

The old Kabūtarhāng carpet, with its camel or red field covered with a small repeating diaper pattern; its satisfying medallion, usually in dark blue; its rather awkward corners, often with a bit of sage green in them; and its undistinguished border—was an honest carpet. The yarn was spun from sound wool, and dyed with indigo, madder, walnut husks, pomegranate rinds, vine leaves and weld. It was a thick, dense carpet, with the wear of two generations in it. Above all, it had character, individuality. It was unmistakable and it belonged to the place. In no other locality in the world could just such a carpet have been woven.

Alas for Kabūtarhāng; alas, too, for Daghadaghabād (a village with a fine tradition of good weaving) and for their neighbouring villages! In or about 1936 word reached the area that America—rich and powerful, the world's greatest market for Persian carpets—did not like their medallion design. If the villagers would weave the patterns which were wanted, America would buy all the carpets which they could produce. A design was brought from Sultānabād—it was a type of design which had been introduced there in the early twenties, and had permeated the Sarūk quality ever since (see p. 141).

The Kabūtarhāng weavers found the fern-like motives of the design a little difficult at first, because they had always woven in straight lines. But they managed them somehow. Then they had trouble with the ground colour: their madder red was too dark and too yellow. A lighter, rosier shade was called for. That too was managed. What could be easier, indeed, than to use less madder and to top the shade with a little aniline from the bazaar—especially when the operation saved them money!

The design took on. It spread from village to village. Before the war the carpets were coming into the Hamadān bazaar in scores—all similar in

---

[1] It is most unlikely that workaday village-woven carpets such as those (for they are in an entirely different category from the finely woven pieces of the great period) could last for more than a hundred years, if that. The great carpets lasted longer because (a) they were closely woven by skilled craftsmen; (b) because the best materials were used in their manufacture; and (c) because it has been an immemorial custom in Persia for exalted persons to adorn their little-used reception rooms with their finest carpets. There they lay, secluded and forlorn, but happily preserved from wear; while the more commonplace pieces carpeted the lesser apartments where the day-to-day affairs of the household were conducted. Thus, the excellent tended to survive and the good to perish —a lucky disposition!

design, in colour and even in size (for most of them measured 12 × 9 feet). They were, indeed, so uniform that they were no longer sold by measurement, but by the piece.

Production dwindled during the war. But no sooner was trade with America resumed than looms were working once more at full capacity. Today the output of the area is over 2,500 carpets a year.

The result of this uninformed activity was deplorable. The carpets rapidly deteriorated in quality and design. The quantity of yarn required for such an output was far in excess of the supplies available in the area; so that the weavers were compelled to buy the inferior product of the Hamadān bazaar. Weaving with the *jūft ilmeh* or double knot (see p. 27)—that evil practice which is, unhappily, spreading through Persia like the plague and threatens to impair the quality of many of her most famous weaves—became the rule in the Kabūtarhāng villages. Dyeing with aniline increased, and the use of black in the place of dark blue became habitual. The Kabūtarhāng carpets of today are hardly recognisable as the descendants of the carpets that were woven there twenty-five years ago. They are, indeed, among the poorest products of the Hamadān plain.

The importers discovered, in due course, that the Kabūtarhāng carpets that were being shipped to them were not what they appeared, at first sight, to be. They found out that the dyes were bad and that the material was inferior. In consequence, the carpet did not give honest service. The American Ambassador in Tehrān was requested to make representations to the Persian Government. Instructions were in due course sent to the Governor of Hamadān to amend this unhappy state of things. Appropriate orders were sent to the villages. At the same time, the Governor very properly enquired why the traders continued to buy the carpets. To this pointed question no adequate reply was forthcoming. After a period of some hesitancy on the part of the villagers and traders, the traffic went on as merrily as before.[1]

How different is the district marked "Mehribān" on the map of the Hamadān weaving districts. (p. 90). This is a large and prosperous area which extends for some 40 miles almost due north from Hamadān. It comprises about forty villages. The weavers of Mehribān—in contrast with those of Kabūtarhāng—have been left alone. Few attempts have ever been made to give them new designs or to improve their colours. Year in, year out, they spin the wool from their own sheep, dye it in their own way and weave their own traditional patterns (see Plates 83, 84). These are simple in character and the colours which they use are few. The predominant shades are dark madder red and indigo blue. Their materials are good, their dyes are good and their weaving is close and even. Hence the rugs and strips (and the few carpets) which they produce are rightly regarded in the bazaar as among the best in the Hamadān area; and they command high prices.

The town of Tuisarkhān may be reached by car from Hamadān by a circuitous road round the base of Mount Alvānd; or on horseback over a steep and stony pass. It is the administrative centre of a large and prosperous area of the same name. Some thirty villages lie tucked away in its valleys.

Weaving is carried on in the town and in most of the villages. The town looms have recently begun to produce a double-wefted fabric similar to the Hamadān town weave (see p. 96). The villages, however, continue to weave their traditional single-wefted rugs.

In general, the villages in any one of the weaving districts of Hamadān produce rugs which are similar in quality and style. This is not true of the Tuisarkhān villages, where striking differences exist between the products of one village and another. Thus, Plate 88 depicts a rug of very simple design and coarse stitch; whereas Plate 81 represents a rug woven in another village (Bergendeh) which produces some of the most attractive rugs in the Hamadān area.

However much the Tuisarkhān rugs may vary in merit, they possess two valuable qualities in common: the yarn which is woven into them is spun from local wools; and is dyed in the time-honoured Persian manner. Thus, a rug from Tuisarkhān may be coarse in texture and of simple design, but because it possesses these two essential qualities it will give good service and pleasure to its owner.

The district which is known in Hamadān as Khamseh lies beyond the Hamadān plain, to the north and east of Mehribān, and extends almost to Zenjān. It does not, in any sense, correspond with the administrative district of Khamseh which stretches farther northward beyond Zenjān itself. Small rugs of very inferior quality (known in the trade as Zenjān Mosūls) are woven in this northern area and are marketed in Zenjān and Tabrīz (see p. 58).

[1] My authority for the above was the Governor of Hamadān himself.

The area known to the Hamadan *dellals* as Khamseh lies to the south of this. It includes about a hundred villages, the majority of which produce excellent rugs. Their designs are mostly of the medallion type (see Plates 92–95).

The rugs of Khamseh are not, on the average, as good as the rugs of Mehriban, because the Khamseh weavers supplement their home supplies of yarn with inferior yarns from the Hamadan bazaar. Their rugs, too, are not as tightly woven and are less weighty than the rugs of Mehriban. Their dyes are, on the whole, good. Since the war, however, a few Khamseh rugs dyed with synthetic dyes of Swiss manufacture have appeared in the Hamadan bazaar.

Sard Rūd (Cold River; loc. Sard-e-Rūd) is a rich agricultural district of the Hamadan plain. It lies almost due north of Kabūtarhāng. Its administrative and market centre is the important village of Damāq.

In appearance the rugs of Sard Rūd are not unlike those of Khamseh which lies beyond it. But they are inferior to the Khamseh weaves; for the Sard Rūd villagers buy all their yarn in the Hamadan bazaar. Although their dyes are good, the cheap yarns which they use produce a fabric which is dull, lustreless and somewhat harsh to the touch.

Many hundreds of new, cheap and short runners are woven in this district every year and shipped to the West. They measure about 9 × 2.6 feet, with cream, camel or red grounds and small repeating medallions. They are good value for the price at which they sell (see Plate 89).

The adjoining districts of Chahār-rā (loc. Charrāh) and Bozchelū (loc. Borchelū) begin about 30 miles east by south from Hamadan and extend for another 30 miles beyond.[1] When I came to Hamadan, thirty-five years ago, half the rugs which were offered in the bazaar from Chahār-rā had black grounds—probably because of the high percentage of black sheep in the local flocks. The villagers have since learnt that black rugs are not much in demand in the West.

The Bozchelū[2] used to weave handsome *dozars*, mostly in the Herātī pattern on red and cream grounds. Recently they have adopted a curvilinear medallion-and-corner design. This is the only district in the plain where rugs in curvilinear design are woven. They also weave fine quality strips for the New York market and a few *kellegis* and carpets (see Plates 78, 79).

Unhappily, during recent years, the dyers of this excellent weaving centre have succumbed to the lure of the cheapness and fatal facility of anilines. The effect on their rugs has been disastrous. The mellow tones of the native dyes have given way to strident notes of crimson, grass green, electric blue and primrose pink. Unless drastic steps are taken to stay this disease the rugs of Bozchelū will suffer irreparable harm.

The large administrative area of Saveh comprises several separate clusters of villages where good rugs (and some good carpets) are woven. The largest group is centred round the village of Noberān. It lies a little to the east of the Dergezin district and comprises some twenty villages. The so-called "lightning" design (Plate 90) is woven in Kerdar, a village close to Noberān. At Imamzadeh, another nearby village, carpets are woven in the "Boteh Kharqai" (large pine) design. At Sefiabād, another Noberān village, one may encounter the unusual sight—in the Hamadan area—of a carpet being woven flat on the ground, in the manner of the nomad tribes. This clearly indicates that the weavers of Sefiabād were, until recently, tent dwellers. They have not yet had time to adopt all the amenities of village life.

Still farther to the east lies another cluster of villages which is centred round Tafrish. The Tafrish rugs are as finely and evenly woven as any that appear in the Hamadan bazaar. Their dyes, too, are good; the Tafrish weavers have a preference for the lighter shades—cream, light reds and light blues—which is unusual in the Hamadan area. Their designs, however, are poor. They appear to know only two or three: one has an ill-drawn circular medallion, and the other is an all-over design in birds and trees —equally ill-drawn (Plate 97). The output of the Tafrish villages is small. During recent years these rugs are being marketed, more and more, in Tehrān.

This survey of the Hamadan weaving area would not be complete without a reference to half a dozen

---

[1] The combined area comprises about thirty villages; of the two, Bozchelū is much the more important.
[2] The local pronounciation of the name is Borchelū, but this is inaccurate. The Bozchelū are a known Mongol tribe, vestiges of which exist to this day in the Caucasus. Like the Karageuzlū, the Hudabandalū and the Baharlū, they probably invaded the Hamadan province in the thirteenth century with Hulagū Khan and settled there. (Professor V. Minorsky.)

villages which extend in line, almost due south from the outskirts of Hamadān, along the foothills of Mount Alvānd.

The most renowned among them (and renown is not too strong a word to use about a village which is known by name by rug men of two continents) is Injilās. The men of Injilās are a proud, independent and stubborn community. For thirty-five years —from near and far—I have followed their fortunes. During that time they have never permitted their women to weave rugs unworthy of the high standard of the village. Neither fair fortune nor adversity has sapped their resolution or blunted their integrity.

Their women weave only two designs—both on madder grounds: the "Boteh Mīrī" (small leaf pattern) and the Herātī. When I first knew them they gave preference to the Mīr design; they now weave more of the Herātī pattern. Both designs are always well and truly executed. They spin and dye their yarns in their own village.

Their neighbours of Everū weave similar rugs and strips. These are well enough, but at best they are only good seconds to the rugs of Injilās. The other villages of the line also weave clean and honest rugs. But there is only one Injilās.

A few miles east and south of Kabūtarhāng, on the other side of the Hamadān–Kazvīn trunk road, are two villages which deserve mention—Bubukabād (loc. Bibikabād) and Ainabād. Like Kabūtarhāng, they weave large sizes, and have done so for generations. Bubukabād is of particular interest because the carpets and *kellegis* which are woven there today are much the same as those of fifty (and perhaps of a hundred) years ago; except that the quality has somewhat deteriorated (see Plate 76).

The Ainabād carpets of today are, on the other hand, very different from the carpets that were woven at the beginning of the century. Plate 98 depicts an Ainabād *kellegi, circa* 1910. Those of today are much inferior and hardly distinguishable from the carpets of Bubukabād.

General Characteristics of the Village Weaves

What are the qualities and characteristics which distinguish Hamadān village rugs from the rugs of other tribes or villages of Persia; and how can we determine if a rug was woven in this area? The rugs of Hamadān possess four principal distinguishing characteristics: (1) the knot; (2) the weight; (3) the weft and back; and (4) the design.

(1) The knot is the first distinguishing characteristic. Almost without exception the rugs and carpets of Hamadān are woven with the Turkish knot (see p. 26). For the majority of the inhabitants of the province—particularly the peasants who live in the hundreds of weaving villages—are of Turkish race; and Turkish weavers everywhere weave the Turkish knot.

(2) The second distinguishing feature is the weight. With the exception of the Bijār weave—which is unmistakable—the village rugs of Hamadān are thicker and heavier than those of other villages of Persia. The handspun yarn is of ample thickness and the pile is cut high. These characteristics produce a dense, rugged, weighty and hard-wearing fabric. The rugs lack the refinement of the more sophisticated weaves of Persia; but they possess instead a sturdiness and solidity which is lacking in some of the finer productions. They are, by and large, the best value of any of the Persian weaves.

(3) The third distinguishing characteristic of the Hamadān weave is its single weft. With few exceptions, the thousands of rugs which are produced in the villages of Hamadān are single wefted. This construction is not usual in Persia, except in tribal rugs—such as the Balūchī rugs of northern Khurāsān, the Afshārī rugs of Kermān and most of the tribal rugs of Fārs. Those, however, are easily distinguishable from the rugs of Hamadān. The urban weaves of Tabrīz, Meshed, Kermān, Isfahān, Kāshān and Qūm possess two or sometimes three wefts.

A single-wefted fabric may easily be distinguished from one with a double weft by examining the back. The back of a single-wefted fabric is flat and even, as both warps to which the knots are tied are visible, side by side. The back of a double-wefted fabric, on the other hand, is made up of close, parallel ridges running "north and south". Each ridge is formed by one of the two warp strings to which the knots are tied: the other has been diverted into the body of the carpet and is invisible. The fact that in the single-wefted fabric *both* warp strings are visible (instead of only one) causes the back to appear much finer than that of a double-wefted weave of the same quality.

(4) The designs of the Hamadān village weavers are, on the whole, simpler than those of most of the tribal rugs of Persia. This can be clearly seen by comparing the reproductions of Hamadān rugs

(Plates 109–110) with those of the tribal rugs of Fārs (Plates 293–327). Both are rectilinear—like the designs of all the Persian tribal rugs—but the designs of Fārs are more detailed and more ingenious than those of the Hamadān villages.

The only rugs which closely resemble the Hamadān village weaves and which may be confounded with them are the so-called Bakhtiari rugs (see p. 307). Like the rugs of Hamadān, they are woven with the Turkish knot; and they are weighty and single wefted. They can be easily distinguished, however, by their characteristic lozenge or panel designs (see Plates 354–361) and by the fondness of the Bakhtiari weavers for yellow—a shade not commonly used in the Hamadān area.

The Decline of the Village Industry

Rug weaving in the Hamadān villages is, beyond peradventure, a declining industry. Official figures of production do not exist; but *dellals* and traders well remember the profusion of rugs which used to pour into the bazaar each day before World War I. The output today is barely half what it was then.

The decline is due to a number of causes—some general, some local. First among them was the derangement of the industry by the two world wars. During the first the Hamadān area was occupied successively by Russian, Turkish and British armies. The countryside was stripped of food. In 1918 there was a drought and the crops failed. As the reserves of grain had been seized and devoured by the soldiers, there was a serious famine. Thousands died of hunger. As if that disaster was not enough, in the following year the Spanish influenza struck the province and thousands more succumbed. Rug weaving in the villages came almost to a standstill.

Between the wars, however, prosperity slowly returned to the province and slowly the weaving industry revived. But the triple disaster of war, famine and disease had left their mark upon it; for there had been little weaving during the period of adversity and no opportunity for young girls of the villages to take their places besides their mothers at the looms and learn the craft. Thus, output was lower than before the war.

The advent to the throne of the reforming monarch, Riza Shah Pahlavi, gave rise to a period of unusual activity throughout Persia. Hamadān alone of all the important towns failed to benefit from the wave of prosperity which followed. None of the new state factories was built there. The new railway passed it by. Furthermore, the unique position of Hamadān in the import trade and its importance as a financial centre were undermined by feverish expansion at the capital. Its trade languished; and its merchants, in despair, closed their offices and transferred their activities to Tehrān. This general decline in the prosperity of the town was very soon reflected in the villages.

To these more general causes for the decline in output must be added a more particular cause—the steady rise in the price of wool. Such rises had always, in the past, temporarily affected the output of carpets, until the disparity had been adjusted by a corresponding rise in carpet prices. But the rise in the price of wool between the two wars—and particularly since World War II—has been almost uninterrupted. The result of this phenomenon has been twofold: (1) peasants or tribesmen who possessed sheep of their own preferred to sell their wool rather than weave it into carpets; (2) and those who had no wool of their own were either frightened by the high price or had insufficient funds to buy. The result in either case was the same—a decline in output.

Is this decline a passing phenomenon? Will the rugs—in all their profusion and variety—pour in once again from the villages as in the years before World War I? Only the unwise would dare to prophesy on such a matter—for Persia is a country where often the unexpected happens. Thus, in the town of Hamadān itself, which, as we have seen, experienced a period of adversity, production is higher than before. The increase in town weaving has not made good the decline in the villages; but the fact that output in the town has actually increased during the last decade indicates the danger of prophecy. Nevertheless, I think it is improbable that production in the area as a whole will again reach the volume which it had attained in 1913, or even in 1927.

The Hamadān Town Carpets

Carpet weaving in the town of Hamadān is a comparatively recent development. There is no evidence that it ever existed before 1912; nor is there any tradition (in a country where traditions persist) which might lend support to a speculation that it might have existed there in the past. Certainly, when I first came to Hamadān in 1912 there was not a single loom in the town.

This, then, will be an account of the rise and development of a comparatively recent industry. I trust that the reader will not consider it improper if I record that I had a hand in setting up the first looms in Hamadān thirty-six years ago. The satisfaction which I feel is that of a person who contemplates a great tree which has grown from a seed which he himself has planted. For there are now a thousand looms in the town, producing some fifteen hundred carpets a year.

Eight looms were set up in 1912 in a house which was rented for that purpose. I was fortunate in being able to engage, at the outset, an expert village weaver who had recently settled in the town. Through her influence and skill the little factory was soon in operation. When I returned to Hamadān in 1948 to write this chapter, I was pleased to find that Kobra Khanūm was now technical superintendent of a factory of 120 looms—the largest in the town.

The production of a new textile fabric is an affair of trial and error. Even the most experienced technician cannot, by taking thought, hit upon the construction which will produce the fabric which he has in mind. This is a matter of balance between a number of factors: the kind of knot which is to be used; the number of knots per unit of measurement each way; the twist and thickness of the warp strings and of the two wefts; the thickness and twist of the woollen yarn; the nature of the dyes. A slight variation in any of these basic factors will change the appearance and the "handle" of the fabric. Finally, the vital matter of cost must be considered.

I had in mind a double-wefted fabric possessing the characteristic weight, ruggedness and solidity of the Hamadān weaves. It should resemble, I thought, the Bijār weave—but with a cotton instead of a woollen foundation. For cotton is superior to wool for warps and wefts: it is more durable, less elastic and more manageable.

The knot should be Turkish. For Hamadān is basically Turkish and all her villagers weave the Turkish knot. To introduce the Persian knot would be to bastardise the product. Furthermore, the Turkish knot produces a somewhat thicker, weightier fabric than the Persian.

A number of trial rugs were woven—and rejected; until at last we hit upon a satisfactory fabric. It counted 10 × 11 knots to the inch—10 east-and-west and 11 north-and-south. This was a quality which would do justice to a design of medial fineness, without being too costly. It weighed 12 lb. to the square yard, which is about the weight of a good Bijār. The new fabric could not be called "Hamadān" as that name is associated in the public mind with a different style of carpet. It was named "Alvānd" after the mountain which towers above

72. A Beauty shows her Face in a Hamadān Factory

73. Sorting out the Colours from White Wool, Hamadān

74. Washing Carpets, Hamadān

the town. In America the carpet is known as "Kazvīn"—I don't know why.

Our wools were bought in Kermanshāh, which is the market for the Kurdish wools of western Persia. The Kurds were then, and still are (in spite of Riza Shah's efforts to settle them in villages), mostly a nomadic, pastoral people. Their mountain sheep produce an excellent crossbred wool—lofty and long in staple. It is similar to Anatolian, and as good. Every year, during the months of June and July, the Karasū River—outside Kermanshāh—is thronged with women, knee-deep in the water, washing the season's clip. The wool is placed in baskets which are raised and lowered in the water until most of the grease is scoured away. The method is crude and not fully effective; so that the wool loses another 10 per cent in weight in the spinning and dyeing.

The scoured wool was at first carded and spun by hand. Some years later, however, a power-driven carding machine was installed and carded wool was given out to the women for spinning. This produced a more even, more uniform yarn, and enabled the spinners to increase their output. Today there are several small carding plants in Hamadān and many thousand spinners.

We employed an Armenian dyer who had been schooled in the use of German synthetic dyes. He regarded the Persian method of dyeing with the amused tolerance of the family doctor for the remedies of the family nurse. For some years we used none but synthetic dyes; but they were never satisfying. When new, they produced a hard, metallic effect in the carpet; while the passage of time—which adds a glow, a mellowness to colours dyed in the Persian manner—dulled the colours mordanted with chrome. In the end we abandoned chrome dyeing and adopted the time-honoured methods of the Persian dyers.

The standard of dyeing, I am glad to say, has been well maintained during the last thirty-five years. It compares favourably with that of any in Persia. Some of the dyers may occasionally use a synthetic dye, but when they do, they use it with skill and discrimination.

The next problem was that of design. What type should be adopted for the new fabric?

The only style of carpet with which the name of Hamadān was associated in the public mind was a rectilinear design of a medallion or multiple medallion type, with a small diaper pattern in two tones of camel in the field. It is illustrated in Plate 109.[1] A few such carpets might be woven; but the demand

[1] Camel hair is hardly ever used in rugs in Persia. The confusion arose, no doubt, from the fact that the warm, yellow-brown shade, which was a characteristic of the Hamadāns of a generation ago, is called in Persian *shuturi*, i.e. camel.

for them would obviously be limited. Nor were the few and simple carpet designs which were in vogue in some of the villages more suitable. It was clear that inspiration must be sought outside the Hamadān area.

We decided to go back to the sixteenth century and to base our designing upon those unmatched classic models. Plates 100, 103 indicate the trend of design which was adopted. Later, the styles were expanded to meet American demands half-way. But the essential Persian character of the motives was, wherever possible, maintained. On the whole, the many new factories which have since been established in Hamadān have followed this lead; so that today the great majority of the carpets produced in the town (unlike the Sarūks of Arāk) possess an unmistakable Persian character.

Thus was the Hamadān carpet born and brought to maturity. Today it has attained full stature and occupies an honoured place among the weaves of Persia. The carpet lacks the supreme artistry of the Kermān; the fineness of stitch of the Kashān; the ingenuity of the Tabrīz; and the high competence of the Arāk. But it surpasses them all in one basic quality: it is the most honest and the most durable of all the present-day Persian weaves. It will serve two, and maybe three, generations. I shall have occasion in this book to record a deterioration in the standards of excellence of many Persian weaves. But this melancholy task has not been mine in surveying the Hamadān town carpet.

Labour in Hamadān

Labour conditions in Hamadān are better than they were, but are still below the standards called for by the Labour Law of 1938. By that law children below the age of fourteen are precluded from working in factories; yet children under that age were working in the carpet factories of Hamadān—most of which are State controlled—in 1948.

On the other hand, there has been some improvement in social amenities for the weavers. Thus, the State factories add 3 per cent to the cost of their products which is expended on medical care and other welfare work.

Weaving is organised in the factories as follows: each loom has its *ostad* or head-weaver, who is expected to bring her own *nakhcheh nevis* (lit. design writer) and *shagirds* or apprentices. The *ostad* is not only a skilled and fast weaver: she must be able to read and execute the design from scale paper, to pass the wefts properly, to trim each row of knots when finished and to superintend the work of her assistants. The *nakhcheh nevis* is her second-in-command. She and the *ostad* tie on the knots which, in each row, mark the beginning and end of every motive or flower. The *shagirds* or apprentices then fill in the spaces between the two limiting knots. Thus, row by row, the design is executed.

The *ostad* is paid at the end of each week at the rate of 1.10–1.50 rials per thousand knots woven by herself and her assistants; the difference in the price rising with the fineness of the quality. From the sum which she receives she pays her assistants. A good *ostad* with her *nakhcheh nevis* and two *shagirds* tie about 25,000 knots a day;[1] so that the four weavers together would earn about 30 rials a day. Out of this the *ostad* receives 12 rials, the *nakhcheh nevis* 8 rials, and the two *shagirds* together 10 rials.[2]

In addition to these payments a bonus is paid to the weavers when the carpet is finished, if it has been well woven. A further bonus is paid if the quantity of yarn consumed is not above the standard rate.

A NOTE ON MALAYER

The town and district of Malayer cannot be regarded as one of the weaving areas of Hamadān—like Mehribān or Dergezin. It is a good deal more than that. Malayer is a prosperous market town of 14,000 people and the administrative centre of one of the richest agricultural areas of north-west Persia. It has been included in this chapter because it is only 50 miles from Hamadān; because its villages are partly Turkish and its weavers use the Turkish knot; and because most of the rugs and carpets produced in the area are marketed in the Hamadān bazaar.

The area comprises the town of Malayer and about 120 weaving villages. The total number of looms in the area amounts to about 2,500 of which 100 are in the town. Of these, about 800 looms weave carpets; the remainder are rug looms. The total annual production in a normal year is about 5,000 pieces, large and small.

The district may be roughly divided into two: (1) a north-western area which marches with the

---

[1] Weaving in Tabrīz is faster and the rate of pay is higher.
[2] It is difficult to establish the value of the rial in foreign currencies, because of the double rate of exchange which prevails in Persia—the official and the "bazaar" rate. The matter is further complicated by the instability of the "bazaar" rate. For purposes of rough comparison, however, a rate of 150 to the pound sterling may be taken (or 55 rials to the dollar). On this basis an *ostad* will earn 1s. 7d. (23 cents) a day; a *nakhcheh nevis* 1s. 1d. (15 cents); and two *shagirds* together 1s. 4d. (18½ cents).

75. A Weaver's Cottage, Nenej Village, Malayer

southern extremity of the Hamadān plain; and (2) a south-eastern area which marches with the Arāk province.

In the first of the two areas a State organisation controls about 500 looms. In the large village of Nenej they have over a hundred. The company supplies the weavers with yarns which are dyed in Hamadān, and with scale-paper designs. Inspectors go round from village to village to inspect the work. The materials employed are sound and the dyes excellent. The fabric is single wefted and counts 7×8 knots to the inch. It is, on the whole, one of the most serviceable of the less expensive Persian weaves (Plates 109, 110).

There are another 200–300 looms in the area which weave single-wefted carpets, *kellegis* and rugs which are indistinguishable from the products of the nearby Hamadān villages. Unhappily, the dyeing here has deteriorated: indigo is used (as always) for the blues and greens; but the villagers use aniline red as a substitute for madder—because it is cheaper and much easier to manipulate.

The second of the two areas (which marches with Arāk) comprises some of the best weaving villages of north-west Persia. A double-wefted fabric, mostly in rug sizes, is produced. Half a dozen of these villages are strung out, one behind the other, in a broad, fertile valley which extends east and south from Malayer. In summer the valley is green from side to side with vines—for its raisins are hardly less renowned than its rugs.

Although the weavers in these villages (like those of Hamadān) are Turks and weave the Turkish knot, their rugs possess a greater affinity with the rugs of Arāk (which are purely Persian) than with those of Hamadān.

Of the six villages of the valley, Jozān produces the best rugs. This little village possesses a reputation which extends all over Persia (Plate 106); and another village, Manizān, is a close second (Plate 108). The local oracles maintain that there is something in the water of Jozān which imparts a softness and brilliancy to the yarns which are dyed there. It may be so. Perhaps, however, the undoubted superiority of the Jozān rugs is due less to the virtues of its water than to the pride which the villagers take in their work; and especially to the care which they exercise in every stage of production—from the washing of the wool (which I was assured they do three times) to the final clipping, which produces a surface as smooth as fine velvet. The designs of Jozān and of the valley generally are somewhat lacking in variety; yet happily the designs are their own. The fabric which they weave counts about 14×14 knots to the inch.

The products of the rest of the weaving villages of this area are not up to the standard of the six villages. The handiwork of the unscrupulous town dyer is to be seen plainly in the reds and pinks. In fineness of texture their rugs are considerably below that of six-village standard, for they rarely count over 12×12 knots to the inch. Nevertheless, they are well woven, well finished and on the whole attractive. Most of them are marketed in Hamadān.

Production in the whole of the Malayer area (as in almost every weaving centre of Persia) stands at about half the pre-war figure. The reasons are not far to seek: since the end of the war demand from the West has been spasmodic, while costs in Persia have continued to rise. Under such conditions merchants and weavers were loth to risk money, materials and labour.

If, within a reasonable period, conditions in the West improve and the demand for Persian carpets is restored to normal or something near to normal, and at the same time in Persia a more stable price level is reached, production will no doubt increase and may attain the pre-war figure of about 5,000 pieces, large and small. The danger is that the restoration of normal trading conditions in the West may be long delayed. In that event many of the village matrons will forget their craft and many of the girls will never learn it.

77. A Rug probably woven in Tafrish
The design is popularly known as Zil-i-Soltan, after a Qajār prince who was governor of Isfahān in 1890.

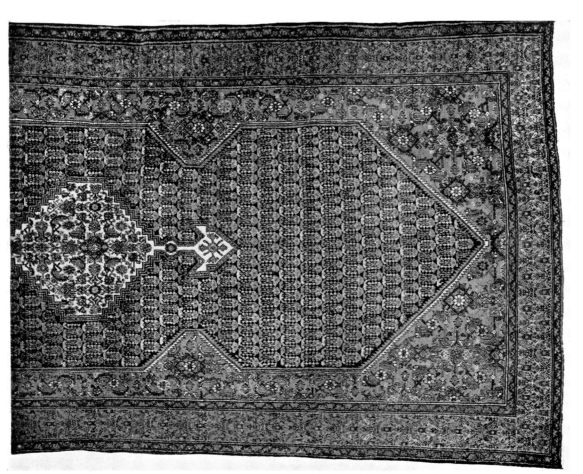

76. A "Mian Farsh" (Middle Carpet) woven in Bubukabād (loc. Bibikabād) (c. 1910)

79. A Bozchelu (loc. Borchelu) Rug (c. 1940)
This is the only area in the Hamadān plain where curvilinear designs are woven.

78. A Bozchelū (loc. Borchelū) Rug (c. 1940)
This is the only area in the Hamadān plain where curvilinear designs are woven.

81. A Bergendeh Rug, Tuisarkhān District (c. 1940)
This design, on a camel ground, is characteristic of the village.

80. A Tuisarkhān Rug of Good Quality (c. 1940)
The border is characteristic of the neighbouring district of Malayer (see Plate 106).

82. A Rug from Gombād Village (c. 1945)

83, 84. Mehribān Rugs, showing Kurdish Influence (c. 1945)
Mehribān adjoins the Kurdish weaving area of Shirishabād.

85. A Jechaneh Rug, Tuisarkhān District (*c.* 1940)

86. A Tuisarkhān Rug (*c.* 1940)

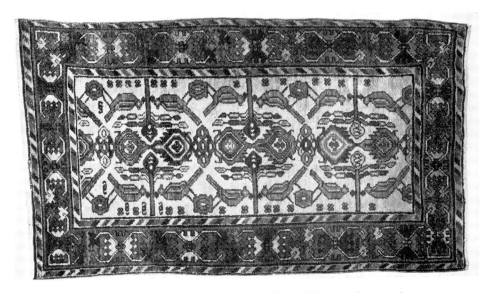

87. A Joraghān Rug with a Bird Motive (*c.* 1940)
The village is situated on the outskirts of Hamadān.

89. Detail of a Strip from Sard Rud
(c. 1936)

88. A Rug from Tuisarkhān (c. 1940)
The border has been taken from a Malayer rug (see Plate 106).

HAMADĀN AND ITS ENVIRONS

91. A ZARĀND RUG FROM THE SHRINE COLLECTION, MESHED (c. 1920)
The inscription expresses the repentance of the donor, Bahriman, for his sins.

90. A KERDĀR RUG FROM THE ZARĀND DISTRICT (c. 1935)

93. A Kalajūk Rug, Khamseh District (c. 1940)

92. A Rug from the Khamseh District of Hamadān (c. 1945)

95. A Rug from the Khamseh District (c. 1945)

94. A Rug from the Khamseh District (c. 1940)

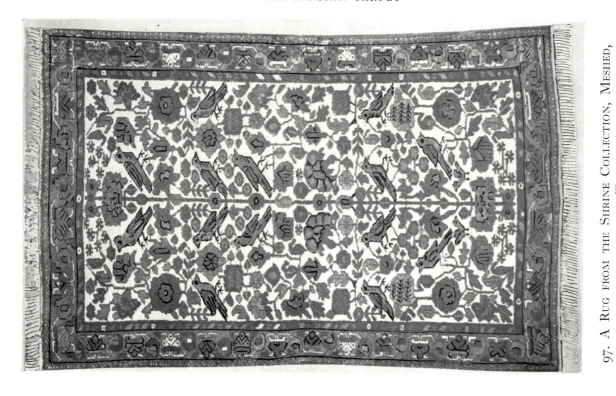

97. A Rug from the Shrine Collection, Meshed, probably woven in Tafrish (c. 1925)

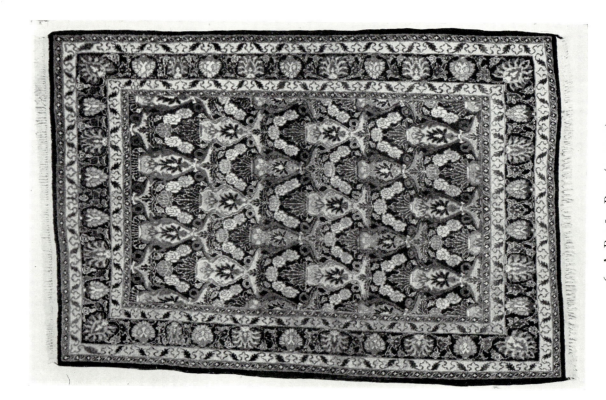

96. A Bahār Rug (c. 1945)
Bahār is a large and historic village situated close to Hamadān. In the thirteenth century it was the capital of a province under a Seljūk prince, Suleiman Shah.

98. A "Mian Farsh" (Middle Carpet) of Fine Quality, probably woven in Ainabād (c. 1910)

99. A Hamadān Town (Alvānd) Carpet (c. 1935)

100. Medallion and Corner Design for a Hamadān Town (Alvānd) Carpet (c. 1933)

101. Design for a Hamadān Town (Alvānd) Carpet (c. 1935)

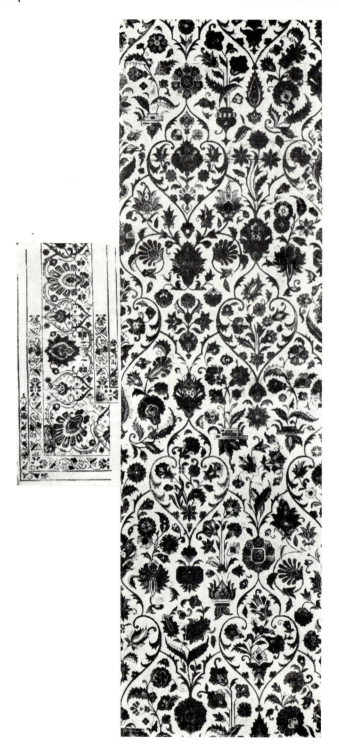
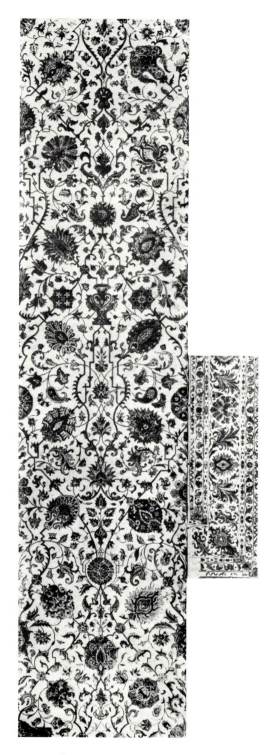

102. Design for a Hamadān Town (Alvānd) Carpet (c. 1935)

103. Design for a Hamadān Town (Alvānd) Carpet (c. 1935)
This is a fine interpretation of the sixteenth-century vase design.

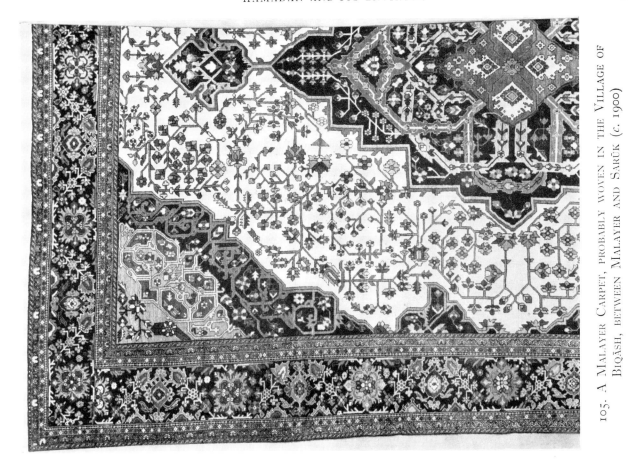

105. A Malayer Carpet, probably woven in the Village of Biqāsh, between Malayer and Sarūk (c. 1900)

104. A Rug in the Grape-vine Design, woven in one of the Malayer Villages (c. 1900)
The border is characteristic of the period.

107. A Malayer Rug (c. 1905)

106. A Jozān Rug (c. 1935)
The delicate, lace-like edging of the Medallion-and-corners—with the same motive in the border—is a characteristic of the best rugs of the Malayer area.

108. A Fine Malayer Rug of Unusual Design, Woven in Jozān or Manizān (c. 1935)

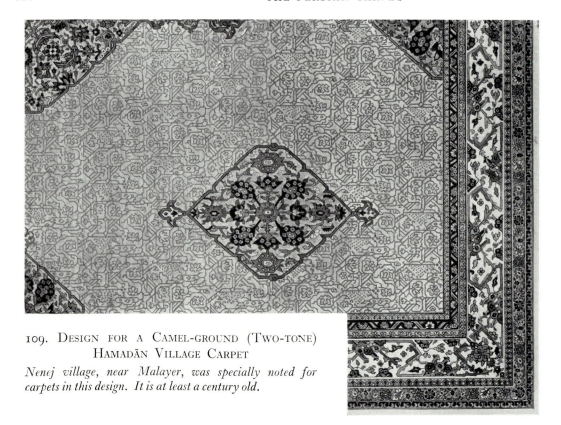

109. DESIGN FOR A CAMEL-GROUND (TWO-TONE) HAMADĀN VILLAGE CARPET

Nenej village, near Malayer, was specially noted for carpets in this design. It is at least a century old.

110. A REPEATING DESIGN FOR A HAMADĀN VILLAGE CARPET (*c.* 1945)

CHAPTER VIII

THE KURDISH WEAVES: SENNEH, BIJĀR AND THE KURDISH TRIBAL RUGS

The Kurds

The weaving tribes of Persian Kurdistān inhabit a large area which extends westwards to the Irāq and Turkish frontiers from a line which begins at Hamikasi (on the Hamadān–Bijār road, after it crosses the northern spur of the Alvānd range) and terminates at the southern end of Lake Urumiah. On the south the area is bounded, roughly, by the Kanagavar–Kermanshāh road.

This geographical definition does not in any way correspond with administrative boundaries. It merely indicates the territory which is mainly inhabited by Kurds. It excludes Lūristān which the Kurds regard as one of the Kurdish lands. Their claim has some justification; because the Lūrs (whose territories extend as far south as Fārs) are closely allied with the Kurds in race and language.

The area is very mountainous; and its inhabitants, until recently, were mainly nomadic. Riza Shah Pahlavi succeeded in forcibly settling most of the tribes of the eastern and less mountainous region. But the western tribes, secure in their inaccessible mountains, were left alone and continue to pursue a nomadic or semi-nomadic existence.

There has never been a proper census in Persia, so nobody knows how many Kurds there are in the country. Estimates vary between 800,000 and 1,000,000. The higher figure is based upon the statements of Kurdish tribal chiefs and may be exaggerated.

The Kurdish language is an Indo-European tongue, allied to ancient Persian and possessing many modern Persian words in dialect form. A Persian who has a mind to do so can pick up most of the Kurdish dialects easily and quickly.

It was the lack of communications with Persia proper, more than any other factor, which has enabled the Kurds to maintain their distinctive language and way of life. In their remote valleys they were secure from the interference and pressure of the central government. The early Shahs attempted from time to time to exercise authority over the tribes; but without lasting results. Indeed, it was not until Riza Shah Pahlavi had driven a few motorable roads into their country that the Kurds became fully aware of the existence of a paramount power at the centre.

Besides the lack of communications, a difference in religion—as significant as the differences of race and language—has tended to keep the Kurds a separate entity or nation within the Persian state. The Persian Moslems (with the exception of a few negligible sects) are Shi'as; whereas the Kurds are Sūnnis to a man. And—as so often happens with a minority sect—their religious leaders tend to emphasise the orthodoxy of their faith and to proclaim the heresy of the Shi'a doctrine. As a result, there is a streak of fanaticism in the Kurds which is lacking in the more easy-going, sceptic Persians.

Nevertheless, the Kurds are an engaging people—gay, hospitable, cleanly in their habits; and fond of dancing and fine clothes. A roystering, quarrelsome, independent race; and one, it must be admitted, which entertains elastic views upon the sacredness of property.

The Kurds have been described as a race of poltroons—which is absurd as some of the tribes are brave enough. But the view that a semi-nomadic people with a leaning for banditry is necessarily contemptuous of odds must be received with caution. For the Kurds, being reasonable robbers, prefer not to attack unless—by organised surprise or a comfortable superiority in numbers—they are assured of victory. And it has been observed that if serious opposition is encountered they prefer not to prolong the battle.

The movement for the unification of Persian, Turkish, Irāqi and Syrian Kurds and the establishment of an independent Kurdish state is an offspring of cloudy idealism rather than of political reality. For the Kurdish peoples are kept asunder by inexorable frontier lines; the four governments to which they owe allegiance are watchful and determined; and the Kurds are so divided by tribal jealousies that they have been hitherto incapable of concerted action. From time to time (as in 1945) the machinations of Russian agents remind the world that the Kurdish question still exists. Unless, however, the Russians decide upon a forward policy in Persia and succeed in carrying it through, the probabilities are that the *status quo* in Kurdistān will be maintained for still another generation.

The Three Kurdish Weaves

There are hardly to be found in the whole of Persia three weaves which differ more widely from each other than the three weaves of Persian Kurdistān: the Senneh weave, the Bijār weave and the weave of the Kurdish tribal rugs. The first is carried on exclusively in the town of Senneh; the second in the town of Bijār and in some forty villages surrounding it; and the third is common to the semi-nomadic and settled tribes of Qulyahis, Gurānis, Senjabis and Jaffis—who weave tribal rugs in their tents and cottages.

The Town of Senneh

The pleasant town of Senneh (or to give it its official name Sanandaj or Senneh Castle) is situated in a hollow in the hills 105 miles north-west of Hamadān. The road from Hamadān is fairly good—though very dusty in summer. In winter the hair-raising Salavatabād Pass—which crosses the first spur of the Kurdish mountains a few miles before the town is reached—is generally closed with snow.

Senneh became the capital of Persian Kurdistān some 200 years ago. Before that time it was little more than a village and the seat of government was in a castle situated five miles farther west. The ruins of the fortress can still be seen crowning an eminence which overlooks the village of Hassanabād. The astute Persian monarchs no doubt preferred to have their deputies reside in a locality which was easier to master than a castle planted on the top of a hill.

The population of Senneh is estimated at 20,000. Except for the garrison, the government officials and about a thousand Jews, the inhabitants are Gurāni Kurds. They are kinsmen of the great Gurāni tribe whose territories lie farther south in the direction of Kermanshāh.

Senneh is a clean and kempt little town, prettily

111. SENNEH (SANANDAJ)

situated in a narrow valley planted with orchards and vineyards. It boasts two broad avenues which meet in a circular *meidan*. It possesses only one building of architectural merit, the Mesjid-i-Jum'a, which dates from the early nineteenth century.

The Rugs of Senneh

For the amateur, the rugs of Senneh have a peculiar fascination. The best examples possess a refinement of texture, an originality and a *naïveté* in colour and design which are delightful and unsurpassed by any other Persian weave. They are also unique in style and unmistakable: none of the rugs of Persia remotely resemble them. For the weavers of this remote little Kurdish town are among the few in Persia who have preserved a style and a dignity of their own. For 200 years they have continued to weave in their own way, undisturbed by the whims and fashions of the West. May they long continue to do so.

The Senneh weave presents a problem to the enquirer: how has it come to pass that the Kurdish weavers—who normally produce coarse and clumsy tribal rugs—have woven in the town of Senneh (and only in that town) some of the most exquisite pieces that have ever been produced in Persia?

This apparent contradiction may perhaps be explained as follows: We know that two centuries ago Senneh—then little more than a village—suddenly became the capital of the province of Kurdistān. Offices had to be provided for the government

113. IN A GENTLEMAN'S HOUSE, SENNEH

departments and homes for the Persian officials who had been ordered to take up their residence there. The new buildings had to be carpeted; yet the refined Persians no doubt discovered that the only floor-coverings available were small (and to their minds) coarse and clumsy tribal rugs—which no Persian gentleman would put on his floor if he could help it. What was to be done?

What would be more in the course of things than for these gentlemen to set up looms in the town, to bring in weavers from the nearby tribes and to order carpets to be made specially to fit their floors? But their refined taste (I suggest) revolted against the clumsy tribal weaves. It demanded something finer in texture and more elegant in design. So they ordered their carpets in a quality with twice the number of warp strings found in the Kurdish tribal rugs; and with cotton instead of wool for warps and wefts—to give strength and stability to the fabric.

The Kurdish weavers laid the warps as directed; but they had to spin the yarn very fine because of

112. WEAVING A SENNEH RUG (1948)

the closeness of the weave. They wove—as they were accustomed to weave—a single-wefted fabric with the Turkish knot. But they soon discovered that in order to obtain a quality that was approximately "square" (i.e. having the same number of knots each way—in this case about 16 × 16 knots to the inch) they had to use a very thin weft indeed. Furthermore, the refined gentlemen from the capital wanted a fabric which would show up the detail of the design—so Kurdish women had to clip the carpet thin.

Thus, I suggest, was born the Senneh weave; and thus it has come to pass that in Senneh alone this thin, refined, single-wefted fabric is woven to this day. While over the hill, a few miles away, the Kurdish women still weave their rustic, unsophisticated tribal rugs.

This unique and delicate fabric—woven, as it has been during the last 200 years in comparatively few designs—has brought renown to the little town of Senneh. Is this honourable record coming to an end? In June 1948, when I revisited the town, barely a hundred rugs a month and hardly any carpets were being produced there. The quality had sadly deteriorated and most of the rugs were of the same design: a Herātī pattern on a cream or red ground with a dark blue geometrical medallion—also in the Herātī pattern. Where, I enquired, were the old designs which had made the name of Senneh famous? The Vekilli (Plate 120); the Gol-i-Bolbol or Flower and Bird (Plate 118); and the Gol Mohammedi (pink roses on a medium-blue field). All lost and forgotten.

My charming host showed me, on the floor of his magnificent *talar*, a huge carpet and some rugs to match in a design which he called Gol-i-Mirza Ali; or (which seemed more appropriate) Gol-i-Frank, i.e. European Flower (Plate 121). This design—and one or two others of like character—seems to have been copied from a fragment of French carpeting. The only other area in Persia where it is known is Bijār—another (and contiguous) Kurdish district. All these designs, I reminded my host, were woven forty or fifty years ago. What were the prospects for the industry today? He drew a sombre picture of its present state: weavers could make no money on their rugs because of the high price of wool. Production had almost come to a standstill.

Perhaps, I suggested, the Senneh weavers were making no money because they kept on weaving the same design—the Herātī—and the West was tired of it. That vicious circle could be broken. The ancient patterns might be revived and the Herātī abandoned. It was a mistake, too, I suggested, to weave rug sizes only: small carpets should be woven as well—which would be more profitable to the weaver.

He promised to see what could be done. He is a scion of one of the two great rival families of Senneh, and his influence is such that he could do much for the industry—if he would. For unless it is taken in hand by some knowledgeable person who would guide the distracted and discouraged weavers, the prospects of rug weaving in Senneh are grim indeed.

The weavers in Senneh spin their own yarn, very thin and with considerable twist. You meet them in the street—men and women—spinning as they walk. The Senneh dyers are skilled and careful, and the dyes which they use are good. Their medium blue is as fresh and clean as any dyed in Persia; and their yellow (which they dye with vine leaves mordanted with alum) is as rich as guinea gold.

While I was in Senneh I had the satisfaction of establishing—beyond the possibility of doubt—that only the Turkish knot is woven there. I trust that from now on the word Senneh will not be misused (as it has been misused for so long) to indicate the Persian knot.

The Town of Bijār

Bijār, a little town of some 7,000 inhabitants, lies in a green and pleasant valley about 120 miles north-north-west of Hamadān. Behind the vineyards and orchards which surround it, a line of reddish hills—some of them capped with crags of fantastic shape—rises out of the plain.

The road from Hamadān is rough and dusty in summer, but—unlike the Hamadān–Senneh road—it is passable for motors throughout the year. About 60 miles from Hamadān the traveller enters a rolling, semi-arid country, intersected with deep gullies and dry river-beds. Before him, on the distant sky-line, frowns a high formidable ridge—as level as though it had been drawn with a ruler. When, at the finish of the dusty day, the traveller reaches the summit of the scarp, let him look back (as he can) for 50 miles across the nebulous and opalescent plain.

In the fifteenth century, Bijār was a village, the property, it is said, of Shah Ismail, the first Sefavi monarch. About a century ago its inhabitants had acquired sufficient wealth and consequence to gain possession of their land and houses—which in Persia is the mark of emancipation. Bijār became a town. Its geographical position, however, was not such as to make it a commercial centre. It remained a

114. BIJĀR

market town for an agricultural area of no particular importance.

Of all the towns of western Persia which were fought over and occupied by the opposing armies during World War I, the town of Bijār suffered the most. It was first occupied by the Russians. They commandeered as much grain as they could find, but otherwise they appear to have been friendly. The population, never imagining that the Russians would evacuate Bijār, accommodated themselves, as best as they could, to the new order. But the Russians did not remain: they retreated before the pressure of the Turkish armies; and the Turks occupied the town. The hapless population was then subjected to Turkish retribution for alleged co-operation with the Russians. What little food they had left was taken from them. The beams were torn from the roofs of their houses and were burnt for firewood. Terror was let loose in Bijār.

The famine of 1918 completed the disaster. For many months the people died in the area at the rate of 200 a day. Bijār issued from the war wrecked and decimated. It has never properly recovered. Before 1914 it was a prosperous town of 20,000 people; today it is little more than a large village.

The Bijār Carpet

The weaving area of Bijār comprises the town itself and about forty villages within a radius of 30 miles.

During the early years between the wars hardly a carpet was woven there. Then, in the middle twenties, the industry began slowly to revive; until, in 1938, about a thousand looms were in operation and the output had reached the respectable total of about a thousand pieces a year.

Then came the second war. That cataclysm did not adversely affect production in many of Persia's weaving centres, because an important local demand for carpets arose in the capital. Unhappily, Bijār did not benefit much from this demand; because its heavy, rather clumsy carpets did not appeal to the *nouveaux riches* in Tehrān. Production in Bijār again sank to a low level.

When I started out from Hamadān in 1948 to revisit Bijār I expected to find (in spite of its misfortunes) some signs of renewed activity in the town. I hoped to see a fair number of carpets on loom in Bijār itself and in the villages. I was disappointed. There was only one piece on loom in the whole town! The position in the villages was hardly any better. Output was down to a bare twenty pieces a month for the whole area.

There seemed to be no valid reason for this. The price of wool, it is true, was high; but so was the price of Bijār carpets in the Hamadān bazaar. I was surprised to learn that politics had a good deal to do with the inertia of the citizens. It appeared that the spellbinders of the Tūdeh party had created unrest which had been liquidated (at the instance of the government) by a local *condottiere*. This is an ancient and accepted technique in Persia; but it is one which involves tribulation for rich and poor alike. The exploits of the *condottiere* were happily ended; but uneasiness and lack of confidence still persisted. Both townsmen and villagers preferred to wait rather than to weave.

The same problem confronted me in Bijār as I had encountered in Senneh. How did it come about that the weavers of eastern Kurdistān abandoned their small, traditional tribal rugs to weave great carpets of unique construction in Bijār and in the surrounding villages?

From the many varied and picturesque replies which I received to my enquiries I hazarded a theory which seemed to fit the facts.

For centuries past the paramount chiefs of eastern Kurdistān have not been Kurds, but Turks. Most of them are Turks to this day. And many of these Turkish tribes—unlike the majority of the tribes of Persia—weave double-wefted fabrics, like the Bijār. Among these are the Turks of the Herīz area and of Tabrīz; the Qashqāīs of Fārs; and some of the Afshārs of Kermān. It may well be that some of these Turkish chiefs of eastern Kurdistān (perhaps a chief of the Afshār family which still owns villages north of Bijār and is connected, historically, with the Afshārs of Kermān (see p. 212), wanted some large and solidly built carpets for their castles. How would they obtain them? By ordering them to be

116. BIJĀR: A KURDISH WOMAN SPINNING

made, in their traditional tribal manner: with the Turkish knot, woollen warps and two woollen wefts. Just as, to this day, the Turkish carpets of Ushāk are woven. The Bijār carpet may, indeed, be a distant cousin of the Ushāk of Turkey.

If this hypothesis is correct, the rest inevitably follows. For wool (unlike cotton) is a springy material, and to obtain a quality counting (say) 12 × 12 knots to the inch the two woollen wefts must be vigorously pounded in. The resulting fabric is inevitably tough and dense—outstanding characteristics of the Bijār carpet. It could not be otherwise.

So difficult is it to beat the woollen wefts into place that the Bijār weavers have been compelled to devise a special instrument for the purpose, in addition to their heavy wood-and-iron "comb". The instrument is like an iron nail about 12 inches long. They bring it down hard upon the weft at close intervals—a tedious but necessary process—to get the proper number of rows of knots per inch.

Carpet weaving in the Bijār area is a cottage industry. There are no factories either in the towns or the villages. The looms are primitive—more often than not the beams are bent or uneven—which partly explains the fact that Bijār carpets are so often crooked. This, however, is not the only reason for their lack of symmetry: the use of woollen yarn for the warp is a more frequent cause. For wool is elastic and is difficult to lay with an even tension.

115. A DOORWAY, BIJĀR

And a warp in which the tension is uneven will invariably produce a crooked carpet.

I was glad to note, therefore, that the Bijār weavers were abandoning woollen warps for cotton. Cotton is far better material for the purpose and the change has made no difference to the appearance or "handle" of the Bijār carpet. Cotton is also being used in place of wool for the thin weft. This, too, is an improvement. For the thick weft wool is still being employed—as it must be. If that too should be changed for cotton the character of the Bijār carpet would be inevitably altered.

The construction of the carpet is undergoing further modification: twenty-five years ago, when I first visited Bijār, the heavy woollen weft which was in use was as thick as a lead pencil. The husky weavers, using their 12-inch nails and heavy combs, hammered it in with vigour. The result was a fabric so tightly packed that it could hardly be folded without cracking the warps. The somewhat thinner weft which is in use today is an improvement. The old Bijār was an over-packed fabric.

The designs of Bijār have always been few, simple and generally rectilinear. The professional designer —often an honoured member of the community in places like Tabrīz, Kashān and above all Kermān— is unknown in Bijār. Occasionally some local aspirant to fame produced a new design; but it was invariably bad.

Formerly a design was associated with a particular village. It was well known by the villagers and invariably woven there. The introduction of the *wagireh* system—whereby a mat was woven which showed one repeat of the design and was used as a pattern by the weaver—enabled the merchants to distribute the better designs more widely. The more recent introduction of scale-paper patterns has still further simplified the distribution.

Nevertheless, the few Bijār carpets which are being woven today are lacking in variety of design. The Herātī pattern, with a centre medallion and usually without corner pieces, predominates over every other (Plate 124). But even that simple pattern is often mutilated by the inexperience or indifference of the weavers. If the industry in Bijār is to revive once more (and the indications are—in spite of the present period of stagnation—that it will revive) the first necessity will be to re-introduce into the area a series of carefully and correctly drawn Bijār patterns which have been lost or forgotten.

One of the most interesting designs produced in the Bijār area is the so-called "Audience" or "Triclinium" design. Who, I wonder, was the graceless dealer who first applied the Greco-Roman word *triclinium*—which meant a couch extending round three sides of a table—to a Persian carpet? And who was the dealer, only one degree less graceless, who first called the pieces "Audience Carpets"; explaining, no doubt, that the prince, ruler or overlord sat on a raised dais which was covered by the upper section of the carpet, while his obsequious retainers stood in two lines on the side-pieces with their backs to the walls!

There is no truth in all this. The word *triclinium* sounds impressive, but when applied to a Bijār carpet it makes no sense at all. As for the "Audience" legend, these carpets were never used for "audiences", as some inventive dealers have affirmed. They were woven "four in one" because some local *khan* wanted the usual four pieces which the Persians are fond of laying in a pattern on their floors (see p. 55)—the *kellegi*, the *mian farsh* and the two *kenarehs*—to appear as one, probably to fit a room. The carpet was woven; it looked impressive; it was repeated; and the idea has been carried out many times since.

The Bijār dyers have always been skilled craftsmen, and there is no evidence that they have lost their technique. They employ the same dyestuffs which are in use in Hamadān (see p. 98). The special method which they have for dyeing with madder has already been referred to (see p. 32). Yet, during my visit, the unhappy word alizarine was mentioned by the *dellals* and traders. There is no evidence yet of its extensive use; but I fear that before long there will be.

The Bijār carpet occupies a special place in the estimation of the world. Like the Senneh, it is a unique fabric. There is none like it in Persia or in any other country. Like the Senneh, too, it has remained untouched—no foreign decorator has obtruded his baleful influence in Bijār. Weave, colours and designs—the last often crude and ill-drawn, yet full of character—are all the weavers' own. May they continue to preserve their heritage intact.

The Kurdish Tribal Rugs

We have now examined two of the Kurdish weaves —the Senneh and the Bijār. The former is confined to a single Kurdish town; the latter to a small region on the eastern border of Persian Kurdistān. We have now to consider the products of a much wider area—the rugs of those settled or semi-nomadic

117. A KURDISH VILLAGE
The slabs in the foreground are dried cowdung for use as fuel.

Kurdish tribes who live within the frontiers of Persia.

We have seen that the Senneh and Bijar weaves, although produced by kindred people, differ widely in almost every particular. In the same way most of the Kurdish tribal rugs differ widely from either.

The principal area of production of the Kurdish tribal rugs lies within a rough circle of about 50 miles radius, centred a little to the west of the large village of Qorveh. This area includes the Qulyahi villages, with their little market town of Songūr, and a second group, to the north-west of Qulyahi, of which the principal centre is Shirishabād.

Twenty years ago the output of the Qulyahi area ran into many thousands of pieces yearly. It has continued steadily to dwindle; but the district still produces as many rugs as all the other Kurdish areas put together.

The Shirishabād group—which produces rugs with some affinity with those of nearby Bijār—is next in importance. The other important Kurdish tribes—the Herki, the Senjabi, the Gurāni, the Jaffi and the Kalhors—are no longer weavers on an important scale. A few Senjabi and Jaffi rugs (with their lovely tones of medium blue) still come into the market. But the output is certainly not more than a tenth of what it was in the early thirties.

The decline in output is due to two main causes: the disruption of tribal life caused by the settlement policy of Riza Shah Pahlavi and the unprecedented demand and consequent high price of wool. Of the two, the second is probably the decisive cause; because the tribes weave so that their surplus wool may be put to a profitable use. But that incentive no longer exists because the whole output can now be sold immediately at a good price. The danger is that when the pendulum begins to swing the other way and wool becomes less easy to sell, the weaver's craft will have been—in many areas—forgotten.

KURDISH WEAVES: SENNEH, BIJĀR AND TRIBAL RUGS

119. A SENNEH RUG (c. 1890)
The iris border is characteristic of the period.

118. DETAIL OF A SENNEH CARPET, IN THE GOL-I-BOLBOL (FLOWER AND BIRD) DESIGN (c. 1890)

120. Detail of a Senneh Rug in the Vekilli Design (c. 1905)

121. Detail of a Senneh Carpet in the Gol-i-Mirza Ali or Gol-i-Frank (European Flower) Design (c. 1910)

123. AN EARLY BIJĀR RUG

It is inscribed "El Sultan Afghān Nadir Shah", i.e. the Afghān King Nadir Shah (a reference to the fact that Nadir Shah was an Afghān tribesman); and it is dated (top centre) A.H. 1158–A.D. 1745. The inscriptions in the upper left and right-hand corners are illegible.

122. A BIJĀR CARPET (c. 1890)

124. A Bijār Carpet in the "Anchor" Design, with Medallion, Ground and Corners in Herātī Pattern (c. 1930)

The anchor is no doubt a corruption of a sixteenth-century form.

126. Detail of a Carpet from Helvai Village, near Bijār (c. 1935)

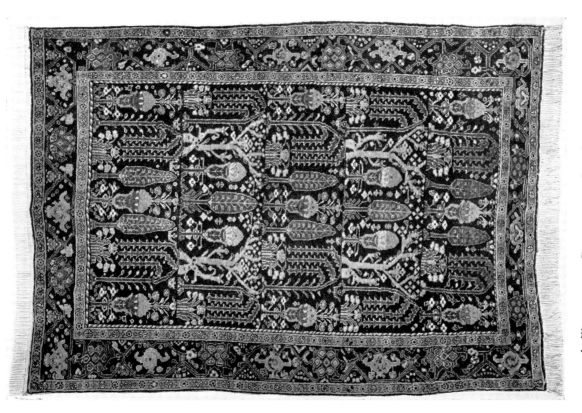

125. A Tekentepeh Rug in the Bid Majnūn (Weeping Willow) Design (c. 1935)

The village lies north of Bijār and its rugs resemble those of Bijār, but are not so heavy.

128. A QULYAHI (KURDISH) RUG (c. 1925)

127. A SENJABI (KURDISH) RUG (c. 1935)

130. A Qulyahi (Kurdish) Rug (c. 1940)

129. A Shirishabād (Kurdish) Rug in the Tulip Design (c. 1940)

131. A Shirishabād (Kurdish) Rug in the "Anchor" Design (*c.* 1940)
(*See note on the "anchor" design under Plate* 124.)

CHAPTER IX

ARĀK (SULTĀNABĀD) AND ITS ENVIRONS; WITH A NOTE ON SERABAND

ARĀK (SULTĀNABĀD) AND ITS ENVIRONS

Of the Town and District of Arāk[1]

If the lack of a history be accepted as an indication of well-being, the province of Arāk must be counted fortunate. For it escaped most of the triumphs and disasters which afflicted its less happy neighbours. Being a purely agricultural area of mud villages and containing no towns of importance (for Sultānabād itself was founded in the beginning of the nineteenth century by Fath Ali Shah), there was nothing much for a predacious soldiery to sack. Because it lay beyond the fringe of the Seljūk invasion, it has remained—in contradistinction to the provinces of Hamadān and Azerbaijān—for the most part Persian in race and speech. It is one of the richest granaries of north-west Persia and supplies Tehrān each year with important quantities of wheat.

Sultānabād, the capital (now called Arāk), is a modern town without archaeological or architectural distinction. Its position and surroundings are not as inviting as those of its neighbour Hamadān, 90 miles to the north. It is, in fact (in summer), a hot, dusty and rather unpleasant town. In winter it is cold and equally unpleasant. Its water supply is so bad that the more fastidious citizens have their water brought to them in barrels from a *qanat* several miles away. The indifferent majority wash their clothes and drink from the same water channels.

Like all Persian towns it possesses a main street, straight and of tolerable width, with another crossing it at right angles. These arteries were built by the orders of that resolute and single-minded town planner, the late Riza Shah. He applied the same simple and effective technique throughout Persia: it consisted in ordering the local governor to draw two parallel lines through the middle of the town and to demolish the few hundred mud houses, shops, baths and caravanserais which happened to lie between. And when that was done, to draw two more—at right angles to the first—and repeat the process of demolition.

132. A Street in Arāk (Sultānabād)

The town enjoys a fairly healthy climate, and possesses an industrious population. It is a centre for two important activities—agriculture and carpet weaving.

The Arāk Weaving Industry: Historical Sketch

The town of Arāk is one of the four most important carpet centres of Persia. We have seen (p. 89) that Hamadān is the home of the inexpensive rug; in the same sense Arāk has been, for nearly a century, the home of the cheap carpet.

We possess no proofs that the weaving industry of the Arāk province is much more than a century old. It may be. But if it were, there are no indications that any outstanding carpets were produced in the province at an earlier period. We do know, however, that Arāk, during the nineteenth century, was producing sound, serviceable and inexpensive carpets; at first for home consumption, and towards the end of the century, for export.

Production for export was started in Arāk by the Tabrīz merchants about the year 1875; and in 1883, a British firm of Swiss origin, Messrs. Ziegler and Co. of Manchester, established an office there. They

---
[1] The reader must not confuse the name of this province with the extensive area to which the Mongol rulers of Persia gave the name "Irak Ajemi", and of course the name has nothing to do with the kingdom of Irāq in Mesopotamia.

were importers of Manchester piece goods and their first office was in Tabrīz. Their business prospered, but they found difficulty in remitting the proceeds of their sales to London. Their principal method was to purchase gold coins—mainly Russian "Imperials" —which they forwarded in "groups" by special messenger to Russia, whence the counter value was transferred to London through normal banking channels. One of Ziegler's staff, a German called Oscar Strauss, suggested that it might be to the firm's advantage to use their funds for buying carpets in Sultānabād (as it was then called)—which they could turn into money in England. The plan was adopted, and in 1883 Strauss was sent to Sultānabād to begin operations. He was an able and enterprising man. Before many years Zieglers possessed a large compound in Sultānabād, with houses for their staff, offices, dyehouses and stores; and were placing orders for carpets in the town and the surrounding villages. It was they who established the system of giving out the yarn ready dyed to the weavers. They used both native and European dyes. Their designs were mainly repeating patterns (Plate 137). The repeat was first woven in the form of mats—twenty or more mats of a pattern—which were distributed among the weavers to be used as models for their carpets. In course of time these mats or *wagirehs* were replaced by scale-paper designs which are now used exclusively in the town and villages alike. The business grew in importance, until by the turn of the century, Zieglers were controlling 2,500 looms in the area. The undertaking, after a long and honourable record, was voluntarily liquidated shortly before the last war.

It was not until the first decade of the present century that other European and American firms established themselves in Sultānabād. Like Zieglers, they built dyehouses, offices and stores; engaged designers; and proceeded to place orders for carpets in their own designs and colours, with town and country weavers. Most of the carpets were of medium quality, counting about 7×8 knots to the inch. They were shipped direct to New York and London via the Caspian and Batūm.

Until the outbreak of World War I the foreign firms continued, with great rapidity, to extend their operations throughout the area, until there were 3,000 looms in Sultānabād alone; while in the surrounding villages every house seemed to be weaving a carpet. It was estimated that a million pounds of foreign capital was invested in the small town of Sultānabād and its environs before World War I.

An important part of the trade, however, still remained in the hands of the Tabrīz merchants. Until World War I they continued to ship large quantities of the two cheaper grades of Sultānabād carpets—known in the trade as Mūshkabāds and Mahāls—to Istanbul; where they were sold to buyers from all parts of the world, particularly from Germany and Austria.

The collapse of the Central Powers after World War I was, therefore, a serious blow to the weaving industry of Sultānabād; and it almost put the Tabrīz merchants out of business. The industry was saved by the sudden demand from the United States for a new and better grade carpet—the Sarūk. Important quantities of this new quality were absorbed by America during the boom period of the twenties.

But with the advent of the American depression the crash came. One after another the American firms closed down and liquidated their assets. Having been deprived of the European market by the world war, Sultānabād temporarily lost the American market as well.

Nevertheless, no sooner did the United States emerge from the crisis than the demand for Sarūks revived. The situation, however, in Sultānabād had changed. Production, which had been abandoned by the American and European firms, was now firmly in the hands of local Persian merchants. The foreign firms decided that it would be impracticable for them to begin all over again on the old lines— with large staffs, offices, stores and dyehouses; and big stocks of wool and yarns. The power and prestige which they had previously enjoyed—which had enabled them to advance money and materials to penniless villagers without undue risk—was gone.[1] They preferred, therefore, to abstain from direct production and to obtain their supplies from the Persian merchants through local agents. This has been the procedure since the middle thirties, and it will probably continue without substantial change.

Conversation Piece

Have you ever encountered, Reader, a name more singular, yet more respectable, than Ebenezer Gentleman? I can assure you (lest you should suppose that I invented it) that a worthy, middle-aged person of that name really lived in Persia (of all places) half a century ago. He was in the employ of Ziegler

---

[1] It was a common practice thirty-five years ago to lock a defaulting weaver in the stable—until his relatives came forward with guarantees that his carpet would be finished or the advance refunded. This was a rough-and-ready technique; but on the whole it worked satisfactorily for all concerned—including the weaver, who preferred it to the attentions of the local authorities of those days.

and Co., a house (as mentioned above) of credit and renown who were pioneers in the Persian trade.

It happened one day that Mr. Ebenezer Gentleman was travelling across country on horseback, when he was set upon by robbers. Resistance on these occasions was useless; because Persian highwaymen wisely abstained from molesting travellers unless they possessed an undoubted superiority in arms and numbers. Mr. Ebenezer Gentleman found himself, therefore, brusquely deprived of his horses and his effects. The bandits, however, were not content with those: they ordered him to hand over his clothes too—until he stood, naked as a pole, by the roadside.

Mr. Gentleman viewed with detachment the loss of his horses and his baggage; but to be deprived of his clothes was, he thought, too much. He therefore addressed the leader of the band as follows: "I do not complain of the loss of my horses and my effects; for this is an inconvenience which may happen to any traveller. But I am surprised that your Eminence should wish to deprive me of my apparel as well. Consider how unseemly it would be if I were to enter the refined city of Isfahān, my destination, unclothed! Pray, therefore, order your men to return to me at least a pair of shoes and something to cover my nakedness."

The bandit (I have no doubt) was taken aback by Mr. Gentleman's observations; and being amenable (like every Persian) to the seductions of courtesy, he gave a sharp order. One of Mr. Gentleman's bags was opened and ransacked, and a pair of slippers with a swallow-tail coat were extracted from them and thrown at his feet. Then, in a trice, the band remounted, clattered down the road and was lost to sight.

Mr. Ebenezer Gentleman viewed with despair the slippers and the swallow-tail. The former, he decided, might last, if carefully nursed, for a few miles. The swallow-tail, though more durable, appeared to lack some of the essentials of decent attire.

That same evening a company of indolent citizens of Isfahān were smoking the *qalian* of sunset at a wayside teahouse, when they suddenly perceived upon the highroad a person of singular deportment. He was barefoot and (what was more unusual) bareheaded; and he was wearing a dress of peculiar and unnatural pattern. It was open behind—exposing his back, his buttocks and his legs—for he wore no trousers—to the public eye. In front, however, his members were effectually concealed; for his coat possessed two pendant queues which hung from the waist down ...

The Arāk Weaving Area

The weaving area of Arāk as shown on the accompanying map (p. 138) cannot be properly surveyed by districts, like that of the Hamadān. For, as we have seen, in the Hamadān area each village produces a rug or carpet which differs in some respect from the products of every other village; whereas the Arāk area proper produces only three qualities: the Mūshkabād, the Mahāl and the Sarūk.[1] These qualities are not rigidly confined to special villages or districts. Two of them—the Mūshkabād and Mahāl—are closely allied, and the weavers sometimes switch from one to the other. During recent years the town weavers and those of some of the more important villages have abandoned the cheaper qualities altogether and are weaving Sarūks.

I propose, therefore, to survey the Arāk weaves by quality and not by district. Before doing so, however, some observations and enquiries of a general character are indicated.

How many looms are there in the Arāk area? Nobody knows. The wildest and the most improbable estimates were given me by traders who should have known better. By cross-checking the number of villages, the monthly shipment of goods and the sales of exchange, I arrived at a figure of about 10,000, of which about 1,500 are in the town. But

133. WEAVERS' INSTRUMENTS, ARĀK VILLAGE
On the left is the beater used for hammering in the wefts; on the right is the comb, used for combing out the ends of the yarn, after the knot is tied.

---
[1] The Kemereh and Seraband weaves are different and will be considered separately.

134. Spring in an Arāk Village

Below is a list of the principal weaving areas of Arāk, with the kind of carpet woven in each, in 1948.

Arāk (town)	Sarūks: Extra, I and II.
Mūshkabād	Mūshkabāds.
Ferahān	Sarūk rugs, Mahāls, Mūshkabāds.
Dulakhor	Mūshkabāds and Mahāls.
Chahār-rā	Sarūk rugs.
Mahallāt	Sarūks: Extra, I and II.
Kezzāz	Sarūks: II and III.
Khonsār	Sarūks: I and II.
Kemereh	Lilihān carpets and rugs: Reihān rugs.
Japalāk	Low-grade (mostly aniline) Mūshkabāds.
Seraband	Serabands: and some very low-grade rugs and carpets for home consumption.

these figures are only vague approximations, because no proper statistics exist.

With the exception of the few Armenian villages of Kemereh—which are mentioned below—and the less important Turkish and Georgian villages of

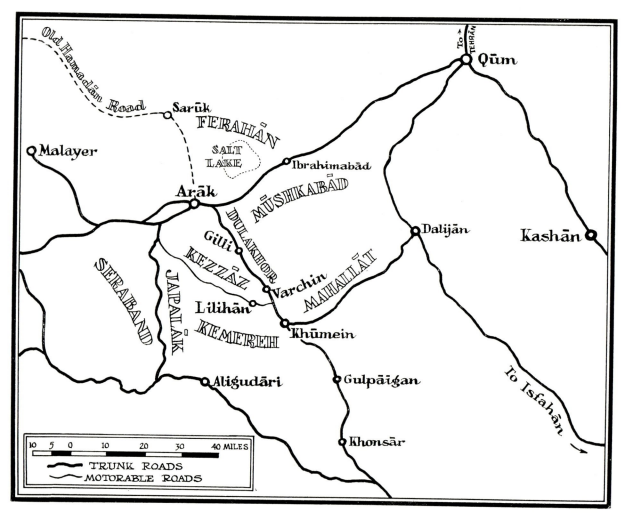

Map IV. The Arāk Weaving Area

Fereidān, the weaving area of Arāk is inhabited exclusively by Moslems of the Persian race, who weave the Persian knot. The most important weaving districts—outside the town of Arāk (Sultānabād)—are Mūshkabād, Ferahān, Dulakhor, the Mahallāt, Kezzāz and Khonsār. The Mahallāt is the richest agricultural area of the province and some of the best Sarūks are produced in its prosperous villages. One of them—the important village of Mahajirān—is reputed to produce the best Sarūks in the whole province.

The Mūshkabād Carpet

As indicated above, the majority of the carpets woven in the Arāk province are of three grades, which are known locally (as in the West) as Mūshkabād, Mahāl and Sarūk. The Seraband and Kemereh weaves are different in character from these and are less important.

The trade name Mūshkabād—by which the lowest of the three grades is known the world over—was well and properly chosen. Over a century ago Mūshkabād was an important market town and the administrative centre of the Ferahān district. It is said to have produced the best wheat in the plain. The story goes that there was some disturbance in the district—probably over a matter of taxes—and that Fath Ali Shah ordered its principal town to be pounded to pieces with artillery. When the job was done he caused the town of Sultānabād to be founded, so that Mūshkabād might not be given the chance to rise again out of its mounds of rubble. For over a century it has remained a melancholy monument to a stupid prince. Today the site lies, grim and desolate, on the right side of the Qūm road 16 miles from Arāk. Here and there, among the shapeless hillocks, I saw little patches of yellow wheat waiting for the sickle. Those little patches, and a solitary peasant, were the only signs of life in Mūshkabād.

There is no doubt that the old dark-blue Ferahān carpets, which were a feature of the more cultured Victorian households, were woven in Mūshkabād and the surrounding villages. In Ibrahimabād, a few miles away, I saw on loom a lineal descendant of those famous carpets. It was correct in every detail of design, colour and construction. For more than a century this family had woven the same style of carpet, over and over again.

These old Ferahāns were formerly collected by the Tabrīz merchants from the houses of well-to-do Persian gentlemen, and were shipped to Istanbul; whence they found their way into the houses of the well-to-do Victorian gentlemen—a happy transmigration!

The Mūshkabād is one of the coarsest of the more important Persian weaves. Its only rival, indeed, for that distinction is a low-grade carpet from the Herīz area. The Mūshkabād, which counts about 5×6 knots to the inch, is a little more closely woven than its northern rival, but it is not so heavy. Both warp and weft are made of handspun cotton. The wool from which the yarn is spun is mostly skin wool from Tehrān, Isfahān or any other place where cheap wools can be bought. The weavers rarely spin it themselves; they buy it ready spun in the bazaar. As with most bazaar goods, the blues, reds and greens are dyed by the local dyers; the creams, yellows, fawns, camels and browns are dyed by the weavers themselves, with local dyestuffs. The Mūshkabād carpet is therefore, in every sense, a bazaar carpet; by which is meant that it is woven by villager weavers for their own account and sold in the bazaar for as much as it will fetch. The carpets are mostly woven in twenty villages in the vicinity of Mūshkabād, and in some of the Ferahān villages east of the Salt Lake.

The designs used in the Mūshkabād quality are generally repeating classic patterns—such as the Herātī, the Gol Henaī, the Mina Khanī, the Harshang; with simplifications of Shah Abbasī, Jōshaqānī and other classic designs (see p. 36). Medallion designs are uncommon, as they are not easy to weave without scale-paper patterns.

The Mahāl Carpet

The name "Mahāl" does not possess either the authority or the romance which is attached to its humbler brother, the Mūshkabād—indeed, the origin of the name is obscure. One trader will affirm that it is derived from the Mahallāt district, where the best Mahāls were formerly woven—but which today is weaving nothing but Sarūks. Another will explain that the word is derived from the Arabic word for locality, and that it was used to denote the placing of an order for a carpet in a certain area or village. Between one or the other of these elucidations the reader may take his choice.

There is no basic difference in weave between the Mahāl and Mūshkabād carpet. The difference is merely one of quality and material; the Mahāl counts about 2 knots per inch more both ways than the Mūshkabād. The yarns used in it are generally better and the colours are clearer and fresher, as greater care is taken in the dyeing. The carpet is denser, somewhat thicker in pile and better finished. The designs are more varied, more accurately drawn and more carefully executed. Altogether, the Mahāl carpet may be described as the more respectable member of the Mūshkabād family. The principal weaving areas of Mahāl carpets are Ferahān and Dulakhor (see Map, p. 138).

The Mahāl carpet, like the Mūshkabād, is a "bazaar" carpet, but in a lesser degree; as some of the Arāk merchants place orders for them on their own designs and supply the weaver with the dyed yarn for their manufacture. Both these qualities, which were formerly produced in the town of Arāk (Sultānabād) as well as in the villages, are today purely village carpets. The town looms produce nothing but Sarūks.

The output of Mūshkabād and Mahāl carpets—90 per cent of which was formerly shipped to Europe—is today mainly absorbed by Persia itself. Some are still shipped to the West and a few to Palestine, Irak, Syria and the Lebanon. As long as the present import restrictions continue shipments to the West will be unimportant.

The Sarūk Carpet

About 25 miles north of Arāk on the old road to Hamadān (which is almost impassable to motors) lies Sarūk, a large village of about 800 houses. It is an ancient village: it was mentioned by the Moslem travellers Yakūt and Mustaufi in the twelfth and thirteenth centuries. Today its name is renowned the world over.

At the end of last century Sarūk was already known in Persia for the excellence of its weaving. Only rug sizes were woven there. In 1912, when I visited the place for the first time, this was still true. It still is. The rugs which were produced then were as stiff as boards, tightly woven, clipped thin and beautifully finished. The designs were of the medallion type.

Early in the present century the name Sarūk began to be applied as a trade name to any closely woven carpet or rug produced in western Ferahān. Those early Sarūks were very different from the Sarūks of today: they were mostly in medallion designs, and on cream or dark blue grounds. Rose grounds were unknown. They were closely woven and the pile was cut short.

In many of the earlier pieces the design was wrongly executed, because the village weavers had not yet mastered the art of weaving from scale-paper designs (Plates 141, 142). After 1913, however, the execution improved considerably (Plate 143). From that time on weaving from scale paper gradually spread throughout the whole Arāk area.[1] It is now the accepted technique in weaving all qualities—except the Mūshkabād and Mahāl qualities in traditional designs, which the weavers know by heart.

That early type of Sarūk was not, however, what the New York importers required—and it was they who commanded the only steady market for Persia's finer qualities in the years which immediately followed World War I. Their interpretation of American demand prescribed three characteristics, which they regarded (and still regard) as essential in the production of a proper Sarūk carpet: (1) a sturdy construction, with a pile 11–12 millimetres thick, to stand a double wash with alkalis;[2] (2) floral designs covering the whole field of the carpet; and (3) 90 per cent rose grounds.

Thus, thirty years ago, out of these strange prescriptions, the modern Sarūk carpet was born. It counts from 9×10 to 11×12 knots to the inch. Machine-spun cotton is used for the warp and the thin weft—handspun for the thicker weft. The yarn, too, is handspun and of good quality. The designs—

135. WEAVING A SARŪK CARPET, ARĀK (SULTĀNABĀD)
Weaving is carried on almost entirely in the houses. There are usually two or four looms in a house.

[1] The technique was introduced into Sultānabād by Mr. George Stevens in 1913.
[2] There is little advantage to be derived from this extreme length of pile. It produces a thick fabric which blurs the detail of the design. The peculiar quality of Persian art is its fine and delicate craftsmanship—which can only be revealed in an appropriate medium. The contention that a pile of 11–12 millimetres is required if the carpet is to withstand the finishing treatment with alkalis is unconvincing. In a properly constructed carpet a pile of 9 millimetres is ample to withstand this treatment; and will, at the same time, provide the necessary definition.

such as they are—are on the whole well executed. The Persian knot produces a clean and regular back. Altogether the weaving is good, as the Arāk weavers are among the most skilled in Persia.

It was fortunate for them that the demand for the Sarūk quality arose from America after the collapse of the Continental demand for the two cheaper grades. The striking change which took place in the output of the three qualities can best be judged by the following table. It does not pretend to be statistically accurate, but it was compiled in consultation with a number of authorities in Arāk and fairly represents the position as it was in 1914 and as it is today.

Distribution of the total yardage of the principal Arāk weaves

	1914 %	1948 %
Mūshkabād quality	75	25
Mahāl quality	15	10
Sarūk quality	5	60
Kemereh, Seraband and others	5	5
	100	100

It will be seen from the above table that today 60 per cent of the yardage produced in the Arāk province is in the Sarūk quality; or, if reckoned by value, about 75 per cent.

The Poverty and Sameness of Arāk Designs

Arāk—which once challenged Kermān in the importance of its output—has never produced great designers like its rival. This is due to the fact that Arāk was mainly distinguished for its cheap and medium-priced qualities. Even the Sarūk of today is a comparatively coarse weave. In consequence, Arāk has never possessed a school of eminent designers.

This, however, does not account for the poverty and monotony of the Arāk designs; for variety and interest can be as happily introduced in a coarse quality as in a fine. In the lower grades the sameness is, up to a point, understandable; because these qualities are woven by the villagers for their own account for sale in the bazaar; and the villagers are left very much to their own devices. But this explanation does not account for the wearisome monotony in the output of the Sarūk quality; for this quality is mostly woven against special orders placed by the Persian merchants of Arāk.

Until the middle twenties the monotony was not pronounced, because Persian classic patterns were still in vogue. But about that time the style of the Sarūk carpet changed: a new type of design was introduced which has dominated the carpet ever since.

The person who, twenty-five years ago, was instrumental in introducing this surprisingly persistent design into Sultānabād was Mr. S. Tyriakian, the local representative of the firm of K. S. Taushandjian of New York, now defunct. Mr. Tyriakian was himself a designer of ability. Wearying, perhaps, of the old Persian motives, he prepared a design in a new style which he thought might sell in America, and ordered some carpets to be made in it. Although the design was hardly Persian, it was good; and it was successful beyond its creator's fondest imaginings. The orders poured in to Sultānabād—first from Taushandjians and then from the other importers as well. Before long Sultānabād was weaving little else. It has been weaving little else ever since. For twenty-five years the same type of design has persisted—almost unchanged—in the Sarūk quality.

Unhappily, the story does not end there. The new style radiated outwards from Sultānabād and spread its baleful influence over the designers of Kashan, Meshed, Kermān and Hamadān. Tabrīz alone escaped—because there is little demand in America for Tabrīz carpets.

In 1948 it was my misfortune to examine the stocks of the Arāk merchants. Carpet after carpet was opened for my edification: all had rose grounds and dark blue borders; and the field of every one was covered with detached floral motives, all very much alike (Plates 151, 152). Some of the pieces were a little closer woven than others; but, by and large, the Sarūk carpets of the Arāk bazaar were all the same. They have indeed been much the same for the last twenty-five years!

The suggestion that a little variety in colour and design might, perhaps, add interest to their stocks was received by the merchants with coldness or derision. "Why should we bother?" they said. "We have only one market: New York. This is what the New York customers want; and we give it to them."

Who is responsible for the strange monomania? The American public—which loves variety, which makes a fetish of change, and is always interested in hand-woven fabrics of character and individuality? Surely not. The American public must be bored to see displayed in the stores, year after year, the same rose-ground Sarūks in the same type of floral pattern.

The public puts this down, perhaps, to the imbecility of the Persian weaver. But the Persian weaver (however much he may be pleased to receive orders in the same design, year in, year out) is certainly not to blame.

The responsibility, I fear, must rest squarely upon the shoulders of the importers of New York. They have failed to make use of the immense range and variety of designs and colours which the Persian weavers have paraded at their feet.

Dyeing in Arāk

The dyers of Arāk carry on their craft in a couple of long, ramshackle buildings on the north-eastern edge of the town. Before I visited their dye-houses I had been assured by several of the merchants that no synthetic dyestuffs were used in Arāk. This proved to be, in the main, correct. No anilines are used by the dyers and (with the exception of synthetic indigo, which is used everywhere in Persia) I was able to trace only one synthetic dyestuff—a Swiss product of good quality.

The usual Persian dyestuffs are used: indigo for the blues; madder for the reds and the rose; vine leaves, with some madder added, for the yellows; tan bark for the camel shades (instead of walnut husks as in Hamadān) with pomegranate rinds as an auxiliary. A Swiss synthetic dyestuff is used for one of the medium blues and also for the green (on vine-leaf yellow). It gives a pleasant irregular shade, unsuitable for grounds but good for motives. Alum is invariably used as a mordant. The method employed in dyeing the famous *dūghi* rose of Arāk has been already described (p. 32). The shade produced is fairly fast to light but it is fugitive to the finishing treatment with alkalis. As the demand from America for rose-ground Sarūks persisted, it would seem reasonable to suppose that immediate steps would have been taken to correct this imperfection. It is, after all, a comparatively simple matter to dye any shade of rose which would be fast to alkalis. The Persian dyers themselves could have solved the problem in their own way, if they had been approached; and for a scientific dyer it was no problem at all. The New York importers, however, met the difficulty in an unenlightened manner: they continued to import their Sarūks as before, knowing that the ground colour would partly disappear in the finishing process; and they connived with the carpet-finishers to paint back the colour by hand— at considerable expense to themselves. They have been doing this for twenty-five years. In other words they have been content to sell carpets, year after year, in which the ground colour has been painted in! One hesitates to say which is more gross—the immorality or the stupidity of this device.

Surely the time has come to put an end to these follies. The designers of Arāk—who have been compelled to draw the same style of design for a quarter of a century—have lost their invention; but there are still designers left in Persia. While the problem of dyeing a fast rose can be solved in a few hours.

I appeal, therefore, to the younger men who are in the Persian rug business in New York to ponder over these matters before it is too late. The writing is already on the wall. During a period of great prosperity in America and in spite of the fact that the duty on Persian rugs has been more than halved, sales of Arāk carpets have fallen considerably.

Let the younger men with taste and ideas and some sympathy for a craft which is in a parlous state go to Persia and take stock of the position. Let them no longer rely—as their fathers have relied for forty years—on the narrow and uninformed views of bewildered agents. Let them eschew methods born of mass production—in an industry in which every weaver must put something of herself into her work. And, above all, let them give rein to the inventiveness of the Persian designers and master-weavers.

Conversation Piece

A tea house in Sarūk village. A group of children has gathered in the courtyard and is staring at us.

I: Is there no school in this village?
First Citizen: There is a school.
I: Do not the children go to school?
Second Citizen: No.
I: Why?
First Citizen: The teacher, sir, is an old man. Every day he smokes three *miscals* of opium; so that he often forgets to open the school. Therefore there is no advantage. It is better that the children should work with us in the fields.
I: It is better.

Kemereh and the Armenian Villages of Southern Arāk

The Armenians of north-west and central Persia constitute—both socially and historically—one of the most interesting of the Persian minorities.

Early in the seventeenth century Shah Abbas transferred no less (it is said) than a quarter of a million of his Armenian subjects from their homelands in the neighbourhood of Jūlfa, Erivān and Kārs to his capital and to the fertile but sparsely populated areas to the north of it. His object was, no doubt, to secure his frontier. For the ancient kingdom of Armenia had been divided between himself and the Ottoman sultan; and thus the frontier ran through territories inhabited by an alien and hostile people. He therefore forcibly transferred his Armenian subjects to a locality where they could give little trouble. Their descendants aver that a third of these displaced persons died on the way—which we may well believe in the light of more recent experiences nearer home.

However this may be, a great many of them did reach their destinations and founded a number of separate, but closely linked, Armenian communities in west central Persia—where they still remain. The principal and only urban community was settled in a suburb of Isfahān, which was named Jūlfa, after the northern Jūlfa on the Araxes, where some of the emigrants had formerly lived. Others were settled in Kemereh, Chahār Mahāl, Japalāk and Fereidān.

The Armenian peasants are a sober, sturdy race. They are cleaner, more orderly, more industrious, more thrifty, and better cultivators than the Persian peasants. Their villages are usually large and surrounded by plantations of poplar and willow and extensive vineyards. They are invariably owned by Moslem landlords, who are pleased to have the Armenians as tenants.

From time to time the Armenian communities have been subjected to religious persecutions; but under the leadership of their bishops and priests, they have invariably succeeded in circumventing their oppressors. Today they are accepted by the Persians as one of the recognised communities of Persia, with the right to elect a representative in the Majlis (Parliament).

The most notable group of Armenian villages is situated in the Kemereh district (see Map IV). Of this group the village of Lilihān is the most distinguished. Its name is, indeed, well known by merchants and rug fanciers in America, although in Europe few people have ever heard of it. Lilihān is the largest of a group of seven Armenian villages (with a total population of 2,500) which are situated within sight of each other in a beautiful and fertile valley a few miles north-west of the market town of Khūmein. All of the seven are weaving villages. They weave rug sizes and carpets up to 12 × 9—all very much alike in design and colour (see Plate

136. LILIHĀN

The largest of a group of seven Armenian weaving villages situated in a fertile valley near Khūmein, Arāk province.

149). The rugs are generally known by the name of the principal village, Lilihān. They weave a single-wefted fabric of close texture, beautifully finished, with a soft, velvety surface. The villagers use wool from their own sheep, which is spun and dyed in their own villages. They use the *dūghi* rose for their ground colour (sometimes, I fear, topped with aniline) and some aniline for their secondary shades. They have the good sense to admit this openly.

For such an excellent fabric their designs are unimpressive. Like the weavers of the thousands of Sarūk carpets, the villagers of Lilihān appear to be under the impression that the American public will buy only one type of design; and this they weave, year in, year out. There is nothing Persian about it.

The Jūlfa community are not weavers and are, therefore, outside the subject of this survey. The community of Chahār Mahāl will be referred to on p. 309. Most of the Armenians of the Japalāk district have recently returned to the Soviet Republic of Armenia; and the remainder of them have sold their properties with the intention of following their fellows.

Scattered among the Turkish, Bakhtiari and Georgian villages of Fereidān are eighteen more purely Armenian villages. There are looms in many of them. Like their neighbours farther north, these Armenians produce closely woven, single-wefted and well-finished rugs. But their designs lack variety and they use a good deal of aniline.

There is one more village in the Kemereh area

which deserves special mention—the Moslem village of Reihān. It deserves to be recorded because it is the only village in the area which has refused to follow in the wake of all its neighbours and to weave the so-called "American design". The villagers of Reihān are (I doubt not) a proud, independent, recusant community. For many generations they have been weaving their design (Plate 149) on a red ground with white border—and they refuse to weave any other. All honour to them. If the other villages had done the same we should have a pleasant variety of rugs from the Kemereh area—instead of the dull uniformity of the "American" design.

Conversation Piece

In the house of the Headman of Lilihān village.

I: I understand that many of your people have left this area and have emigrated to Russia?

The Headman: To Russia? No.

I: No?

The Headman: Three hundred and fifty years ago our ancestors were forcibly deported from Armenia —our motherland—to Persia. Now, the descendants of those who survived that deportation have been invited to return to our motherland, Armenia. Many have already gone. Many more will follow. But not to Russia. No. To Armenia.

SERABAND

The large district known as Seraband is not marked on any map that I have seen. It lies outside the limits of Arāk, and is cut off from it by a formidable barrier of mountains. Its inhabitants are racially divided from the Arāk people and its weaves differ fundamentally from theirs. Strictly, therefore, Seraband should not be regarded as one of the weaving districts of Arāk. It should, indeed, have a chapter to itself. But interesting as the district is, it is hardly important enough for that. It has therefore been included in this chapter from convenience rather than propriety.

The district lies to the west of the railway which runs southward from Arāk. It is a mountainous area, difficult of access except on horseback, and therefore little known. The best approach to it is from Būrūjird, whence a car can, with some trouble, penetrate into it for a dozen miles. Beyond that the journey must be performed on horseback. Seraband is a rich agricultural area of some 300 villages. The inhabitants are nearly all of the Turkish race and speak a dialect of Turkish. Only a few villages on the northern border of the district are Persian, and one village near its centre.

The Turks of Seraband are probably an offshoot of the Seljūk invasion which transformed Azerbaijān and Hamadān into Turkish-speaking provinces. Under what circumstances an important Turkish enclave came into existence in this remote mountainous area—with a Persian population on three sides of it and Lūri tribes on the fourth—is one of those problems which seem always to exist in countries which have been overrun and partially settled by semi-nomadic peoples.

In the West the name Seraband is more commonly used to denote a pattern rather than a weave of carpet. The particular small leaf or pine which is woven in the area is called by this name to distinguish it from the great variety of leaf patterns which are found in Persia (see pp. 39–40). It has been copied in every country of the world where pile carpets are manufactured. The origin of the pattern has been discussed elsewhere (see p. 38). In Persia the Seraband pine is known as the *Boteh Miri*—*boteh* meaning bush or cluster of leaves; *Miri* no doubt refers to the Mir carpets of the early nineteenth century which were the prototypes of the present-day Serabands.

The origin of these famous carpets has been shrouded in a good deal of unnecessary mystery. There is no doubt at all that they were woven in Seraband. The carpets of today are their direct lineal descendants. The details of the ground, border and guards are the same; the knot is the same; the construction—except for the inevitable deterioration in quality—is the same. Indeed, there is hardly a weave in Persia (except perhaps the Jōshaqān) which is more closely related to its early prototype than the Seraband. The origin of the name "Mir" is not so easy to explain. It is probably connected with the village of Mal-e-mir—the administrative centre of the district—but the connection is not clear.

Mr. Nasrullah Mostaufi of Ahwaz—an authority on the geography, manners and customs of his country—informed me that during the period when these carpets were woven, a considerable number of *mirs*[1] were living in the Seraband district. The Seraband *mirs*—unlike most of the *sayyids* of Persia—were among the best elements of the population, and it was in their homes that the Mir carpets were woven. It is conceivable that the village of

---

[1] A descendant of the Prophet: a person whose father or mother was a Sayyid.

Mal-e-mir (i.e. the property of the Mirs) became their principal seat. The fact that this village is today the most important in the district, and is the only Persian village in a purely Turkish area of Seraband, would point to its having possessed a certain distinction in times past. Another explanation is that these carpets were woven to the order of a certain Emir Kabir, a wealthy landlord of the Seraband district; and that the name "Mir" is a corruption of the word "Emir". I prefer Mr. Mostaufi's interpretation.

There are about 3,000 looms in Seraband. Of these only about half weave the Seraband which is known in the West. These looms are concentrated in about thirty villages. The remainder of the looms produce what must be among the poorest carpets woven in the whole of Persia. Their material is inferior, they are coarse and ill-woven, and the dyes are all aniline. A 7×4 rug is woven in a week. These goods are marketed in Arāk and Būrūjird for consumption in Persia itself and, in a lesser degree, in Baghdad.

The Seraband proper, on the other hand, is an honest carpet. It is a sturdy, double-wefted fabric, woven with the Turkish knot. Warps and wefts are of cotton, the latter dyed blue. The villagers use their own wool, or buy it in Būrūjird from Lūri tribesmen. They dye their own yarns with the commoner Persian dyestuffs: indigo, madder, vine leaves, tan bark and pomegranate rind. Their system of dyeing with madder is defective: they use less of the dyestuff than the depth of the shade requires and after the operation is finished they darken the yarn by immersing it in potash (wood ash) liquor. The resulting shade is partly fugitive to weak acids.

137. AN EARLY REPEATING DESIGN BY ZIEGLER & CO. OF SULTANABĀD (c. 1885)
Mats were woven from the design for distribution to the weavers, who made carpets of them.

138. CLASSIC DESIGN FOR A SMALL-SIZED MŪSHKABĀD CARPET (c. 1945)
Drawn by Tahir Zadeh Bihzad, School of Art, Tehrān

140. Design for a Mahāl Carpet; drawn by Tahir Zadeh Bihzad, School of Art, Tehrān
The design first appeared c. 1910.

139. Design for a Mahāl Carpet (c. 1912)

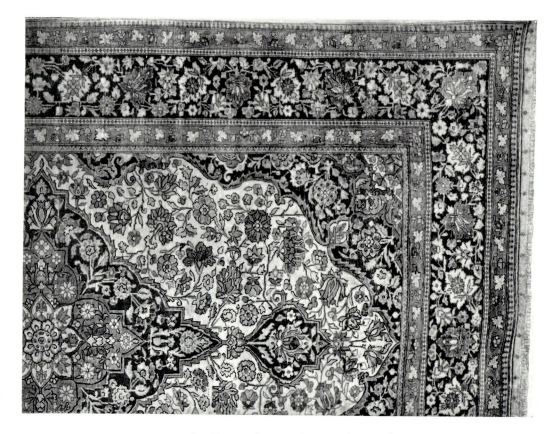

141. An Early Sarūk Carpet (c. 1905)

142. A Sarūk Carpet (c. 1910)

143. Design for a Sarūk Carpet (c. 1920)

144. Working Drawing for a Sarūk Carpet (c. 1948)

145. Design for a Sarūk Carpet (c. 1923)
Courtesy of M. Mustafa Kemal

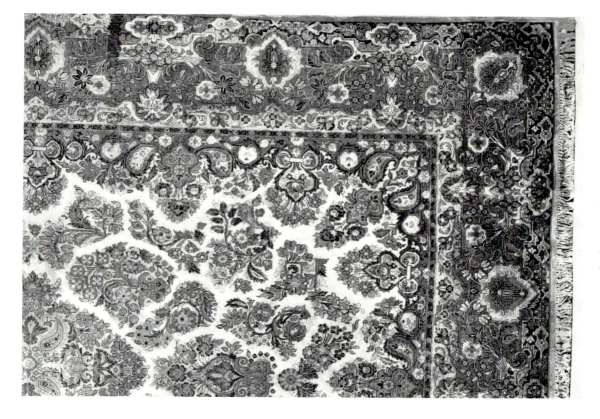

147. A Sarūk Carpet (c. 1935)

146. A Sarūk Carpet (c. 1935)

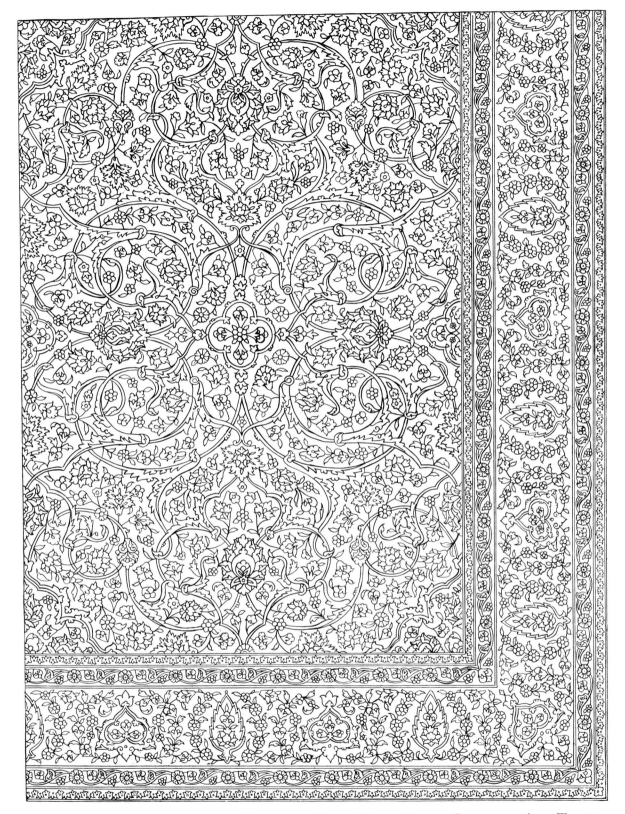

148. Design for a Sarūk Carpet, Drawn by Tahir Zadeh Bihzad, School of Art, Tehrān
The Design first appeared c. 1910.

149. Characteristic Lilihān (*above*) and Reihān (*below*) Designs.

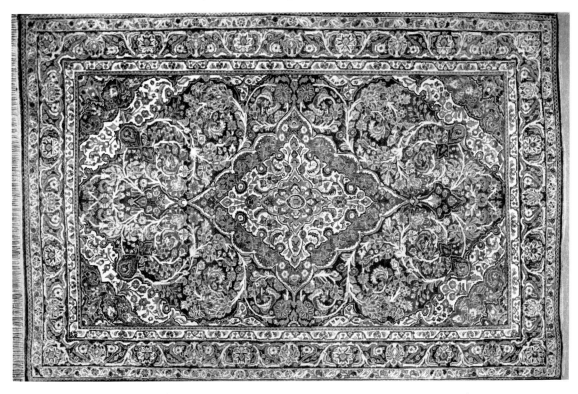

150. A Sarūk Carpet in the Traditional Style (*c.* 1915)

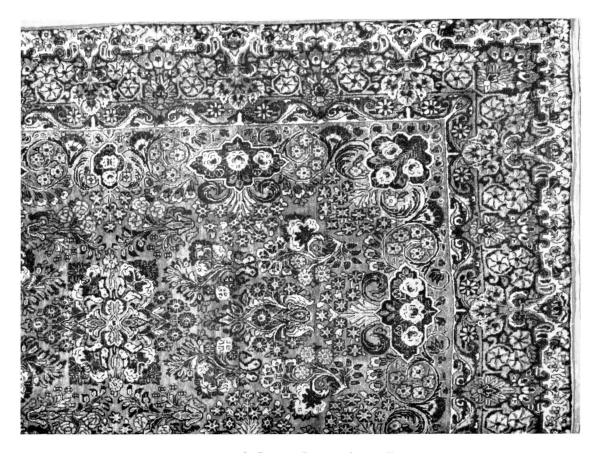

151. A Sarūk Carpet (*c.* 1948)

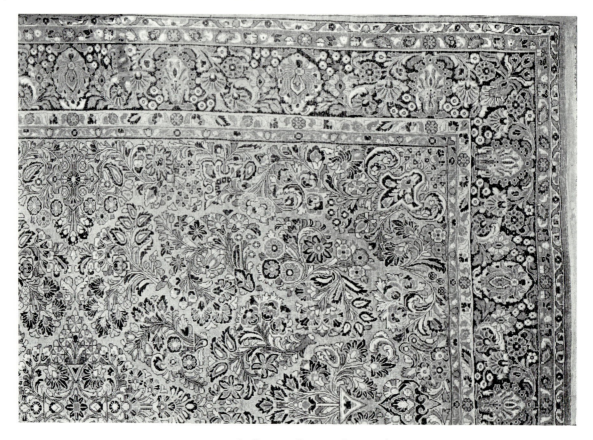

152. A Sarūk Carpet (*c.* 1935)

This type of design was introduced into Sultānabād twenty-five years ago and has been prevalent there ever since.

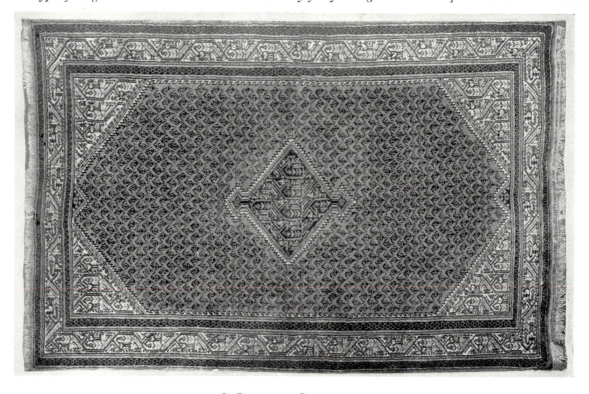

153. A Seraband Carpet (*c.* 1948)

CHAPTER X

THE TURKOMAN RUGS OF THE PERSIAN STEPPE

Preliminaries

I was in two minds whether or not to include the Yomūt Turkoman rugs of the Steppe in this survey. For they are not Persian in character: they belong rather to the great family of the red rugs of Transcaspia—the Mervs, the Bokharas, the Beshirs, the Kizil Ayāks, the Kara-Kalpāks and the Afghans—none of which are Persian. We used to buy Yomūts years ago—I remembered—in bond, in Meshed; but they were woven on the Russian side of the border. If the important quantities of these rugs which I saw in the Tehrān bazaar were of Russian origin also (and had been smuggled into Persia), then, clearly, they had no place in this survey.

A friendly dealer in Tehrān bazaar gave me some useful information on this question. He assured me that his rugs were woven by Turkomans who lived on the Persian side of the border. Had they emigrated recently from the Russian side into Persia? He was not sure; but he believed that some of them had done so. I determined to visit the Steppe to find out.

This was not so simple as it at first appeared. Like the Herīz district, the province of Gurgān is a frontier area, and no foreigner was allowed there except by a special permit from the military authorities. A formal request from the British Embassy was indicated.

The officer in charge of Frontier Security appeared to be politely sceptical of the real object of my proposed visit to Gurgān. He assured me that all Persian carpets were woven in the same manner; and that when I had seen one weaving centre, I had seen them all. Why, therefore, endure the headache and discomfort of a journey to Gurgān? I replied, with deference, that certain differences, in fact, existed between the carpets of one area and another (which, of course, he knew as well as I) and that I was recording these diversities in a book. Perhaps the courteous officer decided that, on the whole, the Russians were unlikely to employ an Englishman to spy for them. He granted me the permit.

I had just arrived from Tabrīz where I had witnessed the sad effects on the industry of the invasion of western dyes. And I was happy to think that on my forthcoming visit to the Yomūt Turkomans I should be spared a repetition of that distressful experience. It happened, however, that I encountered an old acquaintance in the Park Hotel, Tehrān—a Swiss merchant of repute—who was importing Swiss dyestuffs on a considerable scale. While exchanging views on this and kindred subjects, I happened to mention that I was contemplating a visit to the Turkomans of Gurgān. "They are good people," said he, "and good customers of mine. I sell them a dyestuff which we call Rouge d'Orient. They use it for the ground shade of their carpets." Thus are our fondest illusions brutally destroyed!

Gurgān and Gombad-i-Kabūs

The approach to the Persian Steppe from Tehrān is easy. You can go by rail to Bandar Shah on the Caspian, and thence by bus to Gurgān and Gombad-i-Kabūs. Or you can make the whole journey by car. The town of Gurgān can be reached in two days of leisurely driving.

Gurgān (formerly Asterabād)—the administrative centre of the province of the same name—lies close to the border of the Turkoman country, but is not in any sense a Turkoman town. After passing through it, the highway turns north-east, enters the Persian Steppe and ends—83 miles beyond Gurgān—at the little town of Gombad-i-Kabūs. Here, at last, we were in the Turkoman country. The streets were thronged with serious, bearded, gabardined individuals wearing black sheepskin hats and talking in low voices a dialect of Turkī which was quite beyond my comprehension—schooled as I had been in the Istambuli speech.

In contrast with the sombre appearance of the men, the women flaunted gay head-dresses and crimson skirts of generous yardage. Unlike the Persian women they made no special effort to conceal their full, flat, Mongol features.

The Gombad (i.e. dome) of Kabūs—after which the town is named—is not a dome at all, but a handsome shaft of brick about 100 feet high. Le Strange, quoting the Arab geographers, states that during the tenth century, Jurjān (Gurgān) and Tabaristān (Mazanderān) were ruled by a native dynasty, the Ziyarids; and that one of their most famous princes was Kabūs, who died in A.D. 1012.

154. A Turkoman "Yurt"
The top is made of felt and the sides of matting.

He was a warrior, a patron of letters and a poet. The brick tower which was erected in his honour is hollow; and at ground level the hollow enlarges to form the tomb chamber. It is now empty; for the tomb was long since pillaged—either by the Ghūzz in the twelfth century, or by the Mongols in the thirteenth. The shaft bears an inscription in Kufic which states that it was built by Shams-ul-Maali, the Amir, son of the Emir Kabūs, son of Washingir, during his lifetime in A.H. 375 (A.D. 997).

Gombad (to call it by its more common, abbreviated name) is a little town of 5,000 people. It has the usual Pahlavian avenues—lined with trees and crossing at right angles—with the inevitable roundabout at their intersection. The built portion of the town soon fades away into open spaces, dotted irregularly with the movable *yurt* huts of the Turkomans. Here and there beyond the town and stretching far away over the brown Steppe to the horizon there are villages formed by clusters of more *yurt* huts. It would seem as if the Turkomans had accepted village life with reservations; shunning more permanent dwellings, and keeping an eye, as it were, on the wide spaces beyond; ready—if their luck should change—to pack up their felt and matting huts and return to the old, roving life of the plains.

The Yomūt Turkomans of Persia

The Yomūt are a Turkoman tribe, a part of whom live in Persia and the remainder on the east shore of the Caspian in the Turkmen Socialist Soviet Republic. In religion they are bigoted Sūnnis. That part of the tribe which lives on the Persian side of the border occupies the extreme south-western corner of the vast Turanian Steppe. Their territory is bounded on the west by the Caspian Sea, on the south by the Gurgān River and on the north by the Russian frontier. The level plain which they inhabit formed part of classical Hyrcania, later Jurjān—a province of the Eastern Caliphate. In classical times it was a highly fertile area; but the Turkomans who have occupied it for many centuries were, until recently, a race of horse breeders, forever moving their *yurt* huts from place to place in search of fresh pasture for their animals. To horse breeding they added a little marauding as a sideline. Until Riza Shah Pahlavi built his new highways and made them safe for travellers, it had been their practice to raid the Tehrān–Meshed road on their swift horses, to rob a caravan or two and a few travellers, and then ride back helter-skelter into the Steppe with their booty.[1] No gendarmes or troops had dared to follow them. For months on end the Tehrān–Meshed road was empty of traffic. Travellers to Meshed made the long detour via Enzeli (Pahlavi), Baku, Kraznovodsk and Ashkabād—rather than run the risk of the direct overland journey.

That was the situation which a monarch of the mettle of Pahlavi could not tolerate for long. As soon as his highway to Gurgān was finished he gave the Turkomans a sound walloping. When it was all over he treated them with fairness, and made a practice (to their great delight) of attending their annual horse-races in person.

Thus, for the last twenty years the Turkomans have been deprived of the profits and delights of banditry; while their noble occupation of rearing and trading horses has suffered grievously from the advent of the lorry and the car. For a time they suffered serious economic distress. During recent years, however, they have turned to agriculture and carpet weaving, and they are now somewhat better off than they were.

The Turkoman Carpets of Persia

The Turkoman carpets of the Persian Steppe are woven mainly by three tribes—the Atabaī, the Jafarbaī and the Tekkeh. Only the first two are Yomūt Turkomans; the Tekkeh are an offshoot of the important Tekkeh Turkomans of Transcaspia. Of the three, the Tekkeh are the best weavers. They emigrated into Persia from the Turkmen S.S.R. fifteen years ago and settled in Jarghalān, an area

---

[1] When on these raids they are said to have fed their horses on balls of meat and fat.

155. A TEKKEH WEAVER

about 50 miles north-west of Gombad. Their principal centre is the small town of Maravehtepeh. Most of their rugs are marketed in Bujnūrd or Qūchān and are despatched from these centres to Meshed. Their output is small: not over 500 pieces a year. Before the emigration, all the Tekkeh rugs were woven on the Russian side of the border in the neighbourhood of Ashkabād (Turkmen S.S.R.) and were exported to Meshed, where they were sold in bond to the West. Rugs are still being produced in the Turkmen S.S.R., but the market for them is no longer Meshed, but Moscow.

The next best weavers are the Atabaīs, and their production is the largest. Most of them live in Gombad-i-Kabūs itself, and in the neighbouring villages. Nearly the whole of their production is sold to traders in Gombad, who forward them to Tehrān or Meshed. About 1,200 pieces are woven annually in the town and about an equal number in the villages of the area. Thus the district of Gombad produces approximately 2,500 pieces—which is about half the total production of the Persian Steppe.

The Jafarbaī rugs and carpets are, on the whole, inferior to those of the Atabaī, and their production is smaller. Most of them are sold at the Pershembeh or Thursday Bazaar, which is held once a week at a place called Pahlavi Diz, on the Gurgān River, about 15 miles north of Gurgān. Here the Turkomans of the west Persian Steppe bring their fruits and vegetables, their chickens, their hides and skins,

their horses, their wool and their carpets and sell them to the merchants of Gurgān. The Jafarbaī also market some of their rugs at Gomshān, a small town north of Bandār Shah on the Caspian. The best time for buying from the tribes is during the month before Kurbān; for then the output is largest, as the Turkomans need money to buy clothes in preparation for the annual feast.

The Turkoman women weave their rugs with wool from their own sheep, and they spin and dye it themselves. They weave a single-wefted fabric on a loom which lies flat on the floor of their *yurt* huts. Both the warps and the wefts of their rugs are of wool.

After visiting these round, tentlike habitations I began to understand why it is unusual to find a Yomūt carpet which measures over 11 × 8 feet: there is no room on the circular floor to weave larger pieces. Indeed, so much of the tent was occupied by the horizontal loom that I wondered how the family found space to eat and sleep, and how the women contrived to discharge their household tasks —meagre as they were.

Their horizontal looms are similar to those in use by most of the nomadic and semi-nomadic tribes of Kurdistān, Lūristān, Kermān and Fārs. This type of loom and its operation has been described on pp. 22–24.

The native dyestuffs which were for centuries the basic colours of the family of the red rugs of Transcaspia were madder and (in a lesser degree) *kermes*, an insect dye closely allied to cochineal[1]—both of which are found in Transcaspia. Reference has already been made to the sad fact that these dyestuffs, which have made the red rugs famous throughout the world, have been replaced in the Persian Steppe (as they were long ago replaced in the so-called Bokhara rugs) by synthetic reds. The war put an end to the importation of the German synthetic red, Dianil. As long as the stock lasted, it was preferred by the Yomūt Turkomans to Rouge d'Orient—its Swiss counterpart. But as the stock of Dianil became exhausted, the Swiss product gradually replaced it, and now holds the field. Unhappily, however, the Turkoman weavers—who have always been in the habit of dyeing their own yarns—are unfamiliar with the technique required to produce the best results with synthetic dyestuffs. It is to be feared, therefore,

---

[1] "This is one of the Scale Insects, which in various forms, chiefly deleterious, are of very great importance. It is *Coccus ilicis*, or *Kermes ilicis*, which infests the stunted oak, *Quercus cocciferus*, so common in the Mediterranean district. . . . The female insect assumes the form of a sort of gall, and it was only in 1714 that its animal nature was discovered. In the spring, when they are full of reddish juice, the galls are collected, dried, made into a paste with vinegar, and exported under the name pâté d'Ecarlate. This was the red dye of antiquity, *granum tinctorium*. The name *kermes* is said to have come from Persia, and it is the origin of our word crimson."—Malcolm Burr, D.Sc., F.R.Ent.S., etc., *The Insect Legion*.

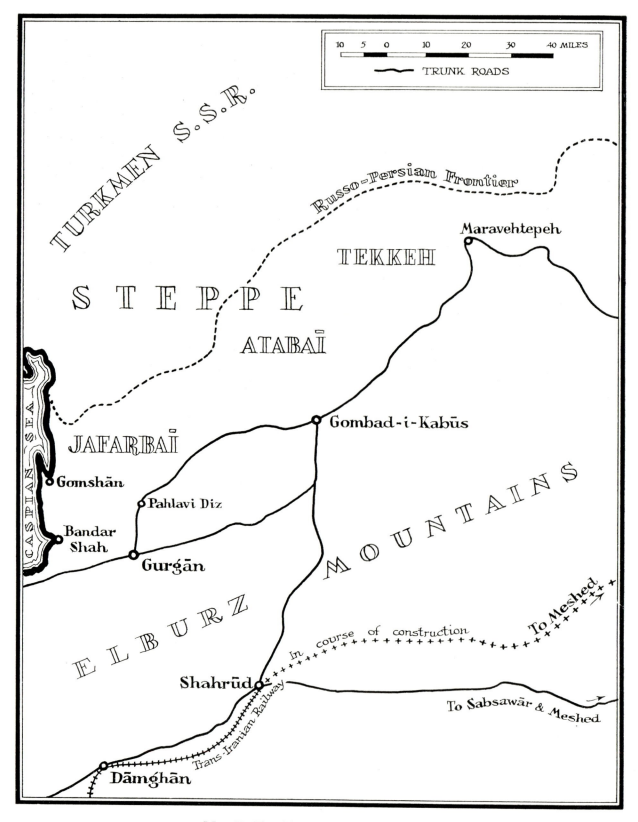

Map V. The Turkoman Weaving Area

156. Yomūt Rug: Old Style

157. Yomūt Rug: New Style

that the dyeing of the Yomūt rugs of the Persian Steppe may be, in many cases, defective. In any event, the new pieces will not acquire, with the passage of time, that depth of colour, that softness and that glow which is possessed by the older Yomūt rugs.

Until recently the Yomūt weavers possessed a few designs of their own (Plate 156) which they wove on dark, plum-coloured grounds—an unmistakable characteristic of their carpets. Since the war, however, the carpets which are woven on the Persian side of the border have undergone a sudden and unhappy change. The characteristic Yomūt designs on plum-coloured grounds have been almost abandoned; and today most of the tribes are weaving the well-known Bokhara pattern on a red ground. The reason for this is simple: during the war the production of the so-called Bokhara rugs and carpets (most of which are woven in the Merv Oasis) declined considerably. As soon as the war was over, there was a keen demand for them; but the price was so high that traders began to look about for a substitute. The Yomūt Turkomans were already familiar with the design, and they were encouraged to weave more of it on red grounds—for which the merchants provided the dyestuff.

I was astonished to find that the chaffering for rugs in the remote, outlandish Steppe is conducted on a square foot basis. Thus, when a stolid, bearded Turkoman spread his rug on the floor of the shop of my friend Mahmūd Noberī, that astute Tabrīzi measured it in feet and then explored a tattered copy of Trickey's *Table of Square Measurements* to find the area, which he communicated correctly to the vendor; and then the bargaining began.

Besides their carpets and rugs, the Turkomans of the Persian Steppe weave handsome *gilims*, on dark red grounds, with small, repeating geometrical patterns in dark blue, maroon, cream, tan and white. They usually measure about 10 × 7 feet.

CHAPTER XI

MESHED, THE QAINĀT AND TURSHĪZ (KASHMĀR)

MESHED

The City of Meshed[1]

Meshed, the capital of Khūrasān, is not an ancient city as Persian cities go. It owes its renown to the fact that it is the burial-place of Ali-al-Riza (died A.D. 818), the eighth of the twelve Imams (commonly known in Persia as Imam Riza); and of the famous Harūn-al-Rashīd, Caliph of Baghdad. The two men died within ten years of each other in a garden about 15 miles south of Tūs—then the second largest city in that part of Khūrasān. The tomb of the venerated Imam (who was also Caliph designate) became at once a sanctuary and a place of pilgrimage. Around it gradually grew the city of Meshed; while nearby Tūs was abandoned after it had been sacked by one of Timūr's (Tamerlane's) sons in A.D. 1389. Its dismal ruins may still be seen to the north of Meshed, close to the Ashkabād road.

As the capital of an important district, Meshed was involved in most of the east Persian campaigns of the Seljūk sultans—who ruled in Ghazni in the eleventh and twelfth centuries—and in those of the Mongols and Timūrid sultans. During the reign of Shah Rūkh, the most illustrious of Timūr's sons—who restored many of the Persian cities which his forerunners had destroyed—Meshed was enlarged and beautified. His wife, Jawār Shādh, was its greatest benefactor, for she built the noble mosque which has immortalised her name. During the sixteenth century the city was taken and sacked many times; even the sacred Shrine was not always respected by its Moslem conquerors. The worst offenders appear to have been the Uzbegs, who raided the district repeatedly during the reign of Shah Tahmasp—while the young Prince Abbas (afterwards Shah Abbas) was the nominal governor. The Uzbegs finally captured and sacked the city in 1589, two years after Shah Abbas had been proclaimed king in Kazvīn. It took him nine years to recover it.

Situated as it was near the eastern frontier of Persia, Meshed was one of the first towns to fall before the Afghan invasions of 1721. But Nadir Kuli (afterwards Nadir Shah)—himself a native of the district—retook it for the Sefavi monarch, Tahmasp II, five years later.

In 1736 Nadir was proclaimed Shah of Persia. He made Meshed his capital, and during his reign of eleven years the city reached its zenith. It then possessed a population of a quarter of a million, and became a great emporium and trading centre.

After the death of Nadir Shah the unhappy city was again taken by the Afghans and it remained an Afghan fief until it was retaken and restored to Persia in 1795 by Aga Mohammed Shah, the first Qajār prince. It was recaptured by the Afghans after his death; but was finally wrested from them by Fath Ali Shah in 1803. Thereafter, except for occasional raids by Turkoman tribes of the border, Meshed enjoyed a measure of tranquillity; until, in 1912, its peace was senselessly disturbed by the bombardment of the Shrine by the Russians—for the avowed purpose of overawing the inhabitants. No great damage was done, but the cynical action made a profound impression on the Moslem world.

If I were asked to name the city which I liked best in Persia, I should answer, without hesitation, Isfahān. But after Isfahān, I would place Meshed. Its climate is less rigorous in winter than that of Hamadān or Tabrīz and less oppressive in summer than that of Shirāz or Isfahān. Unlike Tehrān, it possesses a character of its own, with no Western veneer. It contains the incomparable buildings of the Shrine enclosure, and many notable mosques, sacred colleges and caravanserais, and it possesses a museum in which the unique Shrine Collection of oriental art is beautifully housed and displayed. The recent improvements in the layout of the city are sensible and have preserved much of its old charm. In the Paīn Khiaban—the eastern half of the broad avenue which bisects the city—the visitor can study a greater variety of physiognomies and costumes than in any other street in Persia. I was happy to note that the medley of battered European hats—which Shah Riza had stupidly compelled the villagers of Khūrasān to wear—were being discarded;

---

[1] Al-Māshād, a sepulchral chapel, primarily of a martyr of the family of the prophet. Le Strange defines it as "a place of martyrdom".

An unusual and attractive Meshed Carpet woven c. 1910.

Facing page 160

and that the people were resuming their picturesque white turbans. Turning to more mundane excellencies, I affirm that the melons, grapes, peaches and partridges of Meshed are without rival in Persia.

A variety of crafts are practised in the town, and much of the workmanship is admirable. In Tehrān, if an article is wanted, catalogues are ransacked and in due course it is ordered from abroad. In Meshed a craftsman is called in; and in a few days he will produce, as likely as not, a serviceable answer to the need. But best of all, in a country where to be gracious is regarded as one of the primary arts of life, the kindliness and hospitality of the people of Meshed are outstanding.

When the railway reaches the city, and when the shops which at present obscure the sacred Shrine are removed and the area is laid out as a garden (which is what the Shrine officials plan to do), Meshed will doubtless become a place of pilgrimage, not only for pious Moslems, but also for many thousands who will wish to pay homage to its majestic monuments for their own sake.

The Shrine of Imam Riza

The sacred area in Meshed—which is known as the Bāst or Sanctuary[1]—lies across the wide central avenue which bisects the city in a straight line. The avenue is called "Bala" and "Paīn" Khiaban—the Upper and Lower Avenue—and it was built by Shah Abbas in the sixteenth century. The sacred area, which measures about 300 × 250 yards, is like a town within a town. It is surrounded by a broad circular road, and contains mosques, courtyards, colleges, caravanserais, baths, shops and dwellings.

The area is the absolute property of the late Imam himself—if, indeed, a person, however estimable, who has been dead a thousand years, can be said to possess an estate. The Persians, who should know, maintain that he can. In which case he must be the wealthiest person in Persia. For his estate includes not only the priceless buildings and treasures of the sacred area, but properties in almost every part of the country. To these capital assets must be added the pious and infallible revenues arising out of gifts from unending processions of visionary pilgrims; and fees for ceremonies, funerals and tombs. The goodly and widespread estate is administered in the name of the Imam by an ecclesiastical body, at the head of which is the Mutevelli Bashi, who is one of the most important officials in the country. The appointment is made by the Shah himself and its incumbent is responsible to the Shah alone. Strange as it may appear, the present incumbent is an old Harrovian and a Cambridge graduate. He has twice been Minister of Finance and is one of Persia's most distinguished statesmen.

The sacred area contains a number of notable buildings. In the centre rises the gilded dome of the mausoleum. To the north of it is the great rectangular courtyard known as Sahn-i-Kohneh or Old Court; to the east the Sahn-i-Nō, or New Court, built by Fath Ali Shah in 1808; and to the south lie the extensive buildings of the Mosque of Jawār Shādh. Historically the most important is the mausoleum, raised by the piety of princes round the Tomb Chamber. For many centuries the sight of the gilded dome of Shah Abbas,[2] burning in the distant haze, has brought comfort to millions of pilgrims hurrying forward on the last lap of their dolorous journey.

The Tomb Chamber itself is believed to be the original mausoleum built by the Caliph Mamūn over the remains of his father, Harūn-al-Rashīd. A few years after the entombment of the Caliph, the eighth Imam, Ali-al-Riza, was also buried there.[3] The mausoleum was restored and embellished by Mahmūd of Ghazni and by Sultan Sanjār in the twelfth century; and again two centuries later by the Mongol Sultan Uljaitu Khodabanda. Jawār Shādh, the pious wife of Shah Rūkh, built the fine hall and the adjoining chamber west of the tomb. Under the Sefavis more magnificent buildings and embellishments were added. Shah Tahmasp erected a minaret of which the upper part is covered with gold, and Shah Abbas two towers, 100 feet high. The Emperor Akbar the Great of India—who made a pilgrimage to Meshed in 1695—brought important gifts to the Shrine.

One of its greatest benefactors was the Sūnni and ex-robber monarch, Nadir Shah, who made Meshed his capital and devoted a considerable part of the loot which he brought back from his Indian campaigns to its embellishment.[4] He decorated the southern gateway of the Sahn-i-Kohneh with gold. He also erected a second golden minaret to match the minaret of Shah Tahmasp.

---

[1] From *bastan*, to enclose.
[2] Shah Abbas made the pilgrimage from Isfahān on foot and ordered the dome to be built out of his personal funds. The inscription round its base is by Riza Abbasi, the famous painter and calligrapher.
[3] There is no longer any trace of Harūn-al-Rashīd's grave.
[4] Nadir Shah built himself a magnificent mausoleum in the city, which was destroyed after his death. The memorial building in the Bagh-i-Nadiri is modern.

158. COURTYARD BEFORE THE TOMB CHAMBER
The tomb of the Imam Ali Riza lies under the gilded dome in the upper right-hand corner.

But the noblest building in the sacred enclosure is the Mosque of Jawār Shādh (pronounced locally Gauhār Shādh). This pious lady was the wife of the first and greatest of the Timūrid sultans, Shah Rūkh. The mosque which bears her name is one of the supreme achievements of Mongol architecture. Sir P. M. Sykes has described it as the noblest building in Central Asia—superior to the sacred colleges of Samarkānd.

Meshed is the most important among the places of pilgrimage in Persia, and sixth or seventh in importance among the shrines of the Moslem world. Every pious Shi'a longs to be buried in the vicinity of one of these shrines, and for the Persians Meshed takes precedence over every other. It has been affirmed, indeed, that a pilgrimage to Meshed is as meritorious as eighty pilgrimages to Mecca. Thousands of corpses are brought every year for entombment in the vast cemeteries which surround the town; but the demand for space is such that the bodies are removed every few years to make room for newcomers.

The number of pilgrims who visit the Shrine averages about 120,000 annually. Each pilgrim has to conform to a special ritual which includes three circumambulations of the tomb and the cursing three times of all the enemies of the Imam—with special curses for the Caliph Harūn-al-Rashīd and his son, the Caliph Mamūn.[1] Every Moslem who performs the pilgrimage is entitled to call himself Meshedi, i.e. of Meshed. The title, however, is often used as an honorific in polite conversation.

Meshed is renowned for its religious colleges, of which it possesses no less than twenty. Architecturally the most important is the Madrasseh-i-Mirza Jaffar, which was built in 1650 by a rich Persian of that name. It is regarded as the finest building outside the Shrine enclosure.

The present population of Meshed (excluding the floating population of pilgrims) is about 175,000.

[1] P. M. Sykes, *The Glory of the Shi'ah World*, a valuable and amusing book which every visitor to Meshed should read.

159. PORTICO LEADING TO THE TOMB CHAMBER WHERE THE IMAM ALI RIZA IS BURIED

The Persian Shi'as constitute probably 90 per cent of the people—about a fifth of whom are Turkish speaking. In addition, there are considerable numbers of Afghans, including Huzaras—a Sūnni tribe from western Afghanistān with marked Mongol characteristics—Turkomans, Indians and Jews. The latter are an interesting minority. They were settled there by Nadir Shah, who transplanted them from Kazvīn. In 1839, following an accusation by the Shi'as of sacrilege, the Jewish quarter was plundered. Many Jews were murdered and their synagogue was destroyed. The rest were forcibly converted to Islām. They have since been known as Jadids, or Newcomers. Although they conform outwardly to the prescriptions of the Moslem faith, it is doubtful if even the Shi'as regard them as true believers. They form an able and industrious community of traders. Among them are a number of carpet merchants of standing who have branches in London and Istanbul.

The Early Carpets of Eastern Persia

We have already remarked (Chapter II) how meagre and unsatisfying is the information which we possess regarding the period carpets which were woven west of the Great Desert which divides Persia from north to south. We have not yet been able to determine precisely when or where most of these carpets were made. Although our attempts to answer these questions are based upon a considerable volume of research, they are, at best, only guesses.

This is true also—and to an even greater degree—of those early carpets which are attributed to localities east of the Great Desert. Because—except for a particular type of so-called Herāt carpet—we do not know for certain that they were woven in those localities at all. It is, however, unlikely that in such centres of culture as Herāt or Meshed—which produced painters and calligraphers of renown—the kindred art of carpet weaving should have been entirely neglected.

The great Seljūk sultans who reigned in Ghazni in the eleventh and part of the twelfth centuries, and who gathered round them the foremost painters, architects and calligraphers of the age, failed to appreciate the possibilities which lay in the development of the weaver's craft. And the succeeding two centuries were periods of turmoil and destruction. It was not until the reign of the enlightened Shah Rūkh (1408-1456)—who did his best to rebuild and restore the Persian cities which had been destroyed by his forerunners, Jenghiz Khan, Hulagū and Timūr—that a condition of society arose propitious to the development of a new art.

There is no evidence, however, that Shah Rūkh established a royal factory in Herāt, his capital. Yet, judging from the reports of travellers and the evidence from contemporary miniatures, he may have patronised and encouraged the master-weavers of the realm. Their carpets—some of which are depicted on contemporary miniatures—were rectilinear in design; an indication that the art had not yet progressed very far.

None of these carpets has come down to us. We do, however, possess a later group of carpets with characteristics of texture, colour and design which recall the Khūrasān carpets of today, and which were probably woven in east Persia during or immediately after the Sefavi period.

A distinctive characteristic of these east Persian carpets was the use of "lac" or cochineal (instead of madder) for dyeing the reds. This technique has persisted down the centuries; for to this day in Meshed, Birjānd and Kermān the reds are dyed, almost exclusively, with cochineal—madder being used merely as an auxiliary. Conversely, in west and south-west Persia, i.e. in Tabrīz, Herīz, Hamadān, Arāk, Kashān, Qūm, Isfahān and Fārs, the reds are dyed almost exclusively with madder and cochineal is hardly used at all.

So far as I know, this striking difference in the method of dyeing red has never been turned to account in exploring into the origins of period carpets. May I suggest that the directors of our museums institute research on these lines? A few knots of red yarn extracted from a carpet can easily be tested for cochineal (or "lac") on the one hand, or madder on the other. The result of such a test would be of assistance in determining whether the carpet was woven in eastern or western Persia.

It is generally accepted in the West that these "east Persian" carpets were woven in Herāt—at that time the administrative capital and principal city of Khūrasān. We may, however, properly question the claim of Herāt city to these carpets; because, as far back as men can remember, no carpets have been woven there; nor does any tradition of weaving exist there. And I know of no locality in Persia where carpets were once produced and which today is producing none.

I suggest, moreover, that because the Persians used the name Herāt in referring to some of these carpets, they did not necessarily mean that the carpets were woven in Herāt city; for (as I have had occasion to point out in Chapter V) Persians are in the habit of describing the products of a province by the name of its capital. Thus, they invariably refer to the tribal rugs of Fārs as Shirāz rugs, although no rugs are woven in Shirāz. It may well be, therefore, that the word Herāt—as applied to the period carpets of east Persia—was used in its broader sense, meaning the province (Khūrasān) of which Herāt was then the capital. In that case, these carpets may have been woven in another locality, or perhaps in several different localities, in Khūrasān.

I would suggest, further, that if—during the sixteenth century or later—great carpets had been produced in Herāt, some vestiges of that craftsmanship would appear in the carpets which have since been produced in Afghanistān. If not whole designs, some motives would have survived. Yet there is no trace whatever of Persian influence in any of the carpets of Afghanistān today. And I suggest that as the carpets of Afghanistān do not possess the imprint of the sixteenth century (which exists in practically every Persian carpet) it is because the prototypes were never produced as far east as Herāt.

Perhaps what happened was something like this: the wealthy inhabitants of Herāt—the capital of Khūrasān and its richest and most important city—must have needed carpets for their homes. So the merchants of the city ordered them from the weaving districts of the Qaināt. When, in time, some of these carpets were sold by their owners and found their way to the West, they were called Herāt carpets, because they had come from Herāt; and not because they had been woven there.

If then it be accepted that the so-called Herāt carpets were not woven in Herāt, where were they woven?

The carpets of the sixteenth, seventeenth and early eighteenth centuries which have been generally attributed to east Persia fall into three main groups:

(a) Carpets in the Herātī design.
(b) Carpets introducing the *islim* or snake *motif*, i.e. spiral curves.
(c) Certain *shikarga* (hunting carpets) or animal and floral carpets.

(a) All Western authorities are agreed (and the Persians who have given serious thought to the matter would support them) that certain unmistakable types of carpets in the Herātī design, woven probably in the early eighteenth century, on dark blue or dark red grounds; generally in dark tones with all their colours harmonised by age; closely woven; with an exceedingly soft velvety pile and a natural sheen; usually, but not always, possessing guards in light yellow—were produced in east Persia. Long before Western scholars began to attribute other types to the same area, these pieces were known in Persia and the West as Herāt carpets.

Thirty to forty years ago long and narrow Khūrasān *kellegis* in the Herātī design—which bore a strong family resemblance to the so-called Herāt carpets described in the preceding paragraph—were fairly common. They were coarser in quality; but they had the same type of Herātī pattern, they were similar in colour and they had the same light yellow guards. The less scrupulous dealers used to call them Herāts and raised the price accordingly. They were woven, without any doubt, in the Qaināt. I suggest that the so-called Herāt carpets of an earlier period (in the Herātī design) were not woven in Herāt city but were the forerunners of the nineteenth-century Qain *kellegis* and were woven in the Qaināt.

(b) The early carpets in the *islimi* type of design, with large sweeping spirals, possessed no marks of kinship with the carpets of the Herātī type. Unlike those pieces—which might have been woven in

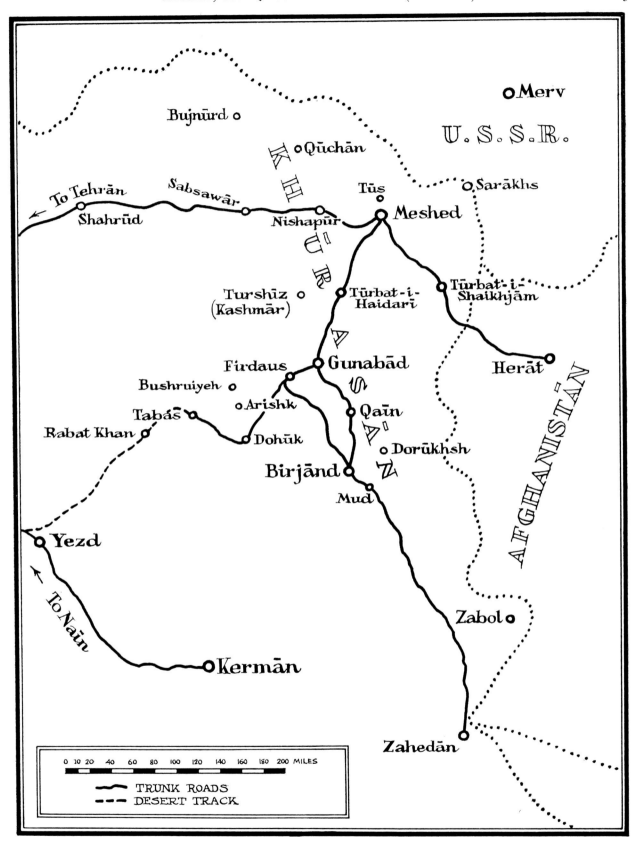

Map VI. Eastern Persia

any village of the Qaināt—the *islimi* type of carpet is a town fabric and must have been woven under the control of a master-weaver. No villager could carry out this type of design correctly (see p. 168).

A fine example of this design in a sixteenth-century carpet is the *pièce de résistance* of the Shrine Museum in Meshed.[1] The carpet is said to have been woven in the city itself. I enquired from the Treasurer of the Shrine whether this statement was supported by documentary evidence. He informed me that a catalogue of the possessions of the Shrine had been prepared about twenty-five years ago, and that it was there stated that the carpet had been woven in Meshed by the order of Shah Abbas, for the Shrine. The statement, he added, was based on tradition and had been confirmed by the opinion of experts; there was, however, no documentary evidence to prove it. It may be stated, in support of the accuracy of the entry in the catalogue, that the *islimi* type of design is traditional in Meshed. Indeed, there is hardly a factory in the city without a carpet or two on loom in a design of this general character (Plate 172). It might well be, therefore, that the prototypes of this *islimi* style of carpet were woven in the seventeenth century in the city of Meshed. And yet—if they were—it must follow that the industry expired very soon after. Perhaps the Afghan invasion of 1721 put an end to it. For I am not aware that carpets were produced in Meshed between the end of the Sefavi period and the end of the nineteenth century. If carpets had been woven there during those 180 years, surely the Shrine would possess a few today. Yet the oldest Meshed carpet in its possession is dated, and it is not more than eighty years old. Moreover, I was informed by the most respectable of the Meshed dyers that his grandfather (who had been a dyer in Kashmir) had emigrated to Meshed about 1860 and had settled there; and that when he had arrived in Meshed the carpet-weaving industry did not exist. It started, in fact, in the late nineteenth century. I well remember, in 1899–1900, the early arrivals in Istanbul of the new Meshed carpets, produced for export. Before that time shipments from east Persia had consisted almost exclusively of old long-and-narrow pieces from the Qaināt.

(c) Of those authorities who have attributed to "east Persia" some of the most famous carpets in the world—such as the animal and floral carpet of the Austrian Museum described on p. 13—few have ventured to suggest where in that vast area they were woven. Yet they were undoubtedly woven in a city (see pp. 27–8), and the only two possible cities were Herāt or Meshed. I have ventured to cast a doubt upon Herāt; that leaves Meshed as a probable—if, indeed, these carpets were woven in east Persia at all.

All of which goes to show—as stated in a previous discussion of this subject (Chapter II)—that we are not certain when or where these Sefavi carpets were woven. I fear that we must leave it at that.

Meshed as a Carpet Centre

Meshed was formerly of greater importance as a carpet centre than it is today. The reasons for its relative decline are patent: the first is the closing of the European markets on which Meshed almost exclusively depended (because America—the other important market—was only mildly interested in Meshed carpets, and not at all interested in carpets from the Qaināt). The second reason is to be found in the Meshed carpet itself. That will be examined below (p. 169).

Meshed is the principal distributing centre for all the varied weaves of eastern Persia. These include (1) the two qualities of Meshed carpets—the Farsibaff and the Turkibaff—which are woven in the city, in its suburbs and in a few neighbouring villages; (2) the carpets from Birjānd, the Qaināt and Turshīz (Kashmār); (3) the Balūchi tribal rugs of Khūrasān and Seistān; and (in a lesser degree) (4) the Yomūt rugs of the Persian Steppe. The present chapter will be devoted to a survey of carpet manufacture in Meshed itself, the Qaināt and Turshīz. The Balūchi tribal rugs will be considered in Chapter XII which follows. The Yomūt weaves have already been dealt with in Chapter X.

The Meshed Carpet

Northern Khūrasān is one of the principal wool-producing areas of Persia. In normal times, indeed, wool is an important export to Russia and the West. The best wool comes from Tūrbat-i-Haidarī, where the grazing is superior to that in other areas of the northern province. Good wool is also produced in the Nīshapūr, Sabsawār and Qūchan areas and in the neighbourhood of Meshed itself.

The sheep in northern Khūrasān are clipped twice a year—in May and again in mid-September. The spring clip is strong, lofty and long in staple; the autumn clip is softer and the fibre is much shorter. Unhappily, the yarns which the master-weavers of

---

[1] See p. 169 for a description of this carpet.

Meshed use in their carpets are spun from autumn-clip wools. This is not done on the score of cheapness—as the autumn clip is often the more costly of the two. It is done, firstly, because the master-weavers believe (quite wrongly) that soft wool produces a better carpet than hard; and, secondly, because the problem of carding has not yet been adequately solved in Meshed. Until quite recently there was no carding plant in the city; and as carding by hand is a slow and tedious process, the wool is carded with the bow—a technique which is usually employed in the East for carding cotton. The carder holds the bow—which is about 5 feet long—in his left hand and plucks the bowstring with an instrument like a pestle. When the vibrating bowstring comes into contact with the cotton (or wool) it causes it to "fluff." Only autumn-clipped wools of short staple can be thus carded; because the long fibres of the spring clip curl round the bowstring. I have seen a carder in Meshed deliberately cut long staple wools in two with scissors, to enable him to operate his bow! It is to be hoped that the master-weavers will make use of the carding plant which has recently been set up in Meshed, and feed it with spring-clip wools. Long-established customs, however, die hard in Persia and the prejudices of technicians die harder.

It is this use of autumn-clip wools which is the source of the widespread legend that the wools of Khūrasān are "soft", and that in consequence Meshed carpets do not give adequate service. That many of them have not given proper service in the past is notorious; but the autumn wool used in their manufacture is only one of the contributing causes. There are two other practices, far more pernicious:

The first has to do with the dyeing of the yarns. The Meshed dyers apparently believe that they cannot obtain an even shade with cochineal red unless they steep the yarn in lime for 24 hours before dyeing. This pernicious practice greatly weakens the red yarn, which is largely used for the grounds of Meshed carpets.

The second is the use of the *jūftī* knot. This practice, however, is confined to the Farsibaff weave, as explained below.

There are two systems of weaving in common use in Meshed: (*a*) the Farsibaff, or Persian weave, and (*b*) the Turkibaff or Turkish weave. The former outnumbers the latter by about three to one. Meshed is the only weaving centre of Persia where both systems are in use—sometimes on different looms in the same factory.

(*a*) *The Farsibaff weave.* This quality is woven with the Persian knot, as its name implies; but the knot is the fraudulent variety (see p. 26). I have had occasion earlier in this book to deplore the steady increase in many weaving districts of Persia of the use of the *jūftī* knot, which is tied on four strings of the warp instead of two. By that method, only half the number of knots are tied to a given number of warp strings than would be tied by the ordinary method; accordingly the resultant fabric possesses only half its proper density and does not, in consequence, stand up to hard wear (see p. 27). This system was not, in Meshed, a malpractice recently adopted by the weaver for personal gain at the expense of the quality of the product. It was one of the two standard methods of weaving which have been in use there since the industry was established at the end of the nineteenth century.[1]

Thus the Farsibaff Meshed carpet suffered from three weaknesses—it was made with yarn spun from autumn wool; its principal ground colour was dyed after the yarn had been steeped in lime for 24 hours; and it was woven with the *jūftī* knot. It is not surprising, therefore, that such a carpet gave inadequate service.

I arrived in Meshed in the autumn of 1948 having in mind these shortcomings. I feared that the general retrogradation of carpet weaving which had followed the war, operating upon an already defective fabric, would have resulted in a further debasement of the Meshed weave. But in Persia the unexpected happens. I found, to my surprise and satisfaction, that during the war the principal master-weavers of Meshed—realising, at last, that there was something seriously wrong with their fabric—had determined to set it right. They had been able to reduce, though not to eliminate, the *jūftī* knot; and they had prevailed upon a few of their dyers to abandon the foolish practice of steeping their yarns in lime. Thus the infirmities of the Meshed carpet are being treated; and in its old age it has become a more honest fabric than it used to be. I visited many factories in the city and suburbs and was pleased to find that the carpets which I saw on the looms were, on the whole, properly constructed.

It could not be expected that a revolution of this kind, in a long-established industry, would be completely effective. The *jūftī* knot was still surreptitiously inserted by the less responsible factory

---

[1] The weavers may have been brought to Meshed from the Qaināt where the *jūftī* knot already existed.

weavers; and it is, no doubt, common in the carpets which are woven singly in the houses. That could hardly be avoided. But the fact remains that the old *jūftī* Farsibaff fabric is no longer an openly admitted standard quality in Meshed.

This fabric was constructed differently from any other Persian weave. Thin wefts were passed above the first and second rows of knots, and thick wefts above the third; and then the operation was repeated. This produced the characteristic back of the old Meshed carpets. The Farsibaff fabric of today, however, is a double-wefted fabric throughout—similar to the weaves of Arāk, Kashān and other areas where the Persian knot is used.

(*b*) *The Turkibaff weave*. The Turkibaff weave[1] is not indigenous to Meshed. It was introduced there by the Tabrīz merchants who established looms in the city and began to weave carpets for export some fifty years ago. Being Turks, the Tabrīzis introduced the Turkish knot. Hence the name Turki-baff, i.e. Turkish weave. The weavers of the Turkibaff quality, like the weavers of Tabrīz, tie the knot to the warp with a hook (p. 24), and are therefore unable to tie a *jūftī* knot—even if they wished to—because the hook can only deal with two strings of the warp at a time. (The Farsibaff, on the other hand, is knotted with the fingers so that the weaver can tie the *jūftī* knot on four strings of the warp.) In both fabrics the same thickness of millspun cotton yarn is used for the warp. For the thick weft handspun yarn, made from low quality cotton, is used. It is much thicker than that generally used in Persia for the purpose and is unevenly twisted and dyed grey. The thin weft is machine spun and hardly thicker than pack thread. It is dyed blue.

Most of the weaving in Meshed and in nearby villages is carried on in factories of from six to forty looms. There are sixteen such factories in the town and half as many more outside. The factories are owned by master-weavers who either sell their carpets in the bazaar or weave against orders. In addition to the factories there are about 300 individual looms in the houses. The carpets which are woven on these looms are generally inferior to those produced in factories under the eye of a master-weaver. Altogether there are about 700 looms in Meshed itself and about half as many more in the villages. Between the wars there were three times as many—an index of the decline which has taken place in the carpet industry of eastern Persia since 1939.

When I revisited Meshed in 1948 the general standard of design and workmanship was unworthy of the renown of the city as a weaving centre. Most of the designs lacked refinement and originality. The draftsmanship was poor. There were scores of carpets with grounds of cochineal red and with clumsy medallions, borders and corners in dark blue. The weaving, too, in some of the factories was none too good. Errors were frequent. The selvedges on either side were coarsely woven.

The master-weavers of Meshed usually dye their own yarns; whereas the smaller men, who operate one or two looms, give their yarns to be dyed by the town dyers. Although the dyes employed are generally good, the dyers lack invention; for the ground shade of nearly every carpet is deep cochineal red, and in every carpet the same dozen secondary colours appear. The dyers of Meshed are sadly in need of outside instruction and guidance.

Cochineal red[2]—the characteristic colour of the Meshed carpet—is one of the most interesting and valuable resources of the Persian dyer. In the hands of skilled technicians—like the dyers of Kermān—a variety of fine shades can be obtained from it, either directly or by combination with madder, weld and other Persian dyewares. The Meshed dyers, however, are unable or unwilling to make full use of its varied qualities.

Why, I asked myself, do the master-weavers of Meshed use practically nothing but cochineal red—a shade which is difficult to furnish to—for the grounds of their carpets?

This is a question which cannot be readily or surely answered. Why do the Dutch and the French, the Italians and the British paint differently? It is, presumably, because someone in each country started to paint in a certain way; and people liked his manner and asked for more of it; so that his *atelier* became popular; and before long many young painters were learning to paint like the master. Perhaps, in the same way, a master-weaver of Meshed produced a fine red carpet with cochineal; and other weavers liked it and copied it. And so, perhaps, the Meshed school of cochineal red carpets was born.

The blues in Meshed carpets are dyed with indigo (although I noticed that in a few factories a virulent synthetic medium blue from Switzerland was being used); the greens with indigo on vine-leaf yellow;

---

[1] This quality is sometimes called in America "Isfahān".
[2] For a full description of this dyestuff, see Chapter IV, "The Craft of the Dyer", p. 29.

the browns and camels with walnut husks; the yellows with vine leaves or weld (a local product) with the addition of a little madder; the light and dark copper reds with madder; and the pinks with cochineal. The worst colour in common use in Meshed is a greenish mustard—the basis of which is pomegranate rind.

Thus the verdict on the Meshed carpet of 1948 must be, I fear, on the whole, unfavourable. In most of the factories the standard of craftsmanship was low; and there was a lack of variety in design and colour. Had the master-weavers of the previous generation—men like Mehmelbaff, Emogli and Khamenei—been present in 1948, they would have had something to say about the carpets which were being produced. Emogli might have recommended the weavers of today to view a carpet which he had woven for a rich merchant, Kuzekenani, some twenty years before; and to ponder, in the light of that carpet, their present handiwork.

For the Kuzekenani carpet is, indeed, a marvel of craftsmanship. During the last fifty years I have seen proud carpets in every part of Persia and the West. But this carpet—woven by Emogli in Meshed—was among the best modern carpets that I had seen. Plate 164 renders feebly its beauties and fails utterly to reveal the high technique which was exercised in its production. The design of both the ground and border was of the very essence of refinement. The *islimis* or spirals—which are so often tiresomely salient in Meshed carpets—were just prominent enough. The larger motives were just sufficiently large to impress, but not to overpower; and the smaller details—distinct and beautifully drawn—constituted a pleasing background for them. Everything was in balance. The dark blue of the ground, the red of the border, and all the secondary colours were clean and clear and made a perfect harmony. Not a shade stood out, pretentiously, above the rest. I was not carrying a magnifying glass, so that I was unable to count the knots; but as near as I could judge the carpet counted from 30 to 33 knots each way to the inch—which meant about 1,000 knots to the square inch. The carpet measured 13.6 × 8.3 feet.

To my very mild protestations at the failure of the weavers of today to maintain the standard of their fathers, I invariably receive the same answer: "The only market which we have left is Tehrān; and in Tehrān they want cheap carpets like these. If we had the orders for finer pieces we would make them."

With the principal European markets (except Switzerland) closed, what orders could they expect to receive? Kermān, Arāk and Hamadān were being kept alive by America; but America had long since turned her back on Meshed. I fear, therefore, that the Meshed weavers, like those of Tabrīz, must continue in the doldrums until western Europe is once more on the road to recovery.

The Shrine Collection

During my stay in Meshed I had the good fortune to be invited by the authorities of the Shrine to examine and report upon a collection of carpets and rugs which had been lying, almost forgotten, in one of their stores. These pieces had been presented to the Shrine by devout Moslems in times past; and many of them had been used to cover the floors of the buildings within the sacred enclosure. Unhappily, they had been kept in use too long and no officer had ever been detailed to look after them. Some were in fragments. From most of them the nap had long since disappeared. In this condition they had been left—decade after decade. There were many pieces of ungainly size—as 40 × 12 feet or 36 × 10 feet. And there were quite a number which had been cut in two, lengthwise, for use as curtains.

An unusual feature of the collection was the number of pieces bearing inscriptions. Some of them were dated, some bore the name of the donor, or the names of both the donor and the weaver. Some were inscribed with the name of the reigning Shah or the Mutevelli Bashi of the time—which fixed the date of the carpet. There is no collection of Persian carpets in the world which contains so many inscribed pieces.

The collection contains only one Sefavi carpet, to which reference has been made on p. 166. It measures 16 × 11 feet. The ground is *laqi* red and the border indigo blue. The flower stalks, the leaves, the cloud-bands and the centres of some of the floral motives are in silver or silver gilt. The inner guard is also in silver. The design is a fine example of the *islimi* type of the Sefavi period. The carpet has been wonderfully preserved and is practically intact, except for a tear in one corner.

It may well be that other carpets of the great period were presented to the Shrine. If so they have been carried away or destroyed by the Turkomans or Uzbegs; because the Shrine possesses no other Persian carpets over 150 years old. It does, however, possess two outstanding pieces which, I believe, were woven in Lahore in the late seventeenth century; for they closely resemble in colour, texture and design other Lahore carpets in collections abroad. Both pieces have red grounds and blue borders. The pile of both is intact, but both pieces are badly torn in many places and the guards are missing.

Next in importance to the two Lahore carpets are three very interesting Ravār Kermān carpets. All three are badly worn. One is almost intact, the others are in pieces. One of the three is clearly dated: 1286 of the lunar year, which would make the carpet seventy-one years old. The date is important, because this carpet is one of the very few Kermāns of the period which bears a date. It will enable us to date other early Ravār Kermāns of the same general style (Plate) 199.

Important as the carpets above mentioned are, the great value of the collection lies in the number of early nineteenth-century pieces from Khūrasān which it includes. I was able to set aside about seventy pieces which are worthy of being preserved. Some of them are mere fragments; others are so badly worn in places that they will have to be cut down to half their size and pieced together to form presentable carpets. Nevertheless there is no museum in the world which contains such a collection of east Persian carpets as the Shrine of the Imam Ali Riza in Meshed.

In addition to the Qaīn, Dorūkhsh, Birjānd and Turshīz (Kashmar) carpets, from fifty to one hundred and fifty years old, the Shrine possesses some twenty large Meshed carpets which were woven early in the present century and which are worthy of being preserved. They are all very much worn; but if carefully repaired they would form a very interesting and representative group of carpets of Meshed manufacture of the early twentieth century. In another fifty years they will be regarded as antiques; even today they are irreplaceable.

The remarkable museum in which the priceless collection of Shrine antiquities is housed is one of the best examples of modern Iranian architecture. Unfortunately, it is not large enough to house the collection of carpets. But I was informed by the Shrine authorities that they hoped in time to complete a second building for the special purpose of exhibiting their carpets. If this is done, Meshed will possess the most interesting exhibition of Iranian carpets in the country, and the largest and most varied collection of east Persian carpets in the world.

Conversation Piece

He was a dark, handsome young man of about twenty-five; active, arrogant and voluble. He lacked all traces of that affability and courtesy which are the most attractive qualities of his race. I had to listen for half an hour—with as much forbearance as I could muster—to a farrago of Marxian slogans and communist clichés, obviously his stock in trade. He assured me of the solidarity of Persian with British labour; and expressed contempt for the British lords who were grinding down the faces of the poor. I ventured to suggest that he had got hold of the wrong story: that in England it was the faces of the lords which were being ground down. But the remark failed to register.

The next day he and four of his associates were arrested for fomenting disturbances and were carried off by car to Tehrān, 600 miles away.

Among the persons arrested was a friend of mine, an intellectual, who—like the young man—had identified himself with the Tūdeh movement. But he belonged to the other, the moderate section of the party. He came from a well-to-do Kermān family. His father had sent him to school in Poona, where he learnt English, which he spoke remarkably well. He then went to Berlin to study medicine. He spent eight years in Europe and then returned to practise in Kermān.

Like so many intellectuals (not only in Persia) he was drawn into left-wing politics, through association with poverty, suffering and disease. What he told me about conditions in Kermān would have been true of most cities; with the difference that in Kermān it was true of three-quarters of the population. He continued, therefore, to pester the authorities for beds, drugs and equipment; until, to get rid of him, they packed him off to Meshed and told him to practise there. He decided then that there was no hope for Persia under the existing order; so he joined the Tūdeh party. For him its political or economic theories were without significance. For him it meant the overthrow of blind authority, and afterwards—beds, drugs and equipment. I suspect that many members of the party have found their way into it, like my friend, through bitterness and frustration, engendered by the indifference of those in power.

THE QAINĀT AND TURSHĪZ (KASHMĀR)

The Carpets of the Qaināt

The Qaināt is no longer a department of the huge province of Khūrasān. It is today merely a convenient geographical term used to denote a mountainous upland about 300 miles long by 60 miles wide which extends in a south-easterly direction from a pass 20 miles south of Juimānd to about 80 miles south of Birjānd. The area falls away gradually on the west to the Great Desert. On the east it declines rapidly to the lower level of the Afghan frontier region.

Carpets have been woven in the Qaināt for many centuries. Mukaddasi stated at the end of the tenth century that these highlands were already famous for their carpets and prayer rugs. He did not specify the localities where they were produced, but it is probable that weaving went on (*a*) in Gunabād[1]—a prosperous and well-cultivated area; (*b*) in Qaīn—which was formerly the capital and the most important town in the province; and (*c*) in Dorūkhs, a village in the hills 45 miles north-east of Birjānd. There are no indications that (*d*) Birjānd itself became a weaving centre earlier than fifty years ago.

(*a*) Gunabād is mentioned by no less than four of the Arab geographers of the tenth, thirteenth and fourteenth centuries. It was a considerable town with seventy villages around it—all well watered.[2] The name is applied today to the same prosperous and well-cultivated area; but the principal village and the seat of the local governor is now Juimānd. Very few carpets are woven there; but there are some fifty rug looms in the area. The fabric which they produce is, for the most part, poor in quality. Yet I was informed by two of the oldest and most respectable carpet merchants in Khurāsān—one in Meshed and one in Turbat-i-Haidari—that the so-called Herāt carpets in the Herāti design were woven in Nūghāb and Bagh-i-Siah, two villages in the Gunabād area. When I enquired what authority they had for making that interesting statement, they answered (though not so briefly): "Tradition".

(*b*) Qaīn was described by Ibn Hawkal (A.D. 978) as the chief town of the province of Kūhistān and the seat of the governor. It was protected by a strong fortress surrounded by a dry moat (for water was too precious to keep the moat filled, except in times of trouble). Its gardens were not very fruitful or numerous, for the cold in winter was severe. The town possessed a fine mosque.[3] Today an ancient and imposing *mesjid* which has recently been repaired overlooks Qaīn. It may be the very one that Ibn Hawkal saw.

Qaīn—with a population of about 4,000—is now little more than a large village; its premier position among the towns of the Qaināt was long ago taken by Birjānd. No doubt the wealth and influence of the great Birjānd families—which were, and still are, the most powerful in the Qaināt—helped to bring about this change.

The town is certainly an old weaving centre. The oldest carpet in the Shrine Collection (with the exception of its one Sefavi carpet) is a Qaīn dated 150 years ago; and most of the antique Khurāsān *kellegis*, in small repeating patterns, which were fairly common fifty years ago were Qaīns. Yet Qaīn today, like Gunabād, produces very little. Its carpets are similar to those woven in Birjānd (see below).

(*c*) The Dorūkhsh area is situated in the hills about 45 miles north-east of Birjānd. It also possesses a long tradition of carpet weaving. Some of the finest pieces in the Shrine Collection are inscribed as having been woven there. Old Dorūkhsh carpets are recognisable by their close weave and their large bold medallions, usually on plain fields—either cochineal red or cream. The cochineal is a peculiarly satisfying shade of old cerise, very frequently combined with old pistache green. The carpets are sometimes decorated with birds. Another favourite design of old Dorūkhsh was the large pine of *boteh* pattern. It was always woven in rug sizes. The pines were usually in pistache green on old cerise grounds.

Sir P. M. Sykes, who visited the district some fifty years ago, stated that weaving in the Qaināt was almost entirely confined to the Dorūkhsh area. There were, he says, at that time about 400 looms there. The figure is probably not exaggerated. Before and shortly after World War I the Dorūkhsh area was producing important quantities of inexpensive but interesting carpets, mostly in repeating all-over designs and occasionally in designs of a simple medallion type. They were known in the West as Qaīn or Khurāsān carpets. Although a good deal of aniline was used in them and they were all woven with the *jūftī* knot, they commanded a ready sale in Europe. Germany and France were the principal markets for them.

Between the wars the popularity of the Birjānd carpet, with its graceful medallion, tempted the weavers of the Dorūkhsh area to embark on the difficult task of weaving medallion carpets in a village area without scale-paper designs and without expert control. The result has been disastrous: hundreds of carpets have been produced there during recent

---

[1] Gunabād is not strictly in the Qaināt because the frontier of the old province lay 20 miles south of the town. It is included under the Qaināt for convenience.
[2] Le Strange, *The Lands of the Eastern Caliphate*, p. 359 (Cambridge University Press).
[3] Le Strange, op. cit.

160. BIRJĀND

years, coarse in stitch, faulty in execution, with black borders and salmon pink guards 3 inches wide—and all alike. They are sad travesties of the graceful and well-woven Birjānd carpets of the thirties. There is a somewhat difficult market for them in Tehrān. Weaving is carried on in Dorūkhsh itself—where there are some 20 looms; and in some fifteen villages besides—some of which contain only 2 or 3 looms each. Today (1948) there are about 120 looms in the area. The local khans have recently built a serviceable road from Birjānd to Dorūkhsh.

(d) Birjānd is a rather dismal town of some 10,000 inhabitants, situated in the treeless valley of the Rūd-i-Shahrūd. Its principal product, other than carpets, is barberry—a dark red berry which is used instead of citric acid in dyeing with cochineal; and sometimes as a flavouring in cooking rice. The town possesses no buildings of architectural interest.

It was largely due to the patronage of the carpet industry by the great land-owning families of Birjānd that the town became, next to Meshed, the most important carpet centre of Khūrasān. Factories were established by the khans in the town itself and in some of the nearby villages which were their property. The villages vied with the town in producing presentable carpets which became known in the West as Birjānds. The level of design, quality and workmanship was raised, so that the Birjānd carpet—in spite of certain defects in its construction (which will be examined below)—was sought after in the markets of Europe. It was never popular in America.

Production in the Birjānd district increased; so that before the war, Birjānd and a few villages in its vicinity, together with nearby Mūd and the Dorūkhsh area, produced nearly all the carpet sizes of the Qaināt. A careful count was made in the early thirties of the looms in the Qaināt: they totalled 3,645.

The Birjānd carpet in the middle thirties was in the heyday of its renown. The designs which were being woven, though lacking in variety, were good; the dyes were excellent; the workmanship was skilled. There was a grace and a refinement in the carpet which was lacking in any but the best Mesheds. In the markets of Europe it was generally preferred to the Meshed.

Unhappily, the war put an end to the demand. One by one the factories were closed, and the industry declined not only in output, but in excellence. Today, in Birjānd itself there are barely 80 looms (against 200 which existed formerly); and a like decline has taken place both in output and quality, in the carpets of the surrounding villages.

The Birjānd carpet, like the Meshed Farsibaff, possessed inherent defects of construction. Like its rival, it is woven with the *jūftī* knot. That method of weaving, as has been explained above, produces only half the number of knots per unit of measurement than the *tai* knot—which is correctly woven on two strings of the warp instead of four. If the warps are laid closely—say fourteen or more to the inch—a carpet of sufficient density to give good service can be produced with the *jūftī* knot; but most of the Birjānd carpets do not possess that quality. Also, as in Meshed, autumn wools are used, which lack the wearing qualities of the spring clip.

Because of its poor wearing qualities, the Birjānd carpet, like the Meshed, is not popular in America. When, therefore, Europe ceased to buy, Birjānd (like Meshed) could not turn to America—as did Kermān and Hamadān. Tehrān was the only market available; and Tehrān demanded cheap carpets—which Birjānd endeavoured to supply.

Thus, nearly all that had been done to raise the level of the industry was lost. In a short time Birjānd and the villages around were producing that most dishonest of Persian fabrics—a *jūftī* weave of coarse quality. The standard of design, too, rapidly deteriorated; and the dyeing became careless and inefficient. By 1948 the industry had fallen to its lowest ebb since the end of World War I.

The present deplorable position is a source of anxiety to the khans of Birjānd. For the area is poor agriculturally and largely depends for its well-being upon the carpet industry. Its decline coincided with five years of drought, and added to the general distress.

Nevertheless, I do not despair of the industry of Birjānd. If and when the markets of the West reopen, there will be a renewed demand for its carpets. I cannot believe that the enterprising khans of the district—who were mainly responsible for the improvement in the weave which took place between the wars—will not again take the lead in its restoration. They have in the meantime learned a lot. They now know that though the carpets which they formerly wove were graceful and refined, these qualities are not enough. They are aware of the weaknesses which have given the Birjānd carpet a bad name. If they have the wisdom to correct them, Birjānd may yet win an honoured place among the weaving districts of Persia.[1]

Turshīz (Kashmār) ranks fourth in importance—after Meshed, Birjānd and Dorūkhsh—amongst the carpet-weaving centres of Khūrasān. It is a very ancient town. Ibn Hawkal described it in the tenth century as a very populous city with fertile lands. Mukaddasi, writing a few years later, said that its principal mosque rivalled that of Damascus in magnificence. Its bazaar was renowned and was considered to be the storehouse of Khūrasān. It carried on an extensive trade with Fārs and Isfahān. In the twelfth century it fell into the hands of the Assassins; but was wrested from them (and plundered) by the army of the Seljūk Sultan Sanjār. Yet it recovered from this misfortune, and in the fourteenth century Mustaufi described it as one of the chief cities of Kūhistān. Its prosperity was short-lived. At the end of the fourteenth century—like so many other Persian towns—it was sacked by the Mongols. It never fully recovered from this disaster.[2]

Some twenty years ago its ancient and time-honoured name was changed by Shah Riza to Kashmār.[3] The Great Shah displayed a fancifulness in the choice of this name, which was foreign to his rather ponderous nature.

Every Persian knows the story of the cypress tree which Zoroaster brought from Paradise and planted in Kishmār, or Kashmār. The tree grew to be the tallest cypress ever seen before or since. It was felled by the order of the Caliph Mutawakkil in A.D. 861, and was transported in pieces to Samarra, where the Caliph was building a new palace. The Caliph, however, was murdered by his son before the pieces arrived. Kishmār (or Kashmār), the home of the famous cypress, is a village near Turshīz. Hence the new name.

Today Turshīz (Kashmār) is a small town of some 8,000 people, situated in a fertile valley about 60 miles due west of Tūrbat-i-Haidarī. There is a good motor road to it from Tūrbat.

The area, like that around Tūrbat, is among the most productive of northern Khūrasān, and its people are, on the whole, prosperous. Why they have not long since succumbed to some fell distemper I cannot explain; for they have failed to observe those nice prescriptions which recommend that water channels should not be used both for washing and drinking.

It is doubtful if Turshīz has been weaving carpets for very long. None of the pieces in the Shrine Collection are over fifty years old; nor do I ever remember having seen a piece elsewhere that was older. This may be, however, because the Turshīz weave has always been so poor that none of the older carpets have survived.

For, until the middle thirties this area enjoyed the distinction of producing some of the worst carpets in all Persia. They were coarse in quality and clumsy in design; the *jūftī* knot was used and the favourite ground colour was an aniline orange-red. During recent years, however, the weave has improved. The iniquitous *jūftī* knot is still used, but the carpets are more closely woven than they were. At least two of the master-weavers of Turshīz are now producing presentable carpets. The rest are still using an acid red for their ground shades, and their designs are crude and ungraceful.

There are at present, in Turshīz itself, some fifty looms in operation; in Mahvalat, a village on the

---
[1] Since this paragraph was written, the khans of Birjānd have once more taken the lead in the restoration of the industry.
[2] Le Strange, op. cit., p. 354 (Cambridge University Press).
[3] No monarch in history changed so many place-names as Shah Riza Pahlavi; the lists of the Royal Geographical Society include over a hundred.

Tūrbat road, there is a small factory with twenty more; and in Forūtah and other nearby villages there are another twenty or thirty. Which brings the total for the area to about one hundred.

Conversation Piece

I had related how, after the Bolshevik revolution, the Soviet Government had offered to sell me a quantity of carpets, which (to my astonishment) I discovered were carpets which they had stolen from us the year before.

"I am reminded," said my friend, "of the depraved young man who engaged in the discreditable practice of removing the carpets from his father's house and selling them in the bazaar. When the elder person at last discovered these improprieties he expostulated with his son. But to no purpose; for he soon perceived, with despair, that the transactions continued; and that before long there would be no carpets left on his floors. He therefore spoke to his son again, as follows:

"'It is evident that in spite of my admonitions you persist in your unfilial conduct; but why allow my possessions to fall into the hands of strangers? Pray do me the favour of selling them to me instead.'

"'I fear,' replied the unprincipled young man, 'that such an arrangement would be damaging to our fortunes. For you, my father, are such a hard and skilful bargainer, that if I were to sell the carpets back to you, they would undoubtedly be sacrificed at prices far below their real worth.'"

161. DESIGN FOR A MESHED CARPET IN THE ISLIMI (SERPENT) STYLE (c. 1910)

162. Design for a Meshed Carpet introducing the Royal Hat
Drawn by Ibrahim Rizai after a Meshed carpet woven c. 1900

163. A Meshed Carpet in the Islimi (Serpent) Style (*c.* 1910)
Probably woven by Haji Jelil Khamenei.

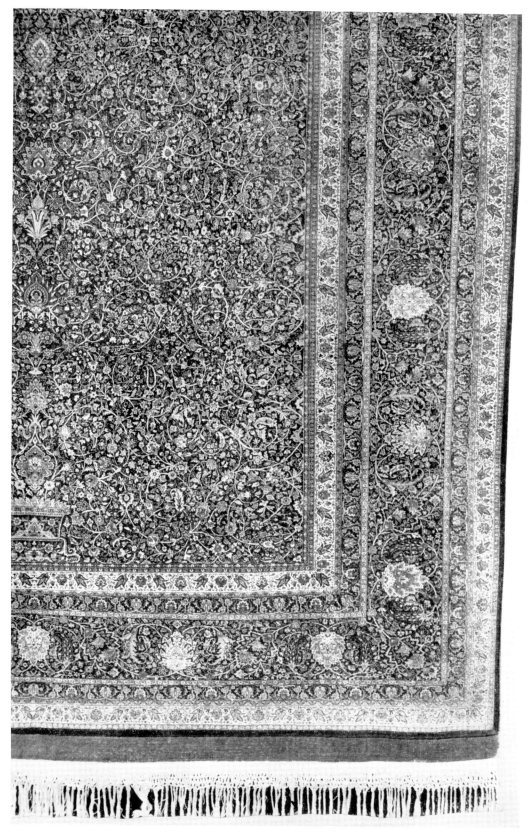

164. A Meshed Carpet woven by Emogli (*c.* 1924)
Property of Aga Kuzekenani, Meshed.

165. A Meshed Carpet (*c.* 1925)
The design is taken from a Dorŭkhsh carpet of the early nineteenth century.

164. A Meshed Carpet woven by Emogli (c. 1924)
Property of Aga Kuzekenani, Meshed.

165. A Meshed Carpet (*c.* 1925)
The design is taken from a Dorūkhsh carpet of the early nineteenth century.

166. A BIRJĀND CARPET (c. 1935)

167. A Meshed Carpet (*c.* 1935)

168. DESIGN FOR A MESHED CARPET IN THE CLASSIC PERSIAN STYLE (*c.* 1945)
School of Art, Tehrān

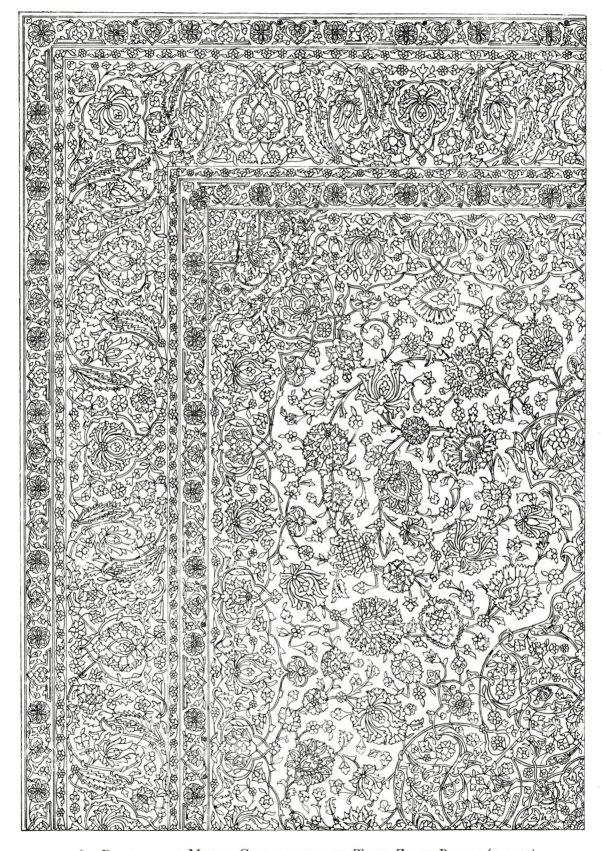

169. Design for a Meshed Carpet drawn by Tahir Zadeh Bihzad (*c.* 1945)
School of Art, Tehrān

171. A Meshed Carpet (c. 1945)

170. Design for a Meshed Carpet in the Islimi (Serpent) Style (c. 1945)
School of Art, Tehrān

172. A Meshed Carpet (*c.* 1945)

CHAPTER XII

THE BALŪCHI TRIBAL RUGS OF KHŪRASĀN

The Balūchi Tribal Rugs of Khūrasān

It has been long assumed—by writers and rug fanciers alike—that Balūchi tribal rugs were produced in the frontier area marked "Balūchistān" on the map of Asia; an area which lies partly in Persia and partly in Pakistān.

Balūchi rugs are not, however, woven in Balūchistān—Persian or Pakistāni. They are woven by the Balūchi tribes of northern Khūrasān—particularly in the areas around Tūrbat-i-Haidarī, Turshīz (Kashmar), Sarakhs, Tūrbat-i-Shaikhjām and Nīshapūr. A few are woven farther south, in Seistān.

The writer who attempts to produce an objective and intelligible account of the Balūchi tribes of Khūrasān is confronted with a mass of vague and contradictory statements and reports which render his task difficult and distracting. One authority states that the Balūchis entered Persia in the sixth century A.D. from the Caucasus, and that they were the last Iranian people to settle in the country. But he does not state whence they came; nor does he explain how it happened that having entered the comparatively fertile area of Azerbaijān, they abandoned it, crossed into east Persia and now inhabit—in small and scattered communities—a huge and mainly arid region of the world, which extends from Sarakhs in the extreme north-eastern tip of Persia to Karāchi, the capital of Pakistān.

After making every allowance for the seeming inconsistencies which attend the migration of peoples, I find this hard to believe. I prefer the testimony of Professor V. Minorsky. He states that the earliest references to the Balūchis which we possess are by Moslem writers of the tenth century A.D. who included them among the tribes which then inhabited the Kermān province. Professor Minorsky adds that the Seljūk invasion probably pushed them farther south and east.

According to Mr. Sijadi of Meshed, who is an authority on the tribes of Khūrasān, the Balūchis of northern Khūrasān were brought there from Balūchistān by Nadir Shah in the eighteenth century, and today form the core of the Balūchi population of the province. They are known as the Old Balūchis, to distinguish them from the New Balūchis of a second migration, which took place about sixty years ago—first into Seistān, and later, because of a famine there, into northern Khūrasān. The Old Balūchis consist of about 1,500 families; the New Balūchis of about 600. Thus, the total Balūchi population of Khūrasān numbers about 2,100 families or about 12,000 people. The different tribes belong to one or other of these two groups.

The Old Balūchis, who have lived in northern Khūrasān for nearly 200 years, have intermarried to a considerable extent with the local population and have become converts to the Shi'a faith. The New Balūchis, too, have mixed with local elements—Tajik, Arab or Brahui; but they are mostly Sūnnis.

The tribal organisation of these two groups is not fixed. From time to time a forceful personality emerges who gathers round him a sufficient number of followers and throws off his tribal allegiance, to found a new tribe of his own.

The principal weaving tribes belong to the first group, the Old Balūchis. The tribes of the second group, the New Balūchis, either do not weave at all, or, if they do, their rugs are generally poor in quality. They are mainly shepherds; but the younger men are prone to vary their pastoral pursuits with occasional bouts of banditry. Both groups are confirmed smugglers. They probably make more money out of selling oil in Afghanistān, or tea and sugar in Persia, than they do out of their more legitimate pursuits.

The principal weaving tribes of Khūrasān—nearly all of which belong to the Old Balūchis—are:

Tribe	Locality
Bahlūlī:	Khaf and Jangal (Tūrbat-i-Haidarī)
Baizidī:	Mahvalat (Tūrbat-i-Haidarī), Qain
Kolah-derazī:	Tūrbat-i-Haidarī and Turshīz (Kashmar)
Jan Mirzaī:	Zaveh and Ali-Ek (Tūrbat-i-Haidarī)
Rahim Khanī:	Tūrbat-i-Haidarī and Sarakhs
Brahui:	Tūrbat-i-Haidarī and Sarakhs
Kurkheillī (Salar Khanī):	Tūrbat-i-Haidarī and Jangal
Hassanzaī:	Various
Jan Begī (New Balūchi):	Roshkhar (Tūrbat-i-Haidarī)

It will be seen from the above list that most of the weaving tribes live in the neighbourhood of Tūrbat-i-Haidarī—an important commercial and agricultural centre—situated in a fertile valley about 100 miles south of Meshed. Most of the Balūchi tribes of this area market their rugs in Tūrbat, which is the most important collecting centre in northern Khūrasān. Meshed itself is also an important collecting centre. So, in lesser degrees, are Turshīz (Kashmar), Nīshapūr and Sarākhs. Sarākhs, although a tribal centre of some importance, is producing fewer rugs than formerly, because of the increased trade in Karakūl lambskins. Grey and black sheep are bred for this trade, so that there is an insufficiency of white wool for carpet weaving.

Like all the nomad rugs of Persia, the Balūchi rugs are woven on horizontal looms. It is a convenient system. Even if the rug is only half finished, it can easily be taken up from the tent floor rolled up on its two loom beams, and carried to the next camping-ground on a pack animal.

Every true Balūchi rug, so far as I am aware, is woven with the Persian knot and is single wefted. Formerly the warps and wefts were invariably of wool, generally black; but in recent years cotton is being used as well. This is a pity; because the decorative *gilim* at both ends of the rug—often in parallel stripes of two or more dark colours—is one of the most interesting and attractive features of the Balūchi weaves; and a *gilim* made with cotton yarn is never as fine as one made with wool. Another peculiarity of the Balūchi rug is its selvedge. This is generally made of black goat hair, a material which is not used elsewhere in the rug.

The characteristic dark colour of the Balūchi rugs is due to the use of three shades of dark red, a dark and medium blue, and black. The impression of colour left by these rugs is one of sombre redness; yet the ground colour of most of them is actually dark blue. Black is commonly used for the outlines—which further deepens the effect of the deep reds and blues. Two shades of camel and a little green are added in the minor figures. White is frequent (and is quite out of place) in the guards. During recent years—perhaps because of the rising cost of dyeing with indigo and madder—there has been a notable increase in the number of camel-ground rugs. This shade is generally combined with reds and blacks to produce a very pleasing effect of colour.

The dyestuffs used by the best Balūchi weavers are indigo for the blues; madder for the red; walnut husks for the camel shades; and willow leaves for the yellows. The greens are dyed with indigo on willow leaves. Henna is used for the oranges and as an ingredient for the browns. Alum is generally used as a mordant (except, of course, for the indigo). It is sometimes obtained by baking a local clay—melanterite. Black wool is used for the blacks, but is generally dyed with a ferruginous litharge, known as *mak*, to give it an even shade. This is an unfortunate practice because, if the liquor is strong in iron, it will in time destroy the yarn. I was informed that in the case of the Balūchis of the north the black was sound because it was produced by dyeing dark-coloured yarns with indigo. This may be true—in some cases.

Unhappily the standard of dyeing among the Balūchis is not what it was. The use of aniline red is spreading. In Meshed I visited the dyers and found that they were selling yarn to the Balūchis which had been dyed a painful crimson with an imported acid red. Also, the proportion of rugs in which black has been used in place of dark blue is on the increase.

To build up a fairly accurate and comprehensive list of the principal Balūchi weaving tribes—together with the localities which they inhabit—is one thing; to attribute every Balūchi rug correctly to its proper tribe is quite another. Even the dealers of Meshed were at sea in this matter. Rarely was the same tribal name attached to a rug by two independent experts. I have, therefore, refrained from attaching tribal names to the Balūchi rugs illustrated in Plates 175–182. To do so would be spurious and misleading. Formerly, the women of each tribal family knew one pattern by heart and rarely wove any other. This is no longer true; because, during the last twenty years, the motor bus and motor lorry have so far eliminated the barriers of space and time in Khūrasān that a style or pattern has ceased to be the property of a single tribe or tribal family. If a pattern is in demand, it soon becomes common to half a dozen localities; for the women are skilful copyists. Thus, the so-called Bokhara design has been adopted by many of the Balūchis of the northern part of the province, by those of Seistān, by the Timūris and even by the Arabs of Firdaus; the Herātī or Fish design is woven in half a dozen localities—as far apart as Sarākhs and Seistān; and the conventional Tree design—with its vertical trunk and diagonal branches, each bearing a single trefoil leaf—is common to a number of tribes in Seistān and in the Tūrbat area.

Camel hair is seldom used. I was informed, however, that the centres of prayer rugs, or rugs made for priests or *Sayyids*,[1] are sometimes woven with it; the reason being that the camel is regarded as a sacred animal because the Prophet rode on one. The story is picturesque, however doubtful. Camel hair is also used in the finest quality Balishts, which are small bags measuring about 32 × 16 inches with a carpet fabric on one side. They are filled with down and used as pillows in the tents. Camel hair is also sometimes used in the Jahizi or dowry rug which the bride-to-be weaves as part of her dowry. These pieces are regarded as the best among the Balūchi rugs and are not easy to acquire.

The Timūri rugs of Tūrbat-i-Shaikhjām

There are other weaving tribes besides the Balūchis in northern Khūrasān. The most important are the Timūris of Tūrbat-i-Shaikhjām and Zūrabād and the Arab tribes of Firdaus (Tūn) and Tabas.

The Timūris are a small tribe of Mongol descent and of the Sūnni persuasion. Their rugs have all the characteristics of the true Balūchis, although they are in general somewhat thinner. The best are woven by the Yaqūb-Khanī sub-tribe. The Timūris are now dyeing their orange-red with aniline. Although they are of Mongol descent they use the Persian knot; which is an indication that they learnt the art of weaving from their Persian neighbours.

The Balūchi rugs of Seistān

An inferior type of Balūchi rug is woven by nomad Balūch tribes—and in lesser degree by villagers—who inhabit the Zabol (Nasratabād) area of Seistān, and the Helmānd delta. They are generally lighter in colour than the Balūchis of northern Khūrasān, the principal ground shades being a light reddish brown or camel. Thus they lack the richness and depth of colour of the true Balūch. The deeper shades of blue and red are, however, fairly common in the older pieces. The rugs have single wefts and the Persian knot is used.

In design, too, they are inferior to most of the Balūchi rugs of the north, though the attractive trefoil pattern (Plate 181) has been adopted extensively. The three-panel ground—each panel containing a series of diamonds one inside the other —is common among the older rugs. In the late thirties an enterprising merchant of Zabol—dissatisfied, seemingly, with the local designs—imported some medallion rugs from Fārs and distributed them amongst the weavers as patterns. However irregular the union, the result was not unlovely.

The principal merit of the Balūchi rugs of Seistān is their size. They usually run about 10 square feet (4 feet × 2 feet 6 inches), which is smaller than the true Balūch. There is a demand for rugs of this size in the West. The output has fallen considerably during the last decade. Today (1948) it is probably under 1,000 pieces a year.

The most interesting type of Seistān rug is the Balisht which is sometimes adorned along the selvedge with a pattern of cowrie shells. They are usually more finely woven than the rugs. Indeed, some of the finest examples of Balūchi weaving are to be found among them.

The Arab rugs of Firdaus and Tabas

The so-called Arab rugs of nothern Khūrasān are woven in the town of Firdaus (Tūn) and in some dozen Arab villages in its vicinity. A lesser quantity is produced in villages in the neighbourhood of the oasis of Tabas.

I decided to travel from Birjand (where I had been staying) to Firdaus on a track which skirted the eastern extremity of the Great Desert, a few miles from the western base of the Qainat massif. On our left stretched the level plain—brown, stony and bare of any sign of life—to a horizon of huge mountain masses—blue-grey, jagged and forbidding. To us, who were planning to cross the Great Desert to Yezd, they were ominous and unexpected. For there was no hint of their existence on the map.

Firdaus (or Tūn, to give it its older and more famous name) is a small town of some 10,000 people situated in the north-eastern corner of the Great Desert about 250 miles from Meshed. Mukaddasi, who visited it in the tenth century, described it as a populous place protected by a castle and possessing a fine mosque. Nasir-i-Khūsraw, in the following century, stated that there were 400 carpet looms at work there when he passed through. It may be doubted, however, if the carpets which Nasir-i-Khūsraw saw were woollen pile carpets. They were more probably cotton *gilims* in repeating patterns of white and blue.

Firdaus is the principal collecting centre for the so-called Arab rugs of north-eastern Khūrasān. The rugs are woven in the town itself as well as in villages which lie at long distances apart in that semi-arid

---
[1] Persons who claim descent from the Prophet Mohammed.

173. WEAVERS AT AYASK, NEAR FIRDAUS

region. They are mostly strung out along the foothills of the Qaīn massif between Firdaus and Birjānd —the route which we followed. The rugs are known in Meshed as Arabs, because most of them are woven by villagers of Arab descent, some of whom still speak a dialect of Arabic. In Firdaus itself, however, where a good proportion of the rugs are woven, the people are almost wholly Persian speaking. Although only a small percentage of the rugs are woven by nomadic tribes, the women still use the horizontal loom—both in Firdaus itself and in the villages— which indicates that they, too, not long ago were nomads and roamed with their black, goat-hair tents in search of pasture for their flocks among those stony, inhospitable plains.

The rugs of the Firdaus area are woven with the Persian knot, and like most of the tribal rugs of Persia they are single wefted. Until recent times they closely resembled Balūchi tribal rugs, in style and colour. So much so that the better pieces were as well regarded by the merchants of Meshed as the true Balūchi rugs. That, unhappily, is no longer true. The fall in the demand for the cheaper grades of Balūchi type of rug (the principal market for them was Holland, and since 1939 Holland has closed its doors to Persian rugs) hit the Firdaus area very badly. When I visited the place in 1948 the weavers seemed to be at a loss as to what they should do. Some were weaving *kellegi* sizes about 10 × 5 feet in a reasonably good quality; others were making 7 × 4 feet rugs; others again were copying Afghan carpets —and copying them fairly well. Most of them were busy with their traditional small rugs of about 12 square feet—but the rugs were of the very lowest quality. It was obvious that the weavers were trying out various sizes, qualities and designs in an endeavour to find a market for their wares. There seemed to be no one in Firdaus able or willing to advise them.

If the weavers of Firdaus wish to find a steady market for their goods they will have to mend their ways. For the well-dyed, fairly well-woven Arab rugs of fifteen years ago are no more. The dyes which are being used there now are about as bad as they can be. Even the dark blue—which used to be excellent and which, so far as I am aware, has never yet been prostituted in any Persian quality— has been replaced by black; and the black which they are using is an imported acid dye of the cheapest quality. Their red is no better.

The output of the area is in the neighbourhood of 1,000 pieces a month in all qualities and sizes.

Crossing the Lūt

One of the few ancient caravan routes across the Lūt—the Great Desert which divides eastern from western Persia—begins at Firdaus (Tūn), passes through the oasis of Tabas and ends on the other side at Yezd.

Often, as I surveyed the map of Persia, I wondered what mysteries that huge, almost blank space might harbour; and I had secretly desired to be one of the small band of Europeans who had crossed it. Twenty-five years ago I had done so—many miles farther south—from Kermān to Zahedān; and I imagined that the more northerly route was of the same general character: a vast, empty, salt-encrusted plain, varied with high sand dunes; gravelly and hard underfoot (except at one fell spot where, I remembered, the soft sand had held us up for hours). The northern crossing, however, proved to be very different.

174. TABAS

A dozen years ago the Persian Government widened and improved the track to make it passable for lorries and buses, both for purposes of trade and for the convenience of pilgrims on their way to the Shrine at Meshed. No culverts or bridges were built: the road—such as it was—followed the natural contours of the land, which had been gouged into a thousand miniature canyons by the courses from the melting snows. Nothing had been spent on the track since it was first improved. Thus at one moment the nose of our car was high in the air; and at the next it was pointing downwards into the trough of an undulation. We were like a tramp-ship in a heavy gale.

Our first stop after leaving Firdaus was Tabas—an oasis which consists of Tabas itself with its half-dozen satellite villages. They looked, from a distance, for all the world like green atolls asleep in a misty sea. For each one is a grove—large, medial or tiny—of tall and graceful palm trees.

Tabas, like Firdaus, is an ancient town—the first to be encountered by the traveller on his way across the desert from Yezd to Meshed. It was therefore named the Gate to Khūrasān. Ibn Hawkal mentioned its "forest of date palms". Mukaddasi wrote of its fine mosque, its great water-tank and its baths. Nasir-i-Khūsraw passed through it in 1052 and described it as a fine, populous town with gardens and palm groves. In the eleventh century, Tabas, like Firdaus, was occupied by the Assassins, and like Firdaus it was recaptured from them by Sultan Sanjār, and partially destroyed.

A friend of mine once told me that when he became too old to work he intended to retire to Tabas and live there for the remainder of his days. Because I knew him to be a person of discernment, I had ever since been curious to visit the place. Having done so, I think I understand my friend's enthusiasm.

For Tabas possesses an undoubted charm. I shall not easily forget the witchery of the courtyard of the house in which we stayed. We occupied an arched *talar*—a kind of raised dais with a large vaulted room behind it. Before us lay a white, three-sided courtyard with a long rectilinear water-tank in the centre. Beyond the tank and reflected in the brimming water were the tall, incredibly graceful palm trees of the small walled garden. At night, in the light of the full moon, the white arches of the courtyard and the ghostly palms trembled in the water.

Yet Tabas is a town of lost prosperity, of departed splendours. Its walls are tumbling; the great mosque with its two stunted minarets is a ruin; two-thirds of its covered bazaar has fallen in. Some of its finest houses are abandoned wrecks. Fully a quarter of the town is a shapeless mass of crumbling earth walls.

As a rug centre Tabas is unimportant. There are a few carpet looms in the town which are superintended by a master-weaver from Yezd, who is weaving carpets there in the Yezd manner. Some Arab rugs are woven at Dohūk, Arishk and other villages. But they appeared to be marketed in Firdaus or Bushruiyeh, whence they are despatched to Meshed.

Beyond Tabas the character of the country changes. This part of the Lūt is in fact not very different from many other parts of Persia—except that it is wilder and more desolate. It consists of a succession of undulating stretches, from 10 to 50 miles wide, which lie between rugged or mountainous massifs. There are no high passes. Time and again we approached a mighty range with apprehension, only to find that the caravans—those ancient pioneers—had discovered a gorge, a notch or a low saddle, which led, without undue hardship, to the farther side.

There are no serious engineering difficulties in the way of building a first-class motor road across the Lūt between Firdaus and Yezd. There is only one really tough spot—a space of about four miles of soft and shifting sand. It lies about midway between Tabas and Yezd.

The Lūt at this crossing is not entirely uninhabited. Between Firdaus and Tabas there are a few isolated villages—particularly the village of Dohūk which lies at about two-thirds of the distance from Firdaus. Here the track bifurcates: one fork turns northwestwards; the other, a mere caravan track, winds south to Naibānd, Ravār and Kermān. When the proposed transdesert roads are built, Dohūk will, no doubt, become the Piccadilly Circus of the Lūt—for half a dozen roads will converge there. Already motor lorries have made the passage from Dohūk to Kermān. Between Tabas and Yezd there are half a dozen inhabited places—either tiny villages or a welcome tea-house, where water and sometimes even petrol is obtainable.

The distance across the Lūt between Firdaus and Yezd is about 408 miles. We stopped four days in Tabas and had a few hours' rest between Tabas and Yezd. The journey took us about thirty hours of actual driving-time.

When we reached Yezd—that most upright and industrious of Persian towns—the map indicated that we had passed from the desert to the town. But we were not aware of it. For Yezd, like Tabas, is an oasis. Around it stretched, as far as the eye could see, the brown, forbidding, desiccated plain.

Conversation Piece

He stood with arms folded and bent head, facing the setting sun. His loose blue shirt, faded and patched, hung almost to his knees, outside his loose blue trousers. His sinewy brown feet were bare. His wrinkled features were almost concealed by an unkempt white beard, which gave to him an appearance a little wild, yet kindly and benign. His lips were moving, but no sound came from them.

Suddenly he lifted up his arms and put his thumbs behind his ears, in one of the ordained motions of prayer.

It was then that I perceived the heavy chains which hung from fetters round his wrists to fetters round his ankles.

I thought: so old, so childlike; what could this man have done? I enquired from the trooper:

"What is his offence?"

"His? Nothing," answered the trooper.

"How, nothing?"

"Nothing," repeated the trooper. And then nonchalantly: "They say his son spoiled a woman."

I thought: a gentle, benign old man; manacled, mumbling prayers in the courtyard of an out-of-the-way post of gendarmerie—because they said his son had spoiled a woman! But what had the old man to do with it? Why was he in chains? And what had happened to the young ravisher? And the lady?

I suggested these questions in the indirectest manner possible, fearing that an undue exhibition of curiosity might dry up the fountain of talk.

She was the daughter, it appeared, of a small landlord of the neighbourhood—a small landlord, who was, nevertheless, a prince of Persia. (I thought: one of their thousand princes; a scion, perhaps, of some half-forgotten dynasty. I remembered that I had met a clerk once—in a small telegraph office in Mazanderān—who called himself a prince: rightfully, no doubt.)

The old man in chains was headman of her father's village. He had a younger son. I warranted him to be a tall, upstanding, flashing-eyed scamp of a young peasant. It is easy in the villages for a youth to look upon a maiden. They saw. They loved. She, swearing she would ne'er consent, consented.

Discovery. A hue and cry. The ravisher mounts the fleetest horse in the prince's stable and flees to the mountains!

Then His Excellency the Governor of the province, apprised of these scandalous proceedings, but unable to secure the son, orders the arrest of the father! Heavy chains are fastened to the old man's wrists and ankles, and he is cast loose in the sun-baked square of this caravanserai of gendarmes.

"But why the father? What had the father to do with the affair? A white-beard?"

The trooper looked at me with surprise and turned away—as if to indicate that these Feranghis understood nothing. He then proceeded, with deliberation, to fill the bowl of his pipe and set a match to it.

There was a loud knocking at the broad, unpainted gate. The trooper ran to his post, drew the bolt and opened the door a few inches. I heard a rapid interchange of volubilities. The door was opened wide.

Two men entered, followed by a third, whose arms were bound behind his back with stout, black goat-hair cords. The prisoner was young, tall, well favoured. They led him across the courtyard towards the far corner where the old man sat, squatting in the sun.

When the young man caught sight of him, he cried "My father!" and ran forward. Then halted and stood with bent head, anxious, humble, penitent, before wronged and stricken age.

Suddenly he threw back his head and said proudly: "They could not catch me, the gendarmes."

Then tenderly: "My brothers told me that they had taken thee and put chains upon thy wrists and ankles. I could not sleep any more. So I have come."

The trooper of gendarmes drew a key from his girdle and unlocked the old man's fetters; and the youth, unbound, held out his wrists.

175. BALŪCH RUGS FROM THE TŪRBAT-I-HAIDARĪ AREA

176. Balūch Rugs from the Tūrbat-i-Shaikhjām Area

177. Balūch Rug from the Turshīz (Kashmār) Area

178. Brahuī Balūch Rug from the Tūrbat-i-Haidarī Area

179. Balūch Rug woven by Kurds who live in villages north of Meshed

180. Balūch Rugs from the Nīshapūr Area

181. SEISTĀN BALŪCH PRAYER RUGS
The middle rug is from the Shrine Collection, Meshed. The inscription on the field is a salutation to the saints; the border and cover inscriptions are illegible. Dated A.H. 1322–A.D. 1904.

182. BALŪCH RUGS FROM THE SARĀKHS AREA
Note the hand of Akbar (bottom right).

183. Arab Rugs from Firdaus and the Surrounding Area

CHAPTER XIII

KERMĀN AND ITS ENVIRONS; THE AFSHĀRI RUGS; AND A NOTE ON YEZD

KERMĀN AND ITS ENVIRONS

The Province and City of Kermān

The long history of the province of Kermān is confused and often sanguinary. Under the Achaemenian and Sassanian kings it enjoyed a happy obscurity. Because of its remoteness and inaccessibility many adherents of the old religion of Zoroaster—who had refused to embrace Islām—took refuge there, and it became a centre of resistance. It was not finally conquered by the Arabs until a century after the decisive battle of Nehāvend (A.D. 641). There is, to this day, a considerable community of Zoroastrians in the city.

In the eleventh century the province came under the sovereignty of the Seljūk sultans of Ghazni. It was preserved from the horrors of the Mongol invasions by its remoteness, and the diplomatic skill of one of its ruling princelings. In the thirteenth century a notable figure among the heterogeneous rulers of the province was a lady, Turkhan Khatūm, who possessed (for those days) unusual and decided views on femininity. It was during her beneficent régime that Marco Polo visited the city, of which he gives a lively description. The lady was buried under the turquoise dome of the Gombad-i-Sabz—which was unhappily destroyed by an earthquake in 1896.

Under the Sefavi kings the province enjoyed a long period of tranquillity. Nor does it appear to have suffered unduly when the Afghans marched through it on their way to Isfahān in 1720 and 1722. The most terrible event in its long history occurred in more recent times: after the death of the benevolent Kerim Khan Zand—whose seat of government was Shirāz—there was a struggle for power between his heirs and Aga Mohammed Qajār, who later became the first Qajār monarch. The gallant Lutf'Ali Khan —the last Zand prince—was finally besieged in Kermān city by Aga Mohammed. After a bitter siege,

184. KERMĀN: OUTSKIRTS OF THE CITY

185. KERMĀN: DESIGN FOR THE BORDER OF A HUNTING CARPET BY HASSAN KHAN

the city was finally captured in 1794. Its inhabitants "were treated with almost inconceivable cruelty. Not only were its women handed over to the soldiery, who were encouraged to rape and to murder, but the Qajār victor ordered that 20,000 pairs of eyes should be presented to him. These he carefully counted."[1]

Under the phlegmatic rule of the successors of Aga Mohammed Shah, the city slowly recovered from this disaster. But it is still poor and hapless. For its surroundings lack an essential element of all prosperity—water; and it is too remote from the more affluent provinces of Persia to share their fortunes—such as they are.

The province of Kermān is about the size of England and Wales, or the state of Illinois. It is bounded on the north and east by the Great Desert; on the west by the province of Fārs; and on the south by the Gulf of Omān. It is the poorest of the five great provinces of Persia. The greater part of it is incultivable—hard or sandy desert or barren upland. The rest—because of the lack of rivers and the inadequate and unbalanced rainfall—is fruitful only in those few and scattered areas where the soil is irrigated by meagre streams or ancient water channels.

Nevertheless, the province produces a variety of food and other commodities of quality. The most important are wheat, barley, rice, cotton, wool, asafoetida, opium, and pistachio nuts. Its fruits are varied and excellent.

Le Strange points out that in medieval times the province had two capitals—Sirjān and Bardāshīr—and that of the two Sirjān was the more important. In the tenth century, however, the seat of government was concentrated in Bardāshīr. By reason of a light-hearted usage common in Persia of calling a province and its capital by the same name, Bardāshīr became known as Kermān. The twin capital—Sirjān—has disappeared;[2] but it has given its name to an important district in the western part of the province.

Kermān is the last of that important line of towns and cities which fringes the western limits of the Great Desert along the ancient highway to India: the line Tehrān–Qūm–Kāshān–Ardistān–Yezd–Kermān. It owes its location, no doubt, to the fact that it lies at the intersection of the Indian highway with one of the principal caravan routes across the Lūt; for the town possesses no strategic strength, nor is the district which surrounds it of any agricultural importance.

Its elevation of 6,000 feet above sea-level—next to Hamadān the highest among the larger provincial towns—has endowed it with a pleasant and, on the whole, a healthy climate. The summers are hot, but not intolerable; and the winters are far milder than those of the cities of the north-west. Snow is uncommon. Although the country around is arid and inhospitable, there are some attractive valleys in the Jūpār mountains south and south-east of the city.

Kermān has a population of about 58,000. Except for a small minority of Afghan and Indian traders and a few Jews, the inhabitants are of the Persian race. There are no foreign consulates. (The Government of India maintained a consulate there for many years, but it was closed in 1947.) The Church Missionary Society—to which the city and district owe an incalculable debt—is now precluded from carrying on its former educational and religious work. But it continues its invaluable medical service and maintains an excellent hospital.

---

[1] Sir P. M. Sykes, *History of Persia*. One cannot help doubting these revolting figures. Aga Mohammed was no doubt a cruel brute, but accuracy is not among the many virtues of Persians, upon whose testimony historians have had to rely.

[2] Its ruins were discovered in 1900 by Sir P. M. (then Major) Sykes.

[3] Curzon (*Persia*) refers to a Persian tradition that the Great Desert was once an inland sea. The ancient city of Rhages or Rey, south of Tehrān, is said to have been on its northern and Kermān on its southern shore. This may be true, because there are huge salt depressions in the north and south. The latter is only 1000 feet above sea level—the lowest point on the Persian plateau.

Ancient Buildings

Kermān is said to contain ninety mosques, but most of them are undistinguished. Two, however, possess considerable architectural merit. The larger and more ancient foundation is the Masjid-i-Mālek, built by the Seljūk Mālek Turān Shāh in the eleventh century. It was a ruin in the sixteenth century and has been practically rebuilt since that date. The second is the Masjid-i-Jumah, which dates from the fourteenth century, though a good deal of the tilework is much later. The Vase design (see p. 17) has been used in one of the panels, which probably dates from Sefavi times.

Another notable building is the Madrassah or religious college of Ibrahim Khan, Zahir-u-Dōleh—a distinguished governor of the province in the early nineteenth century.

But unquestionably the most memorable monument in the area is the mausoleum of Shah Nimatūllāh—a saint and sage of the fifteenth century.[1] It is situated in the village of Māhān (loc. Māhūn) some 25 miles south-east of Kermān, on the Bām road. The tomb chamber is under a beautifully tiled dome, flanked by twin, graceful minarets. There are three courtyards—each adorned, in the Persian manner, with brimming pools. Cypresses, pines and plane trees add quiet and dignity to the enclosure. It is a place for repose and contemplation (Plate 186).

Kermān possesses a handsome covered bazaar, of which the longest alley runs in a straight line for 600 yards. A number of imposing—howbeit somewhat battered—caravanserais lead off from it, their large, square, arcaded courtyards open to the sky (Plate 187).

There is not much left of the great mud wall and its six gates. Only the imposing Gate of the Unbelievers (so called because it guards the section of the town where the Zoroastrians live) still stands (Plate 189). The Castle of Ardeshir and the Castle of the Maiden—which formed part of the defences—are nothing but huge mounds of earth.

187. CARAVANSERAI OF GANJ ALI KHAN, KERMĀN

186. MAUSOLEUM OF SHAH NIMATŪLLĀH, MĀHĀN (KERMĀN)
It was built in A.D. 1437.

188. WIND TOWERS, KERMĀN

[1] Sykes called him the Persian Nostradamus, and added that the Kermānis still believe his prophecies. If so, they must have grown more sceptical since Sykes wrote *Ten Thousand Miles in Persia*.

189. The Gate of the Unbelievers, Kermān

The Rise and Development of the Carpet Industry in Kermān

Such is Kermān—a mud-built city partly in ruins, poverty-stricken and undistinguished. Yet a city which possesses a name renowned throughout the world: for the best carpets in the world are conceived and woven by its people.

Kermān possesses a long tradition in the weaver's craft. But there are no indications that it existed before the sixteenth century. Marco Polo, who visited the place in the thirteenth, gives a detailed list of the activities of its inhabitants. Embroidery is included; but not carpet weaving. Nor did Le Strange—who so carefully perused the works of the twenty-four Moslem geographers—find any reference in their writings to carpet weaving in Kermān. It would appear, therefore, that the craft did not become established there until Sefavi times. We know that it was in existence then, because in the chronicle of Shah Abbas—the *Alamara-i-Abbasi*, which was composed by the monarch's secretary—the carpets of Kermān are mentioned. So they are by Chardin, who was in Persia in 1666 and again in 1672. We know, too, that carpets were shipped from Kermān to India in the time of Akbar the Great, who was a contemporary of Shah Abbas.

The end of the Sefavi dynasty was followed, as we have seen, by a hundred years of turmoil; and that period by the peaceful reign of Kerim Khan Zand. I am not aware of any references to carpet weaving in Kermān during that century and a half. We have already noted that Sir John Malcolm—who visited the neighbouring province of Shirāz early in the nineteenth century and who devoted a chapter of his History to a survey of the commerce, the industry, and the arts of Persia during the reign of Kerim Khan—did not even mention carpet weaving.

It does not follow, however, that the industry in Kermān had ceased to exist. For the Kermān carpet has always been a favourite among the wealthier classes in Persia. It may well be, therefore, that a small demand persisted through the troublous times —which may have kept the industry alive.

Weaving seems to have been going on also in the remote village of Ravār,[1] 100 miles north-east of Kermān, on the edge of the Lūt desert. Ravār was a place of some importance in ancient times. Mukaddasi states that in the tenth century it had a strong castle which served to protect the frontier. Marco Polo passed through it in the thirteenth century. It lies on the ancient caravan road across the Great Desert to Meshed. When this desert road is opened

190. A Doorway, Kermān

[1] The name of this village is frequently mispronounced (but only in the West) Laver.

up to regular motor traffic (which may not be long delayed) Ravar may regain its former importance.

Ravar carpets are the oldest in existence which can be ascribed, without hesitation, to the Kermān area.[1] In the Shrine Collection there are three (one of them a fragment) which were almost certainly woven in Ravār. They are dated A.H. 1286 (A.D. 1866). There are, no doubt, still older pieces in existence.

It is a curious fact that, generations ago, this inaccessible village should have become a weaving centre—in preference to a dozen others, equally populous, better favoured and less remote. I sought for an explanation of this phenomenon in Kermān; but did not find one that was satisfying. Perhaps, in those troublous times, it was the very remoteness of Ravār which induced some khan or master-weaver to set up looms there; for a carpet in distant Ravār would be less likely to enlist the solicitude of an official or of a troop commander than a carpet in Kermān itself, or in a nearby village.

The industry in Kermān—although probably maintained at a high level of excellence during the nineteenth century—was on a small scale, and did not attain to any importance until its end. Thus, in 1871, Colonel Euan-Smith reported that there were only six carpet "factories" in the city. Actually, there were no factories at all in Kermān at that time —in the sense in which that word is used today. The largest establishment contained only a few looms, so that the total number of looms in the city could not have been more than thirty. Again, E. G. Browne, who spent several months in Kermān in 1888, says nothing about its carpets; though he gives some details of the shawl manufactury, and notes that it appeared to be declining. Curzon, writing in the early nineties, devoted half a page to the manufacture of Kermān shawls, but hardly mentioned carpet weaving. The shawls of Kermān, as well as the kindred products of Kashmir, had been in considerable demand by the ladies of the mid-Victorian era. But Curzon appears to have been unaware that the industry of which he spoke so feelingly was doomed to disappear; while the craft of carpet weaving—which he dismissed in a few sentences—was soon to bring the city honourable and world-wide renown.

Sir P. M. Sykes[2] (then Major Sykes) who established the first British Consulate in Kermān in 1895, and who spent a number of years there, wrote (at the turn of the century) that there were about 1,000 looms in Kermān itself;[3] 100 in Ravār; and in the villages of the area only 30. He dilated on the excellence of the weaving and added that if the carpets of Kermān were widely known "they would become the fashion, especially for drawing-rooms and dainty boudoirs". Fifty years ago the Kermān carpet was, indeed, little known abroad.

Sykes protested against the introduction of European designs in Kermān by H.H. the Ferman Ferma —who had been governor there. He may have been referring to a fine rug which that prince had ordered to be woven for himself by one of the most prominent master-weavers of the time. The design is taken from the picture "Fête Champêtre" by Watteau, of which His Highness probably possessed an engraving. The rug bears inscriptions which record that it was woven to the order of Ferman Ferma by Ali Honari—one of whose descendants is today a prominent master-weaver of Kermān. It was presented to the Victoria and Albert Museum by Sir Charles Marling.

Sykes also stated that the usual quality woven in Kermān at that time counted 640 knots per *zar* of 39 inches, which is equivalent to 16×16 knots to the inch; and that the price was £1 per *zar*, or about 2*s*. a square foot! He too, like Curzon, described the shawl industry; hinting, moreover, that the competition of Kashmir was serious. The more serious competition of Paisley and the change in fashion which was to destroy the craft completely had not yet appeared.

The decline in the demand for Kermān shawls happily coincided with the sudden expansion of the carpet industry. The same deft fingers which had formerly woven and embroidered her shawls were quickly taught to master the art of weaving carpets. This, no doubt, accounts for the speed with which the carpet industry expanded; for the labour was there and was already half trained.

It has already been stated (Chapter V) that the expansion of the carpet industry in Persia—which began towards the end of the nineteenth century— was due, in a large measure, to the enterprise of the merchants of Tabrīz. In Tabrīz itself, in the Herīz area, in Meshed, in Sultānabād and in Kashan, these pioneers of the industry established factories or placed orders with local weavers. In Kermān, however—where a small but organised industry already existed—they were content, at first, to buy the carpets as they came off the looms, and to despatch them to Tabrīz, whence they were shipped on to Istanbul.

---

[1] See page 170. [2] Major P. M. Sykes, *Ten Thousand Miles in Persia* (John Murray, 1902).
[3] In 1948 two "fathers of the industry" in Kermān told me that they considered this figure exaggerated.

This system did not long endure. As more buyers from Tabrīz arrived in Kermān—and they soon numbered over a dozen—there were not enough carpets to go round. Furthermore, the Tabrīzis—always restless, always inventive—sought to introduce new designs and new variations of colour in their carpets; and to do this they were compelled to place orders with the existing weavers, or to set up looms or factories of their own. Thus, at about the turn of the century, the industry in Kermān entered upon a long period of steady and almost uninterrupted expansion.

It was about this time that the first foreign firms established offices in Kermān. The first to come was the Eastern Rug and Trading Company of New York (which was afterwards absorbed by the Fritz and La Rue Company of the same city). The late Mr. Otto Brandly went to Kermān for them in 1909, and was thus the first foreign carpet man to take up his residence there.

Some years before that, Nearco Castelli—who belonged to a respected and well-to-do Italian family of merchant-bankers of Istanbul—had begun to interest himself in the Persian carpet trade. The banking house was already in business relations with the Persian merchants of Istanbul and Tabrīz; and Nearco's brother, John Castelli, was already established in Tabrīz, and had been the first agent there of the Imperial Bank of Persia. So that Persia, to the Castellis, was not a remote, mysterious, or seemingly impenetrable country.

Nearco Castelli, trading as Nearco Castelli & Brothers, began operations in Tabrīz and New York at the end of the nineteenth century. Some years later the firm appointed a Tabrīz merchant, one Mirza Ali Ekber, as its representative in Kermān. He was transferred to Kashān in 1909 and was succeeded by George Stevens, who arrived in Kermān about a fortnight after Otto Brandly. It is fitting that the names of these two men—Brandly and Stevens, who were pioneers in the carpet industry of Kermān—should be recorded here.

During the decade which followed, the leading importing firms of Britain and America established offices in Kermān; and the industry continued to expand, with increasing momentum. Whereas in 1900 Sykes had reported that there were 1,000 looms in the city and 130 in the surrounding villages, by 1914 the number had tripled. The increase was mainly in the villages—particularly those within a radius of 25 miles of the city.

World War I inevitably produced a set-back in the industry. Kermān was for a short time in the hands of German agents; but the position was restored by a brigade of Indian troops and local levies under the command of Brigadier-General Sykes—the same Sykes who, twenty years before, had established the first British Consulate in Kermān.

As soon as the war was over the demand for Kermān carpets from America became greater than ever. The firms which had been formerly represented in Kermān quickly resumed their activities; and a number of other concerns established agencies as well. Under this fresh impetus, production continued to expand. The number of looms in the town increased and carpet weaving was introduced into many more of the surrounding villages. Between 1922 and 1929 the Kermān weaving industry reached its peak—both in output and in excellence. About 5,000 looms were in operation. By that time the Tabrīzis had almost faded out of the picture. The trade had passed into the hands of foreign firms.

The American depression of the early thirties was for Kermān a calamity of the first order. The town possessed one and only one major activity—carpet weaving; and 90 per cent of its production was being shipped to the United States. When it became evident in America that the crisis was not a mere passing phenomenon, orders for Kermān were cancelled, one by one. And one by one the American firms gathered in their carpets, closed their dye-houses, their designing rooms, their godowns and their offices, and withdrew.

The effect on the carpet industry of Persia of this wholesale withdrawal—for it took place from Sultānabād, Hamadān and other centres as well—was momentous and far reaching. When, at long last, America issued from the depression, the firms which had survived found themselves faced with a Persia very different from that which they had previously known. Nationalism, under the dynamic impetus of Shah Riza Pahlavi, was dominating men's minds. Foreign firms no longer enjoyed their former prestige; and the privileges—to which they had presumed that they were entitled—had ceased to exist. Under such conditions, advancing money to penniless weavers was, they decided, unthinkable. Most of the firms resolved that they would not return to Persia. The most important of them all, which had maintained its installations throughout the crisis, sold out to a newly formed company, organised and capitalised by the State.

Meantime, the Persian merchants and master-weavers had not been idle. There was no lack of capital in Persia; for the feverish activities of the reigning monarch—in every department of the State and in every part of the country—were beginning to produce boom conditions. The abandoned looms and installations were taken over by local interests; so that when the orders began once more to trickle in from abroad, the carpets were made by Persian, and not by Western firms, as before; and were purchased from them by agents appointed for the purpose.

By the middle thirties the industry in Kermān was on its feet again, although production did not reach, and has not yet reached, the figure of 1929. A careful count of the number of looms in the whole area was made in 1937 and showed the following result:

Weaving Centre	Number of Looms
Kermān city	1,745
Rafsinjān (Bahramabād) and vicinity	74
Jupār and vicinity	466
Mahān and vicinity	309
Zarānd and vicinity	162
Ravār and vicinity	300
Kuhpayeh district	178
Chatrūd	252
Khanuk	21
Hūdk	62
Sarasiab	67
Dewziah	36
Seredār	58
Mazabād	19
Gōk	200
	3,949

In the autumn of 1948, when the present survey was written, the number of looms in operation was still about 4,000.

World War II did not prove to be so calamitous for Kermān as the American depression. Orders from the United States were not curtailed until Pearl Harbour, and by that time a new and striking local demand had arisen in Tehrān, which kept the industry going until foreign demand was once more restored.

Boom conditions—to which reference has been made—had continued in Persia throughout the thirties with increasing momentum, particularly in the capital. Shah Riza far exceeded his illustrious predecessor, Shah Abbas, in the number and extent of the avenues and squares which he caused to be laid out and in the importance and variety of the public buildings which he caused to be erected. We have seen (p. 53) that he determined that Tehrān should not only be the administrative capital of his realm, but also its financial, commercial, industrial and cultural centre. In this he succeeded in a manner which must have gone beyond his expectations. Tehrān became a magnet which attracted to itself a greater part of the intelligence, the wealth, the ambition—as well as the knavery—of the country. It grew in extent, in lustre, in activity—and in population.

The problem of housing this influx of people, largely of the middle class, was further complicated by the entry of the Allied forces into Persia, which resulted in a second building boom. Soon the new, broad, asphalted avenues were lined with flats and private houses. A vast acreage of floor space was created, which clamoured for the best carpets which Persia could produce. The demand was mostly for plain red grounds with medallions; for the Persians delight in bright cochineal red—unfaded and untamed.

Thus, by this unexpected local activity a serious crisis in the Kermān industry was averted.

After the armistice, and as soon as transport became available, shipments to America were resumed. But they were on a smaller scale than before the war: for the style of furnishing had changed. Plain carpets —the very antithesis of the floral motives, the complicated sinuosities, the whorls and tendrils of Kermān—were in vogue. What demand remained for Kermān carpets was concentrated on patterns of French inspiration. Many hundreds of them—all very much alike—were shipped to the United States. During 1947 and 1948 the demand for carpets in the French style gained momentum. By the end of 1948 Kermān was weaving designs which were borrowed directly from Aubusson and Savonnerie.

The Kermān Carpet: the Technique of Production

Kermān produces the most refined and the most elegant carpets in Persia—which is to say, in the world. That does not mean that no carpets have ever been produced outside Kermān superior to the finest Kermān productions. It may be doubted, for instance, if many carpets have been produced in Kermān which rivalled the one which Emogli wove in Meshed twenty years ago for Kuzekenani (see p. 169). But pieces like that are the exceptions which enhance the truth of the first generalisation.

Thirty years ago Kashān might have challenged Kermān for the premier position. The average

Kashān weave, at that time, was more closely knotted than the Kermān. But there the superiority of Kashān ended. Her designers were humdrum. None of them compared in artistic endowment, in creative ability or in draftsmanship with the designers of Kermān. In colour, too, the Kashān carpets were far below their rivals. Whereas the Kermān dyers prided themselves on the range of their shades, the Kashān dyers were limited in their scope and lacked invention. Virtually all the carpets of Kashān contained the same dozen colours. The attempts of the Kashān weavers to produce cream ground carpets were lamentable.

Thus we can, with assurance, award the palm to Kermān. Forty years ago, when she turned from shawls to carpets, Kermān took the lead and she has held it ever since.

The province of Kermān produces excellent carpet wools. They are similar to the wools of Khūrasān and somewhat lighter and finer than those of Kermanshāh. They are, however, heavier in grease than the northern wools. The principal producing districts are Bām, Rūdbār, Rafsinjān, Jirūft and the vicinity of Kermān city. In the days when land transport in Persia was slow and expensive and when the demand for wool was not so great as it is today, the wool produced within the province was not exported and was sufficient to meet the demands of the carpet industry. Today the situation has changed. The woollen mills of Isfahān and Yezd are frequent buyers on the Kermān market, and in consequence the Kermān weavers have to supplement their supplies from Meshed, Sabsawār and Kermanshāh. In addition to these importations of wool, considerable

192. WASHING WOOL, KERMĀN

quantities of spun yarn are imported every year from Tabrīz, 1,000 miles away. The Tabrīz product, being somewhat harsh and kempy, is less esteemed than the yarns spun from local wools, or wools from Khūrasān or Kermanshāh.

The sheep of the Kermān province, like those of Khūrasān, are clipped twice a year—in spring and autumn. But Kermān—unlike Meshed—possesses three power-driven carding plants, so that the problem of carding spring wools does not exist (see p. 167). Both clips are used for carpet yarns, but the wools from the two clips are not blended as they should be. The yarns spun from each clip are used indiscriminately in the same carpet.

Kermān, like the other weaving centres of Persia, possesses an important hand-spinning industry, which gives employment to some 8,000 women in the city and in the nearby villages, all the year round. They spin the power-carded wool on native spinning wheels, which are, on the whole, quite efficient (Plate 193). The spinners are paid 35 rials a *batman* of $6\frac{1}{2}$ lb.[1]

We have seen that the astonishing expansion which took place in the Kermān weaving industry between 1900 and 1929 was due, primarily, to the demand from the United States; and as America called for a wide range of sizes—from 9 × 6 feet to 30 × 15 feet —looms of the roller type were adopted in Kermān, because this type can carry a carpet from 9 to 30 feet long (see Plate 11).

These looms were set up in the houses—from two to four looms in a house—first in the city, and as the demand for carpets increased, in the nearby villages. Small factories, too, containing from ten to forty

191. HOUSE OF A CARPET CONTRACTOR, KERMĀN

[1] For a note on the exchange value of the *rial* see page 99.

193. Spinning Yarn, Kermān

194. Winding the Yarn on Bobbins, Kermān

looms, were established in the city. Of these there were about a dozen in 1948. A few were established in the villages also, but they were small and of no consequence.

The carpets woven in the nearby villages—as well as those woven in distant Rafsinjān and Ravār—are indistinguishable from those woven in the city; for the city and village carpets are identical in construction and quality. With few exceptions, indeed, every village carpet is planned, the design for it is drawn, and the yarns for it are spun and dyed in the city. When ready, the design and the materials are forwarded to the village and the local inspector superintends the weaving. This is the general practice; although one of the prominent Persian firms maintains dye-houses in the important weaving villages of Mahān and Jupār. They claim that in this way they obtain greater variety in the colours of their carpets—which is no doubt correct.

The weavers of Kermān are Persians and they weave the Persian knot exclusively. Unhappily, a pernicious variation of the knot has been introduced in the Kermān area—and is spreading with alarming rapidity. It is undermining the structure of the Kermān carpet, and unless it is checked it will dissipate the renown of the Kermān weave. This unfortunate state of affairs will be referred to at greater length below.

Kermān and Bijār are the only two weaving centres of Persia where three wefts—instead of one or two—are used. All three wefts are passed, one above another, between each row of knots. The first and third are the same in thickness and are slightly thinner than the warp. The middle weft is very thin indeed—thinner than any weft in common use in Persia. The wefts are passed in the following manner: the first weft is passed immediately above each row of knots; the warps are then crossed by lowering the lease rod (see p. 23) and then the thin weft is passed. The warps are then uncrossed by raising the lease rod; and finally the third weft is passed.

There is no advantage in introducing three wefts into a hand-knotted carpet fabric—instead of the usual two. The appearance of the carpet is not improved—either on the front or back; nor does it handle any better. There is no increase in strength or durability. The practice is, indeed, merely a waste of time. I enquired from several knowledgeable persons in Kermān why it was not abandoned. The answer was always the same: the Kermān carpet has always been woven in this way and the system must not be changed. The argument might carry weight if another change—as fundamental as it is malignant—had not already been introduced into the Kermān fabric.

195. The Last Stage: Clipping the Finished Carpet

Labour conditions in Kermān—which were scandalous twenty years ago—have steadily improved since then, and are still improving. Today conditions are no worse than they are in other weaving centres of Persia. The factories are light and clean; the dark, insalubrious hovels which housed the looms of twenty years ago are no more. Press criticism, the vigilance of the League of Nations, the discussions in the Majlis, and above all the activities of the Tūdeh party, have had their influence on the merchants and the master-weavers. The recent Labour Law—although in great measure disregarded—is on the Statute Book; and the more responsible firms are beginning to take it seriously. The movement for the amelioration of the lot of the Kermān weaver goes on.

The method of payment of the weavers differs somewhat from that in vogue in other centres of Persia. The unit of work is the *nishan* of 160 knots. In 1948 the rate of pay was 34 rials per hundred *nishans*, or 16,000 knots. The weavers of Kermān are fast and skilful, so that a head-weaver can easily earn up to forty rials a day with a good assistant.[1]

We have seen that there are about 1,800 looms in the town. Nearly all of them are in private houses, with two or four looms to a house. The householder is not, as a rule, a weaver himself. He may be a tradesman, craftsman or broker; and he employs a head-weaver, who at the same time weaves and directs the looms. The householder's wife and children supply the labour, which may be supplemented from outside the family.

The carpet industry has brought more prosperity to the villages of the Kermān area than it has to the town. The reason for this is that the villagers are cultivators who, with their families, live almost entirely on food which is produced by the village. Weaving, for the villagers, is a supplementary source of income, which enables them to satisfy many of their simple wants. The cumulative effect of a steady influx, year in, year out, into a village, of several thousands of *tomans* a week, is manifest in the air of comparative well-being which most of the weaving villages possess.

Four qualities of carpets are woven in Kermān. They are known respectively as: 70/35, 80/40, 90/45 and 100/50. The bulk of the production is in the first two. The 70/35 quality is mainly used by the "bazaar" weavers; the 80/40 by the more important firms who produce for the American and European markets. The 90/45 and 100/50 qualities are expensive and are only used to weave specially fine pieces. The first figures shown above—70, 80, 90 and 100—indicate the number of warp strings which are laid per *gireh* of 7 centimetres. And the second figures—35, 40, 45 and 50—indicate the number of rows of knots per *gireh*. As the knot is woven on two strings of the warp, the 70/35 quality actually means 35×35 knots per *gireh*. These qualities, translated into knots per inch, work out as follows:

70×35 quality	12.7×12.7 knots per inch
80×40 quality	14.5×14.5 knots per inch
90×45 quality	16.3×16.3 knots per inch
100×50 quality	18.1×18.1 knots per inch

The above figures are nominal in the case of "bazaar" carpets. The entrepreneur, too, rarely lays his warps in accordance with his contract. He hopes, if the carpet comes up well, to get away with it—and he generally does. The firms, on the other hand, which control their own looms—whether in factories or in houses—have the warps laid as they want them.

In Kermān, as in all the important weaving centres of Persia, a firm which is engaged in the carpet trade has the choice of several methods of procedure: (1) It may purchase carpets ready woven in the bazaar. (2) It may purchase them on loom, partially woven. (3) A contract may be signed with an entrepreneur who controls a number of looms, to weave so many hundred *zars* of carpet, the sizes, designs and colours to be indicated, and the entrepreneur to supply the materials and the scale-paper drawing of the design. Such a contract will call for an appropriate advance in cash and a proviso for further payments to be made as the work proceeds. (4) The firm may purchase the wool, give it out to be spun and have the yarn dyed in its own dye-house; it may engage designers and draftsmen to prepare special designs, and may then contract with an entrepreneur or with individual weavers to produce the carpets with the firm's materials. Or, finally, (5) the firm may itself embark directly on the manufacture of carpets by establishing a factory and engaging weavers to work at so may rials per unit of 100 *nishans*. All these methods are in use in Kermān.

Of Design

The renown which the Kermān carpet enjoys throughout the world is due primarily to happy blending of design and colour. The weavers contribute less to the distinction of the carpet than these

---

[1] For a note on the exchange value of the *rial* see page 99.

two elements; for the weavers of Tabrīz, Arāk or of Kashān are as skilled as those of Kermān, yet their product falls far short of the Kermān carpet.

Of the two elements—design and colour—the former is, I think, the more important. I would hesitate to say this of any other Persian weave; because, by and large, colour is the first element to be noticed in a carpet. Design appeals more properly to the trained and practised eye. But the designers of Kermān have put so much art into the Kermān carpet that it is their work—and not so much the work of the dyer—which has given to the carpet its peculiar refinement, its elegance and its style.

I endeavoured, during my stay in Kermān in 1948, to discover examples of the work of the more famous of the Kermān designers. In this I was successful beyond my expectations. It is with pleasure that I am able to include in this survey no less than 34 plates—some line drawings, some photographs of coloured plates and some photographs of carpets, many of which have long since been in service in Western homes. To most of these plates I have added the names of the designers: for, however famous these men were in Kermān itself, they are unknown to the Western world. It is fitting that their names should be recorded here, for Kermān will not see their like again. I append the names of the most famous among them. All but two of them are dead:

    Mohsen Khan
    Hassan Khan (his son)
    Khashem Khan (his grandson)
    Ahmed Khan
    Ahmed Ali Khan
    Zeman Khan
    Sheikh Hossein
    Azizollah
    Ali Riza

Of these men Mohsen Khan was the earliest. His son, Hassan Khan (Plate 196) who died in 1945, and Ahmed Khan are the most renowned.

Unlike Arāk (which has been weaving one and only one style of carpet for almost a generation) Kermān, for the last fifty years, has been producing a richer variety of lovely designs than all the rest of Persia put together. Her designers have had to follow the trend of fashion in America (as indicated to them by the firms for which they worked), but being creative artists they invariably added something of their own.

The genesis of a definite style of Kermān carpet

196. HASSAN KHAN
One of the most noted designers of Kermān; died 1945.

—on a sufficiently important scale to warrant special recognition—dates from the period of the decline of the shawl industry and its gradual replacement by carpet weaving. That was about fifty years ago. As might be expected, the designers of those early Kermān carpets borrowed freely from the Kermān shawls. It is, indeed, probable that many of those carpets were designed by men who had previously been engaged in designing shawls and the fine woollen materials out of which the coats of Persian grandees were fashioned in those days (Plate 203). The lupin-like motives of this plate and those which surround the "Fête Champêtre" of Watteau (see p. 201) were favourites of those early designers. So, too, were the medallion-and-corner designs of the type illustrated by Plate 202; and (for rugs only) the lovely arboreal patterns, some with singing birds in the field and border (Plates 204, 205, 208).

The characteristics of these early Kermāns were airiness and delicacy of colour. This was achieved by the use of two tone effects in the same flower—rose and light rose, green and light green, blue and light blue—generally without outlines. The art which produced those carpets is almost lost; almost, but yet not quite. It is still enshrined in sackfuls of tattered scale-paper designs which fill the dark store rooms of the more prominent carpet producers in Kermān. This period—which for want of a better name we may call the Shawl Period—lasted from the late nineties until the outbreak of World War I. As we have seen, that catastrophe interrupted and disorganised the development of the industry, which marked time until 1919.

No sooner was the war over than expansion was resumed on a more rapid scale than ever. The American market, however, demanded something new from Kermān. The importers in New York had already discovered that the thin, delicate carpets of the Shawl Period did not stand up to the harsh attentions of the New York finishers. A thicker, more robust fabric was demanded; and with it bolder and more robust designs. The Vienna book[1] was rediscovered; and soon the Kermān designers were busy redrawing, in their own way, the famous carpets of the Sefavi kings. But they were not satisfied with mere redrawings. Borrowing freely from the best classical models, they devised new and exciting combinations of their own: elaborate, well-covered medallion-and-corner designs, all-over repeating patterns; and, above all, the elegant panel designs, which have become famous the world over (Plates 211–244). The Classic Period was under way. It lasted for ten years. Kermān has never produced more carpets or better carpets than those produced during that period.

But the style in America was changing. The well-to-do classes demanded smaller motives, more closely covered grounds and plenty of detail. The versatile designers of Kermān produced them, and the period of Covered Grounds was ushered in (Plates 245–257). This period was caught by the depression, but it lasted until 1937.

It was followed by a demand for floral patterns of a different order. Well-covered grounds were wanted as before, but with larger detached and disconnected motives. In this, the Floral Period, the influence of the type of disconnected floral pattern which had been so long in vogue in Arāk was manifest. Once more the Kermān designer set to work and produced a new style which was highly successful. It was at this period that the ancient Persian convention of the straight line border, with its attendant guards, was breached. It was replaced by the so-called "broken border", which was, in many respects, an improvement on the Persian practice—although sometimes the new type of border appeared to be too wide and to encroach too deeply upon the central field. The new style lasted well into the war and was still in demand after the armistice (Plates 258–265).

But not for long; for in America the stylist had again been busy. This time the inspiration came from France; and soon the cry of the New York importers was for French Florals and nothing but French Florals. In 1946, when I visited Kermān, I counted 700 carpets in the bazaar—all in this type of design (Plates 266–269). During 1947 and 1948 the trend towards French design became more pronounced and more catholic. The unhappy designers of Kermān were kept busy drawing puzzling and unfamiliar forms taken from French period carpets of Aubusson and Savonnerie. I have not included a plate to show an extreme example of this style which the Kermān weavers were producing in 1948. The reader, if he is interested, can find designs of this type in any handbook on French period carpets. But Plates 268 and 285 indicate the wanton miscegenation of French with Persian which resulted from this Gallic invasion.

It would, of course, be absurd to suggest that when these changes took place the entire production of Kermān was suddenly switched over to the new style. For there were always individuals or firms or markets which clung to the established and accepted forms of Persian design, and which viewed with distaste the prostitution of a peculiarly Persian art by the Western decorator. In every case, and understandably, the new styles were dictated by America, which is by far the largest consumer of Kermān carpets. And because in America new modes tend to uniformity, a change in style there was quickly followed by the production in Kermān of a new and uniform style of carpet. The new style became widespread and unmistakable.

Why do the American importers do these things? Why does their passion for something new to sell lead them to destroy an ancient, lovely and endemic art? Their activity during the last forty years has been an inestimable boon to Persia, but they have some sad depravities to answer for.

I beseech them, before it is too late, to examine anew their position. Instead of unwittingly helping to destroy Persia's unique contribution to the world —the art of carpet design—(which, I am confident, they have no desire to do) let them assist the Persians to maintain and perfect that art. Surely there are enough varieties of beauty there to satisfy the most exacting decorator—without calling on France today

---

[1] *Oriental Carpets* (Vienna, 1896).

for inspiration, and perhaps tomorrow on Mexico or Egypt.

Happily the French Period coincided with a demand, both from America and Tehrān, for plain ground medallion carpets in Persian designs. New York wanted them in pastel colours: powder blue, rose and cream; Tehrān in flaming cochineal reds. Here, at least, the Kermān designers were on familiar ground (Plates 270–272).

Of Dyes and Dyeing

Kermān—to its high credit—is the only weaving centre in Persia where foreign dyes are almost entirely banned. This has not always been so. There was a period between the wars when the assiduous German salesmen succeeded in inducing many of the merchants and master-weavers to try their wares. But the Germans failed in Kermān, as they were bound to fail. For in Kermān cochineal is used for dyeing red—and cochineal is a wayward and capricious product. That remarkable dyestuff darkens in water or in sunlight; becomes a fiery red when treated with acids, and a bluish peony when treated with alkalis; it turns brown when oxidised; and can be made to bleed like a slaughtered steer. On the other hand, the synthetic chrome red which the Germans produced, though a perfect match for the red of the Kermān dyers, was immovable.

Unhappily for the Germans, the yarns which had been dyed with their *ersatz* product matched only too perfectly those which had been dyed with cochineal, so that the two shades soon got mixed in the

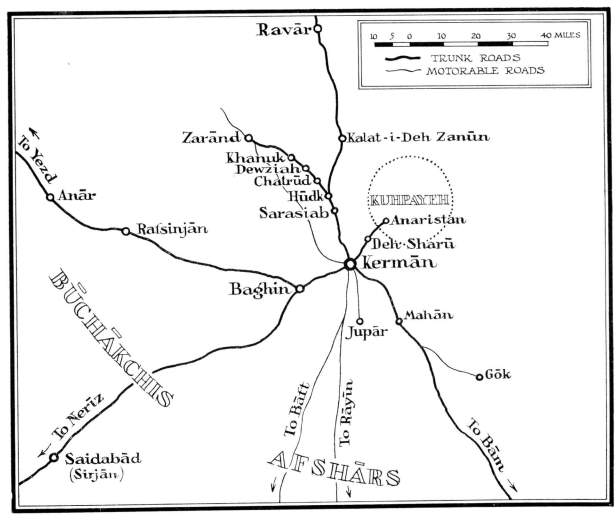

MAP VII. THE KERMĀN WEAVING AREA

yarn stores. And when the first carpets which had been woven with these mixed yarns reached the hands of the finishers in New York and London, pandemonium reigned. The reds in the carpets which issued from their liquors were streaked, or piebald, or mottled. In some cases the carpet was maroon at one end and pure pillar-box at the other. Frantic telegrams were despatched to Kermān, and the Germans were all but booted out of the town. A little of their synthetic red is still used by the less scrupulous weavers; but very little. Some synthetic greens are also used; but even these are being abandoned by the more responsible producers.

Heinrich Jacoby has truly stated that the secrets of the Persian methods of dyeing lie in the quality of the materials; in experience; in the bestowal of unremitting care and attention on every part of the process; and in allowing plenty of time. Fine weather, too, plays its part. It is doubtful, he adds, if any ancient processes have been lost. With all these statements we must heartily agree.[1]

The Kermān dyers follow these precepts more closely than any of the guilds of dyers in Persia. This, no doubt, arises from the fact that they are helping to produce the most aristocratic carpets in the world for the wealthiest clients in the world; and, unlike their less fortunate colleagues, they can afford to do their best and can give rein to their invention. For no Kermān carpet worthy of the name contains less than fifteen colours, and the more sumptuous pieces contain twice as many.

One of the principal claims to renown of the Kermān weavers is that they have mastered the art of producing pleasing carpets on light grounds. The efforts of Tabrīz, Meshed, Hamadān and Arāk in this respect are lamentable: they use the same colours on cream grounds as they do on red.

Not so the Kermānis. Their dyers know how to produce a multiplicity of light, bright and clear colours—as well as soft pastel shades. And their designers know how to apply them. Kermān, therefore, possesses an almost undisputed monopoly in carpets, elegant in design, with light or pastel effects of colour.

The principal dyestuffs which are in use in Kermān are indigo[2] (synthetic), cochineal, madder, walnut husks, weld, pomegranate rind, vine leaves, straw and henna. Alum is the only mordant used —as everywhere in Persia.

The method of dyeing with cochineal is similar to that employed in Meshed; except that most of the Kermān dyers no longer practise the stupid system of first steeping the yarns in lime for 24 hours—a practice which is still common in Meshed. In both places the yarn (and sometimes in Kermān the wool) is first boiled in alum. In Meshed it is afterwards boiled in a decoction of cochineal with barberry, citric acid, or sometimes sour grapes. In Kermān sour grapes are preferred as an acidulant.

The other dyestuffs are used very much in the same way as elsewhere in Persia; except that the Kermānis are cleverer than their colleagues of the north in combining their ingredients to produce a wealth of intermediate shades.

One of the recent important developments of the industry in Kermān is the dyeing of the wool before, instead of after, spinning. By this means complete penetration of the dyestuff is obtained, which produces an evenly coloured carpet. The technique is employed only in dyeing the ground shades of plain ground carpets, or of those with very open grounds.

The Jūftī Knot

It has been my pleasure in this chapter (and I have not experienced this pleasure often in the preparation of this survey) to pay homage to the superb technique of the Kermān designer and to the skill and constancy of the Kermān dyers, who have successfully withstood the wiles of European salesmen, to whom their colleagues in the north long since capitulated.

But what avails the genius of the designers or the skill of the dyers if the weavers of Kermān—expert and industrious as they are—threaten by their malpractices to destroy the good name of the Kermān carpet? For this is what is taking place at present.

I have already had occasion to draw attention to the spread among many of the weaving districts of Persia of the pernicious practice of weaving the *jūftī* knot. This, it will be remembered, consists of tying the knot on four strings of the warp instead of two, so that the resultant fabric contains only half the knots called for by the number of warp strings. The fabric, therefore, lacks density, and its wearing quality is impaired.

Twenty years ago this practice scarcely existed in Kermān; but it took hold in the early thirties and has continued, steadily, to spread. Since the emergence of Tehrān as a market the disease had become more virulent: for as long as the productions of the

---

[1] Heinrich Jacoby, in *A Survey of Persian Art* (Oxford University Press).
[2] Indigo was grown in Jiruft in the tenth century. Le Strange, *The Lands of the Eastern Caliphate* (Cambridge University Press, 1930).

Kermān looms were marketed in Kermān itself—where the buyers possessed a wide experience of the weaver's craft—it could be held in check. The Tehrān buyers, however, possessed no technical knowledge of weaving. They bought the carpet on its appearance only; and this encouraged the Kermān entrepreneurs to produce a cheaper but defective fabric.

The *jūftī* knot of Kermān differs slightly from that in use in Meshed, Birjānd and other localities where the method is employed in combination with the Persian knot. The difference is illustrated on page 26.

Unless the loom inspector keeps his eyes on the weaver, he cannot detect the tying of the fraudulent knot; and unfortunately when once the knot is tied, detection is next to impossible—either from the front or the back of the carpet. It is estimated that half the knots woven in Kermān today are fraudulent, and there is no reason to suppose that the practice will diminish; it is more likely to increase.

No practical method has yet been devised for coping with the evil. Unless one is found and the malpractice is uprooted, the renown of the Kermān carpet will, like that of Meshed, inevitably decline.

East and West in Kermān

It has been pointed out (p. 202) that after the world crisis of the thirties production passed out of the hands of the Western importers into the hands of Persian concerns, some of which were of considerable importance. In 1948 two of these concerns controlled as many as 1,000 looms each and there were others scarcely less important. There are indications, however, that the Western firms are once more beginning to take a hand in the weaving industry. Some of their local agents, who had hitherto been content to buy their goods in the bazaar, are beginning to place orders direct with the weavers or with Persian entrepreneurs. The reasons for this are twofold. First, the Persian firms have failed to produce the variety of designs which the Western markets demanded. For designs are expensive to produce, and the temptation is to weave a hundred carpets from a single pattern, instead of ten or twenty. And secondly, a few of the more important Persian firms have themselves established selling agencies in the West, in competition with the concerns which they were formerly supplying. This has led to retaliation by the Western firms.

If this movement should continue, as it may do, the industry in Kermān may revert once more—at least in part—into the hands of Western importers. It is unlikely, however, to do so on anything like the scale of the late twenties. The Persian firms are well entrenched and will maintain their hold. It is more probable that in Kermān East and West will work together side by side, in friendly rivalry.

Conversation Piece

My friend Ostad Ali Ekber has been engaged for some years in building a house. Having been informed that it was finished at last, I sought his permission to wait upon him, in order to wish him many fortunate hours under his new roof.

197. KERMĀN: A GENTLEMAN'S HOUSE

I was admitted through an imposing gateway into a large, open courtyard. In front of me was a flagged terrace. Beyond it stood a group of buildings dazzlingly white in their new plaster. Rarely had I seen a frontage of rounded arches more elegantly arranged. Between the buildings, sunken gardens had been laid out in trim formality.

When the prescribed enquiries as to our healths were over, I praised my friend's admirable house. But he lifted a refined hand in protest.

"It had been my intention," he said, "to build within this enclosure a house for my family, an office where I could transact my business, a dye-house, a factory, and store rooms for my merchandise. The plans were drawn to my satisfaction, and the building began. But before the foundations had been completed, the war broke out—the second world war within our lifetime. I allowed the work to proceed; but I was no longer interested in it. I thought: after the war, the few will be hungering for money and power, and the many for bread. And so it is—everywhere.

"I am an old man, and I was hoping that I might be permitted to end my days in peace, producing, for my own pleasure, a few fine carpets, here, under my eye. But there is no peace—only headaches, troubles and anxieties. Who would wish to extend such an existence?

"I am reminded of the philosopher who was condemned to death through the machinations of base judges and false witnesses. As he was being led away to the place of execution beyond the city wall, his gaolers noticed that he was laughing, silently, to himself. Astonished at this irregular deportment, they enquired if he were aware that in a few moments his head would be cut off. To which he replied, with every appearance of cheerfulness, that he was well aware of it. 'Wherefore, then, this unseemly behaviour?' they enquired. 'I laugh,' said he, 'at you, who have to return to yonder abominable city; and again I laugh, from satisfaction, at the thought that I am leaving it.'"

THE AFSHĀRI TRIBAL RUGS

It has already been noted (Chapter II) that Shah Ismail, the founder of the Sefavi dynasty, although born in Turkish-speaking Azerbaijān, was not of Turkish race. He was a descendant of Safi-ud-Din, the pious founder of a religious order of dervishes, who claimed descent from the Prophet himself. His father and grandfather, too, were religious men and noted warriors. It was due to the distinction of his family that at the age of thirteen he became the accepted leader of seven Turkish tribes of Azerbaijān. Without the 70,000 lancers provided by these tribes it is doubtful if Ismail would ever have been crowned Shah of all Persia in Tabrīz.

The prestige acquired by Ismail, who was at the same time the founder of a national dynasty and of a national religion, and his martial spirit, enabled him to keep his turbulent henchmen in order. But during the long reign of his successor, Shah Tahmasp, quarrels between the rival chiefs became incessant, and revolts were common. Tahmasp determined, therefore, to give the tribes a lesson. In accordance with an accepted practice of the time he transported a large section of the Afshārs—the most turbulent of the seven tribes—to the distant province of Kermān. There they reside to this day —a Turkish-speaking, semi-nomadic people, surrounded by a population alien in race and speech.

The Afshārs of Kermān province consist of two main divisions—the Afshāris proper and the Būchakchīs.[1] There is no record of the exile of the latter tribe; nor are there any ethnic or linguistic differences between the two. Presumably, therefore, the Būchakchīs separated from the main body after the migration took place. Both are regarded in the province as Afshārs. The Afshārs proper total about 4,000 families; the Būchakchīs 2,000. There is another Turkish tribe, the Shūli, which is apparently not regarded as belonging to either of these two divisions. The Shūli live about 25 miles south of Saidabād, close to the Bandar Abbas road.

Both of the above divisions are nomads. Both spend the long summers in their black-tented encampments on the western slopes of a high belt of country which extends for 150 miles in a south-easterly direction from a line running south-west of Rafsinjan almost to the Kermān-Bām road. The belt has an average width of about 40 miles. The Būchakchī tribes camp in the north-west part of it and the Afshārs in the south-eastern part. From November to March they retire southwards to the warmer foothills and the plains. The principal trading centre of the Būchakchīs is Saidabād (Sirjan) and of the Afshārs, Bāft. But the nomads prefer to barter their rugs against tea, sugar, cotton cloth, needles, thread and other commodities—which the travelling hucksters bring to their encampments— rather than to sell them to the crafty *dellals* of the bazaars of Saidabād and Bāft.

It must not be supposed that the belt of country above mentioned is occupied by the nomadic Afshār tribes alone. The broad valleys—particularly in the neighbourhood of Sirjan—are dotted with numerous Persian villages besides. In spite of the unending feud between predatory tribesmen and peaceful peasants, intermarriage, on an increasing scale, has been going on between them for centuries; so that the linguistic and ethnic differences between Turk and Persian are gradually disappearing. Practically all the tribesmen are today bilingual.

In the same way the so-called Afshāri rugs are no longer an exclusive product of the nomad Afshār tribes; for weaving is now general among the Persian villages of the area as well. In the immediate vicinity of Kermān, however, the villagers—if they weave at all—weave Kermān carpets.

The Persian villagers of this great area far outnumber the 40,000 nomadic Afshārs; and their output of rugs is far greater. They have borrowed designs and colours from the tribesmen; and the tribesmen have, in their turn, borrowed from their neighbours a few designs which are obviously Persian

---

[1] This is the local pronunciation; the more proper Turkish form would be Buchakji—a knife maker or knife dealer.

198. WEAVING AN AFSHĀRI RUG IN SAADATABĀD VILLAGE, NEAR SAIDABĀD
Note the scimitar-like instruments for beating the wefts.

(Plate 276). So that the tribal and village rugs are almost indistinguishable. Both kinds are bought and sold in the Kermān bazaar, and are shipped to the West, as Afshāri rugs; and I propose to use this collective name in writing about them.

There is one element, however, which the Persian villagers have not borrowed from the nomadic neighbours—the Turkish knot. Being Persians they weave the Persian knot. The nomads, on the other hand, who belong to the great race of Turkish weavers, undoubtedly wove the Turkish knot and nothing else at the time of the migration. But four centuries of intermarriage with Persian women have caused a certain amount of infiltration of the Persian knot into their tents.

The Afshār tribe are shepherds, so that the wool for their rugs presents no problem for them. The village weavers, too, usually possess a few sheep; and if their own wool is insufficient to complete their rugs, they supplement it by a purchase from the nomads. Thus, the Afshāri rugs are woven with first-class materials.

Formerly, the nomadic Afshārs and Būchakchīs used nothing but wool for the warps and wefts of their rugs. But owing to the rise in the price, many of them are finding it more profitable to sell the wool and buy cotton, a product of the neighbourhood, for the purpose. The villagers use nothing else but cotton. Thus, comparatively few of the Afshāri rugs which are being woven today have woollen warps and wefts.

The dyeing of the blues and greens—dark, medium and light—with indigo is a complicated process. Formerly the nomads made use of a native variety of the indigo plant, which grows in the region of Bām. But its use entailed the preliminary extraction of the dye from the plant—a laborious process—which has been abandoned. Imported indigo is used instead. Some of the tribes have their own dyers; but the problem is more usually solved by recourse to the dyer of a nearby village, or of an important centre like Saidabād or Bāft. The dyeing of madder (which is the only dyestuff used for the reds by nomads and villagers alike) is a less complicated process and is usually carried out by the weaver herself. The rest of the colours are dyed with the common dyestuffs of Persia—walnut husks, pomegranate rinds, vine leaves, weld, henna (for the orange) and straw for the light yellows. The operation is easy and is invariably carried out by the weavers—both in tent and in cottage. Thus, the dyes in the Afshāri rugs are excellent. The plague of aniline or synthetic dyes has not yet penetrated the area.

Both the nomads and the villagers weave their rugs on horizontal looms which are laid flat on the ground (Plate 198). The system has already been described on p. 23.

By and large, the Afshāri rug (like most of the tribal weaves of Persia) is a single-wefted fabric. Occasionally, however, one comes across a double-wefted piece—woven perhaps by a weaver from Kermān who had found her way to a village and wished to demonstrate that she was one better than her neighbours. Or she may have been a woman from one of the Qashqaī tribes of Fārs, who weave a double-wefted fabric.

The designs used by the Afshāri tribesmen (and borrowed from them by the villagers of the area) are unlike the designs of any of the Persian tribal or village weaves. Occasionally, however, a rug will bear a family resemblance to a tribal rug of Fārs. It may have been copied; or a weaver may have crossed the border from Fārs into Kermān and woven it there.

Many of their designs are original and striking. Like all the tribal rugs of Persia they are woven in straight lines—the horizontal, the perpendicular and the oblique of 45 degrees—for curves must first be plotted on scale paper, and that is hardly a feasible task for blacktenters. One of the cleverest—if not the most refined—of their creations is the *morgi* or Hen design (Plate 284). The weavers of the south seem to enjoy making a pattern out of representations of the domestic fowl; for the same motive appears quite frequently in the tribal rugs of Fārs as well. Their medallion patterns on plain or partly covered grounds (Plates 274, 282) are superior to those of any of the tribal or village rugs of Persia; but their adaptations of some of the floral or vase patterns of Kermān are not so happy. Plates 275, 276 represent the better designs of this type.

As we have seen in the case of the Balūchi rugs of Khūrasān, the design of an Afshāri rug is unhappily no longer a sure indication as to the tribe or village which produced it. For improved communications have made the better designs common to half a dozen localities.

The output of Afshāri rugs—like that of all the tribal rugs of Persia—has fallen far below the pre-war figure. Estimates of production varied, but the general view was that about 25,000 pieces were woven annually before the war; whereas in 1948 the figure was less than a quarter of that. The reasons were the same as those which affected the output of the tribal or village rugs of Hamadān, Kurdistān and Khūrasān: namely, the closing of the European markets and the rise in the price of wool. Until the importation of Persian rugs into the countries of Europe is once more permitted, there will be a limited demand for Afshāris in the Kermān bazaar —because America imports very few. And in Persia a limited demand means that weaving ceases in the tents and cottages. Happily for the tribal and village weavers, there was a good demand for wool, and the price was high.

I am not pessimistic about the future of the Afshāri rug. The product is an honest one: wools, dyes and designs are good. Weaving is not up to pre-war standard, but it should improve when the demand for good rugs revives. The pre-war figure of 25,000 rugs a year is not a large one. When the European markets reopen, it should be once more attained.

A NOTE ON YEZD

The ancient city of Yezd is renowned throughout Persia for the industry of its inhabitants and for the integrity and acumen of its traders, industrialists and bankers. There are, indeed, few bazaars in the country without one or two Yezdi merchants of enterprise and credit. The bill of a Zoroastrian banker of Yezd is accepted as sound paper from one end of the country to the other.

The Yezdis are busy people and traditionally they are weavers of textiles. Almost every house has its handloom where some kind of cotton or silk fabric is woven. During recent years a number of textile mills have been erected and their products enjoy a high reputation in the bazaars of Persia. The expression "Mal-i-Yezd"—a product of Yezd—is used in the bazaars to indicate good value.

Until a few years ago, Yezd was not a carpet-weaving centre of any importance.[1] There were 20 or 30 looms in the town, but no more. Most of the carpets woven were in one of two designs: the Herātī and the design which is shown on Plate 285.

During recent years, however, the industry has expanded considerably. In the early forties the State set up a number of looms there; and a few independent merchants did the same. Today, in the town itself and in a few of the neighbouring villages, there are about 200 looms in all.

The rapid expansion of the industry has had the unfortunate effect of destroying the distinctive character of the Yezd carpet, which was an interesting fabric and worth preserving. But the demand for Kermān carpets for the Tehrān market was such that local merchants imported designers and technicians from Kermān to weave them. Before long, the distinctive Yezd fabric had disappeared, and today Yezd is producing 200–300 carpets a year which are hardly distinguishable from the Kermān product.

Conversation Piece

My friend Tabassi led me down half a dozen steps and ushered me, with pride, into a kind of semi-basement, which was his factory. He had placed it, he explained, below ground level because in Yezd the heat in summer is intense and underground rooms are cooler. The factory was orderly, clean and well lighted from above. Men and women, boys and girls, were busy at the looms. We listened to the familiar drone of voices calling out the patterns and the tap-tapping of the weavers beating in their wefts.

"It would be without profit for me to say," said the gentle Tabassi, after we had completed the round of his looms, "that the carpets of Yezd are equal to the carpets of Kermān. For we belong to the same guild, and I could not deceive you, even if I would. But one thing I will say, and you, who understand such matters, will agree with me: the

---

[1] But Gouvea, who visited Yezd in 1603, said that at Atūd (14 leagues from Yezd) "le pavé était couvert d'un très riche tapis; c'est à Yezda qu'on fait les meilleurs du monde". I can trace no other reference to carpet weaving in Yezd in Sefavi times, and the good Gouvea may have made a mistake—he may have intended Kermān. In any case his note adds more confusion to the problem of the places of origin of the Sefavi carpets (see p. 7).

carpets of Yezd are honest carpets, while those of Kermān . . ."

"Alas," said I.

"You examined the weaving in my factory with attention. Did you discover a single *jūftī* knot in any carpet?"

"I did not," I said.

"You will not find any in Yezd. So far, we have prevented that sickness from entering our city. But for how long shall we be able to keep out a disease which has spread throughout Irān? Recently a weaver from Kermān came to my factory and asked for work. When he told me that he was a Kermāni I rushed off to the Governor and beseeched him to send the man away; because, as I explained, he had a contagious sickness. And it was done."

My friend was right. The Yezd carpet is an honest fabric, for the *jūftī* knot—which may bring about the eclipse of the Kermān carpet—scarcely exists in Yezd. The Yezd fabric is, therefore, denser and it will give long and satisfactory service. The expression "Mal-i-Yezd"—a product of Yezd—may become known beyond the confines of Persia.

199. Ravār Carpet (*c.* 1890)

200. Detail of a Ravār Carpet (*c.* 1900)

201. Classic Period: a Ravār Carpet (*c.* 1914)

202. Detail of a Design for a Kermān Carpet in the Style of the Shawl Period
Courtesy of M. Mustafa Kemal

203. Shawl Period: Design for a Kermān Rug by Hassan Khan (c. 1900)
It is not an uncommon practice in Persia to weave the portrait of a gentleman into a rug.

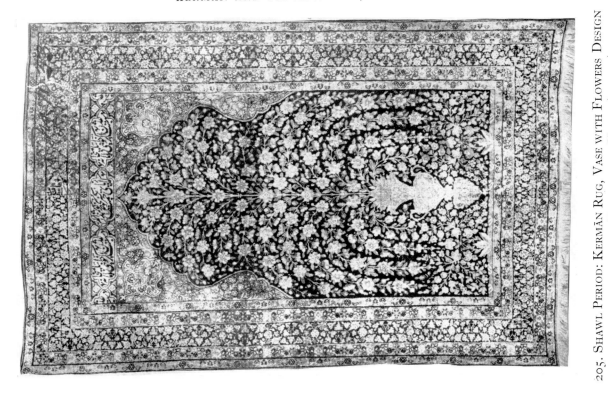

205. Shawl Period: Kermān Rug, Vase with Flowers Design inscribed with a Verse from Hafiz (c. 1910)

204. Shawl Period: Kermān Rug, Arboreal Design with Birds (c. 1900)

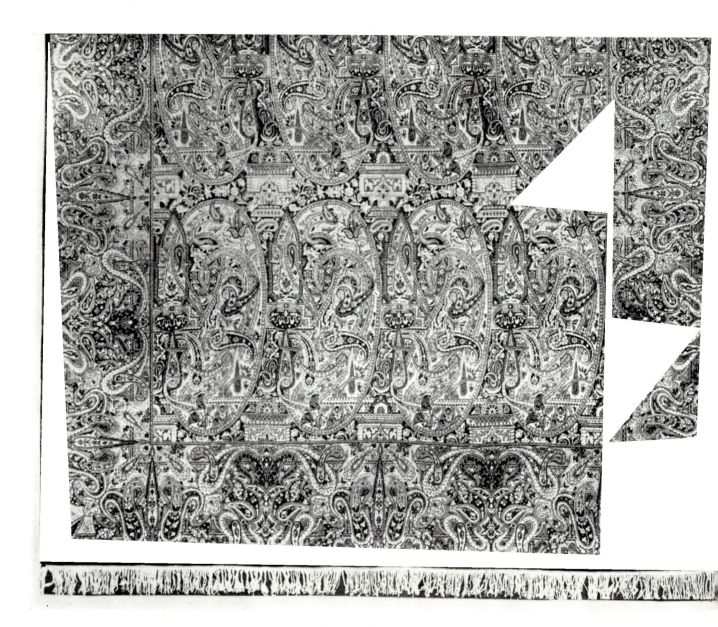

206. KERMĀN CARPET: SHAWL PATTERN (*c.* 1900)
Drawn by Ahmed Khan in 1934, after an original design by Kerbelai Mohammed Ali.

207. SHAWL PERIOD: A KERMĀN CARPET INTRODUCING SHAWL PATTERN MOTIVES ON AN OPEN GROUND (c. 1925)
Designed by Ali Mohammed Kashi.

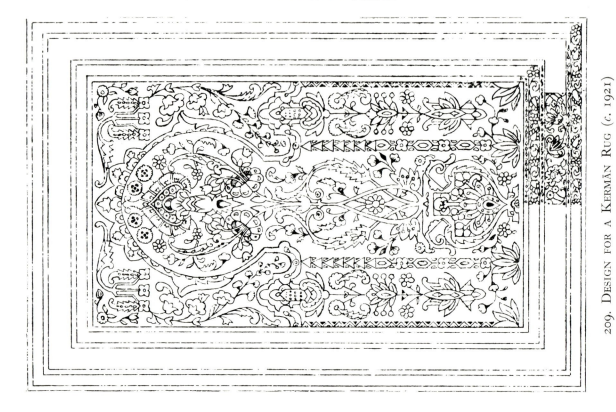

209. Design for a Kermān Rug (c. 1921)
Courtesy of M. Mustafa Kemal

208. Shawl Period: Kermān Rug, Animal and Floral Design (c. 1915)

210. Designs for Kermān Runners (c. 1912)
Courtesy of M. Mustafa Kemal

211. CLASSIC PERIOD: DESIGN FOR A KERMĀN CARPET, CONVENTIONAL MEDALLION AND CORNER
DRAWN BY SHEIKH HOSSEIN (c. 1915)

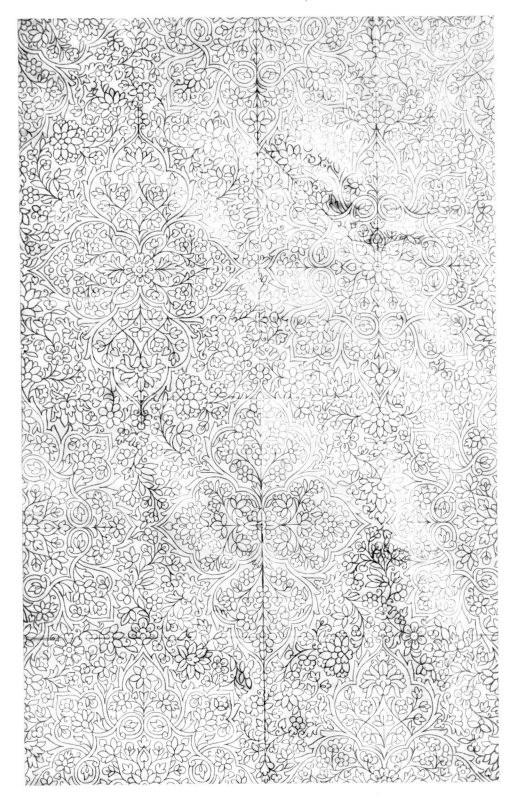

212. Classic Period: Design for a Kermān Carpet in Repeating Medallions (c. 1915)

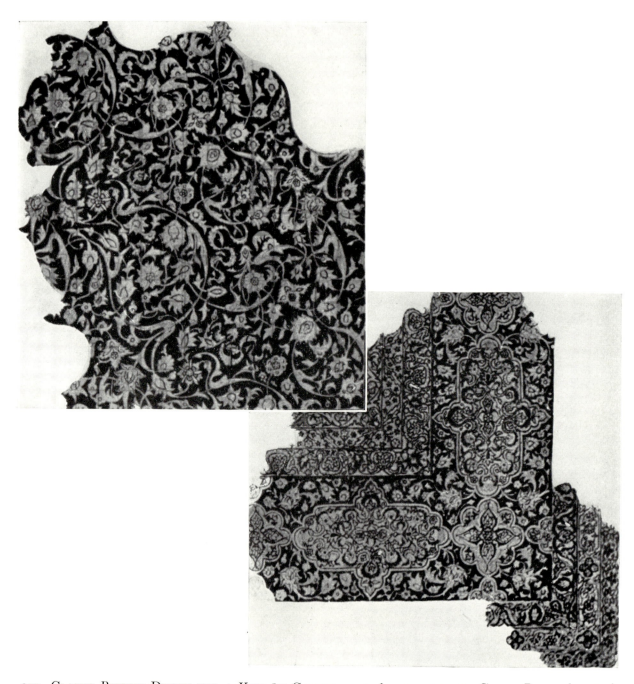

213. Classic Period: Design for a Kermān Carpet with Arabesques and Cloud Bands (c. 1919)

214. CLASSIC PERIOD: A KERMĀN CARPET
The design was drawn by Zeman Khan in 1922, after the Hunting Carpet in the Austrian Museum, Vienna.

215. CLASSIC PERIOD: REPEATING MEDALLION
DESIGN FOR A KERMĀN CARPET (c. 1927)

216. CLASSIC PERIOD: DESIGN FOR A KERMĀN
CARPET (c. 1925)

217. CLASSIC PERIOD: A KERMĀN CARPET WITH REPEATING MEDALLIONS
DESIGNED BY SHEIKH HOSSEIN (*c.* 1925)

218. Classic Period: a Kermān Carpet designed by Sheikh Hossein after a Sixteenth-century Carpet (*c.* 1925)

219. CLASSIC PERIOD: A DESIGN FOR A KERMĀN CARPET IN REPEATING ARABESQUES (c. 1925)

220. Classic Period: a Kermān Adaptation of the Persian Garden Design (*c.* 1928)

221. CLASSIC PERIOD: DESIGN FOR A KERMĀN RUG (c. 1927)
Courtesy of M. Mustafa Kemal

222. Classic Period: a Panel Design for the Field of a Kermān Carpet Designed by Sheikh Hossein (*c*. 1927)

223. Classic Period: Detail of a Kermān Carpet, Designed by Ali Mohammed Kashi (c. 1927)

224. CLASSIC PERIOD: A KERMĀN CARPET IN A COMPARTMENT DESIGN DRAWN BY ALI RIZA (*c.* 1927)

225. CLASSIC PERIOD: A KERMĀN CARPET IN A PANEL DESIGN WITH INSCRIPTIONS: PROBABLY DESIGNED BY ALI MOHAMMED KASHI (*c.* 1928)

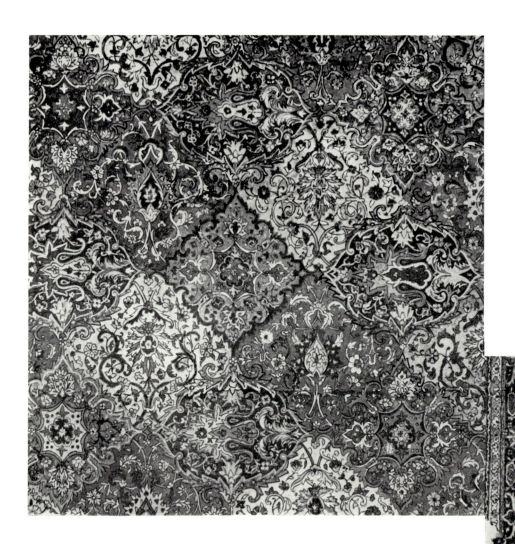

226. Classic Period: Design for a Kermān Carpet Drawn by Sheikh Hossein (c. 1928)

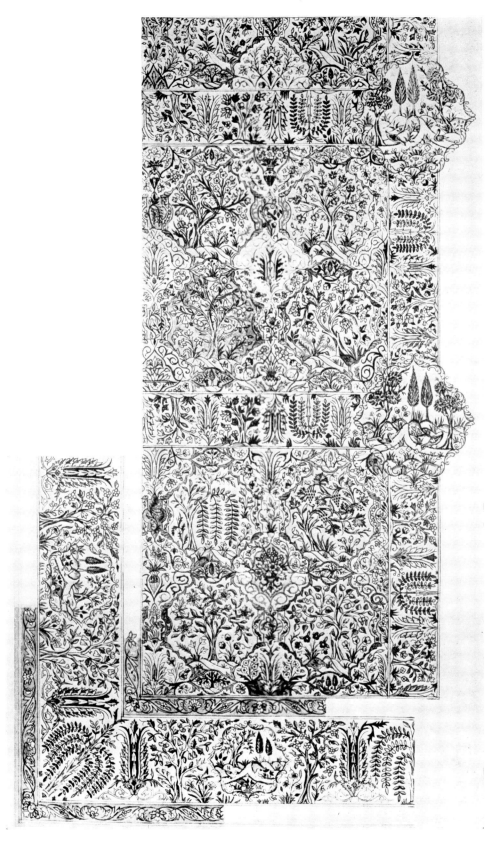

227. CLASSIC PERIOD: PANEL DESIGN FOR A KERMĀN CARPET BY ALI MOHAMMED KASHI (c. 1928)

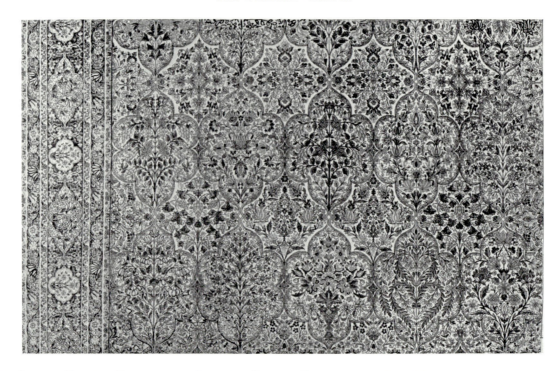

228. Classic Period: Detail of a Kermān Carpet, Designed by Ali Mohammed Kashi (*c.* 1928)

229. Design for a Kermān Rug (*c.* 1912)
Courtesy of M. Mustafa Kemal

230. CLASSIC PERIOD: KERMĀN CARPET; PANEL DESIGN BY ALI RIZA (c. 1928)

231. Classic Period: a Kermān Carpet in a Panel Design; probably Designed by Ali Mohammed Kashi (c. 1928)

232. CLASSIC PERIOD: A KERMĀN CARPET; PROBABLY DESIGNED BY KHASHEM KHAN (c. 1928)

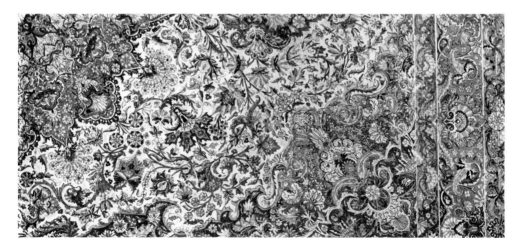

233. CLASSIC PERIOD: MEDALLION AND CORNER DESIGN FOR A KERMĀN CARPET WITH FLORAL AND ARABESQUE MOTIVES; DRAWN BY AHMED KHAN (c. 1929)

234. Classic Period: Kermān Carpet; Medallion and Corner Design embodying Classic Floral and Arabesque Motives; by Riza Bahramand (c. 1929)

235. CLASSIC PERIOD: A KERMĀN CARPET (c. 1929)
The border, being unattractive, has been eliminated.

236. CLASSIC PERIOD: DESIGN FOR A KERMĀN CARPET (c. 1929)

237. Classic Period: Design for the Field of a Kermān Carpet, all over with Floral and Arabesque Motives, by Ahmed Khan (c. 1929)

238. Classic Period: Animal and Tree Design for a Kermān Carpet (c. 1929)

239. Classic Period: Kermān Carpet Panel Design by Sheikh Hossein (c. 1929)

240. Classic Period: Design for a Kermān Carpet with Repeating Medallions; Drawn by Ali Riza in 1931 after an Earlier Model

241. CLASSIC PERIOD: DESIGN FOR A KERMĀN CARPET BY TAHIR ZADEH BIHZAD, SCHOOL OF ART, TEHRĀN

No two of the multiple medallions are alike.

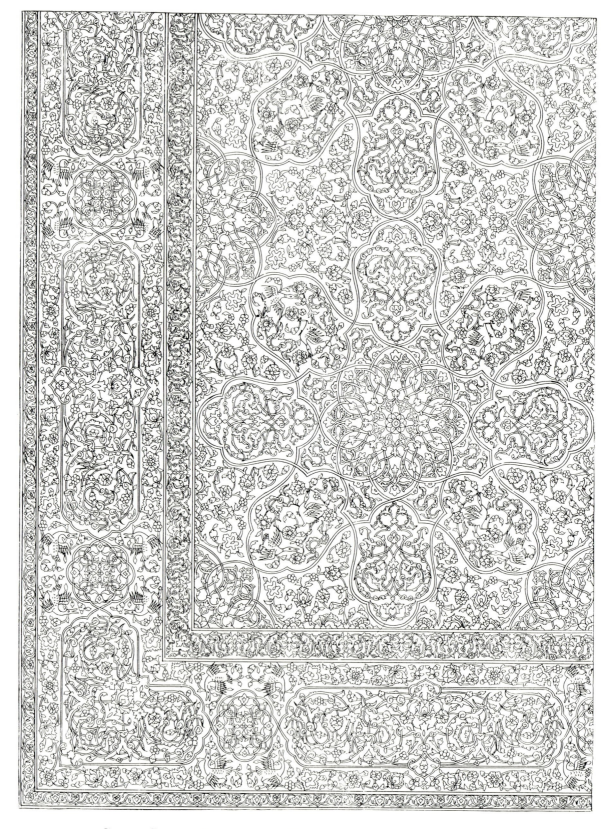

242. Classic Period: Design for a Kermān Carpet by Tahir Zadeh Bihzad, School of Art, Tehrān

243. Classic Period: the Sixteenth-century Vase Design suitable for a Kermān Carpet, Redrawn by Tahir Zadeh Bihzad, School of Art, Tehrān

244. Classic Period: Design suitable for a Kermān Carpet based on a Sixteenth-century Carpet: Drawn by Tahir Zadeh Bihzad, School of Art, Tehrān

245. PERIOD OF COVERED GROUNDS: DESIGN FOR A KERMĀN CARPET BY AHMED KHAN (*c.* 1931)

246. PERIOD OF COVERED GROUNDS: DESIGN FOR A KERMĀN CARPET DRAWN BY AHMED KHAN (*c.* 1929)

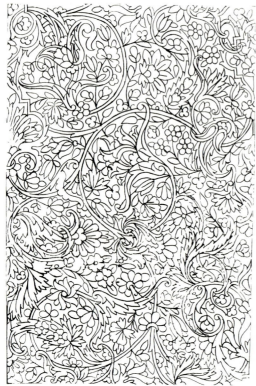

247. Period of Covered Grounds: Detail of an Arabesque and Floral Design for a Kermān Carpet (c. 1935)

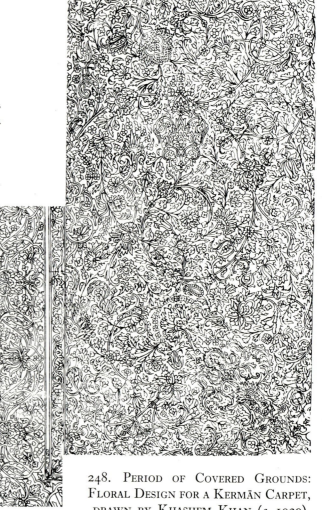

248. Period of Covered Grounds: Floral Design for a Kermān Carpet, drawn by Khashem Khan (c. 1929)

249. Period of Covered Grounds: a Kermān Carpet probably Designed by Sheikh Hossein (*c.* 1930)

250. Period of Covered Grounds: a Kermān Carpet probably Designed by Hassan Khan (c. 1930)

251. PERIOD OF COVERED GROUNDS: A KERMĀN CARPET IN A MOSAIC PATTERN, DESIGNED BY ALI RIZA (*c.* 1932)

252. Period of Covered Grounds: Kermān Carpet embodying the Early Shawl Motives Designed by Ahmed Khan (c. 1934)

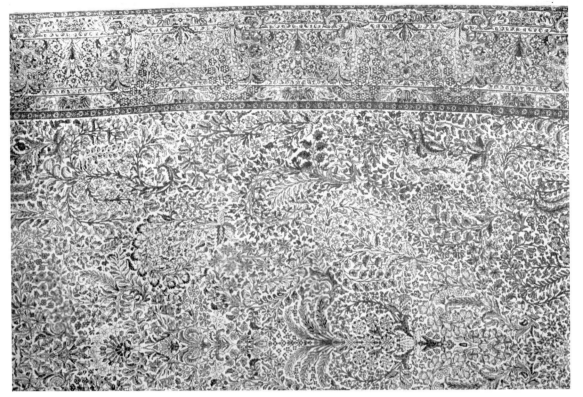

254. Period of Covered Grounds: Detail of a Kermān Carpet Designed by Riza Bahramand (c. 1934)

253. Period of Covered Grounds: Kermān Carpet (c. 1935)

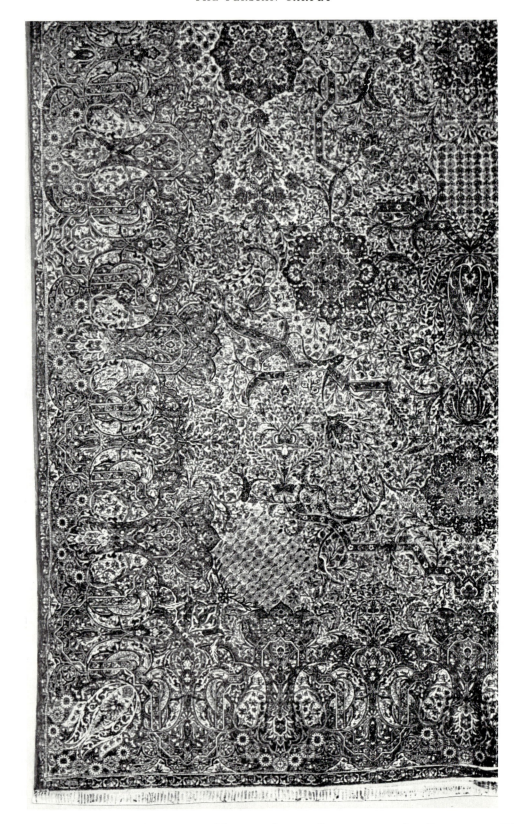

255. Period of Covered Grounds: a Kermān Carpet Designed by Ali Mohammed Kashi (*c.* 1935)

256. PERIOD OF COVERED GROUNDS: A KERMĀN CARPET PROBABLY DESIGNED BY AHMED KHAN (c. 1937)

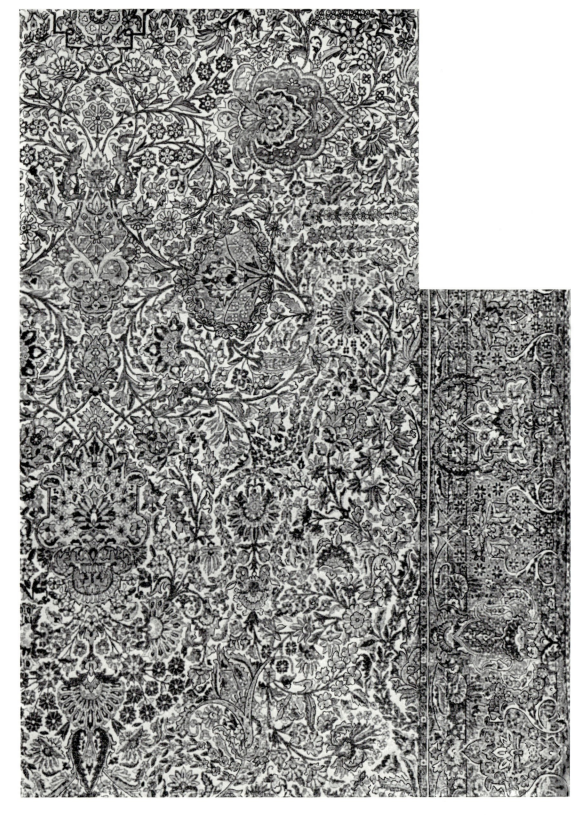

257. PERIOD OF COVERED GROUNDS: A KERMĀN CARPET DESIGNED BY AHMED KHAN (*c.* 1935)

258. FLORAL PERIOD: A TYPE OF DESIGN WHICH WAS MUCH IN VOGUE IN KERMĀN IN 1945-7
DESIGN BY KERBELAI AKBAR (c. 1944)

259. FLORAL PERIOD: KERMĀN CARPET; THE DESIGN CONSISTS OF DETACHED FLORAL MOTIVES
—A STYLE INTRODUCED 25 YEARS AGO IN ARĀK (SULTĀNABĀD) AND STILL PREVALENT THERE (c. 1943)

260. Floral Period: a Kermān Carpet with Detached Floral Motives and Wide, Broken Borders (c. 1944)

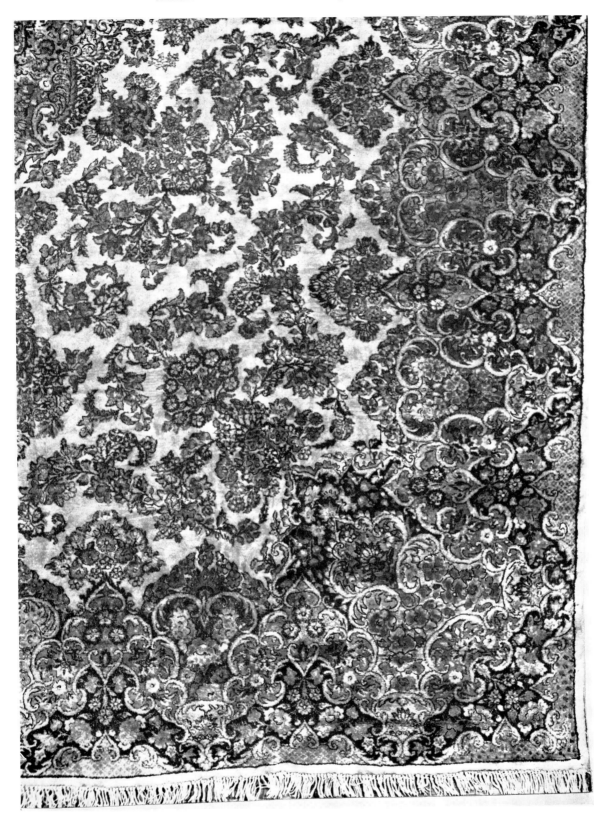

261. FLORAL PERIOD: KERMĀN CARPET WITH DETACHED FLORAL MOTIVES, A STYLE LONG PREVALENT IN ARĀK (SULTĀNABĀD); BUT INTRODUCING THE BROKEN BORDER (c. 1945)

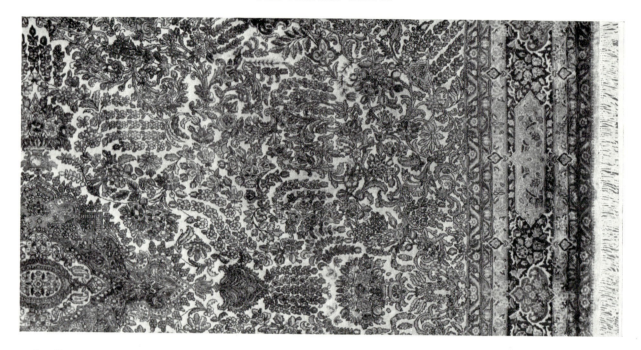

262. Floral Period: a Kermān Carpet with Detached Floral Motives, a Style prevalent in Arāk since 1922 (c. 1945)

263. Floral Period: a Kermān Carpet; the Design embodies both Classic and Floral Motives (c. 1946)

264. Floral Period: Kermān Carpet; the Design of the Ground is made up of Detached Floral Motives—a Style introduced 25 years ago in Arāk (Sultānabād) and still prevalent there (c. 1945)

265. Floral Period: Kermān Carpet with Floral Motives which recall the work of the Arāk (Sultānabād) Designers (c. 1946)

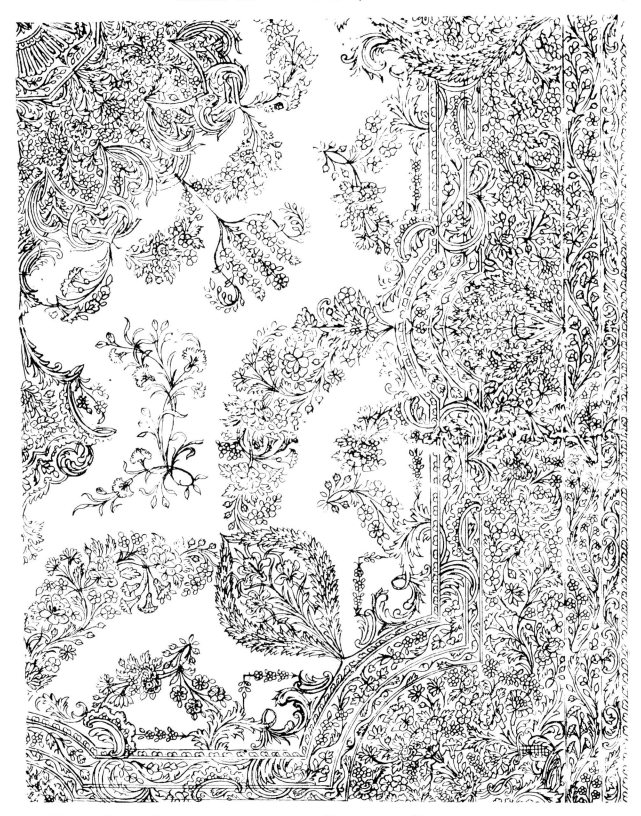

266. French Floral Period: during which the Designers of Kermān were attempting to marry Persian Motives with unfamiliar forms taken from French Period Carpets (c. 1946)

267. FRENCH FLORAL PERIOD: A TYPICAL DESIGN FOR A KERMĀN CARPET TAKEN FROM A FRENCH PERIOD CARPET; DRAWN BY ALI RIZA (*c.* 1948)

268. FRENCH FLORAL PERIOD: KERMĀN CARPET OF THIS PERIOD SHOWING FRENCH INFLUENCE (*c.* 1944)

269. FRENCH FLORAL PERIOD DURING WHICH THE DESIGNERS OF KERMĀN WERE ATTEMPTING TO MARRY PERSIAN MOTIVES WITH FORMS TAKEN FROM FRENCH PERIOD CARPETS (c. 1948)

270. Boom conditions in Persia during and immediately after the War created a local demand for Kermān carpets in medallion-and-corner designs on plain red grounds (*c.* 1947)

271. Boom conditions in Persia during and immediately after the War resulted in a local demand for Kermān carpets in Medallion-and-Corner designs on plain red grounds (c. 1947)

272. Boom conditions in Persia during and immediately after the War created a local demand for Kermān carpets in medallion-and-corner designs on plain red grounds (c. 1947)

273. Detail of an Afshāri (Balvardi) Rug (c. 1935)
The design is not tribal in character; it was probably taken from a Kermān rug.

274. An Afshāri (Kutlū) Rug (c. 1935)

275. An Afshāri (Kutlū) Rug (c. 1935)
The design is a crude rendering of a Kermān vase pattern. The Kutlū rugs are generally double-wefted.

276. An Afshāri (Dashtab) Rug (c. 1935)
The design is not tribal; it has been taken from a Kermān or Ravār carpet.

277. An Afshārī (Deh Shotorān) Village Rug (c. 1938)

The Deh Shotorān weavers are among the best in the area.

278. Afshārī (Saarabād) Rug (c. 1940)

279. Afshārī (Al-Saadi) Rug (c. 1940)

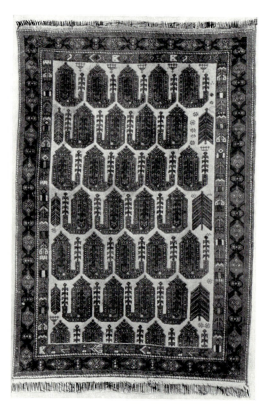

280. Afshārī (Parizi) Rug (c. 1945)

281. Mohammedabād (*c.* 1940)

282. An Afshāri (Deh Shoṭorān) Rug (*c.* 1940)

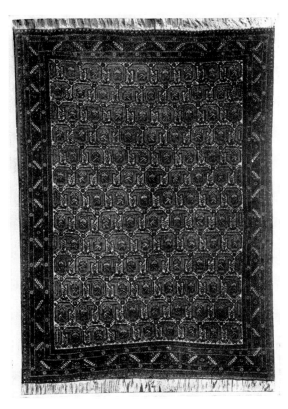

283. An Afshāri (Dehāj) Rug (*c.* 1940)

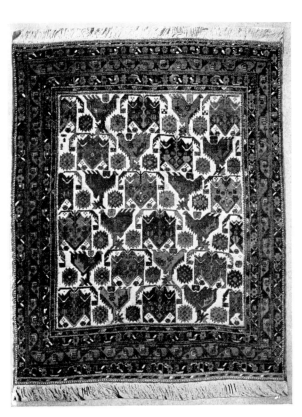

284. An Afshāri (Beilleri) Rug (*c.* 1940)
One of the cleverest—if not the most refined of their designs is the morgi *or hen design.*

285. A Kermān Carpet woven in 1948
The design embodies both classic and French features. The treatment of the border is new.

286. Yezd Carpet
Until a few years ago Yezd carpets were mostly in this design or in the Herāti pattern. Recently, however, Kermān designers and technicians have been introduced and the distinctive character of the Yezd carpet has disappeared.

CHAPTER XIV

THE TRIBAL AND VILLAGE RUGS OF FĀRS

The Province of Fārs

Fārs, one of the five major provinces of Persia, was the cradle of the Persian monarchy—the home of the Achaemenian kings. Cyrus was born there, and his reputed tomb is still to be seen at Pasargadeh. Persepolis—and Istarkhr near by—were respectively the official capitals of the Achaemenian and Sassanian dynasties.[1] Le Strange points out that the area was known to the Greeks as Persis; that they, in error, applied the name to the whole kingdom; and that this misuse has been perpetuated throughout the world.[2]

During the domination of Persia by the Abbasid Caliphate and the Seljūk sultans, the province was visited by several of the Moslem geographers, who left a satisfying picture of its wealth and importance. The Mongol conquerors Jenghis Khan and Hulagū left it alone. Timūr, on two occasions, accepted its submission and appears to have spared the capital city of Shirāz. Under the Timūrids of Herāt and the Mongol princes of Tabrīz, the distant province enjoyed a measure of tranquillity, which—in the Persia of those days—compensated for neglect. In 1510, Shah Ismail, "The Father of the nation", overthrew the petty dynasties of Fārs, Kermān and Khūrasān and thus brought about the unification and consolidation of the Persian kingdom. During the reign of Shah Abbas the province prospered. Under its enlightened governor Imam Qūli Khan, its capital, Shirāz, was surpassed in splendour only by Isfahān itself.

In 1724 the Afghans overran the province. In a few months the prosperity which had been slowly built up under the Sefavi kings was all but extinguished. Nevertheless, after the expulsion of the Afghans, and before the wretched inhabitants had had time to recover, an insensate rebellion against Nadir Shah brought upon them the routine retribution of that inexorable monarch.

The brightest period in the history of Fārs was at the end of the eighteenth century, when the benevolent but illiterate Kerim Khan Zand made Shirāz his capital. That happy period was soon followed by the rule of the brutal Aga Mohammed Shah, the first Qajār monarch. He indulged his hostility to the Zands by destroying the walls of Shirāz and reducing it to the rank of a provincial town. His successors, however, made amends for his imbecility; for, under the three important Qajār monarchs, the province enjoyed a long period of comparative peace; marred only by occasional tribal tumults or the recalcitrance of a royal prince or local grandee. The ill-conceived attempts of the late Riza Shah Pahlavi to settle the turbulent nomads on the land came to an end with his abdication.

The province of Fārs possesses an area of some 60,000 square miles—about the same as Kermān—with a population estimated at about 1,000,000. The coastal belt is hot and semi-arid. Inland the country rises in a succession of parallel ranges—the south-eastern end of the great Zagros chain—and then subsides to the level of the central plateau.

The inland area of Fārs, though mountainous, possesses many fertile and well-watered valleys and a pleasant climate. This is one of the few provinces of the Persian plateau where a few forests still exist and which can boast of a number of rivers. The Mānd and the Shahpūr both rise in the Zagros range and, after many ramifications, empty into the Persian Gulf in the neighbourhood of Bushire. The Kūr—which waters the plain of Persepolis—like so many of the rivers of the Persian plateau, never reaches the sea.

The province is potentially rich; but the devastation of locusts, the occasional droughts, and above all malaria, are evils beyond the capacity of a weak and penurious administration to counter. Furthermore, the hostility which normally exists in the province between the civil and military power is complicated in Fārs by the existence of ancient and powerful tribal families whose authority is not inferior to either of the two agencies of government. Such a situation inevitably leads to jealousy and intrigue; sometimes, indeed, to murder and rebellion.

It is estimated that about one-third of the population of Fārs is nomadic. Large numbers of its inhabitants move twice a year across huge tracts of

---

[1] Sūsa and Babylon were the actual centres of government of the former, and Ctesiphon of the latter.
[2] However this may be, the common language of the whole kingdom became known as the language of Parsā—or Farsī; which is what the Persians call their language to this day.

country, by-passing on their way thousands of tempting and defenceless villages.¹ These nomad tribes differ in speech, race and tradition, so that rivalries, feuds and sometimes open warfare are a common feature of their existence. They live largely outside the pale of governmental authority, and regard robbery as a manly excitement rather than a crime. Thus the province of Fārs is one of the most troublous of Persia. "Whether villager or nomad, man must bear arms and be brave to survive."

The economy of the tribes is pastoral, so that sheep, goats, camels and horses are among the principal products of the province. The villagers, on the other hand, grow barley, rice, millet, cotton, tobacco, opium, almonds, gum tragacanth and excellent fruit. The wine of Shirāz, though rather sweet for Western palates, is renowned in Persia. The principal exports are wool, skins (the so-called Persian lambskins are prized and are not inferior to those of Khūrasān and Afghanistān), almonds, gum tragacanth and tobacco. But of all the products of Fārs the one which is best known to the world is the so-called Shirāz rug.

Shirāz the Capital²

Shirāz is an attractive little city of 130,000 people situated in a pleasant valley some 20 miles long and 6 miles across. It is surrounded by hills except to the south-east, where there is a gap through which a road runs to the salt lake Maharlu—and thence on to Nerīz. In spite of its elevation of 5,000 feet, it is hot in summer; but the autumn and winter are delightful. Snow is infrequent.

The visitor who has read of the charms of old Shirāz—of its gardens of cypress and orange, where the nightingale defied the dawn; of its wine and wit and laughter; and its lazy, musical speech; a Shirāz over which the spirits of Hafiz and Saadi wistfully brooded—may be a trifle disappointed with what he sees today. For new Shirāz is a trim little town with asphalted streets, smart shop fronts and many new, quasi-European buildings. It possesses, indeed, one of the finest avenues in Persia—2 miles long, 100 feet wide and provided with lighting standards which would not be out of place in Oxford Street. The good citizens of Shirāz have named their avenue after their greatest benefactor, Kerim Khan Zand; which was the least that they could do after cutting his fine bazaar in two to build it. Shirāz possesses, too, a new hotel, an up-to-date electric light plant, a small wireless station and an aerodrome. Diminutive British taxis dart nimbly about, ready to carry you from one end of the town to the other for 5d. A water supply, complete with pumping stations and reservoirs, is being provided by one of the city's wealthiest sons. The municipality is active, enterprising and not too dishonest. The old, lazy Shirāz has given place to a brisk businesslike community, which appears to take itself very seriously indeed.

To me—perhaps because from my youth the bazaar has been, as it were, round the corner—the bazaar of Shirāz is one of the most impressive features of the town. Curzon describes it as the finest in Persia. He must have had its architecture alone in mind; for the Shirāz bazaar is far less extensive and exciting than the bazaars of Tehrān or Isfahān. It is, however, an impressive structure—cruciform in design with nave and transept and domed roof—for all the world like a vast medieval cathedral.

Among the notable religious edifices in Shirāz are three mausoleums erected in the ninth century over the tombs of the three brothers of Imam Riza (the eighth Imam, see p. 160)—Ahmed ibn Mūsa, Mir Mohammed and Sayyid Ala-ud-Din Hosain. All three mausoleums have lovely turquoise domes. The most important is that of Ahmed ibn Mūsa—a delightful building in the Arab style—known as the Shah Cherāgh. Another notable building is the

287. A GARDEN OF ORANGE TREES AND CYPRESSES

---

¹ Some of the tribes cover 350 miles each way in their biannual migrations.
² "Here art-magic was first hatched; here Nimrod for some time lived: here Cyrus (the most excellent of heathen princes) was born: and here (all but his head, which was sent to Pisigad) entombed. Here the great Macedonian glutted his avarice and Bacchism. Here the first Sibylle sang our Saviour's Incarnation. Hence the Magi are thought to have set forth towards Bethlehem; and here a series of two hundred kings have swayed their sceptres."—Thomas Herbert, *Travels in Persia*, 1627–1629.

THE TRIBAL AND VILLAGE RUGS OF FĀRS

290. THE TOMB OF SA'ADI

288, 289. THE TOMBS OF TWO BROTHERS OF THE 8TH IMAM (WHO IS BURIED IN MESHED)
Above is the Shah Cherāgh, the tomb of Ahmed Ibn Musa; below is the tomb of Mir Mohammed.

Medresseh Khan, one of the most beautiful religious colleges in Persia. It was founded by Allah Verdi Bak Afshār and his son Imam Qūli Khan, the famous governor of Shirāz during the reign of Shah Abbas. It is in the usual form of a large rectangular courtyard with four arched porches, one in the centre of each of the four sides of the rectangle. The tilework is extraordinarily delicate in design and colour. The building was in a shocking state of repair in 1948: one of the four sides of the courtyard was a ruin; and numberless tiles had fallen from their places—or had been removed and sold. In the courtyard itself some enterprising person was growing vegetables. Repairs were under way; but it is doubtful if the delicate shades of the tilework can ever be matched. The most notable mosque (though not the oldest) is the Masjid-i-Vakil (eighteenth century) named after its founder, Kerim Khan Zand. That wise and beneficent ruler to whom the town owes so much, never assumed the royal title, but called himself Vakil-i-Rayā, or Representative of the People—maintaining that he was acting as regent for the last Sefavi prince.

The Rugs of Fārs

In the geography named *Hudūd-al-Alām* (*The Regions of the World*) which was written in A.D. 892, the unknown author states that rugs were woven at that distant period in Fārs. Le Strange, too, mentions four places: Jahrūm, Darabjīrd, Fasā and Gundijān, where carpets were produced before the fourteenth century. The first three places can be identified.[1] They lie between Shirāz and Lār. The

---

[1] Gundijān no longer exists; but Le Strange quotes the Fars Nameh of the twelfth century, which places it 4 *farsaghs* from Jirrah and 12 from Tawwaj. Both carpets and veils were made there.

Moslem travellers from whom Le Strange culled his information passed through them on their way to the capital.

What kinds of carpets did these travellers find so long ago in Fārs? They gave us no hint. They merely mentioned "carpets"—together with other products of the country—and left it at that. So we cannot be certain as to what they saw; but we can make a good guess.

The three places mentioned are today little more than overgrown villages. They were certainly more prosperous in those days (they could hardly have been less so); but there are no indications that they were much larger. We can, I think, be confident, therefore, that the rugs which these travellers saw were not town or factory made (see p. 28) but were village or nomadic weaves. In that case they would probably be small—because nomads do not weave large pieces; neither do villagers, unless specifically trained to do so. Their designs would be geometrical because, as explained in Chapter V, curvilinear or floral patterns must first be drafted on scale paper, which entails designers and draftsmen and the whole paraphernalia of a carpet factory. Both warps and wefts would be of wool—because nomads use their own wool for the purpose, and in Fārs to this day the villagers do the same.

Thus—by a process of induction—we arrive at the conclusion that the rugs which the Moslem geographer saw six or seven centuries ago probably resembled those which are being produced in Fārs today. And why not? Tribal and village life in the backwaters of Persia has changed hardly at all since the Arab conquest. And like conditions produce like commodities.

There have been a number of references to the rugs of Fārs in more recent times. It is clear in each case that the rugs referred to were tribal weaves—the predecessors of the Qashqaī and the Khamseh rugs of today. For there are no indications that Fārs has ever produced large and fine carpets—except perhaps an occasional piece, specially ordered by one of the khans for his own use.

Shirāz, the capital, is not a weaving centre. There are no carpet factories in the town, nor is weaving carried on in the houses, as in the other weaving centres of Persia. It is, however, important to the merchant; because it is the market for the thousands of rugs and small carpets which are woven by the nomadic tribes and the settled villagers of Fārs.

Every day dust-covered lorries or little caravans of donkeys bring them in from the plains or the mountains, 20–150 miles away; and offer them for sale in the caravanserais, where they are chaffered for by the *dellals*. By nine o'clock the deals are over. Then the rugs are brought to the merchants seated in their stalls in the stately vaulted bazaar of Kerim Khan. The name Shirāz which is commonly applied to these rugs is, therefore, a misnomer. They should be called after the province where they are woven —Fārs. For they are tribal and village rugs of Fārs.

The rugs of Fārs may be classified into four main groups:

Name	Nomad or settled	Speech	Estimated percentage of the rugs of Fārs woven by each group
(1) Qashqaī	Nearly all nomad	Turkī	15
(2) Khamseh	Nomad and settled	Arabic and Turkī	40
(3) Mamassani and Hulagū	Mostly settled	Lūri	1
(4) Persian Village	Settled	Persian	44
			100

(1) *The Qashqaī*,[1] a Turkish tribe, are the most important, the most advanced and the most prosperous of the tribes of Fārs. They are also the best weavers; so I propose to devote more space to them than to the lesser tribes.

They are almost completely nomadic. During eight months of the year they inhabit—in their black goats' hair tents—a high belt of country which extends for about 150 miles northward and slightly westward from a point about 40 miles north of Shirāz. The belt is about 70 miles wide at its widest point. It lies at a height of over 6,000 feet and some of the valleys are 8,000 feet above sea-level; while the mountains attain heights of 10,000–12,000 feet. Within this area live, in their encampments during the summer months, the six important Qashqaī sub-tribes, together with a large number of smaller *taifehs* (see Map VIII for the areas occupied by the more important tribes). They number in all about 50,000 families, or approximately 250,000 souls. In the late autumn they move from the highlands to

---

[1] I am indebted for much of the information on the tribes of Fārs to Dr. Oliver Garrod, M.B.E., M.B., B.S., who spent twenty months among the tribes of western Persia; also to the reports of Mr. H. G. Jakins, H.B.M. Consul, Shirāz, and J. I. McGee of H.B.M. Consulate, Shirāz; and to the Foreign Office Research Department.

291. A QASHQAĪ TENT

the warmer coastal country which lies west, south-west and south of Shirāz. Here the grass is scarce, so that the tribes spread out over a larger area than they occupy in summer.

When or under what conditions the Qashqaī entered Fārs is not definitely known; but they are presumed to be Turkish (probably Seljūk) tribes driven south by the Mongol invasions. They did not, however, achieve cohesion until the reign of Kerim Khan Zand, who died in 1779. It was he who was appointed the chief of the Shahilū clan as the first Il-Khani of the Qashqaīs. The title has remained hereditary in the family ever since.

During the nineteenth century, the Qashqaī, under their powerful Il-Khanis, played an increasingly important role in the politics of Fārs. In World War I they sided with the Germans, but were defeated by a combined force of Indian troops and local levies under Sir Percy Sykes.

The policy of settling the nomad tribes on the land —if necessary by force—which was inaugurated by Riza Shah in the early thirties, brought disaster to the Qashqaī. The lines of march which they followed in their migrations were cut by military forces. Some of the tribes were compelled to settle in the uplands, where there was no fuel and where the cold in winter is intense; others were forced to remain in their low-lying winter quarters, where the heat in summer withers the grass. Thousands of their animals died. The result was an uprising—which was followed by severe reprisals and a more stringent enforcement of the settlement policy.

The abdication of Riza Shah in 1941 was followed by a disintegration of Persia's military strength. The Qashqaī quickly took advantage of the situation and compelled the army to evacuate most of their lands. Their exiled khans escaped from Tehrān, rejoined their followers and soon re-established their power. The tribes resumed their former nomadic existence and began, slowly, to build up their decimated flocks and herds. Today (1948) they are well on the way to recovery.

But the problem of the nomads still awaits solution. Though the methods adopted by Riza Shah were insensate, there can be no doubt that the broad policy was right. Tens of thousands of undisciplined tribesmen with their families, flocks and herds cannot be permitted to march twice a year across a province, looting the villagers and trampling down their crops. Sooner or later they will have to settle and learn to lead the lives of normal peasants. A policy of this kind, however, cannot be carried out rapidly and ruthlessly: it must be planned by experts and executed gradually, over a long period of years.

The Qashqaī are physically the most attractive of the tribes of Fārs. They are tall, wiry, well-set-up fellows. Their features are generally inclined to gauntness, their cheek-bones are high and their noses aquiline. They wear long coats, sometimes bright-coloured but more often grey, with slashed sleeves. Round the waist they wear a voluminous sash, and above it their riflemen cover their chests —as with a cuirass—with rows of cartridges. Their head-dress is notable: they wear a brown or grey felt hat, rounded over the top, with turn-up side flaps—a satisfying frame for their lean, handsome faces. They speak a dialect of Turkish which resembles the Turkish of Azerbaijān. Anyone familiar with Turkish of Istanbul can with ease conduct a conversation with them.

292. QASHQAĪ WEAVERS AT WORK IN THE OPEN
They are weaving 4 × 2·6 rugs "on end" on the same warp.

The Qashqaī are orthodox Shi'a Moslems, generally devout, but not fanatical. Except for their khans, whose sons are always sent to school, they are illiterate. Although the Moslem religion permits polygamy, the Qashqaī are, with few exceptions, monogamous. Their standards of morality are high, and their respect for honesty is certainly above the average in Persia. The proclivity of nomad tribes for banditry is less pronounced in them than it is with the Khamseh or the Mamassani; and incomparably less so than with the Kuhgalū. They are a hospitable people, and provided adequate notice is given them, they are pleased to receive strangers. Living as they do in the open air—remote from the contagions of city life—they are healthy communities, singularly free from venereal diseases, malaria and tuberculosis, which are devastating Persia.

It is an almost invariable rule in Persia that the cleanest, the most orderly and the most prosperous weaving tribe or village produces the best rugs. Indeed, when one enters the courtyard of a villager's cottage, a glance is usually sufficient to determine whether the woman of the house is a good weaver or a bad.

Thus the Qashqaī—who are the most advanced of the tribes of Fārs—are also the best weavers of the province. It is they who weave the so-called Turkī Shirāz rugs (which are sometimes called Mecca

THE PRINCIPAL QASHQAĪ SUB-TRIBES

Name	Number of families	Nomad or Settled	Speech	Some notes about the tribe and its rugs
Qashqūlī	3,000	90 per cent nomad 10 per cent settled	Turkī	Generally industrious, quiet, hospitable—good family men. "They present nomadic life at its highest." Increasing tendency towards agriculture and settlement. Their rugs are among the best of the Qashqaī, but output is small. Double wefted, usually Turkish knot; bright, clear colours; selvedges often decorated with tufts of wool; all wool.
Shish-Būlūkī	5,000	Nomad	Turkī	Largest and wealthiest of the Qashqaī. Little to choose between their standards and those of Qashqūlī. Their rugs are famous and similar to Qashqūlī; but output is small. Double wefted and usually Turkish knot; all wool.
Darashūrī	5,000	Nomad	Turkī and Persian	Darashūrī, Qashqūlī and Shish-Būlūkī form the backbone of the Qashqaī; Darashūrī are wealthy, respectable and hospitable. They were famous horse breeders; but Riza Shah compelled them to spend the winter in the highland when most of their horses perished. Their rugs are good. Double wefted; generally Turkish knot; small output; all wool.
Farsī Madān	2,100	Nomad	Turkī	Of little importance. Standards far below above three. Dirty, ill-clothed, ill-fed. Reputation for robbery. Their rugs are poor and output small; all wool.
Gallehzān	1,200	Nomad	Turkī	Are divided into two sections. Gallehzān Namadī, which are fairly respectable, and Gallehzān Oghrī—a lawless rabble of robbers. Their rugs are poor; all wool.
Rahimī	500	Nomad	Turkī	Considering the size of the tribe, output considerable; but their rugs are on the whole poor. Double wefted; generally Turkish knot; all wool.
Iqdār	400	Nomad	Turkī	Small tribe but respectable. They weave good rugs. Double wefted; generally Turkish knot; all wool.
Safi Khani	200	Nomad	Turkī	Very small tribe and not too respectable. They weave good rugs, however. Double wefted; Turkish knot; all wool.

Shīrāz in the West—for no apparent reason). Like all the weavers of Fārs—tribal or settled—they weave on horizontal looms which lie a few inches off the ground (see p. 285). The loom is taken up when they move forward, following the flocks; and reset at the next encampment.

Rug weaving is not with the Qashqaī—as it is with the Khamseh—a purely commercial proposition. Their women take pride in the rugs which they produce. Care is exercised in washing the wool, in spinning and dyeing it, and in the choice of clear and cheerful colours; for their rugs are much less sombre than those of the Khamseh. The shade for which they are particularly noted is a golden yellow. They are chary about revealing the technique by which they obtain it; believing, no doubt, that they possess a secret of high value. There is no mystery about it, however. The dyestuff is weld, which they call *kaveshk* and which grows wild on their hills. A small quantity of madder is added to give it depth of shade; and alum is the mordant used. Interest is added to their rugs by the selvedge which is neatly overcast in variegated colours; and by the bunches of gay wools with which it is often embellished.

The Qashqaī, being Turks, normally weave the Turkish knot. Occasionally, however, a rug is encountered which has been woven with the Persian knot—the result of a marriage with a Persian or Arab woman. The Qashqaī rugs, like all the tribal and village rugs of Fārs, have woollen warps and wefts. But they possess a characteristic construction which distinguishes them from all the other rugs of Fārs—they are double wefted.

Their designs, like those of all the tribes of Persia, are rectilinear. Two specially characteristic motives appear again and again—and have been copied by the Khamseh and the Persian village weavers (Figs. 304, 327). The first is merely a geometrical figure. The second appears to be something more: the conventionalisation, perhaps, of a stretched lambskin, a turtle, a crab or a beetle. But its form has undergone a change through constant repetition; so that today even those who reproduce it constantly are unaware of its significance.

Unhappily, the output of the Qashqaī weavers is much less than that of their rivals, the Khamseh. The estimate of 15 per cent of the total production of Fārs, which is attributed to them in the table on p. 284, includes the output of some of the smaller settled tribes. The output of these tribes is considerable, but their rugs are poor. The production of the nomad Qashqaī alone is probably only 6 or 7 per cent of the total of the whole province.

A list is given above of the more prominent of the Qashqaī weaving sub-tribes with some particulars of their numbers, mode of life, speech and importance as weavers. There are a number of other sub-tribes in addition to those listed; but they are either very small or else they are unknown as weavers in the Shīrāz bazaar.

So much for the Qashqaī. The next important tribal group on our list is:

(2) *The Khamseh*. This group is not—like the Qashqaī—composed of sub-tribes of the same race, speaking the same language and conscious of a tribal unity and allegiance. The Khamseh are an artificial confederation of five sub-tribes: the Arab, Basirī, Ainalū, Baharlū and Nāfar. They number about 70,000. The first two are of Arab race and speak a corrupt Arabic among themselves. The Ainalū and the Baharlū are of Turkish origin and speak Turkī; and the Nāfar are a mixture of Turkish and Lūri. The Khamseh occupy an area east and southeast of the Qashqaī, with whom they are not on the best of terms. Until recently the Confederation acknowledged the Qavam family (whose present chief is Qavam-ul-Mulk IV) as their titular head. Today, however, they are under the control of a military officer appointed by the Governor-General.

The Arabs, which formed the largest and the most powerful section of the Khamseh Confederation, entered Fārs shortly after the Arab conquest of the seventh century. They are inveterate nomads. When compelled by Riza Shah to settle on their lands, they refused to bestir themselves and waited for the tide to turn. When, in 1941, it did, most of them resumed their nomad existence. Those who remained on the land are bad cultivators and live in poverty and squalor. The main source of income of the nomad part of the tribe is transport: they let out their horses, camels, mules and donkeys for hire.

The Arab weavers of the Khamseh are of special interest to the merchant, because their output is by far the largest of any of the tribes of Fārs. They produce about 40 per cent of all the rugs and *kellegis* which are woven in the province. Their rugs are generally of average "bazaar" quality, rather dark in colour and (like all nomad rugs) rectilinear in design. They weave an astonishing variety of patterns. Unlike the Qashqaī rugs, they are single wefted and woven with the Persian knot. Their warps and wefts are regularly made of wool, although cotton or even goat hair are sometimes used. The selvedges are overcast (as in most of the rugs of Fārs), usually in two sombre colours—not in the gay, variegated shades of the Qashqaī rugs. Nor are the selvedges, like those of the Qashqaī, adorned with bunches of coloured wools. Their dyes are, on the whole, good. In short, the Arab rugs (together with the village-woven rugs which they resemble) are not for the collector or the amateur; but are fair, average, bread-and-butter pieces for the middle-class man.

The Basirī section of the Khamseh Confederation are of mixed Arab and Turkish descent and speak a corrupt dialect of Arabic. They claim to have entered Fārs from Khūrasān. It may be that they are an offshoot of the Arab tribes which live in the neighbourhood of Firdaus (see p. 187). Like the Arab section of the Confederation, they were forcibly settled in 1933, but resumed their migrations after the abdication of Riza Shah. They are the most prosperous and well behaved of the Khamseh nomads. They formerly wove fine rugs. Even today their rugs are, on the whole, better than those of the Arabs. Their output is considerable.

The Turkish Ainalū tribe of the Khamseh Confederation claims to have emigrated into Fārs from Turkestan in the eighteenth century. They are now settled in the district of Fāsā and are rapidly losing their tribal characteristics. They are reliable, honest, hard-working people. Being Turks, they undoubtedly wove the Turkish knot when they arrived from Central Asia; but they are now a settled tribe and have intermarried with their Persian neighbours; so that today many of their rugs are woven with the Persian knot. All are single wefted. Their output is very small.

The Turkish Baharlū tribe of the Khamseh Confederation claims to have entered Fārs in the twelfth and thirteenth centuries. Until 1918 they were nomads; but they are now definitely settled in the Dārāb plain, south of Nerīz. They were formerly bandits and fierce fighters; but like so many of the tribes which have abandoned a nomadic life for a settled existence, their strength and independent spirit has been sapped by disease and squalor. They were once regarded as among the best weavers of

THE TRIBES OF THE KHAMSEH CONFEDERATION
(Formerly under the Qavam family; now under the control of a Military Governor.)

Name	Number of families	Nomad or Settled	Speech	Some notes about the tribe and its rugs
Arab	6,000	Nomad and Settled	Corrupt Arabic	Largest and most powerful of the Khamseh. Suffered greatly under settlement policy of Riza Shah. Most of them have resumed nomad life. Standards much inferior to Qashqaī. Main source of income of nomads is hiring out transport animals; the settled sections live in poverty and squalor. Theirs is the largest output of rugs of any tribal group—about 40 per cent of total Fārs output. Their rugs are mostly medium and low quality; Persian with some Turkī knot; mostly single wefted; all wool.
Basirī	2,800	Nomad	Corrupt Arabic	Forcibly settled in 1933; resumed migration in 1942. Lazy and unclean, but more prosperous and well behaved than the rest of Khamseh. They formerly wove fine rugs; and still weave better rugs than the Arabs. Output considerable. Persian knot; single wefted; all wool.
Ainalū	1,400	Settled	Turkī	Settled near Fāsā since early twenties. Reliable, honest and hard working. Resemble Qashqaī. Economic conditions good. Rugs good, but output not important; Turkish and Persian knot; single wefted; all wool.
Baharlū	700	Settled	Turkī	Settled in Dārāb plain since 1918. Formerly war-like, but degenerating from effects of disease. Formerly among the best weavers of Fārs. Rugs now only average; small output; Turkish and Persian knot; single wefted; all wool.
Nāfar	450	Semi-nomad	Turkī and Lūrī	Lawless robbers, but weave good rugs; output very small; Persian knot; single wefted; all wool.

Fārs and their finest rugs were prized by amateurs. They still weave; but their output is small and their rugs are only of average quality, if that. The Nāfār are of mixed Turkish and Lūri blood. They are a lawless crowd who live in a hot and barren region south of Lār. Their output is very small, but above the average in quality.

A list is given above of the components of the Khamseh Confederation, with some particulars of their numbers, mode of life, speech and importance as weavers.

(3) *The Mamassani and Hulagū*—the next of the four main divisions into which I have classified the weavers of Fārs—are included more out of consideration for two interesting tribal groups than because of their standing as weavers. They are both Lūri tribes and mainly settled. Rice cultivation is their principal source of livelihood. Only a small part of them move up, with their flocks, into the hills. The Mamassani inhabit a series of beautiful and fertile valleys situated about 70 miles north-west of Shirāz—through which Alexander passed on his famous march from Susa to Persepolis. The Hulagū are not strictly a tribe of Fārs, as they live partly in the adjoining province of Khuzistān and depend administratively on the government of Behbehān.

The output of these two tribes is insignificant. Indeed, so few come into the Shirāz bazaar that the local *dellals* have not bothered to enquire into their tribal origin. They call them Lūri rugs and leave it at that. Some find their way into the bazaars of Isfahān, Behbehān and Ahwaz—and so miss Shirāz entirely. During my stay in Shirāz in the winter of 1948 I came across only two pieces—neither of which was of any particular merit. One of them is reproduced (Plate 316). The Shirāzi *dellals* appear to entertain a poor opinion of the Lūri weaves.

(4) *The Persian Village Rugs*. The fourth and last group consists of rugs woven by the Persian-speaking villagers of Fārs. The distinction between the true villagers and the recently settled tribes is, however, sometimes blurred, because both may live in the same plain or valley; and intermarriage may be frequent. It may be difficult, in such cases, to determine the exact origin of a rug from the area.

The Persian weaving villages lie within a circle with its centre in Shirāz and a radius of about 150 miles. Most of them are to be found within the segments to the south-east and north-east of the capital; and many lie within or on the edge of tribal areas. There are no weaving villages in the low-lying coastal belt.

The output of the Persian weaving villages is the largest of the four groups. It amounts to a little less than half the total production of Fārs. Thus, the output of the Arab nomads of the Khamseh Confederation, plus that of the Persian villages, amounts to nearly 85 per cent of the whole production of the province. The bulk of the so-called Shirāz rugs of medium quality which are shipped to the West come from these two sources.

There is little to choose between them. Both weave the four sizes which are usual in the rugs of Fārs, and which measure, respectively, about 4×2.9 feet; 5×3.9 feet; 6.9×4.9 feet and 10×7 feet.[1] Both weave (on horizontal tribal looms) a rather loose, short pile, single wefted, all-wool fabric, with the Persian knot; the rugs of both are rather sombre in colour—with dark and medium blue, and dark brick red as predominating shades: their designs (of which there are a great variety) are similar in character—always rectilinear, invariably consisting of one, two or three bold medallions, with the ground covered in a great variety of small, detached and often amusing little figures. The rugs from these two principal sources are, indeed, so much alike that only the Shirāz *dellals* can tell them apart; and even they are frequently at fault.

Production

The output of the rugs of Fārs is estimated at about 30,000 pieces of all sizes per annum. It has undoubtedly declined since the period between the wars; but not to the same extent as in other weaving centres of Persia. Indeed, in respect of one size only—the *kellegi* (which measures about 10×7 feet)—the output is considerably larger than before the war. The production of the rug sizes, however, has declined considerably, so that present exports include a considerable proportion of rugs collected by the *dellals* from the dwellings, tea-houses, offices and caravanserais. For, as everywhere in Persia, there is always a reserve of used pieces of this kind on tap. As elsewhere, the decline is mainly due to two causes: the rise in the price of wool and the falling off in the demand from the West. In the case of Fārs, however, there appears to be another contributory cause: formerly the landlords (or their representatives) were wont to assist production by supplying the wool and

---

[1] Very rarely in Fārs are carpet sizes woven larger than 10×7 feet. The reason is that both tribal and village women weave at horizontal—instead of vertical—looms; and horizontal looms take up a great deal of space. A loom for a 12×9 feet carpet would take most of the floor space in a weaver's tent or cottage.

advancing the cost of dyeing. Today, however, most of these persons have acquired considerable wealth through the rise in price of agricultural commodities during the war; and, in consequence, they are no longer interested in promoting rug weaving in their villages. Their part in the economy of tribal and village production has, to a certain extent, been taken by the local shopkeepers; but their assistance is proving to be more onerous than that of the chief or squire.

Designs were formerly traditional in the families of the sub-tribes and in the villages—and to a great extent they still are. Each sub-tribe or village possesses from two or three to perhaps a dozen—in accordance with its importance or output. Yet the rugs that are produced are far from being turned out as from a machine—in dozens to a pattern. No two, indeed, are ever the same; for no two women will interpret the design in the same way. Each will produce some variation of her own. Designs are, of course, not recorded, either on paper or in the form of *wagirehs* or sample mats. They are handed down from mother to daughter and are, no doubt, discussed and copied in the tents and cottages. From time to time a weaver with a creative urge will design a new figure or medallion; or will look about her and pick out a tree, a bush, a flower, an animal and weave from it a pattern in straight lines. And thus a new design is born.

As with the Balūchis and the Afshārs, design is no longer a sure indication of origin. Indeed, there are daily wrangles in the Shirāz bazaar between the experts as to whether a rug was woven by this tribe or village or that. For the barriers between them are breaking down and designs are becoming common property. See Plate 305, which represents a Basirī rug in a purely Qashqaī design.

The tribal and village rugs of Fārs are in many respects superior to those of any other part of Persia. The wools of Fārs, although softer than the wools of the north, are, nevertheless, good carpet wools. And they are spun by the weavers themselves—which is generally a guarantee of the soundness of the material. Their colours are on the sombre side; but not more so than those of the Hamadān or Kurdish rugs; and less so than those of the Balūchis. Their dyes are, on the whole, excellent: anilines and synthetic dyes have not yet penetrated, to any extent, into Fārs. In closeness of weave they compare favourably with the rugs of Hamadān, Kurdistān or the Bakhtiari country. And in interest and variety of design they are definitely superior to any of the tribal or village rugs of Persia.[1]

Yet, in spite of these excellent qualities, the rugs of Fārs are not regarded in the West—and particularly in America—as among the best of their class. The reason for this is to be found in their faulty construction; they are "all-wool" fabrics.

Wool is not a suitable material for the foundation of a carpet (see p. 97). It is elastic; so that the warps cannot be brought to the proper tension. And a loose warp produces a flabby fabric, which is liable to go crooked or to cockle. Wool, too, is springy. When used as a weft it does not pack as tightly as cotton—to make a firm foundation for the pile. It is also lighter than cotton. Thus, a fabric with warps and wefts of wool lacks weight and body—particularly if, as in most of the rugs of Fārs, the wefts are single.

Finally, when the all-wool rug has received the attention of the finishers in the West, it issues from their liquors and their drying rooms a sad and sleazy object. Whatever "handle" it possessed has disappeared. It is loose, flabby, without substance. If placed upon a hardwood floor, it becomes a danger. This is why America will have none of it.

We should hesitate long before advocating any radical change in such a natural, spontaneous product as a tribal or village rug. The world does not possess enough of these things; and Persian carpets have been "improved" too much already. I would be the last to recommend any change in the designs, the dyes, or the workmanship of the rugs of Fārs. But the substitution of a cotton for a woollen back would produce a better fabric, without altering in any way the style or the appearance of the rug. The change is already taking place—almost without remark—in Kurdistān and amongst the Balūchis and Afshārs. I recommend it to the merchants of Shirāz. Perhaps, if they could introduce it, they would be able to sell their rugs in the United States—to their own advantage and to the lasting benefit of the weavers of Fārs.

Conversation Piece

"Has a low-born person carrying a rug over his shoulder passed this way?" enquired the merchant breathlessly.

"You appear to be disturbed," replied the dervish.

---

[1] Some of their designs indicate an affinity with the weaves of Shirvān and Kubā—an affinity which may well exist, because many of the weaving tribes of Fārs are Turks who emigrated from the north.

"I should think I am!" exclaimed the merchant. "A rogue came into my shop a few minutes ago, and when my back was turned he seized my most valuable rug and made off with it. Happily I caught sight of him before he got away. I pursued him across the city and beyond the wall; and then I lost him. Has he by any chance entered this cemetery?"

"Why pursue him further?" answered the dervish. "Be seated—and wait. For wherever he may be, to this cemetery, in the end, he must return."

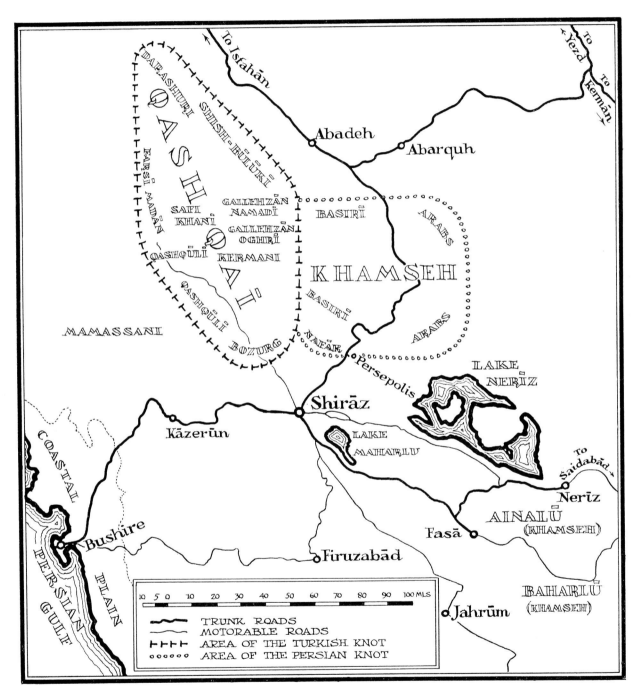

MAP VIII. SUMMER QUARTERS OF THE PRINCIPAL WEAVING TRIBES OF FĀRS

Group 1. Qashqaī

293. Two Shish-Būlūkī Saddle-bags (Turkī, Nomad)

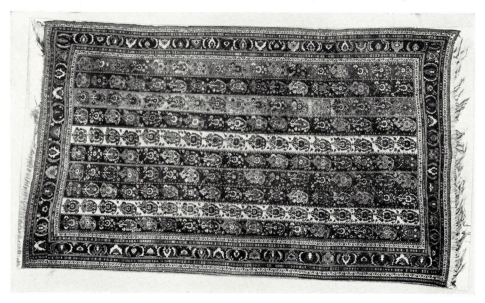

294. An Antique Qashqaī Rug (Turkī, Nomad)

Group 1. Qashqaī

295. Fragment of an Antique Qashqūlī or Būlli Rug (Turki, Nomad) from the Shrine Collection, Meshed

296. A Basirī Kolomec Rug (Turki, Nomad)

297. A Gondashtli (Turki, semi-Nomad)

298. A Safi Khanī Rug (Turki, Nomad)

Group 1. Qashqaī

299, 300. Two Shish-Būlūki Rugs (Turki, Nomad)

Group 2. The Khamseh Confederation

301. An Arab Ghani Rug (Arab, Nomad)

302. A Pir Islami Rug (Arab, Nomad)

303. A Gishni Chahār-rā Rug (Arab, Nomad)

304. An Arab-Farsi Rug (Arab, Nomad)

Group 2. *The Khamseh Confederation*

305. A Basirī Rug (Arab, Nomad)

306. A Basirī Saddle-bag (Arab, Nomad)

Group 2. The Khamseh Confederation

307. An Antique Lab-u-Mahdi Rug (Arab, Nomad)

308. A New Lab-u-Mahdi Rug (Arab, Nomad)

309. A Laverdāni Rug (Arab, Nomad)

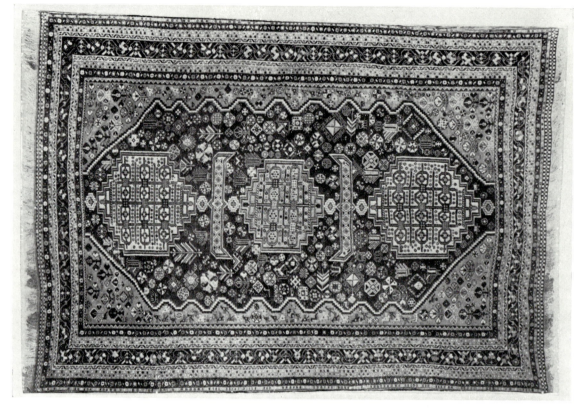

311. A Kurshul Rug (Turki, Settled)

310. A Derazi Rug (Arab, Nomad)

Group 2. The Khamseh Confederation

THE TRIBAL AND VILLAGE RUGS OF FĀRS

Group 2. The Khamseh Confederation

312. AN ARABI SHIRĪ RUG (ARAB, NOMAD)

313. AN ARABI GHANĪ RUG (ARAB, NOMAD)

314. A MAZIDI RUG (ARAB, NOMAD)

315. A GISHNI CHAHĀR-RĀ RUG (ARAB, NOMAD)

Group 3. Mamassanī and Hulagū

316. A Lūrī Rug (probably from a Mamassani Village)

Group 4. Persian Villages

317. A Rug from Kevelli Village

Group 4. Persian Villages

318, 319. Two Rugs from Abadeh Village: the Design of the second is borrowed from Qashqāī Tribes which camp in the vicinity during the summer

Group 4. Persian Villages

320. A Rug from Shuleh Sarūkh Village, near Persepolis

321. A Rug from Goshnaqūn Village

322. A Rug from Deh Bīd Village

323. A Rug from Maligandeh Village

Group 4. Persian Villages

324, 325. Two Rugs from Nerīz Village

326. A Rug from Sirānd Village

327. A Rug from Karftar Village (Turki)

CHAPTER XV

ISFAHĀN AND THE SO-CALLED BAKHTIARI WEAVES; JŌSHAQĀN; AND A NOTE ON NAĪN

ISFAHĀN AND THE SO-CALLED BAKHTIARI WEAVES

The City of Isfahān

Isfahān is without a doubt the most elegant, the most stately and the most agreeable of the cities of Persia. It will not permit the visitor to forget, for an instant, that it was once a capital—and one of the most splendid capitals of that astonishing period of history, the end of the sixteenth century. It possesses an air of tradition, of dignity, of breeding, which is quite foreign to the parvenu modernity of Tehrān.

When Shah Abbas decided that the exposed position of Tabrīz necessitated the removal of his capital to a more secure locality, his choice fell, almost inevitably, on Isfahān. For it lay near the centre of his kingdom and remote from his enemies, the Turks and Uzbegs. From the former it was protected by the great Zagros range[1] and from the latter by an almost impassable desert. The beneficent waters of the Zaindeh Rūd—one of the few rivers of the plateau—made the area one of the most fertile in his kingdom; and it possessed a healthy and equable climate. When in the nineteenth century the Qajārs, in their turn, transferred the capital to Tehrān, they did so, not because its location offered any advantages over that of Isfahān, but rather from considerations of dynastic jealousy and prestige.

Isfahān was already a considerable city before Shah Abbas made it his capital. In the eleventh century it was described by one of the earlier Moslem travellers as the largest city in the Persian-speaking part of the empire. It was surrounded by a wall some 14 miles in circuit, and it contained a magnificent mosque, fifty caravanserais and—"two hundred bankers"!

In the fourteenth century the city was taken by Timūr; and shortly afterwards it had the temerity to rebel against him. The Mongol exacted a Mongolian penalty: 70,000 of its inhabitants were massacred.

But—like so many Persian cities which had suffered similar disasters—it recovered with surprising speed: during the fifteenth and sixteenth centuries it was again prosperous and important. Then, at the end of the sixteenth century, Shah Abbas made it his capital. Before long, rumours of the luxury and splendour of his court spread to the West and stirred the imagination and enterprise of many travellers. We possess numerous detailed records of their journeys and their sojourns in the capital. There is, indeed, no eastern city of the period of which we have a clearer picture than that of Isfahān during the reign of Shah Abbas and his immediate successors.[2]

The Afghan invasions put an end to that illustrious era. In 1722—after an inglorious battle before the capital—the Persian army, superior in arms and numbers, was signally defeated. The city was soon invested and the cowardly Shah Sultan Hosain, the last of the Sefavi kings, surrendered his crown to the invaders.

At first the conquerors treated the inhabitants with clemency. But an insurrection broke out in Kazvīn, and the Afghan ruler became alarmed lest the capital should rise in his rear. He determined to murder the ministers and nobles and then to hand over the city to his soldiery to sack. The order was carried out, and for fourteen days the pillage and massacre went on. Seven years later, the city was relieved by Nadir Qūli (afterwards Nadir Shah) after he had defeated the Afghans in two great battles. In 1736 he became the ruler of Persia. One of his earliest acts was to transfer the seat of government to Meshed, his birthplace. From that time on Isfahān ceased to be a capital city. Kerim Khan Zand made Shirāz his capital; and the Qajārs, Tehrān—where it remains.

For 200 years Isfahān persisted—with rare intervals of respite under an enlightened prince or governor—in a process of slow decay. Happily that extraordinary monarch Riza Shah rescued it in time.

---

[1] Nevertheless, Suleiman the Magnificent captured it in 1548; but he was unable to hold it.
[2] "Pietro della Vale, Herbert, Olearius, Tavernier, Chardin, Sanson, Daulier Deslandes, Kaempfer and Lebrun successively shed the light of an acute and instructed scrutiny upon the scene, and have added to the respective literatures of Italy, Great Britain, Germany, France and Holland."—Lord Curzon, *Persia*, vol. II, p. 22.

328. View of Isfahān

Not only did he ordain and superintend the restoration of its crumbling monuments, but he inculcated in the minds of the more receptive among his people an awareness of the value of that heritage and a pride in its possession.

Isfahān has been described as one of the outstanding cities of the world. The statement can, I think, be properly defended. But what is beyond controversy is that—architecturally and in layout and position—it is the premier city of Persia.

It is, in the first place, unique among the cities of the plateau in that it is situated on a river spanned by two of the noblest medieval bridges in existence (Photos 329, 330). The earlier of the two was built in the fifteenth century by the famous Il-Khani Uzūn Hassan, whose capital was Tabrīz (see p. 52). It was restored by the Sefavi monarch Abbas II. The other—which is the more renowned of the two, though not the more satisfying—is the bridge of Allah Verdi Khan. It was built during the reign of the great Shah Abbas, who named it after his prime minister.

Besides its two splendid bridges, Isfahān possesses one of the most imposing (as it is one of the largest)

329. The Bridge of Hassān Beg, Isfahān
It was built by Uzūn Hassan of Tabrīz and was repaired by Shah Abbas II.

330. The Bridge of Allah Verdi Khan, Isfahān; named after the Prime Minster of Shah Abbas I

square of any city in the world. It measures 512×150 metres, and its axis runs exactly north and south. Polo was played there in Shah Abbas's time: the goal-posts are still standing at each end. The only square which can compare with it is the Red Square in Moscow; but the most single-minded friend of Russia could hardly place the cathedral of St. Basil on a level with the Masjid-i-Shah, or the Tomb of Lenin with the Masjid-i-Sheikh Lūtfūllāh or the Ali Kapū. Nor (in my view) does any system of enclosing a square compare with that of the Persian. They do it with a long line of identical two-storied, pointed arches in brick—a method which is at once simple, restrained and dignified.

Isfahān also possesses one of the finest avenues in Persia—the famous Chahār Bāgh—which bisects the city from the north to the bridge of Allah Verdi Khan; and then carries on through the industrial centre on the farther side of the river to the Shirāz road. It was planned by Shah Abbas for use as a pleasure garden—as its name implies. It possesses three traffic lanes separated by rows of trees.

The oldest and archaeologically the most interesting mosque is the Masjid-i-Jumeh. It dates from the eleventh century—and a still older building had previously existed on the site. Numerous additions were made to it between the twelfth and eighteenth centuries. In 1930 an extensive programme of repairs was undertaken. Unfortunately, so much of the masonry and tilework had to be renovated or renewed that the building appears today more like a modern foundation than a mosque which is nearly a thousand years old.

Students of architecture disagree as to which of the two premier mosques of Persia—the mosque of Jawar Shadh in Meshed or the Masjid-i-Shah of Isfahān—is the nobler edifice. The tilework of the former is, perhaps, more splendid and more varied; but the latter is architecturally more impressive. It was begun in 1612, by the order of Shah Abbas, and was finished in 1638, eight years after his death.

On the east side of the square is the great domed mosque of Sheikh Lūtfūllāh. It is a covered building

331. THE MASJID-I-SHAH, ISFAHĀN

332. DETAIL OF THE TILEWORK, MASJID-I-SHAH

without a courtyard—one of the few of the great mosques of Persia of this type. Its huge dome, the entrance and the whole of the inside of the building are tiled—the inside with tiles of a deep lapis blue. It was designed by Mohammed Riza of Isfahān who completed it in 1619. The mosque was used as a place of worship by the ladies of the court of Shah Abbas.

On the opposite side of the square, facing the mosque, is the Ali Kapū—the Exalted Gate—so called because it was the main gateway to the royal enclosure. Shah Abbas is said to have lived there while he was engaged in building his capital. From the great terrace, with its tapering wooden pillars, the Sefavi kings used to watch the games of polo and the military parades in the square below.

The inside walls and ceilings of the building were covered with paintings and designs in fresco. Many

334. THE CHEHEL SITŪN, ISFAHĀN

of the former have been covered with plaster. Attempts are being made to remove it without damaging the paintings underneath; but unhappily without much success. The designs, however, are mostly intact or have been well restored. As examples of sixteenth-century design they are remarkable.

The Chehel Sitūn—one of the palaces of the royal enclosure—was probably built during the reign of Shah Abbas; but the date is uncertain. The name means "forty pillars", whereas the actual number of pillars is eighteen—with two more to support the royal recess. The probable explanation of the discrepancy is that there were twenty pillars on the west side of the building which was destroyed by fire during the reign of the last Sefavi king, Shah Sultan Hosain. If a more fanciful explanation is preferred, it is that the second twenty pillars may be seen reflected in the tank which faces the building.

The interior of the Chehel Sitūn has been converted into a museum. The most interesting of the exhibits are the historical paintings in the main hall, some of which are probably Italian (Plate 334).

The magnificent tiled gateway of the Medresseh Chahār Bāgh is situated on the east side of the avenue of that name. Like most of the Moslem religious colleges it is built round a square courtyard with a great tiled porch on each of the four sides. The porch on the south side is surmounted by a fine tiled dome with two minarets (Plate 335). Round the courtyard are rooms for 134 students. The Medresseh was finished just before the Afghan invasion (1722), and it is said that the last Sefavi king was murdered there by the Afghans in his private room.

333. THE ALI KAPŪ, ISFAHĀN

335. THE DOME OF THE MEDRESSEH MADER-I-SHAH, CHAHĀR BAGH, ISFAHĀN

Isfahān as a Carpet Centre

Of the nine urban weaving centres which I purpose to survey, Isfahān is one of the least important. The city, indeed, emerged as a weaving centre only about twenty-five years ago. Before that it was merely a collecting point for the comparatively few Lūri and (so-called) Bakhtiari rugs which were then produced; and it was periodically visited by the *dellals* from Hamadān and Tehrān in search of these goods. They were usually able to supplement their purchases with semi-antique *kellegis*, strips and carpets out of the houses—a class of merchandise which is to be found in every important bazaar in Persia. Isfahān at that time was, in fact, nothing but a feeder for the Hamadān and Tehrān markets.

About twenty-five years ago, however, weaving began on an important scale in Isfahān itself and in some of the nearby villages. No sooner was the industry firmly established than a sudden expansion took place in the production of Bakhtiari rugs from the Chahār Mahāl. What prompted the latter movement I am unable to explain, but it took place; and the rugs naturally found their way into the nearby Isfahān bazaar.

Thus the output of the looms in the Isfahān area; the considerable influx of rugs and small carpets from the Chahār Mahāl; and the trickle of Lūri rugs from the Kuhgalū and other Lūri tribes has made Isfahān a small, but no longer a negligible, market. The products of the area fall naturally into the above-mentioned headings, and they will be considered in the same order, viz.:

(1) The weaving industry of Isfahān and the neighbouring villages.
(2) The so-called Bakhtiari weaves from the Chahār Mahāl.
(3) The Lūri tribal rugs.

The carpets and rugs of Jōshaqān and Naīn are not marketed in Isfahān; most of them are despatched direct to merchants in Tehrān. I have, however, included them in this chapter—under separate headings—because both localities lie within easy reach of Isfahān.

(1) *The Weaving Industry of Isfahān and the Neighbouring Villages.* We have seen (p. 303) that the production of fine carpets in Isfahān—an art which the great Shah Abbas himself had promoted and patronised—was brought to an inglorious end by the capture of the city by the Afghans in 1722. There is no evidence that any attempt was made, during the subsequent 200 years, to revive the industry. Here and there a few desultory looms may have existed in the city; but nothing more. There are no eighteenth- or nineteenth-century carpets extant which can, without hesitation, be ascribed to Isfahān.

The re-establishment and rapid expansion of the industry which took place in the early twenties of the present century was due rather to simple economic causes than to the vision or the assiduity of any single person or group of persons. The echoes of the post-war boom in Europe had penetrated as far as Persia, and the people of Isfahān had sensed that there was a keen demand for carpets in the West. Yet they—good craftsmen that they were—were not participating in the trade which was bringing prosperity to the weaving centres. So they, too, began to weave.

At first, rug sizes only were produced. They were fine in quality and their designs were attractive (Plates 337, 338): but the material used was not of the best, the dyes were poor and the pile was cut too low. The price, however, was reasonable; and as the European markets were at the time looking for a light-weight rug of fine quality at a low price, they sold readily. Production continued to increase until, by the middle thirties, about 2,000 looms were producing these rugs in Isfahān alone; plus another 500 in the nearby villages.

The outbreak of World War II nearly brought disaster to the infant industry. It had depended, exclusively, on European demand—for the designs and colours were unsuitable and the fabric too thin for the American market. Thus, when the European demand expired, the whole industry was threatened with extinction. It was saved (as in other parts of Persia) by the increase in home consumption brought about by the boom in Tehrān.

But the *nouveaux riches* in the capital demanded a better class of rug than the Isfahān weavers had been accustomed to produce. They also demanded carpet sizes. So that by the end of the war practically all the looms in the city were weaving a finer and more expensive fabric than before; and about a third of the looms were weaving carpets. The local demand, however, was never sufficient to make up for the disappearance of the trade with the West. So that production fell to about a third of the pre-war figure.

The position did not improve during the post-war period. Indeed, even before the end of the war a large proportion of the weavers had already abandoned their looms for the newly established cotton and woollen mills where the pay was better. By 1949, when I revisited Isfahān, the 2,000 looms which had formerly existed in the city had shrunk to about 600; with perhaps another 300–400 in the four weaving villages near by. The production of the closely woven, but inexpensive, Isfahān rugs—of which many thousands had been woven and sold before the war—had ceased in Isfahān itself; though they were still being woven in the villages. The village rugs, however, were coarse, unlovely in design and crude in colour. They were quite unsuitable for the Western markets; but there appeared to be a demand for them in Tehrān, in Irāq, Syria and Egypt. The city looms, on the other hand, were producing rugs and carpets of the finest quality, many of them with silk warps. They counted from 15 × 15 to 25 × 25 knots to the inch, and the workmanship was as good as any in Persia. There was a tendency, however, to clip the fabric too thin. As a result, these closely woven pieces will not give the service which their ultimate owners will have the right to expect. The materials, on the whole, were good: the finest pieces were woven with mill yarn, spun from Australian wool in the local factory; or with yarn from the mills of Tabrīz or Kazvīn. The pieces of lesser count were woven with handspun yarn either local or imported from Meshed or Tabrīz. A good deal of the local yarn was spun from skin wool from the tanneries. The baleful *jūftī* knot —which is sapping the industry in so many weaving centres—had begun its work in Isfahān; happily, however, the disease—in 1949—had not yet advanced very far.

Weaving in Isfahān is carried on almost entirely in the houses, most of which are situated in the poorer quarters of the city. There are usually two looms to a house. The householders either weave for their own account or for one of the local merchants who supply them with materials and pay for the labour as the work proceeds. There are, in addition, three small factories in the city of ten to fifteen looms each.

In spite of the undoubted competence of the Isfahān weavers their rugs and carpets lacked the charm and the distinction which should attend upon such fine craftsmanship. Most of the designs— which were drawn to order by professional designers in the city—were wanting in variety and invention; and those which gave evidence of originality were lacking in elegance. A few months' tutelage in one of the designing rooms of Kermān would open the eyes of the Isfahān designers to the range and diversity of their art.

The colours of these fine pieces were even less happy than their designs. Nine out of ten had cream grounds, with hard brick-red borders and blue-black or brick-red medallions. The secondary colours were equally commonplace. It appeared, indeed, as if the whole industry of Isfahān revolved around fifteen colours—all hard and all the same.

For this the dyers were mainly responsible; because neither weavers nor merchants troubled to select the shades for their carpets, and to place their orders with the dyers accordingly. They appeared, indeed, to be indifferent as to the shade of red or blue or green or yellow or brown which they received from the dyers' hands. They took the shades which the dyers gave them.

This somewhat haphazard procedure—if practised within proper limits—is not as reprehensible as it

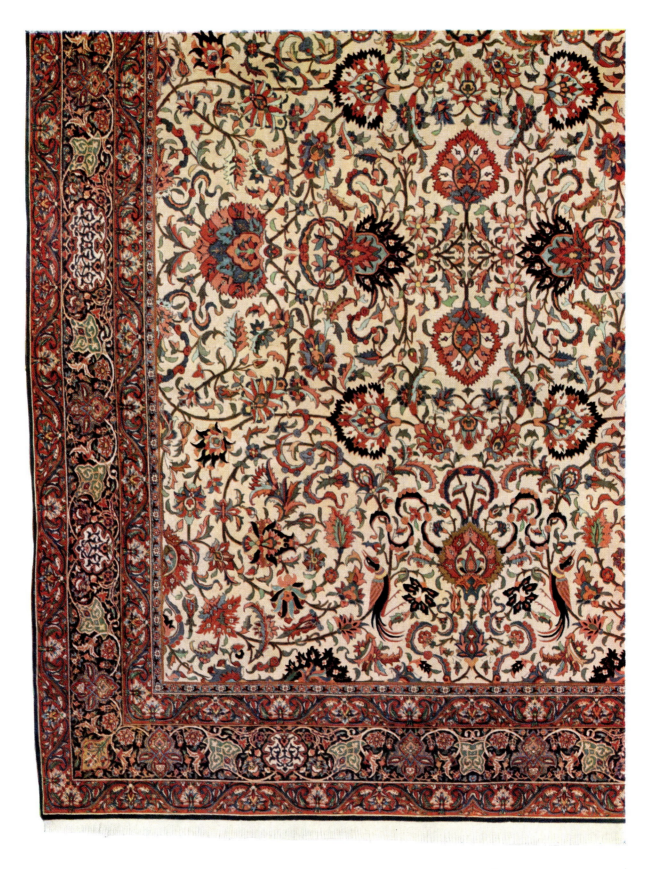

Isfahān Carpet woven c. 1920, introducing motives from the Great Period

appears. Nor is it confined to Isfahān alone. It is, in fact, traditional in many of the weaving centres of Persia; and it is one of the factors which has given to the Persian carpet its sincerity, its lack of sophistication and its charm. The blending of the vivid colours, which chance has thrown together, is left to the adducing hand of time; or, if the time be short, to the cunning of the carpet finishers of the West.

That was well enough so long as the Isfahān dyers were using Persian dyes, which possess the merit of losing their intensity; so that in time, or in the hands of the finishers, they blend together. Unhappily, however, the dyers have replaced the bright but mutable Persian colours with equivalent shades dyed with imported chrome dyestuffs; and neither time nor the cunning of the finisher can ever temper these hard chrome-dyed brick reds and grassy greens.

I spent a morning in the dim half-light of the domed dye-houses which, in Isfahān, are situated in one of the vaulted streets of the bazaar, called the Row of the Dyers. There, while talking to the kindly blue-fisted dyers, and peering into their pots and copper boilers, I listened to the story that I had heard so often in many dye-houses in Persia: the scarcity and high cost of madder; the slow, complicated (and therefore costly) technique which its use demanded; and the cheapness, swiftness and ease of dyeing with synthetic dyes. The dyers of Isfahān are sound and experienced craftsmen. Unlike so many of their fellows who are using synthetic dyes in other parts of Persia, they know their stuff. They were dyeing silk, wool and cotton in a great variety of shades—both in the Persian manner and with imported chrome and acid dyes. They assured me that for the town carpets they used only Persian dyes; which statement, I am afraid, I was compelled to discount—because I had seen plenty of rugs the day before which impugned it.

The dyers made no bones about what happened when the villagers brought in their yarns. It was a repetition of what I had heard in Tabrīz and Meshed: the villager was unwilling to pay the price for an honest job; but he got what he paid for.

What can be done to solve this baffling problem of dyes in Persia? For if it is not solved, the renown of the Persian carpet will inevitably decline. The subject will be examined in the last chapter of this book, which deals with the future of the industry.

(2) *The Bakhtiari Rugs and Carpets of the Chahār Mahāl.* Isfahān is the principal market in Persia for the sturdy rugs and carpets—often woven in repeating patterns of lozenges and squares—which are commonly known as Bakhtiaris. Although the term is used in Persia as well as in the West, it is a

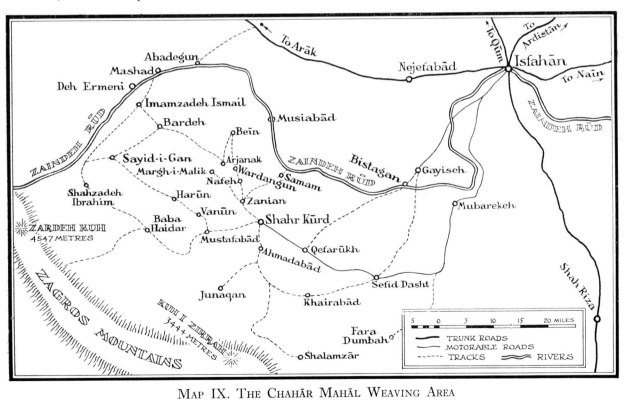

MAP IX. THE CHAHĀR MAHĀL WEAVING AREA

misnomer; for the so-called Bakhtiaris are not woven by Bakhtiari tribes at all.

They are woven in villages, scattered over a fertile, well-watered area known as the Chahār Mahāl, which is situated along the eastern slopes of the Zagros range, 80 miles west and south of Isfahān. The area is bounded on the north by the northern bend of the Zaindeh Rūd (which separates it from the district of Fereidān); on the west and south by the Zagros mountains; and on the east by the Isfahān plain. The majority of the inhabitants of the area are peasants of Turkish race and speech. But there are, in addition, a considerable number of villages inhabited by Persians; and in the northern part (which adjoins Fereidān, with its large Armenian population) there are seven Armenian villages.

Early in the nineteenth century the Bakhtiari khans of the Haft Lang,[1] who had acquired wealth and power, began to covet comfort and security as well—advantages which were denied them by their nomadic existence in the mountainous Bakhtiari country. They therefore acquired lands in the foothills to the east—which is the Chahār Mahāl. There they built country houses for themselves and set up establishments as country gentlemen. They were able thus to enjoy many of the amenities of civilised life—without breaking the tradition of their class by cutting themselves off from contact with their tribes.[2]

During the last hundred years the Turkish and Persian villagers of the Chahār Mahāl have accommodated themselves to their new masters. They have partially adopted the Bakhtiari dress and some of the Bakhtiari customs; and have intermarried with servants and retainers of their khans. But these are insufficient grounds for calling their rugs after the great semi-nomadic Bakhtiari tribe which occupies a large and mountainous area much farther to the west.

These rugs and carpets are woven in almost every village of the Chahār Mahāl. The majority of the villages lie in the vicinity of Shahr Kūrd, which the Bakhtiari khans have made the administrative centre of the area. There is a fairly good road from Isfahān to Shahr Kūrd, and a regular bus service, except in bad weather.

Conversation Piece

We were seated round a charcoal brazier in the principal store in Shahr Kūrd. Our host, Mohammed Riza, was obviously a trader of substance, for an impressive variety of merchandise crowded his shelves and counters and overflowed on to the floor. He was apparently at the same time grocer, haberdasher, draper and oil-and-colour man. Judging from scraps of conversation which I overheard between him and Hosain Aga the merchant (who had accompanied us from Isfahān) he was in the wholesale trade as well and dabbled in the mutton-fat and butter of the district—commodities which are justly renowned in the Isfahān bazaar.

There was also seated with us one Meshed Ali, a *dellal* of consequence from Isfahān. He was a native of the Chahār Mahāl and an authority on the carpets of the district.

Next to Meshed Ali was a tall, thin, voluble gentleman whose name I did not catch, but whose like is to be found in all the rural communities of Persia (and for that matter in other rural communities as well). For want of a better name I will call him Mr. Know-All. Behind him, and sitting silently in the background, was a soldier. His only claim to presentation here (for he took no part in the proceedings) was his appearance: his fair smooth skin, his fine flaxen hair and his guileless blue eyes. He might have been a Norseman.

When the first round of tea had been consumed, my friend Hosain Aga, the merchant from Isfahān, explained the object of my visit. I was engaged, he said, in writing a book about the carpets of Persia. And I had come to the Chahār Mahāl to gather information.

"What will be the use of such a book?" enquired Mohammed Riza, the trader.

This was a disconcerting question which, I confess, I had asked myself more than once in moments of dejection. I explained—in halting and unconvincing phrases—that many thousands of Persian carpets adorned the houses of the West, and that thousands more were being shipped every year. The people of the West might, I thought, desire to learn about the different localities where these carpets were made; and about the wool, the weaving, the designs and the colours of each type of carpet. I had already spent eight months, I said (warming to my subject), journeying from place to place where carpets were woven, to find out these things and to write them down. And now I had come to the Chahār Mahāl.

"When will your journey be finished?" enquired Mohammed Riza, the trader.

"I hope to return to my country within the year, to complete the book."

---

[1] The Bakhtiari tribes are separated into two main divisions: the Chahār Lang and the Haft Lang.
[2] This tradition has been, to a certain extent, disregarded in recent years.

"What!" he exclaimed, "after a whole year in Irān will it not be finished?"

"Alas, no," I said. "There is much work to be done. Perhaps in another year——"

"A journey of one year and then another year's expense on top of it! Where is the profit?"

"Such a task," cried Mr. Know-All with conviction, "is not undertaken for profit. Even if he did not sell a single book——"

"It will not be as bad as that, I hope," I interrupted hastily. "But meantime I should like to ask you all—who know about the Chahār Mahāl—how many villages there are in the district."

"In the Chahār Mahāl there are 240 pieces of villages," said Mr. Know-All, as if he had just finished counting them.

Meshed Ali, the *dellal* from Isfahān (who was born in the area) shook his head. "You exaggerate. There are not over 200 pieces in the Chahār Mahāl."

Our host raised a protesting hand. "For my own benefit I once made a list of them, they number 120."

I made a note of the figure and proceeded with the enquiry. "How many looms do you think there are in these 120 villages?"

"A great many," said our host cautiously.

"Why," cried Mr. Know-All, "here in Shahr Kūrd alone there are a thousand! And two *farsakhs* away, in Qaverūkh, there are a thousand more!"

"In Shahr Kūrd," said our host, "you may say that there are 500 looms. In Qaverūkh there are, it is true, a thousand houses; but many of the householders are too poor to weave. How can they weave a carpet if they have nothing to start it with? You may say another 500 looms for Qaverūkh."

"What do you estimate would be the average number of looms per village in the Chahār Mahāl?" I enquired. "Fifty?"

"What!" exclaimed Mr. Know-All derisively.

"A hundred?" I hazarded.

There was an excited argument. At last our host declared: "More."

"But," I demurred, "if there are 120 villages and there is an average of even 100 looms per village, that would make 12,000 looms. How many *zars* of carpet does a loom produce in a year?"

There was another heated argument. At last our host declared firmly: "Twenty."

"Very well," I said, "12,000 looms at 20 *zars* a year makes 240,000 *zars* of carpet. That is about the production of Hamadān, which is a province and twenty times the size of the Chahār Mahāl; 240,000 *zars* is equivalent to 100,000 rugs. Where do they all go to? I have never seen more than a few hundred at a time anywhere."

"In the Chahār Mahāl," explained Mr. Know-All, as if to terminate the discussion, "every woman and every child is a weaver."

After I had visited the area I wrote in my note book:

Chahār Mahāl, 120 villages; probably average number of looms per village, 30; allowing that they work two-thirds of the time, output must be about 12 *zars* a year; 120 × 30 × 12 equal 43,200 *zars*; or, say, 45,000 square metres. Looks far too much to me; probably very much less.

Thus are estimates prepared in Persia.

When the Turkish invaders from the north-east[1] settled in the Chahār Mahāl they brought the Turkish knot with them, and the villagers have retained it ever since. If occasionally a rug is discovered woven with the Persian knot, it is an isolated case due to an intermarriage with a Persian woman from Isfahān, Arāk or some more distant province. The fabric is generally single wefted; and the designs are rectilinear.

The horizontal loom is still in use—both for rug and carpet sizes. That is why 90 per cent of the carpets of the Chahār Mahāl measure under 11 × 8 feet—there is no room on the floor of their cottages to weave larger pieces. In Qefarūkh (loc. Qaverūkh) I saw two 15 × 12 feet carpets being woven flat on the floor. They took up the whole of the floor space of the two principal rooms in one of the larger houses.

The weavers of Shahr Kūrd alone prefer the upright loom. They have adopted the type which is in vogue in Isfahān. It has a fixed upper beam and the ends of the lower beam fit into slots in the two side-pieces. The warp is tightened by driving wedges into the two side slots. Altogether, the Shahr Kūrd weavers have adopted a more urban style of weaving: upright looms, large sizes, a double-wefted fabric and scale-paper designs in curvilinear patterns.

On the whole the dyes used in the Chahār Mahāl are good, but the dyeing is careless. Too often grey yarns are used instead of white—which produces muddy colours. And too often black is used instead of dark blue. The villagers, indeed, spend very

[1] They were most probably Seljūks.

little money on indigo. Synthetic dyes and anilines are used, but not on an important scale. Like the Qashqaī, the Chahār Mahāl weavers are fond of yellow. They dye it in the same way as the Qashqaī —with weld and madder.

They possess about twenty-five designs—most of which are common to several villages. The majority of their rugs and carpets are in repeating lozenges or square panels in variegated colours (Plates 354–364). The latter is so characteristic of the weave that it is commonly known in Persia as the "Bakhtiari design". They are fond, too, of tree designs (Plate 356) and of an all-over pattern which, I was assured (and can well believe), was taken from a cotton print of Russian manufacture (Plate 363).

To me the rugs and carpets of the Chahār Mahāl are among the most interesting of the tribal village weaves of Persia. For they possess that quality which we call character: that is individuality, sincerity and strength. Most of the examples shown in the plates possess these qualities. When, however, the villagers attempt to ape their neighbours —as in their lamentable efforts to weave medallion patterns (which they appear to have borrowed, in a moment of weakness, from Arāk)—they fail. Unhappily, this type of design is becoming more frequent in the area.

In general, the standard of excellence has declined in the Chahār Mahāl, as it has in most of the weaving areas of Persia. In a few of the villages the weaving was as good, or even better, than ever. But that, unhappily, was not true of most. The rugs, on the whole, were coarsely woven; the colours muddy; and far too much black was being used instead of indigo-blue. The prevalence of ill-drawn, clumsy medallion designs was distressing. I could only hope that when the West begins once more to enquire for Bakhtiari rugs and small carpets, the weavers of the Chahār Mahāl will produce them as well and as truly as they did in the years before the war.

(3) *The Lūrī Tribal Rugs*. The few rugs produced by the Kuhgalū and other Lūrī tribes which occupy the valleys south-west of Isfahan are hardly worthy of notice. The output of the Lūrs was never large, and it has dwindled to nearly nothing. An occasional rug will find its way into the Shirāz bazaar (see p. 298); a few appear, from time to time, in Isfahan (although during a two weeks' stay there in 1949 I only saw two pieces); and some no doubt are marketed in Behbehān, or sold to members of the staff of the Anglo-Iranian Oil Company which operates in the neighbourhood. But, as one of the tribal weaves of Persia, the Lūrī rugs are no longer of any importance.

JŌSHAQĀN

There are half a dozen villages in Persia—each a planless agglomeration of a few hundred flat-roofed cottages built of mud and poplar poles; each with uneven and unpaved alleyways winding between crumbling mud walls; and each inhabited by a poor and ignorant peasantry—which bear nevertheless names which are renowned the world over. Such are Ravār, Sarūk, Jozān, Herīz—and Jōshaqān.

The notoriety of Jōshaqān rests upon the fact that for at least two centuries (and perhaps for twice as long) it has been weaving two (and only two) closely allied designs (Plates 365, 366). There are thousands of villages in Persia which have been weaving for as many centuries as Jōshaqān; but—under the influence of fashion or demand—they have constantly altered their styles. Jōshaqān is one of the few which has pursued its way, down the centuries, indifferent to the importunities of the bazaar or to the clamours of the stylists. The villagers knew that they had a good thing, and they have stuck to it.

In the Victoria and Albert Museum there is a fragment of a Jōshaqān carpet of the eighteenth century; and there are early fragments in other museums and collections in Europe and America. Except that the pile of these fragments is worn and the colours faded, any one of them might have been woven in Jōshaqān last week. The fabric of these antique pieces is the same as that of the carpets of today; the motives of the design are the same; the dyestuffs used are the same. In both the old and new, the weaving is rectilinear: there are no curves in either. Plate 367 is a photograph of the fragment in the Victoria and Albert Museum; Plate 365 of a modern Jōshaqān carpet. The resemblance (after an interval of 200 years) between the design of the fragment and that of the corner of the modern carpet needs no comment. The weavers of Jōshaqān have been right to stick to their two designs. For—with or without a central medallion—they are satisfying compositions.

Jōshaqān is a village of about 500 houses, situated in a valley of the Kuh-i-Varganeh, 76 miles almost due north of Isfahan. It can be easily reached by car. A track runs for 11 miles across the plain from Meimeh—a station on the Isfahan–Tehrān trunk road—to the village. The village is sometimes called

336. Jōshaqān Village

Jōshaqān Qāli, i.e. "Carpet Jōshaqān", to distinguish it from four other villages of the same name which are situated within 100 miles of Isfahān.[1]

Persian villages are, as a rule, unkempt and uncomely. But Jōshaqān, especially in summer, is a charming little place. A stream runs through it, a half-ruined fort, with four tall towers, grimly overlooks it; and an *Imam Zadeh* with conical, turquoise roof, adds to it a spot of colour. The monotony of its drab mud houses is in part relieved and in part concealed by slender poplars. Behind it towers the Kuh-i-Varganeh (Photo 336).

Conversation Piece

On the day on which I revisited the village its *Erbab*, Makhsūd Khan Homayūn (who owns half of it), happened to be there. It was January. We had driven across the plain in the beginnings of a snow storm; by the time we reached the village the alleyways were covered in snow. But Makhsūd Khan soon had the logs roaring in his upper chamber. As we sipped comforting glasses of hot, sweet Persian tea, I informed him, with diffidence, of the object of our visit. Whereat he expressed his pleasure with such cordiality and humour that we were instantly at ease.

"I am delighted," said our host, "that Jōshaqān possesses for you such an interest that you have driven all the way from Isfahān, in winter, to see it. And you were right to do so; because there is no village in Irān whose carpets are more famous. Of that I possess indisputable proof, which I will show you. It is a fragment of a chronicle of the reign of Shah Tahmasp, which I discovered one day in an obscure bookshop. I have kept it here ever since, because I found in it a reference to the carpets of Jōshaqān."

With that he withdrew, and quickly returned with a few sheets of tattered manuscript. And thereupon he read to me how the Emperor Homayūn of India (who was in exile) had expressed the wish to visit the Persian court; and how Shah Tahmasp had ordered a great *istikbal* of 30,000 people to go forward to receive him; and of the rich presents which the Shah had sent: mantles of honour, swords of gold, horses, jewels, embroidered saddles and the like; and three pairs of carpets of Jōshaqān, each of 12 *zars*. I remembered then the painting in the Chehel Sitūn of the meeting between the Shah and the Emperor.

We were soon discussing the past glories and present discontents of the village. Makhsūd Khan deplored the fact that his villagers—who had for centuries maintained a standard of good weaving—had now been compelled, by the high cost of wool, cotton and dyestuffs and by the refusal of the merchants to pay them an adequate price—to reduce the quality of their carpets. I suggested that this was, perhaps, a passing phase; and that when the present abnormal demand for wool was satisfied and the markets of the West reopened, all would be well again.

"Inshallah!" smiled our host contentedly, and then conducted us on a tour of inspection through the village.

There are about 200 looms in Jōshaqān. To my surprise I found that many of them were of the roller type—which is not often seen in villages outside the Kermān province. Our host informed me that they had been set up there about a century ago by a merchant of Kashān. The yarn which the Jōshaqānis use is handspun from local mountain wools (which are very good), supplemented by wools from Isfahān and Khūrasān. The warps and wefts are also handspun from Isfahān cotton.

The villagers use about twelve colours, and all of them are excellent. Indeed, there is no better madder red produced in Persia. They prefer vine leaves to weld for their yellows. Synthetic dyes and anilines are anathema in Jōshaqān.

The fabric is double wefted; and the villagers, being Persians, weave the Persian knot. Men, women and children sit side by side before the looms. The normal quality which they used to

---

[1] And not, as Upham Pope suggests, because the Vase carpets were made there (see p. 17).

weave before the war (and which they were weaving 200 years ago) was about 10 × 10 knots to the inch. Today it is no more than 8 × 8 knots. The result is that the present-day carpet is much inferior in density to the pre-war fabric.

I was grieved to find that the *jūftī* knot had gained a footing there. It was, I was assured, used sparingly; but I had seen enough of its baleful effect in other parts of Persia to realise that the disease will spread and will inevitably undermine the good name of the Jōshaqān carpet.

The output of Jōshaqān's 200 looms was (in 1949) between 4,000 and 5,000 metres a year. Probably more than half was in rug sizes, made for the Tehrān market; normally the production of rugs is small.

In addition to the looms in Jōshaqān there are about 100 looms in Meimeh, the village on the trunk road where the track branches off to Jōshaqān. Meimeh weaves the Jōshaqān design, but in a much finer quality than that woven in Jōshaqān itself. The carpets counted about 13 × 13 knots to the inch, which is somewhat fine for a rectilinear pattern; for in a fine quality, designs of this character are apt to appear stiff and angular. The Meimeh carpets are well woven but they are clipped too thin.

It is, I think, a pity that the Jōshaqān design and style have spread to another village. Before the war the markets of the West had been able to absorb 500–600 Jōshaqān carpets a year—all of the same design and colour. But they might have difficulty in absorbing twice as many. And if that came to pass, the pressure on the villagers of Jōshaqān to weave a different design might be too great for even that stubborn community to resist.

A NOTE ON NAĪN

Naīn (pop. about 6,000) is one of the lesser of the long line of ancient fortified towns which follow the western border of the Great Desert. Like its southern neighbour Yezd, it is an oasis: on every side the brown, desiccated plain extends to the level horizon, or to a distant line of grey and jagged mountains. But, unlike Yezd, Naīn is still untouched by the rejuvenating hand of the planner. It remains a town of narrow, crooked and ill-paved streets flanked by windowless mud walls.

The Persian people—when other activities fail them—turn to carpet weaving; with the firm assurance that they will be able to produce a fabric which the world will buy. We have seen that this is what occurred in Kermān when the shawl industry failed. We shall see that Kashān began to produce carpets when—at the beginning of the present century—the town lost its importance as a textile centre. The same thing happened in Naīn, when the adoption of European dress by the Persians threatened to destroy its traditional industry—the manufacture of fine woollen cloth for the *aba* or Persian cloak.

The industry of rug weaving was started just before the war. The weavers, accustomed as they were to spin fine yarns for their fine cloths and to weave a textile of high pitch, laid the warps for their rugs to a quality of 22 × 22 knots to the inch. They began thus to produce a more closely woven fabric than any that was standard in Persia at the time. The fabric being new and the output small, it sold readily. After that came the war and the boom in Tehrān. Nothing was too good or too expensive for the *nouveaux riches* of the capital. Thus was the Naīn fabric launched; and it became recognised as the closest weave of Persia, and one of the best.

The end of the war brought about a decline in the demand from Tehrān, and the Naīn rugs were too expensive for impoverished Europe; so that Naīn might have again found itself in straits had there not occurred another unexpected turn in its fortunes. A new and hitherto unsuspected market for its cloth was discovered in Palestine and the Arab states. So that today rug weaving is declining (there were in 1949 about 150 looms in the town) and cloth weaving has once more become the principal industry of the little town.

The wools of Naīn are finer in fibre and softer than the average wool of the Persian plateau. And the skilled Naīn spinners produce from them a fine and even yarn well suited to a weave which counts about 450 knots to the inch. The dyes, too, which are used in Naīn are excellent. A fastidious critic might perhaps point out that the Naīn rugs—like those of Isfahān which they closely resemble—lack variety in design and colour. But the output is so small (somewhere about 500 metres a year) that a greater diversity of patterns and shades would add little to the merits of this comparatively rare and excellent product.

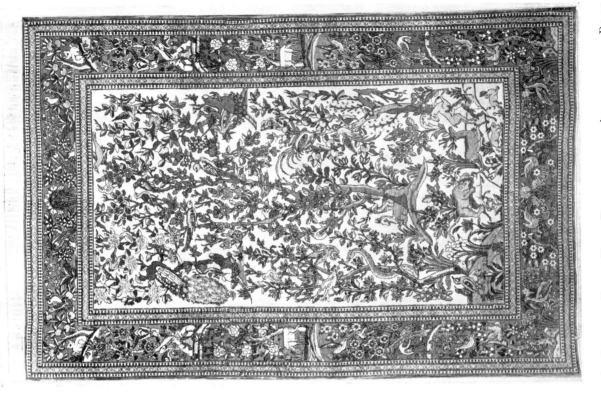

338. Isfahān Rug, Tree Design, with Animals and Birds (c. 1925)

337. Isfahān Carpet in a Medallion and Corner Design (c. 1925)

339, 340. Between the Wars Isfahān produced important quantities of medium-priced rugs of fine quality. They commanded a ready sale on the Continent (c. 1935)

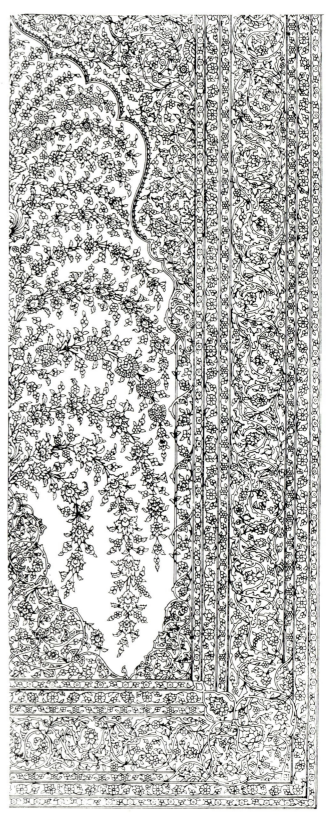

341. Design for an Isfahān rug; drawn by Tahir Zadeh Bihzad, School of Art, Tehrān, from an Isfahān rug (c. 1935)

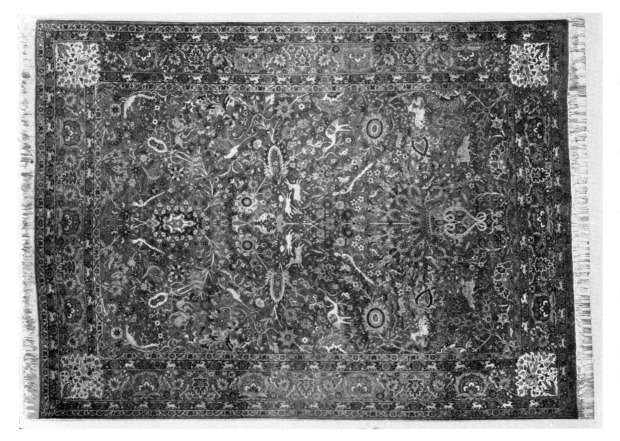

343. An Isfahān Carpet with Animals, Birds and Flowers; a Fine Specimen of Modern Craftsmanship (c. 1935)

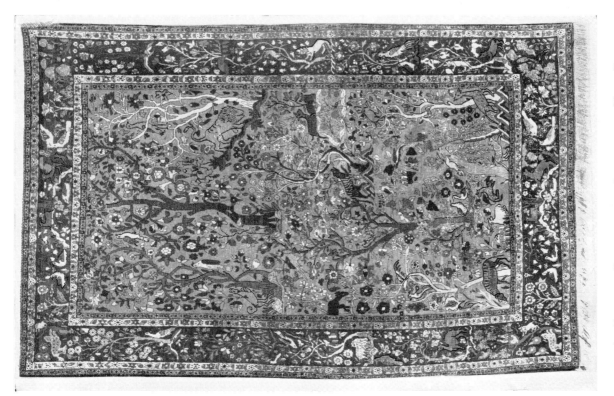

342. An Isfahān Carpet in an Animal and Tree Design (c. 1935)

345. Isfahān Carpet with Medallion and Corners (c. 1940)

344. An Isfahān Rug (c. 1940)

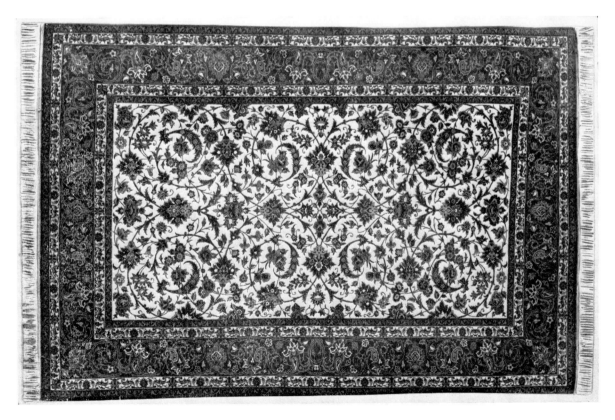

347. An Isfahān Rug, Portico Design, with Vase of Flowers and Vines (c. 1945)

346. Isfahān Carpet (c. 1945)

348. Isfahān Carpet; with Birds and Flowers (c. 1945)

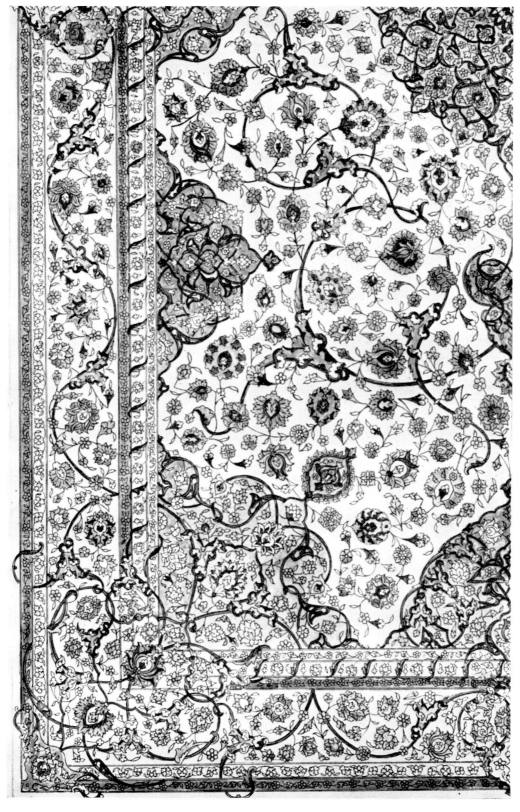

349. Design for an Isfahān Carpet with Medallion and Arabesques; Drawn by Tahir Zadeh Bihzad, School of Art, Tehrān (c. 1945)

350. Design for an Isfahān Carpet; taken from the Fresco in the Alī Kapū, Isfahān; Drawn by Tahir Zadeh Bihzad, School of Art, Tehrān (c. 1945)

351. Animal and Floral Design for an Isfahān Carpet; Drawn by Tahir Zadeh Bihzad, School of Art, Tehrān (c. 1945)

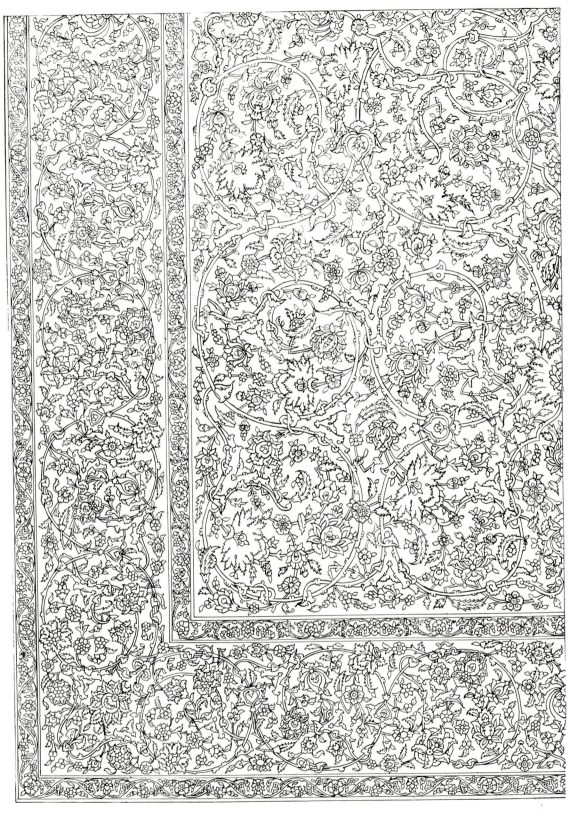

352. Design for an Isfahān Carpet with Spirals and Arabesques; Drawn by Tahir Zadeh Bihzad, School of Art, Tehrān (*c.* 1945)

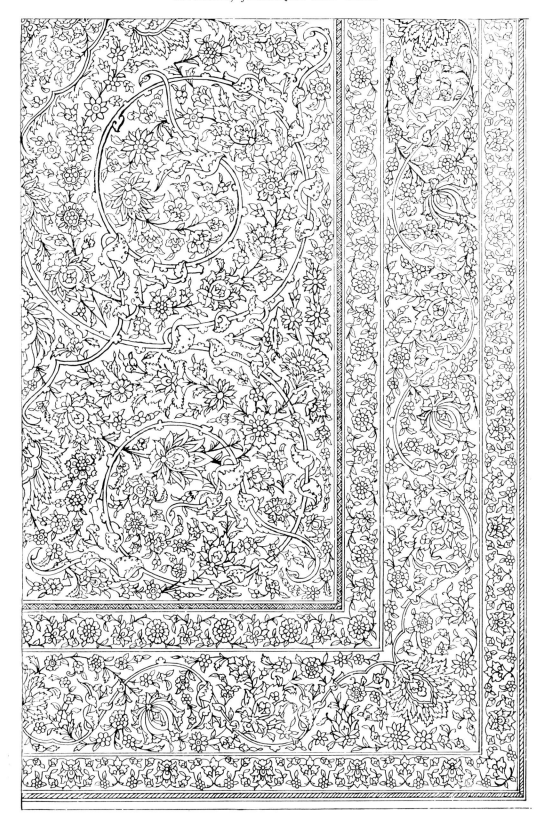

353. Design for an Isfahān Carpet with Spirals and Arabesques; Drawn by Tahir Zadeh Bihzad, School of Art, Tehrān (c. 1945)

354. A "Bakhtiari" Rug from Boldaji Village, Chahār Mahāl (c. 1940)

355. A "Bakhtiari" Rug from the Armenian Village of Hajiabād, Chahār Mahāl (c. 1940)

356. A "Bakhtiari" Rug from Shalamzār Village, Chahār Mahāl (c. 1940)

357. A "Bakhtiari" Rug from Beīn Village, Chahār Mahāl (c. 1935)

358, 359. "Bakhtiārī" Rugs from Chahār Shotūr Village, Chahār Mahāl (c. 1945)

360. A "Bakhtiārī" Rug from Shahr Kūrd Village, Chahār Mahāl (c. 1945)

361. A "Bakhtiārī" Rug from the Shrine Collection, Meshed
It is dated A.H. 1361 — A.D. 1942. *The inscription is illegible.*

363. A "Bakhtiari" Carpet from Destgird Village in the Chahār Mahāl (c. 1940)

This interesting design was said to have been taken from a Russian cotton print; the border is poor.

362. A "Bakhtiari" Carpet from Beīn Village. Chahār Mahāl (c. 1945)

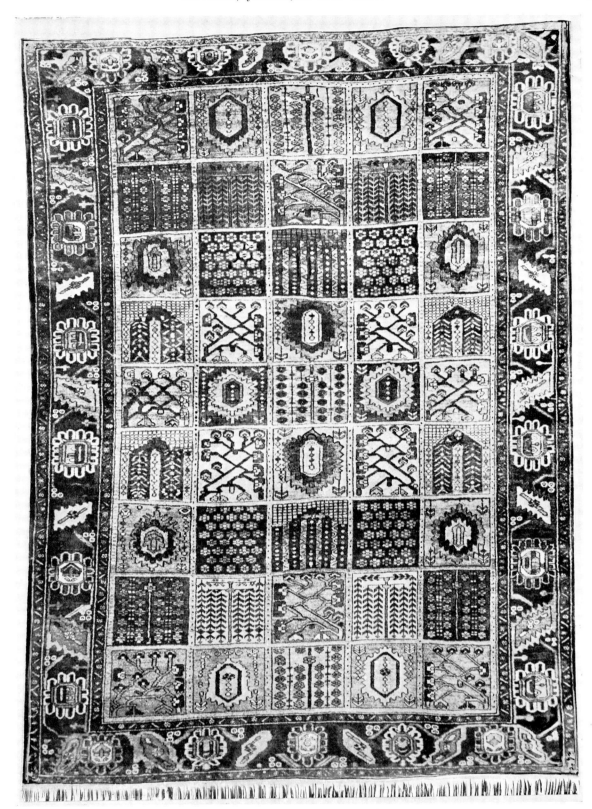

364. A "Bakhtiari" Carpet from Qefarūkh (loc. Qaverūkh) Village, Chahār Mahāl (c. 1945)
This is a favourite design of the area, so much so that it is known throughout Persia as the "Bakhtiari" design.

365. A Jōshaqān Carpet (c. 1920); similar motives—but differently applied—appear in this Carpet as in Plate 35

366. A Jōshaqān Carpet from the Shrine Collection, Meshed

Both carpets have the classic Jōshaqān border.

367. Fragment of a Jōshaqān Carpet in the Victoria and Albert Museum, London

Compare the design with that of the corners of the carpet reproduced on Plate 366. For at least two centuries (and perhaps for twice as long) Jōshaqān has been weaving this design.

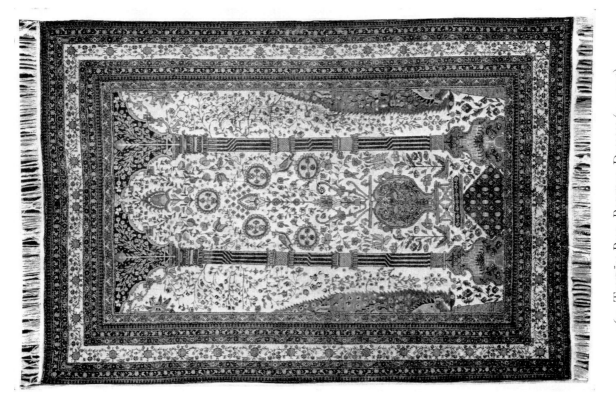

369. Tehrān Rug, Portico Design (c. 1915)
Tehrān is no longer a weaving centre.

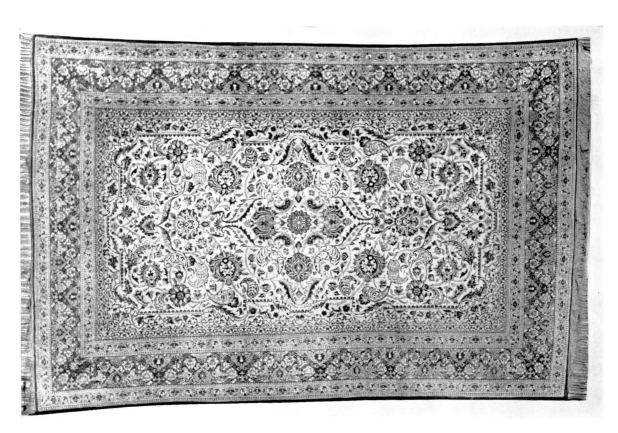

368. A Naīn Carpet (c. 1946)

370. A Tehrān Carpet in a Panel Design (*c.* 1920)

Tehrān was never an important weaving centre, although some interesting pieces were produced there. The industry ceased to exist about twenty years ago.

CHAPTER XVI

KASHĀN AND QŪM

KASHĀN

The town of Kashān is the third in the long line of towns which follow each other at distances of from 75 to 150 miles along the western fringe of the Great Desert on the highway to India. Unkempt, dilapidated and situated in a drab, treeless and almost waterless plain, it is one of the less attractive of the towns of Persia. The area, indeed, is so lacking in water that the unhappy peasants are unable to grow wheat for their needs. They are compelled to grow the less thirsty barley, and to satisfy their hunger with barley bread. The visitor wonders what dream or portent could have induced the wife of Harūn-al-Rashīd (who is said to have founded the town and to have built the formidable wall which surrounds it) to select such a dolorous site.

The altitude of Kashān (3,200 feet) is one of the lowest of the more important towns of the plateau. The town, in consequence, is extremely hot in summer. It is, indeed, so hot and its irrigation channels lie so far below the level of the ground, that the inhabitants have found coolness and water only by an ingenious device: instead of building their houses upwards, in the accepted manner, they build them downwards. Their dwellings consist of large, sunken, rectangular courtyards—some as much as 30 feet below ground—with the living quarters arranged in galleries, one below the other. Kashān,

372. KASHĀN DWELLING-HOUSES
The importation of machine-made textiles from the West undermined the industries of Kashān and the imposing houses of its merchants and manufacturers slowly fell into wrack. To-day most of them are occupied by three or more families of carpet weavers.

is, I dare say, the only town in existence where, to reach the first, second or third floors, you have to walk downstairs.

Yet Kashān, in spite of its disabilities, possesses a long and honourable record; for its inhabitants, unable to gain a livelihood from the inhospitable land, turned their hands to industry and made their town the principal centre in Persia for the production of fine textiles in cotton, wool and silk. Numerous travellers who visited Persia during the sixteenth and seventeenth centuries have testified to the excellence of these tissues. The city at that time is said to have been four times its present size.

The advent into Persia during the nineteenth century of machine-made textiles from the West undermined and finally destroyed the industries of Kashān. The imposing houses of its merchants and manufacturers slowly fell into wrack. Today most of them are occupied by three or more families of poor carpet weavers (Plate 372). While most of the towns of Persia have improved their streets and rebuilt at least the façades of the buildings facing them, Kashān still remains a maze of narrow, tortuous and ill-paved alleys, flanked by crumbling walls and half-ruined houses.

371. KASHĀN
Note the domed roofs of the bazaar.

The Revival of the Carpet-Weaving Industry in Kashān

The question whether or not some of the great carpets of the sixteenth century were woven in Kashān has been discussed in Chapter II. The conclusion was reached that the town possesses as good a claim as any other to the parentage of the Ardebil carpet and to a number of other carpets of the same group. But, as in Isfahān, the industry does not appear to have survived the Afghan invasions. So far as I am aware, no carpets of the eighteenth and nineteenth centuries exist in any of our museums or private collections which can, with definite assurance, be attributed to Kashān.

It happens from time to time in the history of communities that an event takes place which, in itself, is without significance, but which produces, nevertheless, a vital change in the lives of thousands of its members. Such an event took place sixty years ago in Kashān—at a time when the economic position there appeared intractable and forlorn, owing to the collapse of its industries. The portentous event was the marriage of Hajji Mollah Hassan, a merchant of substance, with a lady from Arāk.

The good merchant counted among his activities the sale of merino yarn from Manchester, for use in the textile industries of his native town. But the trade had fallen off and the Hajji found himself possessed of a quantity of fine merino which was unsaleable. He remembered then that his young wife had been a skilled weaver in Arāk, and he suggested to her that she should weave a rug with the yarn in his store. A suitable design was chosen; the yarn was given to be dyed; and in due course the first modern Kashān rug was born.

Its workmanship was of the best; its surface as soft as velvet; its colouring rich and clear. It was examined with critical eyes by the textile experts of Kashān; and it was approved. For, indeed, a rug had never before been woven in Persia with Australian merino.

A second rug was soon started in the house of Burūjirdī and a third in the house of Tabatabai—both prominent merchants of Kashān, whose sons are still producing carpets there. All three rugs were quickly sold. The movement was set in train and began rapidly to expand; for the women workers of the moribund textile industries took up carpet weaving with alacrity.

Thus was revived—after two centuries of quiescence—the carpet-weaving industry of Kashān.

The Early Carpets of the Revival

The Kashān carpets of the first two decades of the present century differed from the weaves of the rest of Persia in one essential particular: they were woven with imported merino yarns. For the weavers of Kashān continued to follow the lead of the lady from Arāk and her first two disciples.

We are too often inclined to assume that the carpets which were produced forty or fifty years ago were superior to the products of today. That this is far from true of the carpets of Kashān is manifest by comparing Plates 377, 378—which are photographs of some of the best of the earlier pieces—with Plates 390–403, which represent the products of today. It is clear that these early designers and weavers had a lot to learn.

The Expansion of the Industry

The speed with which the industry developed is indicated by the following table, which shows the approximate number of looms in the area at successive periods during the last sixty years. It was prepared by one of the prominent merchants of Kashān, who did not pretend that the figures were accurate. However that may be, they certainly do indicate the rapidity of the industry's expansion and its importance to Kashān.

NUMBER OF LOOMS IN KASHĀN AND DISTRICT

Year	Total number	Town	Local villages	Natanz and area
1890	3	3	0	0
1900	1,500	1,500	0	0
1910	3,000	3,000	0	0
1915	5,000	4,000	1,000	0
1920	2,500	2,500	0	0
1925	6,000	4,000	2,000	0
1930	8,000	4,000	2,000	2,000
1935	10,000	4,000	4,000	2,000
1940	12,000	4,000	6,000	2,000
1945	11,000	4,000	5,000	2,000
1949	9,000	4,000	3,500	1,500

I confess that the figures appeared to me to be somewhat exaggerated. For one thing, 4,000 looms seemed excessive for a town of 45,000 people. I was assured, however, that the figure was approximately correct, as there were many looms in the town at which only one or two weavers were working. The figures for the nearby villages appeared to be more reliable; for there are no less than eighty villages within a radius of 30 miles of the town. Of these the most important are Nūshabād, Armāq, Ravānd, Fīn,

373. KASHĀN: WOMEN SORTING WOOL

Tahirabād, Mashad, Rahāq, Aliabād, Mishkān, Abuzaidabād and Qamsār—all of which weave carpets fully equal in quality to those of Kashān itself. In addition to these there are two villages—Aron and Nasirabād—which weave inferior carpets. The remaining weaving villages contain fewer looms and generally weave poor qualities. Natanz, which has developed as a weaving centre since 1930, is a large cluster of villages rather than a town. The area weaves a fine quality, mostly in rug sizes (Plate 408). The fabric is fully equal to that of Kashān, with some characteristics of its own, discernible only by the local experts.

The Industry in 1949

(1) *The Yarns*. The use of merino yarn did not survive the onset of the crisis of the early thirties. For the fabric was too expensive for markets distracted by that depression. Again, it was found that carpets woven with native handspun yarn were not very different—after they had passed through the hands of the finishers abroad—from the more expensive fabrics woven with imported merino. Thus handspun yarn was soon adopted throughout the area. It was mainly spun from wools imported from Sabsawār, Kermanshāh and Isfahān. Shortly before the war a power-driven carding plant was erected in Kashān, and today the wools are machine carded before being spun by hand.

Kashān has never resumed the use of imported yarns. In recent years, however, some of the Persian mills have been producing yarns which—although they are not pure merino—are softer and more even than the handspun yarn which has been in use since the thirties. The new material produces a smoother, more velvety surface than the old, and it takes the dye better. It is well suited to the closely woven and beautifully finished fabric of Kashān. Its cost, however, is higher than the handspun material.

(2) *Qualities*. The Kashān fabric is double wefted and woven with the Persian knot. The quality which is generally woven in Kashān itself and in most of the villages of the area is a nominal 40 × 40 knots to the *gireh* of 6·5 centimetres. This is equivalent to $15\frac{1}{2} \times 15\frac{1}{2}$ knots to the inch. Actually, however, the carpets rarely count over 36 × 36 knots to the *gireh* each way; so that the number of knots in a Kashān carpet of good average quality is about 14 × 14 to the inch. This is about the same as the quality of the superior grade of Kermān.

Below this is a cheap quality carpet which is woven principally in the large village of Aron—8 miles east of Kashān—where there are about 400 looms. The

374. THE WEAVING VILLAGE OF NŪSHABĀD, NEAR KASHĀN

375. THE HOUSE OF THE HEADMAN OF NŪSHABĀD VILLAGE

Aron carpets are coarse in stitch and are unworthy of the renown of the Kashān weave. They usually count only 28–30 knots to the *gireh*—which is no better than the pre-war "bazaar" carpet of Tabrīz. The Tabrīz carpets, however, were woven in a great variety of designs and colours; whereas the carpets of Aron village are all medallion-and-corner designs on brick-red grounds, with dark blue medallions and borders. They all look alike.

(3) *Weaving*. There are no factories in Kashān. All the looms are in the houses—usually two looms to a house. Or if the house is large and occupied by two or more families there may be four to six looms. Each pair of looms, however, works independently. The weavers are given 4 kilogrammes of dyed yarn and 1·50 kilogrammes of cotton yarn per square *zar* (1·08 square metres) to weave their carpet; and they are paid 450–500 rials (or 69*s*.–76*s*., reckoned at the exchange rate of 130) for weaving a square *zar*. Out of this they pay their assistants. In addition, a commission is paid to the person by whom the weaver is introduced, who also acts as her guarantor and who inspects her work. Practically all the weaving is done by women and the standard of workmanship is very high.

(4) *Output*. Weaving is slow in Kashān. The average output per loom, both in the town and in the villages, is about three-eighths of a square *zar* (or about four three-eighths square feet) per month. Thus, it takes an average of two years to weave a Kashān carpet measuring 12 × 9 feet. This does not mean that the weavers who are under contract take so long; because the merchants avoid placing their contracts with slow weavers. A good weaver and one whose work is periodically inspected weaves fully half as much again. My friends estimated that the total output for the whole Kashān area, including Natanz, was something less than 45,000 *zars* per annum or, say, 50,000 metres. It is extremely difficult to determine how near the truth these figures are: but my impression is that they are on the high side.

(5) *The Dyes*. We have seen that the battle of the dyes is being waged with some acerbity in Persia. Arāk (Sultānabād), Meshed, Kermān, Shirāz and Qūm are holding their part of the line fairly well against the onslaught of the European dye manufacturers. Hamadān is wobbling. Tabrīz, Isfahān and, I regret to say, Kashān have almost given up the fight. A few of the more important Kashān merchants still have their yarns dyed in the traditional manner; but European dyes are used in the majority of the carpets produced in the area.

In 1949, when I revisited the town, three-quarters of the output was being produced for the Tehrān market—which called for nothing but red-ground carpets in medallion-and-corner designs. It was, indeed, wearisome to see carpet after carpet—excellent in quality and workmanship (except for the use of the *juftī* knot)—yet all alike in colour and design. Madder was not much used for the grounds of these carpets. It was too expensive and its shade was too mellow for the *nouveaux riches* of Tehrān. They wanted a flashier carpet; and the Kashān merchants gave it to them by dyeing the yarns with a synthetic red of Swiss manufacture, mordanted with chrome and "topped" with aniline to give it greater brilliancy.

(6) *The Designs*. It has been mentioned above that the early designers of Kashān had much to learn about their craft. Their lack of invention was indicated by the fact that in the early carpets the same border was used again and again (Plates 377, 382). It was known in Kashān as the Mustōfi border, because it is said to have been taken from a carpet in the possession of a famous statesman of the late nineteenth century, Mustōfi-el-Mamalek. The Kashān designers have learnt a great deal since then. They do not possess the genius of the designers of Kermān; but they are competent—though somewhat limited—craftsmen. By and large, they were (in 1949) producing only two styles: the medallion-and-corner type with covered grounds; and the so-called Isfahān or Shah Abbas type. Nevertheless, within these limits, their work was excellent. Between the wars some of the American firms which were established in Arāk (Sultānabād) ordered Kashān carpets in the Sarūk design which was popular at the time, and still is (see p. 141). Immediately after the war the demand for this type of carpet was resumed, and most of the Kashān looms were busy producing it. Happily, however, the demand for them fell off as quickly as it started. There were none on loom in 1949.

It is not the practice in Kashān for the merchants to employ their own designers. Formerly some of the foreign firms did so; but they have long since closed their offices. Today, designs are ordered from one or another of the half-dozen professional designers of the town, and generally the merchants take what is given to them by the designer.

(7) *The Jufti Knot*. The reader who has had the assiduity to accompany me to this point in this survey must, I fear, have been wearied by the constant reference to a disease which has infected the weaver's craft in Persia: the *juftī* knot. I must ask

his indulgence if I refer to this malady again; for it is rife in Kashān. Unless checked, it must inevitably impair the good name of the Kashān carpet.

Twenty years ago the *jūftī* knot was unknown in Kashān. Today it is estimated that about a third of the knots woven in the area are fraudulent. It is not as high a proportion as in Kermān (where it is estimated that at least half the knots are *jūftī*): but experience in other centres has shown that the virulence of the disease increases when it has once taken hold. It has already been pointed out that detection is extremely difficult, except at the actual moment of tying the knot; and that no remedy is yet in sight.

Conversation Piece

The conversation (as so often happens in Kashān when a few friends are gathered together) had turned to the subject of scorpions. For the scorpions of Kashān are as renowned as its carpets. My host, Sayyid Hosain, had taken no part in the talk; but when the interest began to flag, he observed:

"Nevertheless, these little creatures have their uses." Whereupon we awaited the promised tale.

"A good many years ago [began my host] there arrived in Kashān one day an Inspector from the Ministry of Finance. He had been sent, it appeared, to resolve certain doubts which had arisen in the distrustful mind of the Minister touching the persistent decline in the revenues of Kashān.

"The Inspector was a person of zeal and industry, and it soon became apparent to the Collector of Taxes in Kashān that he would not be satisfied with those useful devices which had served in the past to moderate and compose the ardour of half a dozen previous inspectors. Nor did he appear to be moved when it was suggested that certain benefits might be expected to accrue to him if his report were favourable. The Inspector appeared, indeed, to be so impervious to these well-tried approaches that the Collector was at his wits' end to know what to do next.

"It was at this dark moment that the Head Carpet Spreader of the Collector's household unfolded his ingenious plan.

"That same evening the Collector, his Deputy, the Inspector from Tehrān and a few of the Collector's relatives were enjoying the cool air of sunset on the spacious *talar* of the Collector's house. The conversation—as so often happens at distinguished gatherings in Kashān—had turned to the subject of scorpions. The Collector had recounted a story of a young girl who had recently arrived from Tehrān to be married, and who had succumbed to the bite of one of those detestable creatures on her wedding day. The Deputy had capped it with an account of a gentleman from Shirāz who had come to visit his relatives. He had been bitten on the hand by one of those odious insects—a large black one—as he lay asleep. In an hour the lower arm had swollen to twice its size. To save the wretched man's life, the arm had had to be amputated at the elbow.

"'These abominable creeping things,' volunteered the Collector's brother-in-law—whose white turban and ample gaberdine proclaimed his association with the church—'appear to sense and to resent the presence of strangers. Your true Kashāni is rarely troubled by them; whereas there are numberless cases on record of visitors being bitten shortly after their arrival. The bite is generally mortal, though there have been cases (as mentioned by my friend the Deputy Collector) when the life of the victim has been saved by the immediate amputation of a limb.'

"It was noted that in the course of these genial remarks the sour visage of the visiting Inspector had assumed a tint which recalled the clay of Natanz, out of which the justly famous pottery of that town is fashioned. He was about to seek further information when he saw the Head Carpet Spreader suddenly dart from his station in the rear of the distinguished company and bring down a large foot firmly on some object on the ground. The assembled company started with cries of alarm, for they had realised at once the significance of that swift action. Meanwhile, the faithful servant, having ground his foot into the carpet, warily lifted it and disclosed the repulsive remains of a black scorpion.

"The Collector at once expressed in appropriate phrases his apologies to his guest; adding that the scorpions of Kashān were in their most tiresome and aggressive mood during that autumn month. At length, the rice was served; but it was observed that the Inspector failed to attack the snow-white mountain with his accustomed diligence. In fact, when the company rose from the table and prepared to disperse to their several apartments, it was remarked that he had hardly eaten anything at all.

"The diligent Carpet Spreader accompanied the Inspector to the apartment which had been reserved for him, and began to unroll his bed. But no sooner had the upper sheet been folded back (for it was too hot for the customary quilt) than a loud imprecation escaped from the devoted servant, followed by a series of invocations to the Deity. For in the middle of the lower sheet lay a black scorpion.

"At the sight of that abominable insect in his bed the face of the Inspector became as white as paper; and for some moments he was unable to speak. Then, in a feeble voice he complained that he was unwell; and he entreated the Carpet Spreader—in spite of the late hour—to order his carriage without delay. ..."

QŪM

If the town of Qūm had not been overshadowed by the capital (Tehrān is only 92 miles away) it would perhaps have acquired greater renown than it possesses. For it enjoys notable advantages which are denied to many of its sister towns: it is situated on an important river, which—for half the year at least—is something more than a dry river-bed, and which helps to irrigate a large area; it is a road and rail junction of growing importance; and above all it possesses (next to Meshed) the most notable shrine in Persia, which is visited by many thousands of pilgrims every year. For here, Fatima, the sister of Ali Riza, the eighth Iman, is buried; as well as four more less important personages—the Sefavi monarchs Safi, Abbas II and Suleiman; and Fath-Ali Shah, Qajār.

The recent and unexpected emergence as weaving centres of such towns as Yezd, Naīn and Qūm, indicates that the carpet industry—however it may have languished in the older localities—is still a vigorous and fertile craft. For Qūm did not begin to weave until the middle thirties. The industry was started there by some merchants from Kashān.

I was the bearer of a letter of introduction from a Kashān friend to a gentleman of holy lineage (as his dark blue turban testified) who was also a carpet merchant of repute. We discovered him in a small dark office in a caravanserai leading from the covered bazaar. He perused my letter with attention and then expressed—in those polite and cordial phrases with which all Persians adorn their conversation —his complete subservience to my wishes.

As the interview proceeded I perceived that the good Sayyid appeared to harbour a measure of jealousy towards the rival city of Kashān. It was probably professional; for the carpets of Kashān are renowned the world over; whereas Qūm was a late starter in the weaver's craft and her undoubted achievements have still to win recognition. My friend enlarged upon the superiority of Qūm over her rival. The population of his native town, he assured me, was nearly double that of Kashān (the difference is actually about 15 per cent in Qūm's favour); the credit and enterprise of her merchants stood higher than that of the merchants of the Kashān bazaar; her dyers—unlike the dyers of Kashān who had ruined the good name of the

376. THE MOSQUE AT QŪM

Fatima, the sister of the 8th Imam, is buried here. Shah Abbas made Qūm a place of pilgrimage, second in sanctity to Meshed. His three successors—Safi, Abbas II and Suleiman are buried here. So is Fath-Ali Shah, Qajār.

Kashān carpet—were honest men and would have nothing to do with European dyes; her weavers, too, were more skilful and more swift. Although there were only 1,000 looms in Qūm, they produced 8,000 *zars* of carpet a year—nearly double the average output of the Kashān weavers.

"Has that malignant disease, the *jūftī* knot, penetrated as far as Qūm?" I enquired. "You know that in Kashān——"

"In Kashān," he interrupted roundly, "they weave nothing else! Every knot, from one end of the carpet to the other, is fraudulent. But not in Qūm. If I catch one of my weavers doing it, I cut the carpet—a whole *gireh* of carpet if necessary—with my knife, and make her reweave it. That is how we treat the disease in Qūm—we cut it out! You can say that in this city the *jūftī* hardly exists." I made a note accordingly.

The rest of the morning was spent in enquiry and discussion. We learned that in Qūm all the looms were in the houses, and that generally there were two looms to a house. There were no factories. Inspection was comparatively easy, because all the looms were in the town itself. (In Kashān, it will be remembered, they are spread over a wide area, which includes Natanz, 60 miles away.)

Qūm, we learnt, did not produce much wool. Most of what was used in the carpet industry came from Sabsawār and was finely and evenly spun in Qūm itself. In addition, a certain amount of spun yarn was imported from Tabrīz.

After the war (the Sayyid informed us) there had been more than 1,500 looms in Qūm; but the number had since declined. In 1949 there were about 1,000. The number, however, was more liable to variation—up and down—than in other localities of Persia; because the weavers were better off and more independent than elsewhere. They wove when it suited them, and they refused to sign written contracts—preferring to weave and deliver the carpet in their own time.

I closed my note-book at last and expressed a wish to visit some of the looms of the town. Our host agreed and suggested that we should visit his looms first. We took a carriage to one of the less fashionable quarters. It had rained hard during the week and the horses waded through a sea of liquid mud. On the way our host informed us that he had given up weaving the regular Qūm quality and was now producing a much finer fabric. His yarns, he said, were specially spun and dyed for him and his designs were drawn by the best designers in Isfahān.

The first carpet which he showed us was certainly impressive. It had an all-over floral design on a cream ground, with sixteenth-century motives partly woven in silk. I noticed that my young companion—who possesses an eagle eye—was examining the knots with suppressed excitement. Then he whispered to me, "The whole of the ground is *jūftī*."

I turned to the good Sayyid and mentioned, with as much indifference as I could muster: "My young friend finds some *jūftī* knots in the carpet. That is a pity. Such a fine piece . . ."

I waited to see the flash of a knife and the tattered ends of the slit carpet. Instead, our host, in a melancholy, deprecating voice addressed his head-weaver:

"Alas, my sister, how often must I entreat you not to do this thing. It is, after all, a wickedness. It will bring trouble, it will bring loss, it will bring——"

He was interrupted by a stream of verbiage which issued from the thin lips of the lady seated at the loom. By His Honour Abbas, she had never woven a *jūftī*. The young man was blackening her face. Was it her fault if the yarn was too thick for a quality of 60 to the *gireh*? How could such a quality be woven with this yarn unless she put in a small *jūftī* here and there? By His Honour Abbas, it was nothing more than that. She was an honest woman. She never wove a *jūftī*. It was because the yarn was too thick. . . .

The shrill voice went on and on while the good Sayyid shepherded us to the door. "As you saw," he said when we had regained the open air, "she is a good weaver—a very good weaver. It is true, she has woven here and there a little *jūftī*; but she says that the yarn is too thick."

"Is it?" I enquired.

"Well," he replied ruefully. "To say the truth, when I gave it out to her she found that it was good."

We trudged from house to house inspecting the looms of Qūm. It was the same everywhere. Qūm—like Kermān, Isfahān and Kashān—had succumbed to the malady. We estimated that something like a quarter of the knots woven there were fraudulent.

Nevertheless, Qūm in 1949 was producing interesting rugs and carpets, which possessed a character of their own and which differed from anything else produced in Persia. In quality the standard fabric counted about the same as the standard fabric of Kashān—a nominal 40 × 40 knots to the *gireh* of $6\frac{1}{2}$ centimetres (which actually counted about 36 × 36). This is about 14 × 14 knots to the inch. The dyes in use were—almost without exception—Persian. This may be due to the fact that most of the carpets of Qūm are woven on cream grounds; so that the problem of providing a red dyestuff, inexpensive and easy to use (to replace the expensive and tricky madder) does not arise. For the small quantity of red which is required, madder is used. The blues are dyed with indigo; and the yellows, tans and browns with the usual Persian vegetable dyestuffs (see p. 32).

But the charm of the Qūm carpet lies primarily in its designs, rather than in its quality or colour. When the industry was started some fifteen years ago it was fortunate in securing the services of a few designers who were devotees of the small repeating patterns which the Persians love. Some of them were traditional; others were invented, and most of them were good. Qūm, at a bound, established a style of its own; and so far the style has endured (Plates 409–419).

If I were asked to name the weaving centre of Persia which—during the last decade—has produced the most original carpets, I should answer, without hesitation, Qūm. Kermān has, of course, produced the best. But in Kermān the weaver's craft has been long established, and it has followed an already existing tradition. Qūm, on the other hand, started from scratch. It would have been a simple matter for her designers and merchants to reproduce the patterns which were current in Persia at the time. But they did not do so. They produced a style which was unmistakably their own, and which was truly Persian. May it survive for many generations.

Conversation Piece

Footsore, and with the bottoms of our trousers plastered with mud, we returned to the Sayyid's office. Having provided us with tea, that gentleman retired to the courtyard, secured a can of water, removed his shoes and socks and meticulously washed his feet. Having performed that preliminary rite, he returned to his office and unrolled a small weather-beaten Balūch rug. Once more removing his shoes he placed a small talisman at one end of the rug, stood upright facing it at the other, held up his hands palms upwards, and began to recite, in low tones, the first Sūra.

He had been engaged for some minutes in devout prostrations and genuflections, when the door opened and a young man appeared. The good Sayyid paused in his adoration of the Deity and said:

"Did he bring the two carpets?"

"He brought them," answered the young man.

The good Sayyid smiled contentedly and then continued, unperturbed, his adoration of his God.

378. A Kashān Carpet (c. 1905)
Design and execution improved as the industry continued to expand.

377. A Kashān Carpet (c. 1900)
The industry in Kashān was revived during the last decade of the nineteenth century, after two centuries of quiescence. The carpets produced in the early years of the revival, though fine in texture, were often crude in design and faulty in execution.

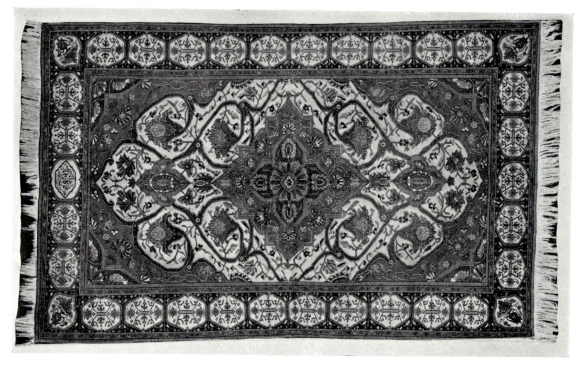

380. A Kashān Silk Rug (c. 1910)

379. A Kashān Carpet (c. 1910)

381. A Kashān Carpet (c. 1915)

382. A Kashān Carpet (c. 1915)

383. A Silk Kashān Carpet; Tree Design with Animals and Birds (c. 1915)

384. A Kashān Carpet with Medallion and Corners on a Plain Field—A Type of Design which is uncommon in Kashān (c. 1915)

346 THE PERSIAN CARPET

386. A Kashán Carpet (c. 1920)

385. A Kashán Rug (c. 1920)

387. A Kashān Carpet (c. 1925)

388. Detail of a Kashān Carpet (c. 1935)

389. A Typical Modern Kashān Carpet

391. Floral and Animal Design for a Kashān Carpet
(c. 1945)
The design represents a quarter of the carpet.

390. Floral and Arabesque Design for a Kashān Carpet
(c. 1945)
The design represents a quarter of the carpet.

392. Medallion and Corner Design for a Kashān Carpet (c. 1945)

393. Arabesque Design for the Border of a Kashān Carpet; drawn by Tahir Zadeh Bihzad, School of Art, Tehrān (c. 1945)

394. Arabesque Repeating Design for a Kashān Carpet; drawn by Tahir Zadeh Bihzad, School of Art, Tehrān (c. 1945)

396. Design for a Kashān Carpet (c. 1946)

395. Medallion Design with Arabesques for a Kashān Carpet (c. 1946)

398. Detail of a Design for a Kashān Carpet with Arabesques and Birds (c. 1946)

397. Repeating Medallion Design for a Kashān Carpet (c. 1946)

400. Detail of a Design for a Kashān Carpet (c. 1946)

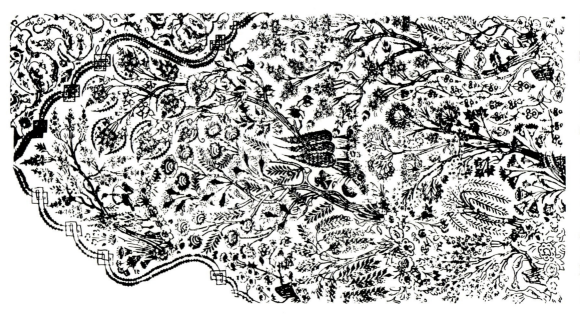

399. Tree Design for the Field of a Kashān Rug (c. 1946)

402. Detail of a Design for a Kashān Carpet (c. 1946)

401. Design for the Field of a Kashān Rug (c. 1947)

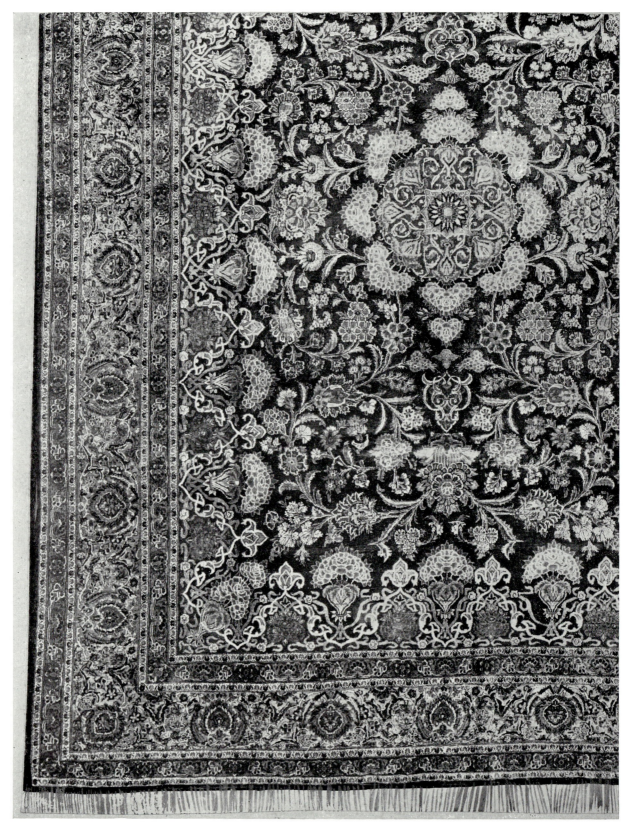

403. Detail of a Kashān Medallion Carpet (c. 1948)

405. Medallion and Corner Design for a Kashān Carpet (c. 1948)

404. Design for a Kashān Carpet; the Design is taken from a Seventeenth-century Carpet in the Mausoleum of Shah Abbas II at Qūm (c. 1948)

407. A Kashán Carpet (c. 1948)

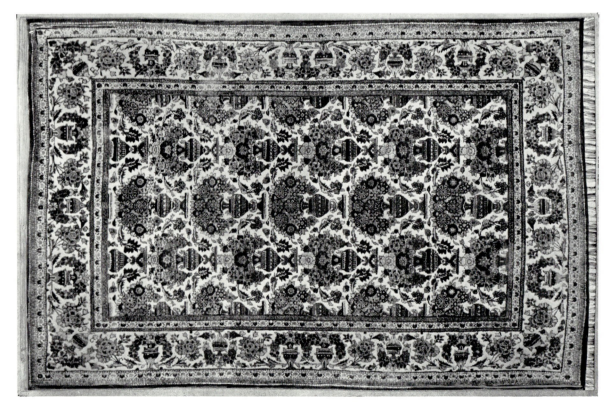

406. A Kashán Rug (c. 1948)

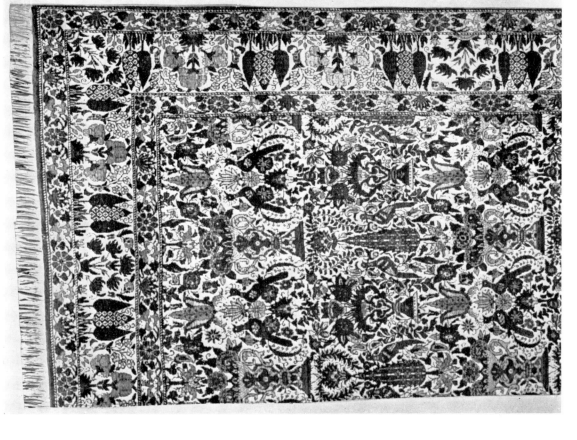

409. Detail of a Qūm Carpet

408. A Natanz Rug (c. 1946)

410. Detail of a Qūm Carpet (*c*. 1940)

411. A Qūm Rug (*c*. 1942)

412. Detail of a Qūm Carpet (*c*. 1945)

413. A Qūm Rug (*c*. 1945)

414. Detail of a Qūm Carpet (*c.* 1945)

415. Detail of a Qūm Carpet (*c.* 1945)

416. Design for a Qūm Carpet (*c.* 1945)

417. A Qūm Rug (*c.* 1945)

418. A Qūm Carpet (*c.* 1946)
Persian landscape designs are not always as pleasing as this.

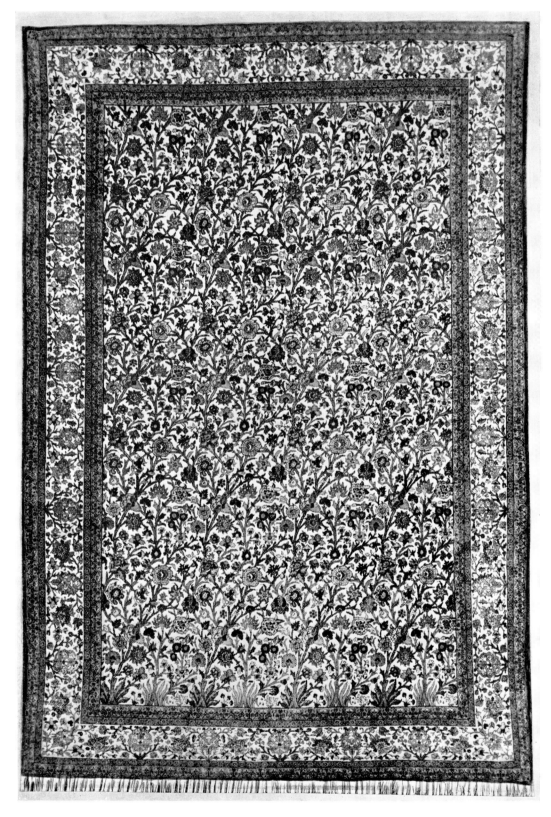

419. A Qūm Carpet (c. 1948)

CHAPTER XVII

THE FUTURE OF THE INDUSTRY

The State of the Industry in 1948

It was the writer's misfortune (as mentioned in the Foreword of this book) to conduct the present survey at a time when the carpet-weaving industry was in its most hapless state since its resurgence from comparative oblivion in the last quarter of the nineteenth century. It was for him a particular misfortune, because he had been for half a century connected with this activity, so fraught with delight; and he would have been far happier proclaiming its virtues than dwelling on its delinquencies. Yet to have praised where no praise was due would have done the industry a disservice. Better far to diagnose its diseases and to suggest remedies for them, if they could be found.

The deterioration in the craft first became noticeable after World War I. It was, indeed, sufficiently pronounced for the pre-war carpets to command a premium over those of the immediate post-war period. Happily the malady was arrested; so that by the middle twenties Persia was again producing quantities of sound and attractive carpets.

For the next fifteen years the standards of production were, on the whole, well maintained. Then came the second world upheaval. Not only were markets again impoverished or destroyed; but for the second time in twenty years Persia was occupied by three belligerents, and her social and economic life again undone. It was inevitable that this second world calamity should have produced a second and more serious decline in production and a deterioration in quality.

It has often been suggested that we are witnessing the beginning of a decline in the carpet-weaving industry of Persia; a decline which (we are told) will continue until the industry reaches the status of an insignificant, *recherché* craft—or perhaps disappears. The protagonists of this idea point to the growth of power-driven industries in Persia which, they declare, are absorbing the materials and the labour. In this connection they draw attention to the decline in output of carpets in Turkey, and conclude that in Persia like causes will produce like effects.

I do not share this view. Industrialisation, no doubt, accounts in part for the decline in the output of carpets in Turkey. But I suggest that it is deceptive to draw a parallel between the two countries; because the position in Persia is, in one important respect, fundamentally different from that which existed in Turkey: in Turkey weaving was concentrated in the towns; in Persia three-quarters of the output is produced in villages and by nomadic tribes. Industrialisation in Turkey was bound, therefore, to affect carpet weaving, because most of her factories were built on urban sites; but a like movement in Persia would hardly touch her peasants in their distant and scattered villages, or her nomadic shepherds. Industrialisation might produce a decline in the output of the towns; but it could not, of itself, seriously weaken or destroy a peasant craft.

The Decline in Production

I do not, therefore, consider that the present decline in production is an indication of decrepitude. It is due rather to a variety of economic and social causes, foreign and domestic, which will probably prove to be temporary and self-liquidating. Without any doubt, the most important cause is the shrinkage in the demand from Europe. This is indicated by the maintenance of production at a high level in Kermān and Arāk—the only two weaving centres which depend for their prosperity on the United States. If and when Europe recovers and orders begin to flow once more from Britain and he Continent in a slowly increasing volume, Persia will, I am persuaded, be able to keep pace with the demand.

The Deterioration in Excellence

I have had occasion many times in the foregoing chapters to refer in some detail to the deterioration in excellence of Persia's carpets; for it exists, in one form or another, in every weaving centre. I do not propose, therefore, in the present chapter to go over the ground again; but to consider only three principal deficiencies which have spread to such an alarming extent through the industry. For I believe that its future largely depends on their correction. If no solutions are found to the problems which they present and if the industry is allowed to drift along on its present bearing, the repute of its productions will be impaired and the industry will lose much of the importance and the renown which it still possesses.

The Decline in the Standard of Design

The first of the three maladies which I propose to consider (and the least mischievous) is the decline in the standard of design. It is the least dangerous of the three because it can be most easily remedied.

Persia's designers are not altogether to blame for the deterioration in their taste, invention and technique. The fault more properly lies in the West; for the centres where the decline is most pronounced are Arāk (Sultānabād), Meshed (with Birjānd) and Tabrīz; and in each of the centres the decline can be traced to causes which lie outside the borders of Persia.

In Arāk it is the New York importers who are the guilty parties. It has already been pointed out (p. 141) that they destroyed the inventiveness of the Arāk designers by persisting, for twenty-five years, in ordering Sarūk carpets which were as much alike as peas in a pod. And they continue to do so. Arāk, it is true, never possessed a school of designers equal to the group which brought fame to Kermān; nevertheless, the Arāk designers, before the early twenties, were producing a variety of ingenious, if not outstanding, designs. They are no longer doing so. The art has been destroyed by the tedious repetition—over a long period—of a single style.

The New York importers, however, had nothing to do with the decline in Meshed and Tabrīz; because America bought very little from those centres. Europe was their market. The war, and the post-war restrictions—which nearly every European government felt bound to impose on the importation of Persian carpets—almost brought the industry in both places to a standstill. Meshed (and Birjānd) found a limited outlet for their products in Tehrān; and Tabrīz discovered a market in the neighbouring countries of the Near East. But the master-weavers discovered that in both these markets price rather than excellence begot custom; and in order to lower their prices they lowered their quality—and dispensed with their designers.

A decline in quality may be restored without serious difficulty; for quality in a fabric is a matter of materials and knots. But the restoration of the standard of design and colouring is a longer and more complicated task. For designers who lose their employment disappear: they find other jobs, or leave the locality, or—for want of practice—they forget their craft. That is what has happened in Meshed, and (in a lesser degree) in Tabrīz.

It is unlikely that the master-weavers of Meshed will be able, unaided, to improve the standard of design in that locality. Their forerunners of twenty-five years ago—men like Mehmelbaff, Khamenei and Emogli—have died, and their successors are unworthy of them. But even in those days the work of most of the Meshed designers was not impressive. Today it is dull indeed. What then can be done to restore the standard—at least to what it was in the middle twenties?

Conference on the State of the Carpet Industry

In the spring of 1949 a conference was held at the Ministry of Economy in Tehrān to discuss the state of the carpet industry and to make recommendations. For the Persian Government was well aware that the position was not as they would wish to have it. A considerable sum of money was to be allocated to the carpet industry under the Seven Years Plan; and it was hoped that the recommendations of the conference would be adopted by the responsible officers of the Planning Commission.

The conference was attended by officials of the Ministry assisted by experts and technicians from every branch of the industry. Having just completed my visits to the weaving centres, I was invited to attend.

One of the subjects on the agenda of the meeting was this question of the decline in the standard of design; and the measures which might be taken to restore it. Particular mention was made of Meshed where, it was agreed, the decline was most pronounced. The conference recommended that a Bureau of Design should be established there—either under the direction of the State or of the School of Art in Tehrān. It should engage two or three first-class designers (probably from Kermān) whose duty it would be: (a) to examine and pass designs before they were issued to the looms; (b) to train local designers; and (c) to furnish designs at low cost to the master-weavers. It was further suggested that if and when the Meshed experiment had proved its usefulness, a second bureau should be established in Tabrīz.

On the whole the plan appeared to be practical and feasible; and—providing that it is carried out with a reasonable degree of efficiency—it should produce results. The State has so far done little for the carpet industry; it now has the opportunity of carrying out a useful and constructive piece of work.

This, then, is the remedy which has been recommended for the least serious of the three maladies from which the industry is suffering. I propose to consider next the formidable problem imposed by the use of dyes of foreign manufacture.

The Use of Imported Dyes

This subject has already been examined at some length in Chapter IV of this survey ("The Craft of the Dyer"). It was there stated that the two main classes of imported dyes—(1) the cheap and fugitive acid and basic dyes (which are known in Persia under the generic term of "anilines"); and (2) the more expensive and fast synthetic chrome dyes—were being imported into Persia in increasing quantities. It was pointed out that the use of anilines was a serious threat to the reputation of the Persian carpet, for they faded quickly into offensive shades. As for the fast chrome dyes, it was contended that fastness was not the only, nor indeed the first, criterion of excellence. The first criterion should be whether or not these dyes contributed to the production of the best Persian carpets. It was maintained that synthetic dyes mordanted with chrome did not.

This question was also discussed at the conference to which reference has been made above. The conference recognised that the use of imported chemical dyes was deleterious to Persia's most famous industry and that the cure of the disease was a most difficult and complicated problem.

It was pointed out at the meeting that there existed among the merchants an important and vocal "free school" which maintained that the Persian dyers should be allowed to use whatever dyes they liked. The protagonists of this view contended that if the dyes were bad, the carpets would not sell; and the disease would, in time, cure itself.

I was unable to share this opinion. The facts were all against it. Aniline dyes have been in use in Persia for sixty years; and although buyers and sellers alike were well aware how unsuitable these dyestuffs were for dyeing carpet yarns, they were, nevertheless, being used more than ever. The protagonists of the "free school" omitted to take note—either from indifference or from design—that if buyers could not find enough properly dyed carpets to buy, they bought the others. They probably paid a little less for them; but the damage was done. Obviously, therefore, a different approach to the problem was indicated.

It was pointed out at the conference that the village dyer was rapidly disappearing, and that most of the dyeing was now carried out in the towns. This fact would make control by a responsible authority more easy—though it was recognised that controls in Persia were, in any event, difficult to apply. Various methods were suggested. The one which appeared most practical and feasible was that the town dyers should operate under licences from the Ministry; that they should be required to use only Persian dyes for carpet yarns; and that contravention of this regulation should be punishable by withdrawal of the licence and perhaps by a fine.

Objections were made to this scheme on the grounds that it would prove unworkable; mainly because the dyers would be bribed to break the regulation. I did not think these objections were well founded; for bribery can only flourish if detection is difficult and if there is an ulterior profit both for the briber and the bribed. Under this scheme none of these conditions would exist: for the detection of spurious dyes is easy; and it is difficult to believe that a weaver would bribe a dyer to dye his yarns badly, or that the dyer would take the risk of losing his licence by breaking the regulations—when he could make as much profit by sticking to them.

I had interviewed a good many dyers in the course of my visits to the weaving centres and, on the whole, I had found that they were decent and respectable men, and frank about their craft. Most of them averred that it made no difference to them whether they used Persian, chrome or acid dyes. They acted on the old Turkish proverb: "So much money, so much madder"—meaning that the customer got what he was willing to pay for.

In my view, therefore, a system whereby the dyers would be licensed and permitted to dye carpet yarns with approved dyes only could be made to work. The scheme might be placed under the control of the local managers of the state-owned organisation, who are efficient and intelligent men.

The question, which dyestuffs should be "approved" for dyeing carpet yarns and which should not, would require careful consideration. Cheap acid and basic dyes—the so-called "anilines"—should, of course, be rigorously prohibited, both for direct use and for "topping" purposes. But a case (though, in my view, not a good case) could be presented for the use of synthetic dyes mordanted with chrome; because, as we have seen, they are among the fastest dyes known. The principal objections to their use have already been stated on p. 30.

There are several solutions to the question, viz.:

(1) To prohibit the use of all imported chemical dyestuffs for dyeing carpet yarns. This would be the ideal solution. But it possesses several disadvantages: (a) the scarcity and consequent high cost of madder; and (b) the fact that it would take three to four years to render Persia independent of foreign supplies of red dyestuffs—because the madder plant does not properly yield its dye until it is three years old. The second disadvantage is further conditioned by the readiness of the cultivators to plant madder. They could hardly be expected to do so (in view of their past experience) without a government guarantee; and that would lead to complications and perplexities.

(2) To permit the use of chrome dyes of proved quality. Such a policy would throw the door wide open to the use of synthetic dyes; and the inevitable result would be that the use of Persian dyestuffs would gradually disappear and in a few years the Persian carpet would lose a great deal of its Persian character.

(3) To prohibit the use (for dyeing carpet yarns) of all imported chemical dyes *except indigo and synthetic madder*; all other shades to be dyed with Persian dyestuffs or cochineal.

This scheme offers, in my view, several advantages over the other two. In the first place it is in keeping with Persian tradition. From time immemorial, indigo alone has been used in Persia for dyeing blues and greens; and (until recently) only madder and cochineal for dyeing reds. By prohibiting the use of all chemical dyes except indigo and synthetic madder this tradition would be preserved; because natural and manufactured indigo are chemically the same, and so are natural and synthetic madder. Manufactured indigo has been in use for a long time in Persia and calls for no comment. A few remarks on a new method of using synthetic madder may be of interest here.

The Persian technique of dyeing with natural madder has already been described in Chapter IV ("The Craft of the Dyer"); and it was there suggested that results very similar to those obtained with natural madder may be obtained with the synthetic product by using alum instead of potassium bichromate as a mordant. The under-mentioned formula will give good results:

Alum 10 per cent (of the weight of yarn).
Oxalic acid 5 per cent (of the weight of yarn).
Supramine 1 per cent (of the weight of yarn).
Alizarine red dry paste 4 per cent (of the weight of yarn).

(Supramine is a levelling and restraining agent. Alizarine red is the tinctorial element in natural madder.) The yarn is placed in the solution *cold*; the vat is raised slowly to the boil and boiled for $1\frac{1}{2}$ hours. The yarn is then thoroughly scoured in cold water.

If this scheme for solving the dye problem in the carpet industry is adopted, only two foreign chemical dyestuffs would be authorised for dyeing carpet yarns: indigo and synthetic madder (alizarine red). All other shades would be dyed with natural Persian dyestuffs—and cochineal. There should be no difficulty in enforcing the use of the common Persian dyes, because they are cheaper than synthetic dyes and just as easy to apply; while cochineal has been for centuries one of the principal resources of the Persian dyer. Thus a full range of dyestuffs would be available to the dyers of carpet yarns, viz.:

For dark blues, medium blues, light blues: indigo.
For reds and roses: synthetic madder (alizarine red); cochineal.
For yellows: vine leaves; weld.
For browns: walnut husks; oak bark.
For camels and tans: walnut husks; pomegranate rind.
For greens: indigo on vine leaves or on weld.
For oranges: henna; vine leaves and synthetic madder.
For creams: walnut husks; pomegranate rind; straw.
For black: indigo and henna.

Almost any shade can be obtained by combinations of the above dyestuffs.

I suggest, therefore, that the Ministry of National Economy acquire the necessary powers to tackle the problem of the use of imported chemical dyestuffs in carpets in the following manner:

(1) that the dyers in the carpet-weaving areas should be allowed to operate only under licence from the Ministry;

(2) that they should be allowed to use only Persian dyes, synthetic indigo, synthetic madder and cochineal for dyeing carpet yarns;

(3) that contraventions of this regulation should be punishable by the withdrawal of licences and a fine.

The Use of the Jūftī Knot[1]

So much for the first two problems—the decline in the standard of design and the use of chemical dyes of foreign manufacture. Both these weaknesses are, I am persuaded, amenable to treatment. We have now to consider the third and gravest asthenia of the weaver's craft: the fraudulent knot.

The renown of the Persian carpet is founded mainly upon two factors: its beauty and its wearing quality. The use of the *jūftī* knot impairs both: it impairs its beauty by robbing the fabric of density and so of definition; and it impairs its wearing quality because the fabric contains less knots and therefore less material than is called for by the number of warp strings.

I have had to refer to the *jūftī* knot a good many times in the course of this survey; for it has spread, like a disease, from one weaving centre to another; so that today there are only a few urban weaving areas which are still uncontaminated. It originated in Khūrasān, where for many generations it was an accepted method of weaving. Until twenty-five years ago it was confined to that province. But, at about that period, the new road system of Persia was born. Communication became easy, inexpensive and swift, so that people began to travel who had never moved out of their villages before. Weavers from Meshed, Birjānd, Turshīz, Dorūksh and other localities of Khūrasān moved south and west and carried the germ with them.

It would be impossible to determine with any degree of accuracy what percentage of the knots tied in a particular area are *jūftī*. For, as has already been explained, their detection (after the weft has been passed) is extremely difficult, even for an expert. Only vague approximations, based upon the "feel" of the fabric and upon the observations of local carpet men, can be presented. It will be observed from the appended list that the tribal and village weavers have been only slightly affected.

Approximate percentage of jūftī *knots woven*

Town Weaves

Tabrīz	None
Arāk	5 per cent
Meshed (Turkibaff)	None
Meshed (Farsibaff)	25 per cent
Hamadān	20 per cent
Kashān	25 per cent
Qūm	25 per cent
Isfahān	20 per cent
Kermān	50 per cent
Birjānd	90 per cent

Tribal and Village Weaves

Herīz area	None
Balūch tribal	None
Kurdish tribal (including Senneh and Bijār)	None
Fārs tribal	None
Afshār tribal and village	None
Arāk village	None
Bakhtiari village	None
Hamadān village	25 per cent
Qaināt villages / Turshīz	90 per cent

That is, roughly, the position. It is serious enough. Out of ten principal town weaves all but two have succumbed to the malady. In the infected areas the percentage varies between about 20 per cent in Hamadān (town) to 90 per cent in Birjānd. Birjānd, however, is in a class by itself; because the *jūftī* knot originated in Khūrasān where it has been, for many generations, the traditional method of weaving. I have estimated permeation in Birjānd at 90 per cent (instead of 100 per cent) because the *jūftī* knot is never used for outlines: 10 per cent has been allowed for them.

The malady is, unhappily, progressive. In the middle thirties the percentage in the Kermān weaving area was certainly less than 20 per cent; today it is probably over the 50 per cent indicated above. And if nothing is done to arrest its progress the figure may reach 90 per cent, as in Birjānd. Isfahān, Kashān and Qūm succumbed later (Qūm quite recently); so their percentages are lower. But in these centres, too, they are rising. Arāk is the only important area where the Persian knot is woven which is comparatively free.[2] For some reason the infection has passed it by.

Can anything be done to arrest or eradicate the malady? It must be admitted that so far no practical and feasible specific has been discovered. But the picture is not quite so sombre as, at first sight, it appears.

In the first place, most of the tribal and village areas (as distinct from the towns) are free from the disorder. It is serious only in the Khūrasān villages where, as we have seen, it is the traditional method of weaving—however bad the tradition may be. But even in Khūrasān the Balūchi tribal rugs are free from it. So also are three-quarters of the Hamadān

---

[1] For a description of the *jūfti* knot see p. 26.

[2] Yezd, too, is free; but it is not an important weaving centre.

villages (the malady is at its worst in the areas round Kabūtarhang and Bibikabād). The Herīz area, too, is free. So are the tribal or village weaves of Fārs, the Afshāri rugs of Kermān province and the so-called Bakhtiari rugs of Chahār Mahāl.

But the most significant and important centre which is completely free from the malady is Tabrīz; for Tabrīz is a large city and, as we have seen, most of the urban centres have succumbed. The reason (as I have pointed out, p. 60) is because the Tabrīz weavers have been taught to tie their knots to the warp strings with an instrument like a crochet hook; *and with this hook the jūftī knot cannot be tied.* So that today the Tabrīz weave is the best of the town weaves of Persia. The Tabrīz carpet has other weaknesses, but this is not one.

There is one more urban centre, Hamadān, where the Turkish knot is used and where, in consequence, hook-knotting could be introduced without difficulty. At present the knots are tied with the fingers, and about 20 per cent are fraudulent. The adoption of the hook would eliminate the *jūftī* knot entirely.

If the use of the hook has kept Tabrīz free from the malady, and could free Hamadān, why cannot the same technique be applied to the other five centres—Qūm, Meshed, Isfahān, Kashān and Kermān? Unhappily the matter is not as simple as it appears.

During 1948 I discussed this problem with the more prominent carpet men in all these localities. Without exception they admitted its seriousness; but they declared that the malady could not be eradicated because an inspector could not be placed by every loom. I pointed out, however, that in Tabrīz, where the hook was used for knotting, the malady did not exist; and that if their weavers could be taught to tie the Persian knot with the hook (instead of with the fingers) the disease might be eradicated.

A trial was made in one of the Meshed factories: four weavers working at the same loom were taught to tie their Persian knot with a Tabrīz hook. It is more difficult to tie than the Turkish knot, so that the four weavers were not able, when I saw them, to weave as fast with the hook as with their fingers. But that may have been because the technique was new to them. Nevertheless it was clear (1) that the use of the hook had kept the malady from Tabrīz; and (2) that the same instrument could be used to tie the Persian knot. It was obvious, however, that none of the master-weavers were prepared to make a large-scale trial. They maintained that the difficulties in the way of introducing the new technique were too great and the chances of success too small.

Here, as with the dye problem, is an opportunity for the Ministry to take a hand. I suggest that Qūm be chosen as the place for a large-scale experiment; because Qūm was the last urban centre to succumb to the malady. The looms there are situated in the town and would in consequence be easier to control than in a centre like Kermān or Kashān, where they are scattered over a wide area. I would further suggest that (1) a dozen Qūm weavers be taught to use the hook; (2) that they be sent into the houses as instructors; and (3) that any weaver who succeeds in passing a test of weaving (say) 2,000 Persian knots an hour with the hook would receive a certificate of proficiency and a money prize.

It is, I think, probable that when a weaver has attained proficiency with the hook she would continue to use it—particularly if some inducement were offered to her at first to do so.

I cannot pretend to be wholly optimistic over the results of such an experiment. It can only succeed if it is conducted by a person with enthusiasm, technical knowledge and monumental patience, supported by all the resources of the Ministry. If, however, by a happy chance a cure of the disease were effected—and if the same treatment were then applied to other centres, with results equally fortunate—a benefaction of incalculable value will have been conferred on the weaving industries of Persia. I suggest, therefore, that it is a piece of constructive work which the Ministry should undertake without delay. The experiment is certainly worth trying.

If it should not be undertaken, or if it should be attempted and should fail, I can suggest no other treatment for the malady. It will probably increase in virulence in those areas already affected and it may spread to others at present immune.

In that event there might be cause for uneasiness, though hardly for alarm. The renown of the Persian carpet might suffer, because some pieces may wear out sooner than they should. But, on the other hand, the tribal and most of the village weaves and the carpets from Tabrīz and Arāk are still unaffected by the malady and will continue to give good service. In Hamadān the trouble could easily be eradicated.

The world, too, will, no doubt, continue to buy Persian carpets—though some of them may fail to outlast their owners, as they used to do. For the tempo of our lives is increasing: a fabric which would last one or two generations was formerly regarded with admiration and content. Is it so regarded today? Are we not so much the slaves of fashion and change that we attach a lessening importance to mere endurance; and is that quality not more and more regarded as a tiresome and redundant virtue?

I have been hearing for fifty years about the decline and ultimate extinction of the Persian carpet. Indeed, one of my earliest recollections of this sombre prognostication was a warning from an uncle (shortly after I entered the business) that I had embarked upon a sinking ship. But for half a century this luxury ship of slender tonnage has battered and buffeted her way through one economic gale after another, and has been pirated (in calmer weather) by the finance ministers of every government the world over. Yet she still rides the Seven Seas—not proudly, but circumspectly; confident that she will continue to make her customary landfalls.

APPENDIX I

A CHRONOLOGY OF THE PERSIAN CARPET

The Achaemenian Dynasty (553-330 B.C.)

553 B.C.	Cyrus founds the Achaemenian dynasty.
491-490 B.C.	Darius the Great invades Greece; Persians defeated at Marathon.
481-479 B.C.	Xerxes invades Greece; Persians defeated at Salamis and Plataea.
401 B.C.	The march of the 10,000 Greek mercenaries from Babylon to the Black Sea.
334-330 B.C.	Alexander invades Persia and overthrows the Achaemenian dynasty.
323 B.C.	Death of Alexander.

Information on the subject of carpets during the Achaemenian era is meagre. The passing references of Xenophon cannot be accepted as establishing that knotted pile carpets existed in Persia in the fourth century B.C. Athenaeus, who wrote from hearsay 200 years later, is even less convincing. The nomadic shepherds of the plateau, however, may have been producing a pile fabric—the forerunner of the tribal rugs of today.

The Seleucid Dynasty (312-120 B.C.)

312 B.C.	Seleucus—one of Alexander's generals—founds the Seleucid dynasty and builds his capital at Seleucia, 40 miles north of Baghdad, on the Tigris.
223-188 B.C.	The campaigns of Antiochus the Great. His defeat by the Romans at Magnesia in 190 B.C.
129 B.C.	Defeat of Antiochus Sidetes by the Parthian Phraates II. Decline and disappearance of the Seleucid dynasty.

No references to carpets have come down to us from the Seleucid and Parthian eras. Again, the nomadic shepherds may have been weaving rugs for their own use, or perhaps for barter.

The Parthian Dynasty (170 B.C.–A.D. 226)

124-88 B.C.	Campaigns of Mithridates II against the Scythian nomads.
53-33 B.C.	The first struggle with Rome; defeat of Crassus. The second struggle with Rome; defeat of Mark Antony.
A.D. 226	Ardeshir defeats the Parthian king near Ahwaz and founds the Sassanian dynasty.

The Sassanian Dynasty (A.D. 224-641)

A.D. 241-361	The wars between the Byzantine Empire and Persia; first period: Shapur I (240-271), Shapur II (309-379).
A.D. 425	White Huns invade Khūrasān.
A.D. 557	Destruction of the White Huns.
A.D. 503-628	The wars between the Byzantine Empire and Persia; second period: Khosrō I (Nushirvan), 531-578; Khosrō II (Parviz), 590-628.
A.D. 633-641	The Persian Empire overthrown by the Arabs.

There are a number of references—however unsatisfying—to carpets during the latter part of the Sassanian era. In the Chinese Sui Annals (A.D. 590-617) woollen rugs are mentioned as a product of Persia. "Soft carpets" formed part of the booty captured by the Emperor Heraclius during his campaigns against Khosrō II (Parviz) early in the seventh century. The huge Garden Carpet of Khosrō I and others which were looted by the Arabs ten years later at the sack of Madain (Ctesiphon) were stated by the Arab historians to have been covered with jewels. It is probable that they were tapestries and not pile carpets; for a pile fabric is not suited to the hot climate of Mesopotamia nor does it lend itself to adornment with jewels, while a tapestry does. Furthermore, a pile carpet of the size of Khosrō's Garden Carpet (it is said to have measured 90 × 90 feet) would have weighed 2½ tons.

Pile rugs, however—woven on the plateau by the tribes or in the villages for barter against other commodities—probably existed and may have been in common use.

Persia under the Caliphate (A.D. 641–1258)

A.D. 661–750	Persia under the Omayyad Caliphate.
A.D. 750	The Abbasid Caliphate founded, with its capital at Baghdad.
A.D. 861–977	Direct rule of the Caliphate replaced by semi-independent dynasties which acknowledged the suzerainty of the Caliph.
	Saffarid dynasty, founded 861.
	Samanid dynasty, founded 874.
	Ziyarid dynasty, founded 928.
	Buwayhid dynasty, founded 932.
	Ghaznavid dynasty, founded 977.
A.D. 1037	The Seljūk Turks conquer Persia and settle in Azerbaijān and Hamadān provinces, where Turkish becomes the predominant language.
A.D. 1138–1194	The Seljūk sultanate overthrown by the Shahs of Khiva.

Some twenty Arab historians and geographers visited Persia during the supremacy of the Baghdad Caliphate, and there are a number of references to carpets in their writings as early as the ninth and tenth centuries. They are stated to have been produced in Fārs; in Mazanderān; in Gilān; and in the Qaināt. Unfortunately, the Arab writers failed to furnish details of the kinds of rugs or carpets which they saw. It is improbable, however, that carpet sizes were woven; production was more likely to have been confined to small nomad or village pieces for sale or barter. Designs were almost certainly rectilinear.

In the eleventh century the Seljūk Turks invaded Persia and soon extended their dominion as far as the Mediterranean. They settled permanently in the Azerbaijān and Hamadān provinces; displacing many of the inhabitants, who fled south. The Seljūk women were weavers and they introduced the Turkish knot into the two provinces—where it persists (with the Turkish language) to this day. The rest of Persia, however, where the Seljūks did not settle, continued to weave the Persian knot, as before.

Although the Seljūk sultans were patrons of the arts, they do not appear to have realised the possibilities of the weaver's craft.

The Mongol Domination (A.D. 1220–1449)

A.D. 1219–1257	Jenghiz Khan devastates Persia.
A.D. 1258	Hulagū sacks Baghdad and destroys the Caliphate.
A.D. 1295–1304	Rule of the great Il-Khani Ghazān Khan. He is converted to Islām.
A.D. 1380–1393	Timūr (Tamerlane) conquers Persia.
A.D. 1408–1446	During the beneficent reign of his son, Shah Rūkh, much of the devastation caused by the Mongol conquerors repaired.
A.D. 1469–1478	Uzūn Hassān of the "White Sheep" dynasty rules the empire from Tabrīz.
A.D. 1499	Shah Ismail I overthrows the "White Sheep" dynasty and founds the Sefavi dynasty.

Half-savage conquerors like Jenghiz Khan and Hulagū paid little attention to the arts. At the end of the thirteenth century, however, the Il-Khani Ghazān Khan (who built an administrative capital in the outskirts of Tabrīz) covered the floors of the buildings with carpets (rugs?) from Fārs. He also sent a present of carpets to the mausoleum of Sayfaddin Khalid ibn Valid in Damascus. Timūr (Tamerlane) in the fourteenth century was probably too busy with his campaigns to pay attention to a village craft. But in the fifteenth century, Uzūn Hassān of Tabrīz and the Timūrid sultans of Herāt covered the floors of their palaces with fine carpets. Their designs were mostly rectilinear, as the craft had not yet reached an advanced stage of mastery. The art of weaving elaborate curvilinear patterns did not originate until the end of the fifteenth century.

The Sefavi Dynasty (A.D. 1499-1722)

A.D. 1514	Ismail defeated by the Ottomans at Chaldiran.
A.D. 1524	Shah Tahmasp succeeds Ismail.
A.D. 1534	Ottomans take Tabrīz.
A.D. 1555	Tahmasp signs peace with Turkey.
A.D. 1587	Abbas the Great becomes Shah of Persia.
A.D. 1588-1590	War with Turkey: Persia cedes Tabrīz, Shirvān, Georgia and Lūristān to Turkey.
A.D. 1590	Shah Abbas moves his capital to Isfahān.
A.D. 1598	The Sherley brothers arrive in Persia. They reorganise and rearm the Persian army.
A.D. 1602-1627	Successful campaigns against Turkey. Persia recovers her lost provinces.
A.D. 1629	Death of Shah Abbas.
A.D. 1630-1638	War with Turkey. Hamadān, Erivān, Tabrīz and Baghdad captured by the Turks.
A.D. 1721-1722	The Afghans invade Persia; they capture Isfahān and overthrow the Sefavi dynasty.
A.D. 1723	The Russians occupy the Caspian provinces.

In 1499, after seven centuries of alien rule, a national dynasty arose in Persia. It is to the high credit of the first three princes of this dynasty—particularly of Shah Tahmasp and Shah Abbas—that they perceived the possibilities of development in the weaver's craft. In the production of their carpets they enlisted the talents of the first painters and master-weavers of the age. The carpets were produced in urban centres, because they called for craftsmanship and equipment far beyond that which the tribes and villages possessed. During this period the most famous of the carpets which today adorn our collections were produced and the classic forms of Persian curvilinear design established.

The century between the death of Shah Abbas and the Afghan invasions witnessed the decline of the art. It was brought to an inglorious end when the last Sefavi king surrendered his capital to the Afghans in 1722.

The Afghan Domination (A.D. 1722-1730)
The Reign of Nadir Shah (A.D. 1736-1747)
The Regency of Kerim Khan Zand (A.D. 1750-1779)

A.D. 1729-1735	Nadir Qūli expels the Afghans, Turks and Russians.
A.D. 1736	He ascends the throne as Nadir Shah.
A.D. 1737	Nadir invades Afghanistān.
A.D. 1738	He invades India; surrender of Delhi.
A.D. 1740	He defeats the Uzbegs of Bokhara and Khiva.
A.D. 1743-1745	His successful campaign against Turkey.
A.D. 1747	Assassination of Nadir Shah.
A.D. 1750-1779	The beneficent regency of Kerim Khan Zand.
A.D. 1794	Aga Mohammed Khan Qajar overthrows the Zand dynasty and establishes the Qajār dynasty.

The short period of Afghan domination was followed by the turbulent reign of Nadir Shah. Little attention was paid to the arts during these 125 years of wars and tumult.

During the regency of the benevolent Kerim Khan Persia enjoyed a period of peace and tranquillity. But there is no evidence that Kerim Khan made any attempt to revive the industry. Weaving went on, no doubt, among the tribes and in the villages; but, however useful, it must have been on a small scale.

Persia under the Qajārs (A.D. 1796-1925)

A.D. 1804-1813	First Russo-Persian war.
A.D. 1825-1828	Second Russo-Persian war. Persia cedes her Caucasian provinces to Russia; the present frontier is fixed.
A.D. 1856	Anglo-Persian war over Herāt.
A.D. 1906	Muzaffar-ud-Din Shah grants a Constitution.
A.D. 1907	Anglo-Russian agreement over zones of influence.
A.D. 1914-1916	Russo-Turkish campaigns in the north-west; British in the south.
A.D. 1921	*Coup d'état* of Riza Khan.

The three important Qajār monarchs, Fath-Ali Shah, Nasir-ud-Din Shah and Muzaffar-ud-Din Shah, endowed Persia with a measure of tranquillity and security which gave to the industry the climate which it needed for revival. The revival began about 1875 under the leadership of the merchants of Tabrīz, who were the first to produce carpets for export. In 1883 Messrs. Ziegler and Company of Manchester established a branch office in Sultāna-bād (Arāk)—the first foreign firm to produce carpets in Persia. They were followed by many other firms, mostly American. The industry expanded rapidly

A.D. 1925	Riza Khan becomes Shah of Persia. End of the Qajār dynasty.

The Present

1927–1930	The Trans-Iranian railway was begun. Reforms and industrialisation policy instituted.
1941	Allies occupy Persia. Abdication of Riza Shah Pahlavi.
1942–1945	Persia becomes the principal supply route for Allied arms to Russia.
1947	Insurgent government of Azerbaijān liquidated.

during the early years of the present century until, in the years before World War I, Persia's export of carpets had reached the respectable figure of about £2½ million.

World War I brought about a serious set-back, both in output and quality. But, by the late twenties the position was restored.

The industry continued to expand until the late thirties, when the economic depression in the West diminished foreign demand. All the American and some European firms closed their offices. The acuteness of the crisis in Persia was, however, mitigated by increased local demand induced by the dynamic activities of Riza Shah.

World War II brought about a second period of deterioration in output, craftsmanship and design. The deterioration unhappily persists. Fraudulent practices in the weaving and the use of imported dyes—some of inferior quality—increased during the post-war period.

For the first time a central distributing market—with stocks of carpets from most of the weaving centres—was established in Persia, in Tehrān.

APPENDIX II

Carpet exports from Persia from 1923 to 1973 expressed in metric tons.

1923–24	4676 metric tons	1945–46	3522 metric tons
1924–25	4209 ,,	1946–47	4645 ,,
1925–26	5035 ,,	1947–48	2667 ,,
1926–27	5114 ,,	1948–49	3528 ,,
1927–28	6092 ,,	1949–50	2799 ,,
1928–29	6115 ,,	1950–51	4601 ,,
1929–30	5315 ,,	1951–52	4097 ,,
1930–31	5380 ,,	1952–53	4885 ,,
1931–32	4809 ,,	1953–54	5271 ,,
1932–33	3646 ,,	1954–55	4557 ,,
1933–34	4636 ,,	1955–56	4955 ,,
1934–35	4038 ,,	1956–57	4583 ,,
1935–36	3972 ,,	1957–58	6392 ,,
1936–37	4516 ,,	**1958**–59	4809 ,,
1937–38	2682 ,,	1959–60	6309 ,,
1938–39	2032 ,,	1960–61	6950 ,,
1939–40	2921 ,,	1961–62	7312 ,,
1940–41	2764 ,,	1962–63	7556 ,,
1941–42	2655 ,,	1963–64	8790 ,,
1942–43	1615 ,,	1964–65	10563 ,,
1943–44	1078 ,,	1965–66	13084 ,,
1944–45	834 ,,	1966–67	9697 ,,

1969–70	11096 metric tons
1970–71	10982 ,,
1971–72	12851 ,,
1972–73	14621 ,,

No values have been given because no accurate figures are available.

APPENDIX III

A SHORT LIST OF PERSIAN MEASURES AND THEIR APPROXIMATE EQUIVALENTS

Qāli	A carpet. The sizes usually range from 9′×6′ (ca. 1·80×2·80 mts.) and upwards.
Kellegi	A long and narrow carpet where the length is usually from two to three times the width, i.e. from, say, 10′×5′ (ca. 1·50×3·00 mts.) to about 20′×7′ (ca. 2·00×6·00 mts.)
Dozar, Khalicheh or *Sedjadeh*	A rug measuring approximately 7′ 0″×4′ 6″ (1·35×2·10 mts.)
Zaronim	A rug measuring approximately 5′ 0″×3′ 6″ (1·05×1·50 mts.)
Zarcherek, Panjcherek or *Zaroquiart*	A rug measuring approximately 4′ 6″×2′ 3″ (0·70×1·40 mts.)
Pushti	A mat measuring approximately 3′×2′ (0·60×0·90 mts.)
Kenareh	A strip or runner from about 2′ 6″ to 3′ 6″ wide (0·75 to 1·10 mts.) by about 8′ to 20′ long (2·50 to 6·00 mts.)
Farsakh	About $3\frac{3}{4}$ miles or 6 kilometres
Zar	Approximately 41 or 44 inches, 104 or 112 cms.
Punzeh or *Gireh*	$\frac{1}{16}$ *Zar*, about $2\frac{3}{8}″$ to $2\frac{3}{4}″$, $6\frac{1}{2}$–7 cms.

Units on which Weaver's wages are based:

In Meshed the MOKATA containing 16,000 knots
In Tabrīz the KABAL containing 14,000 knots
In Kermān the *NISHAN containing 160 knots

* Usually 100 Nishans, i.e., 16,000 knots

Weights and measures vary, sometimes considerably, from district to district and those given above are only meant to serve as a rough guide.

Although officially Persia adopted the metric system some years ago, in actual practice the old measures are still in daily use.

INDEX OF PLACES, TRIBES AND PERSONS

Note. The principal reference is placed first

A

Abadeh (Fārs), Plates 318–19
Abbas, Shah (1587–1629): patron of carpet industry, 4, 5, 7, 8 n., 17; decline of industry after death of, 5, 18; "Vase" carpets of reign of, 43; moves capital to Isfahān, 53; *et passim*
Abuzaidabād (Kashān), 335
Afghanistān carpets, 164
Afshāri: Turkish tribe transferred to Kermān, 27, 212; tribal rugs, 212–14, Plates 273–83
Ahmed Ali Khan (Kermān designer), 207
Ahmed Khan (Kermān designer), 207, Plates 206, 233, 237, 245, 246, 252, 256, 257
Ainabād (Hamadān), 95, Plate 98
Ainalū tribe (Khamseh Confederation, Fārs), 287–8
Aliabād (Kashān), 335
Ali-Ek (Khūrasān), Balūchi tribe at, 185
Ali Honari (Kermān weaver), 201
Ali Mohammed Kashi (Kermān designer), Plates 207, 223, 225, 227, 228, 231, 255
Ali Riza Bahramand (Kermān designer), 207, Plates 224, 230, 234, 240, 251, 254, 262
Alvānd, name given to Hamadān town weaves, 97, Plates 70, 99–103
Amirabād (Hamadān), 92
Anatolia: Turkish knot used, 26; wool from, 98
Antikaji family (Tabrīz merchants), 56 n.
Arab tribes of Khamseh Confederation, Fārs, 287–8
Arāk (formerly Sultānabād): Mūshkabād, Mahāl and Sarūk (*q.v.*) carpets of, 137–44; history, 135–7; Herātī design at, 37; Mina Khanī, 42; Bid Majnūn, 49; Gol Henaī design originated at, 49; *dūghi* rose dye, 32, 60; village curvilinear weaving, 35; skilled weavers, 99; dependence on U.S. market, 362–3; design copied at Tabrīz, Plate 53; famed for cheap carpets, 135; patterns borrowed from, 312

Ardebil: the "Ardebil" carpet, 10; see also under *Famous Carpets* in General Index; "Ardebil strips" at Sarāb, 67
Arishk (Khūrasān), Arab rugs of, 189
Armāq (Kashān), 334
Aron (Kashān), 335–6
Ashkabād (U.S.S.R.), 157, 160
Asleh (Herīz), 64
Atabaī, Turkoman tribe, 157
Azerbaijān: thirteenth-century carpets, 3; Seljūk settle in, 27; Tabrīz (*q.v.*) at centre of, 52
Azizollah (Kermān designer), 207

B

Bāft (Afshāri), 212–13
Bagh-i-Siah (Qainat), Herātī design at, 171
Bahar, Plate 96
Baharlū tribe (Khamseh Confederation, Fārs), 288–9
Bahlūli tribe (Balūchi), 185
Bahramabād, see *Rafsinjān*
Baizidi tribe (Balūchi), 185
"Bakhtiari" weaves, 307–12; a misnomer, 307, 310; resemble Hamadān village rugs, 96; fourteenth-century rug, 3
Bakshaīsh (Herīz), 61, 64; Harshang design at, 49; Herātī design at, 62, Plate 19; rectilinear designs, 62 n.
Balisht, Balūchi tribe of Seistān: bags, 186; rugs, 187
Balūchi tribes of Khūrasān, 185–9, 290; Herātī design, 38; use of goat hair, 25
Balvardi (Afshāri), Plate 273
Bām (Kermān Province), wool of, 204
Barbaro, Giosafa (Venetian Ambassador at Tabrīz): mentions fifteenth-century carpets, 3; described Tabrīz, 52
Bardashīr (Kermān), 198
Basirī tribe (Khamseh Confederation, Fārs), 287–8, 290; Plates 305–6
Beck, Sebastian, 10 n.
Behbehān (Fārs), 289
Beilleri (Afshāri), Plate 284
Beīn (Chahār Mahāl), Plates 357, 362
Bergendeh (Tuisarkhan group), 93, Plate 81

Beshīr (U.S.S.R.), 155; Turkish knot used, 26
Bijār (Persian Kurdistān), 122–5, 120; Herātī design at, 38; Mina Khanī, 42; Bid Majnūn, 43, 49 and n.; thick weave, 95, 205; madder dyeing technique, 32; comb-beater, 24; market at Hamadān, 89; Plates 122–6
Bilverdī (Herīz), 63
Biqāsh (Malayer), Plate 105
Birdwood, Sir George (Orientalist), on earliest pile carpets, 1
Birjānd (Qainat), 170–3, 163; Persian knot used, 27; cochineal, use of, 163; characteristic colour, 60; barberry dye from, 34, 172; depends on Western markets, 363; use of *jūftī* knot, 366
Bode, 7; on "Chelsea" carpet, 13
Bokhara (U.S.S.R.), 155, 159
Boldaji (Chahār Mahāl), Plate 354
Bozchelū or Borchelū (Hamadān), curvilinear village weave of, 94
Brahuī tribe (Balūchi), 185
Brandly, Otto, pioneer in Kermān carpet industry, 202
Browne, E. G. (1888), on Kermān, 201
Bubukabād or Bibikabād (Hamadān), 95, 367
Būchakchī or Būchakjī tribe (Afshāri), 212–13
Bujnūrd (Khūrasān), 157
Būlli (Qashqaī), Plate 295
Burr, Dr. Malcolm: on cochineal and lac, 33–4; on *kermes* insect dye, 159 n.
Burūjird, 145
Burūjirdī (Kashān merchant), 334
Bushruiyeh (Khūrasān), 189

C

Castelli, Nearco and John, at Kermān, 202
Chahār Lang, sub-division of Bakhtiari, 310 n.
Chahār Mahāl: "Bakhtiari" weaves of, 307, 309–12, Plates 354–64; Seljūks settle in?, 27; Mina Khanī design in, 43

375

Chahār-rā or Charrāh (Hamadān): black-ground rugs, 94; weave Sarūks, 138
Chahār Shotūr (Chahār Mahāl); Plates 358–9
Chardin, le Chevalier (seventeenth century): mentions Isfahān court factory 5; Kashān craftsmanship, 11; describes Tabrīz, 53; Kermān carpets, 200; Isfahān, 303 n.
Chatrūd (Kermān), 203
Constantinople, becomes world market for carpets, 56
Curzon, Lord (*Persia*): on Great Desert, 198 n.; Kermān shawls, 201; Shirāz, 282; Isfahān, 303 n.

D

Daghadaghabād (Hamadān), 92
Damāq (Hamadān), 94
Darabjīrd (Fārs), carpets before fourteenth century, 283
Darashūrī, sub-tribe of Qashqaī, 286
Dashtab (Afshārī), Plate 276
Dastajīrd (Hamadān), 92
Deh Bīd (Fārs), Plate 322
Dehāj (Afshārī), Plate 283
Deh Shotorān (Afshārī), Plates 277, 282
Derazi (Khamseh Confederation, Fārs), Plate 310
Derbend (Caucasus), cheap rugs of, 89
Dergezin or Deryazin (Hamadān): sixteenth-century silk carpet from?, 4, 89; were best weavers of Hamadān, 91; now produce poor rugs for export, 92
Destgird (Chahār Mahāl), Plate 363
Dewziah (Kermān), 203
Dilmaghānī family (Tabrīz merchants), 56 n.
Dohūk (Khūrasān), Arab rugs of, 189
Dorūkhsh (Qaināt), 171–2; carpet in Meshed museum, 170
Dulakhor (Arāk), weave Mūshkabāds and Mahāls, 138–40

E

Eastern Rug and Trading Co. of New York, at Kermān, 202
Ehrabi family (Tabrīz merchants), 56 n.
Emogli (Meshed weaver), 169, 203, 363, Plate 164
Euan-Smith, Col. (1871), on Kermān, 201
Everū (Hamadān), 95

F

Famenin (Hamadān), old carpets attributed to, 92
Fārs Province, 280–90; ninth-century rugs from, 2, and thirteenth-century, 3; Shirāz carpets woven in, 23; Herātī designs in, 38; Jōshaqānī design unknown in, 51; "Hen" motif, 213–14; Boteh designs, Plate 21; rugs rich in motifs, 51; characteristic colour, 60; single wefts, 95; Fārs and Hamadān tribal rugs compared, 96; horizontal looms, 22; Turkish tribes of, 27
Farsī Madān, sub-tribe of Qashqaī, 286
Fasā (Fārs), carpets before fourteenth century, 283
Ferahān (Arāk): weave Sarūks, Mūshkabāds and Mahāls, 138–40; Herātī design at, 37, Plate 18
Fereidān district (Arāk): Turkish and Georgian, 139; Armenian and Bakhtiari villages of, 143
Ferman Ferma (Governor of Kermān), 201
Fīn (Kashān), 334
Firdaus or Tūn (Khūrasān): Arab rugs of, 187–8; use "Bokhara" design, 186
Forūtah (Qaināt), 174
Fritz and La Rue Co. of New York, at Kermān, 202

G

Gallehzān Namadī, sub-tribe of Qashqaī, 286
Gallehzān Oghrī, sub-tribe of Qashqaī, 286
Garrod, Dr. Oliver, on Fārs, 284 n.
Genjeh (Caucasus), Turkish knot used, 26
Gentleman, Mr. Ebenezer, 136–7
Georavān, alternative name for Herīz designs, 41, 61
Ghazān Khan, Il-Khani (1295–1304), Fārs rugs of, 3
Ghiordes (Anatolia), Turkish knot used, 26
Ghūzz tribes (Turkey), tribal marks of, 51
Gishni (Chahār-rā), Plates 303, 315
Gōk (Kermān), 203
Gombad-i-Kabūs (Turkoman town), 155–7
Gomshān (Gurgān), 157
Gondashtli (Qashqaī), Plate 297
Goshnaqūn (Fārs), Plate 321
Gouvea (1603), visited Yezd, 214 n.
Gunabād (Qaināt), 171
Gundijān (Fārs), 283
Gurānī tribe (Kurdish), 120, 126
Gurgān (formerly Asterabād), 155–7

H

Haft Lang, sub-division of Bakhtiari, 310 n.
Hajibād (Chahār Mahāl), Plate 355
Hajji Mollah Hassan (merchant), revived Kashān carpet industry, 334
Hamadān Province: village industry, 90–6; town industry, 96–9; famed for cheap rugs, 89; history, 87–8; Afghan conquest, 5; Seljūks settled in, 27; villages speak Turkish, town Persian, 87; sixteenth-century silk carpet from? 4; Turkish knot used, 10, 26, 89, 95; Herātī design in, 38; Boteh, 38; Mina Khānī, 43; Bid Majnūn, 49; Harshang design in Turkish villages, 49; Jōshaqānī design, 50; oak-bark dye, 32; characteristic colour, 60; Tabrīz loom used, 58; carpets wear well, 59
Hassan Khan (Kermān designer), 207; photograph, Plate 196; Plates 185, 203, 250
Hassanzaī tribe (Balūchi), 185
Helmānd delta, Balūchi tribes of, 187
Helvāī (Bijār), Plate 126
Herāt (Afghanistān): once capital of Khūrasān, 37, 164; carpets never made there?, 163–4; name probably given to products of Khūrasān, 164; early "Herāt" carpets described, 164; Vienna carpet probably not Herāt, 13, 166; tradition of Herāt carpets made in Qaināt, 171; see also under *Herātī Designs* in General Index
Herīz area, 61–7, 312; characteristics of, 60, 61; Herātī designs in, 38; rectilinear medallion-and-corner design, 41, 63; Mina Khānī, 43; Harshang design in Turkish villages, 49; Jōshaqānī design, 50; Turkish knot used, 26, 61
Herki tribe (Kurdish), 126
Hūdk (Kermān), 203
Hulagū (Fārs and Khūzistān), 284, 289
Huzaras, Afghan tribe, 163

I

Ibn Batūta (fourteenth-century Arab geographer), mentions Bakhtiari rug, 3
Ibn Hawkal (Arab geographer, A.D. 978): mentions Sarāb, 67; Qaīn, 171; Turshīz, 173; Tabas, 189
Ibrahimabād (Arāk), weave Mūshkabāds, 139

INDEX OF PLACES, TRIBES AND PERSONS

Ibrahim Rizai (Tabrīz designer), Plates 62-4, 162
Idhej (now Izeh, Bakhtiari town), fourteenth-century rug at, 3
Imamzadeh (Hamadān), Boteh Kharqaī design, 94
Injilās (Hamadān), 91; high uniform standard of, 95
Ipekji family (Tabrīz merchants), 56 n.
Iqdār, sub-tribe of Qashqaī, 286
Isfahān, 307-9; history and description, 303-6; Shah Abbas moves capital to, and founds court factory at, 5, 10; "Vase" carpets possibly made at, 17; Shah Abbasī designs at, 43; Bid Majnūn unknown, 49; Persian knot used, 27; cotton and cotton mills, 25; imports wool from Kermān, 204; name applied to Meshed Turkibaffs, 168 n.
Ismail, Shah (1499-1524), restores Persian independence, founds Sefavi dynasty, 4, 52, *et passim*
Istahri (tenth-century geographer), mentions Fārs rugs, 2

J

Jacoby, Heinrich, 210
Jadid, name given Meshed community of Jewish ancestry, 163
Jafarbaī, Turkoman tribe, 157
Jaffi, Kurdish tribe, 120, 126
Jahrūm (Fārs), carpets before fourteenth century, 283
Jakins, Mr. H. G. (Consul at Shirāz), 284 n.
Jan Begī, Balūchi tribe, 185
Jangāl, Balūchi tribes at, 185
Jan Mirzaī, Balūchi tribe, 185
Japalāk (Arāk): weave Mūshkabāds, 138; inhabitants return to U.S.S.R., 143
Jarghalān (Turkoman district), 157
Jirūft (Kermān), wool of, 204
Jōshaqān, or Jōshaqān Qāli, 312-14, 307; home of the Jōshaqānī design (*q.v.* in General Index), 49 and n.; not the origin of the rose-ground Vase carpet, 17
Jozān (Malayer), 100, 312; Plate 108
Juimānd (Qaināt), 171
Jūlfa (Isfahān), 143
Jupār (Kermān), 203, 205

K

Kabūtarhang (Hamadān), 92-3, 91
Kahnuk (Kermān), 203
Kalajūk (Khamseh, Hamadān), Plate 93

Kalhors, Kurdish tribe, 126
Karabāgh (Caucasus): Turkish knot used, 26; Harshang design at, 49
Karajā (Herīz), 62, 63; single wefts, 58; Plate 66
Kara-Kalpāk (U.S.S.R.), 155; Turkish knot used, 26
Karftar (Fārs), Plate 327
Kashān, 333-7; seventeenth-century carpet from, 8; birthplace of Maqsūd, 10; who wove "Ardebil" carpet, possibly here, 11; all-silk Hunting carpet made here?, 11; Boteh design at, 38; Shah Abbasī designs, 43; Bid Majnūn unknown, 49; Jōshaqānī design, 50; Persian knot used, 27; silk rugs made, 25; fine stitch, 99, 203-4; cotton and cotton mills, 25
Kashgār (U.S.S.R.), Turkish knot used, 26
Kashmār, see *Turshīz*
Kazāk (Caucasus), Turkish knot used, 26
Kazvīn: Sefavi carpets not woven at, 10; cotton and cotton mills, 25, 53; spinning factory, 58; name wrongly given to "Alvānd" carpets, 98; capital of Persia for brief period, 10
Kemereh district (Arāk), 142-4, 141, 138; Armenian villages of, 143
Kendrick, A. F.: translated *Old Oriental Carpets*, vi, 7; on "Chelsea" carpet, 13; on "Vase" carpets, 17 n.
Kerbelai, Mohammed Ali (Kermān designer), Plates 206, 258
Kerdar (Hamadān), "lightning" design at, 94, Plate 90
Kermān Province, 200-14; history and description, 197-9; "Vase" carpets made in?, 17 n.; designs, 206-9; pre-eminent in design, 99; Boteh designs, 38, Plate 21; Shah Abbasī designs, 43; Bid Majnūn, 49; and Jōshaqānī designs unknown, 51; characteristic colour, 60; dyes, 209-10; madder, 31; indigo, 33; cochineal and lac, 33; Persian knot, 27, Plate 14; *juftī* knot, 210-11; village curvilinear weaves, 35; ground looms, 22; comb-beaters, 24; trimming shears, 25; cotton, 25; dependence on U.S. market, 362; Afshāri (*q.v.*) tribes of, 212-14
Kermanshāh, market for Kurdish wools, 98, 58, 204
Kevelli (Fārs), Plate 317
Kezzāz (Arāk), weave Sarūks, 138-9
Khaf, Balūchi tribe at, 185

Khamenei, Hajji Jelil (Meshed weaver), 169, 363, Plate 163
Khamseh Confederation (Fārs), 287-9, 284; Plates 301-15
Khamseh district (Hamadān), 91, 93-4, Plates 92-5
Khanabād (Hamadān), 92
Khashem Khan (Kermān designer), 207, Plates 232, 248
Khonsār (Arak), weave Sarūks, 138-9
Khoy, wool, 58
Khūrasān: see *Meshed* and *Balūchi Tribes*; early nineteenth-century carpets, 170; Herātī design in, 36; Boteh designs, Plates 21-2; cultivated weld, 32; use of cochineal and lac, 33; *juftī* knot, 27, Plate 14; wool from, 166-7
Khūzistān: indigo, 33; administration, 289
Kizil Ayāk (U.S.S.R.), 155; Turkish knot used, 26
Kobra Khanūm (Hamadān weaver), 97
Kolah-derazī, Balūchi tribe, 185
Kozlor, 2
Kubā (Caucasus): Turkish knot used, 26; cheap rugs of, 89; link with Fārs, 290 n.
Kuhgalū, Lūri tribe, 312, 286
Kuhpayeh (Kermān), 203
Kurdistān (Persian): Kurdish weavers, 119-26; Mina Khanī design from?, 42; Bid Majnūn, 43; oakbark dye used, 32; market at Hamadān, 89-90
Kurkheillī (Salar Khanī), Balūchi tribe, 185
Kurshul (Fārs), Plate 311
Kutlū (Afshāri), Plates 274-5

L

Lab-u-Mahdi (Fārs), Plates 307-8
Lahore (India), carpets in Meshed museum, 169
Laver, mispronunciation of Ravār (*q.v.*), 200 n.
Laverdāni (Fārs), Plate 309
Lecoq, 2
Le Strange (*The Lands of the Eastern Caliphate*), 67 n., 155, 160 n., 171 nn., 173 n., 198, 200, 210 n., 281, 283-4
Lilihān (Arāk), 138; name given Armenian weaves of Kemereh, 143
Lūristān, oak bark from, for dyeing, 32
Lūri tribes: of Fārs, 284, 288, 289; near Isfahān, 307, 312; Lūri related to Kurds, 119
Lūt Desert, 188-9

M

Mahajirān (Arāk), weave best Sarūks, 139

Mahāl: trade name for one kind of Arāk carpet, 136–40, 141; name may not derive from Mahallāt, 139; Gol Henāī design, 49; Jōshaqānī design, 50

Mahallāt (Arāk), Sarūks woven in, 138–9

Mahān (Kermān), 199, 203, 205

Mahmedoff family (Tabrīz merchants), 56 n.

Mahvalat (Qaināt): Balūchi tribe at, 185; factory at, 173–4

Makū, wool from, 58, 61

Malayer, 99–100; Bid Majnūn design in, 49; market at Hamadān, 89; Plates 104–10

Malcolm, Sir John; description of eighteenth-century Persia, 5, 200

Maligandeh (Fārs), Plate 323

Mamaghāni family (Tabrīz merchants), 56 n.

Mamassani, Lūrī tribe of Fārs, 284, 289

Manizān (Malayer), 100, Plate 108

Mankowski, Tadeusz, 8 n.

Maqsūd (weaver), wove the "Ardebil" carpet (1539), 8, 10

Maravehtepeh (Turkoman town), 157

Marco Polo, 200

Marling, Sir Charles, 201

Martin, Dr. F. R., 7, 11

Mashād (Kashān), 335

Mazabād (Kermān), 203

Mazanderān Province: madder from, 31; cotton mills, 25

Mazidi (Fārs), Plate 314

McGee, Mr. J. I., of Shīrāz Consulate, 284 n.

Mehmelbaff (Meshed weaver), 169, 363

Mehribān (Hamadān), 93–4; madder-dyeing technique, 32

Mehribān (Herīz), 64, 61

Meimeh (Jōshaqān), 314

Merv (U.S.S.R.): "Bokhara" rugs of, 159, 155; Turkish knot used, 26

Meshed (Khūrasān capital), 163–70; history and description, 160–3; Farsibaff and Turkibaff, 166; Vienna carpet from?, 13; Shrine Collection, 169–70 (see also under *Museums* in General Index); Nadir Shah's capital, 160; Herātī design, 38; medallion-and-corner, 41; Shah Abbāsī, 43; Bid Majnūn unknown, 49; characteristic colour, 60; cochineal dyeing technique affects quality, 34; Persian knot used, 27; market for East Persian weaves, 166; dependence on Western markets, 363; cotton, 25; exports wool to Kermān, 204; decline in design, 363

Minorsky, Prof. V., vi, 51, 52 n., 53 n., 94; translator of *Hudūd-al-'Alam*, 2 n.; on Mongol invasions, 2 n.; on Balūchi tribes, 185

Mirza Ali Ekber (Tabrīz merchant), at Kermān and Kashān, 202

Mishkān (Kashān), 335

Mohammedabād, Plate 281

Mohsen Khan (Kermān designer), 207

Morris, William: advised purchase of "Ardebil" carpet, 8; former owner of rose-ground Vase carpet, 13

Mostaufi, Nasrullah, of Ahwaz, on derivation of "Boteh Mīrī", 144

Mosūl (Irāq), misnomer for Hamadān village rugs, 91

Mūd (Qaināt), 172

Mukaddasi (tenth-century geographer): mentions Fārs carpets, 2; and Qaināt carpets, 3, 171; Turshīz, 173; Tūn, 187; Tabas, 189; Ravar, 201

Muratovitz (Armenian merchant, 1601), buys Kashān carpet, 8

Mūshkabād, trade name for one kind of Arāk carpet, 136–9, 141; Mina Khānī design, 42; Gol Henāī, 49; Jōshaqānī, 50

Mustaufi (geographer, 1340): mentions Sarāb, 67; Sarūk, 140; Turshīz, 173

Muzaffar-ud-din, Shah (1900), discourages aniline dyes, 29

N

Nadir Qūli, Shah (1736–47): ejects Afghans, 5; Turks, 53

Nāfār tribe (Khamseh Confederation, Fārs), 288–9

Naīn, 314, 307; recent carpets, 57; characteristic colour, 60; Persian knot used, 27

Nasirabād (Kashān), 335

Nasir-i-Khusraw (geographer, 1052): describes Tūn, 187; Tabas, 189

Nasir-ud-din, Shah, discourages aniline dyes, 29

Nasratabad, see *Zabol*

Natanz (Kashān), 355, Plate 408

Nearco Castelli and Brothers, 202

Nenej (Malayer), 100

Nerīz (Fārs), Plates 324–5

Nīshapūr (Khūrasān): Balūchi tribal rugs of, 185–6; wool, 166

Noberān (Hamadān), 94

Nūghāb (Qaināt), Herātī design at, 171

Nūshabād (Kashān), 334

O

Ostad Mohammed Ali (Tabrīz dyer), 66

P

Pahlavi Diz (Gurgān), 157

Paul Simon of Jesus and Mary (Carmelite Father), visited Kashān 1607, 11

Peter of St. Andrew (Carmelite Father), visited Kashān 1607, 11

Pir Islami (Fārs), Plate 302

Pope, A. Upham: contributor to *A Survey of Persian Art*, vi, 8 n.; on Dergezin, 4 n.; mistaken attribution of carpets by, 13, 17, 49 n., 62 n.; on Jōshaqān, 313 n.

Q

Qaīn: no longer chief town of the Qaināt, 171; antique Khūrasān carpets and *Kellegis* from, 170–1; Balūchi tribe at, 185; Herātī design at, Plate 17

Qaināt, the (Khūrasān), 170–3; tenth-century carpets, 2, 3; early "Herāt" carpets from, 163–4; Herātī design at, 38; Boteh Kharqāī designs, 38; antique Mina Khānī design, Plate 25

Qajār dynasty, 53, 54, 88, 197, 281, 303, 371

Qamsār (Kashān), 335

Qashqāī, Turkish tribe transplanted to Fārs, 27, 284–7: Plates 293–300

Qashqūli, Qashqāī sub-tribe, 286

Qefarūkh or Qaverūkh (Chahār Mahāl), 311; Plate 364

Qorveh (Hamadān), 91

Qūchān, wool, 157, 166

Qulyahi (Kurdistān), 126, 120; Plates 128, 130

Qūm, 338–40, Plates 410–19; new variations of Boteh design at, 38, Plates 21–2; recent carpets, 57; characteristic colour, 60; Persian knot used, 27

R

Rafsinjān or Bahramabād (Kermān), 203, 205; wool, 204

Rahāq (Kashān), 335

Rahimī, Qashqāī sub-tribe, 286

Rahim Khānī, Balūchi tribe, 185

Ravānd (Kashān), 334

Ravar (Kermān), 203, 205, 312; antique carpets, 200–1; in Meshed museum, 170; Plates 199–201

Razān (Hamadān), 91
Reihān (Arāk), 144, 138; Jōshaqānī design at, 50
Riza Bahramand (Kermān designer), see *Ali Riza Bahramand*
Rizaieh, wool used at Tabrīz, 58
Riza Pahlavi, Shah (1921–41), 53, 88, 96, 119, 126, 135, 156–7, 173, 202–3, 285–8, 303–4
Robinson, Messrs. Vincent, and Co., sold "Ardebil" carpet, 8
Roshkar (Khūrasān), Balūchī tribe at, 185
Rūdbār, wool, 204
Rūkh, Shah (1408–46), sumptuary carpets of, 3, 35, 163

S

Saadatabad (Afshārī), Plate 198
Saarabad (Afshārī), Plate 279
Sabsawār (Khūrasān), wool, 166, 204
Sadaqiani family (Tabrīz merchants), 56 n.
Safi Khānī, Qashqāī sub-tribe, 286
Saidabad or Sirjān (Kermān), 212–13
Sainsaraī or Sinsireh (Herīz), 64
Salar Khānī, see *Kurkheillī*
Salmas, wool, 58
Salmasī family (Tabrīz merchants), 56 n.
Sanandaj, 120; and see under *Senneh*
Sarāb (Herīz), 62, 67; Boteh design, 38, Plates 22, 67
Saraī (Herīz), 64
Sarākhs (Khūrasān), Balūchī tribes of, 185–6
Sarasiab (Kermān), 203
Sard Rūd (Hamadān), 91, 94
Sarre, Friedrich, monograph on old carpets, vi
Sarūk (Arāk), 136–8, 140–1, 312; trade-name given successively to three different weaves, 140; modern Sarūk design not Persian, 141, 92, 99, 363, Plates 141–52; carpets wear well, 59; Boteh design, Plate 21
Saūjbulāgh (Kurdistān): Mina Khānī design, 42; Harshang design, Plate 33
Saveh (Hamadān), 94, 90
Sefavi dynasty, 3–5, 49, 161, 169, 306, 371; great carpets of this period, 7–18
Sefiabad (Hamadān), 94
Seistān, Balūchī tribes of, 187, 185–6
Seljūk sultans, 3, 27, 87, 163, 173, 197, 281, 370
Senjabi, Kurdish tribe, 126, 120
Senneh (Kurdistān), 120–2; "Senneh" a misnomer for Persian knot, 26; since only Turkish knot used, 27, 122; Herātī design in, 38; Boteh Kharqaī, 38; marketed at Hamadān, 89; capital of Persian Kurdistān, 120
Seraband (near Arāk), 144–5, 138; alternative name for Boteh Mīrī design, 38, Plate 20; characteristic colour, 60; Seljūk settle in?, 27
"Serape" = Sarāb (*q.v.*), 61 n.
Seredār (Kermān), 203
Shahr Kūrd (Chahār Mahāl), 310–11
Shahseven tribes (Hamadān), wool, 65, 91
Shalamzār (Chahār Mahāl), Plate 356
Shām (Tabrīz), 3, 52, 54
Sheikh Hossein (Kermān designer), 207, Plates 211, 217–18, 222, 226, 239, 249
Sherley, Sir Anthony, on Kashān carpets, 11
Sherley, Sir Robert, mentions Isfahān court factory, 5
Shīrāz (capital of Fārs): "Shīrāz" rugs marketed but not made in Shīrāz, 284, 289; largest of ground-loom products, 22–3; Persian capital in eighteenth century, 5
Shirishabād (Kurdistān), 126, Plates 129, 131
Shirvān (Caucasus): Turkish knot used, 26; Harshang design in, 49; cheap rugs of, 89; link with Fārs, 290 n.
Shish-Būlūkī, Qashqāī sub-tribe, 286
Shuleh Sarūkh (Fārs), Plate 320
Shūlī, Turkish tribe of Kermān, 212
Sigismund III Vasa, King of Poland (1601), buys Kashān carpet, 8
Sijadi (of Meshed), on Balūchī tribes, 185
Sirānd (Fārs), Plate 326
Sirjān, 198, 212–13
Songūr (Kurdistān), 126
Stebbing, E. (*The Holy Carpet of the Mosque at Ardebil*), 6 n.
Stein, Sir Aurel, 2
Stevens, George: introduces scale paper designs to Arāk, 140 n.; pioneer in Kermān carpet industry, 202
Strauss, Oscar, of Messrs. Ziegler, at Arāk, 136
Sultānabad, now Arāk (*q.v.*), founded nineteenth century, 10
Sultan Mohammed (court painter), ? designed all-silk Hunting carpet, 11
Sykes, Major (later Sir) P. M., various works quoted, 162 and n., 171, 198 n., 199 n., 201, 202

T

Tabas (Khūrasān), Arab tribes of, 187–9, Plate 174
Tabatabaī (Kashān merchant), 334
Tabrīz (Azerbaijān), 54–61; history and description, 52–4; Turkish-speaking city since eleventh century, 52; capital of Mongol Empire in thirteenth century, 3, 52; Sefavi capital, 4, 53; Afghan conquest of, 5, 53; Russian conquest (1827) and later interventions, 53, 57; "Ardebil" carpet not made at, 10; led modern revival of carpet industry, 6, 54–6; influence on design, 42, 60; Herātī design at, 38; "Samovar" border, 38; Boteh design, 38; medallion-and-corner designs, 41; Mina Khānī, 42; Shah Abbāsī, 43; Bid Majnūn, 49; Jōshaqānī design, 50; Tabrīz loom, 23–4, 58, Plate 10; Tabrīz hook, 24, 59, Plate 12; hook precludes use of *juftī* knot, 60, 367; trimming shears, 25; Turkish knot used, 26, 61; dyeing methods, 60; characteristics of Tabrīz carpets, 60–1; ingenuity pre-eminent, 99; coarse grades wear badly, 59; factories at, 56, 58, Plate 39; dependence on Western markets, 363; cotton mills, 25; influence of Tabrīzī merchants in Kermān, 201–2
Tafrish (Hamadān), 94; Plates 77, 97
Tahirabād (Kashān), 335
Tahir Zadeh Bihzad, drawings by, 43, Plates 26–31, 59, 138, 140, 148, 169, 241–4, 341, 349–53, 393–4
Tahmasp, Shah (1524–87): encouraged carpet industry, 4; great carpets made in his time, 5, 7, including "Ardebil", 8, 10, and ? all-silk Hunting carpet, 11, and a New York carpet, 18; Jōshaqān carpets in time of, 313; moved capital from Tabrīz to Kasvīn, 53
Tattersall, C. E. C., 7; on "Chelsea" carpet, 13
Taushandjian, Messrs. K. S., of New York, 141
Tavernier, J. B., mentions Isfahān court factory, 5, 303 n.
Tehrān, 94, 96, 169, 203, 209, 214, Plates 368, 370; Coloured Plate facing p. 336
Tehrānji family (Tabrīz merchants), 56 n.
Tekentepeh (Kurdistān), Plate 125
Tekkeh, Turkoman tribe, 157
Timurī tribe (Khūrasān), 187; use "Bokhara" design, 186

Trenckwald, Herman, monograph on old carpets, vi
Tuisarkhān (Hamadān), 93; Plates 80, 81, 85, 86, 88
Tūn, see *Firdaus*
Tūrbat-i-Haidarī (Khūrasān): Balūchi tribes of, 185–6; wool, 166
Tūrbat-i-Shaikhjām (Khūrasān): Balūchi tribes of, 185; Timūri tribes of, 187
Turkman-Chai, Treaty of, 53
Turkoman weaving area, 155–9
Turshīz, now Kashmār (Khūrasān), 173; Balūchi tribal rugs of, 185–6; carpets in Meshed museum, 170; markets at Meshed, 166
Tyriakian, S., responsible for modern Sarūk design, 141

U

Urdubatli family (Tabrīz merchants), 56 n.
Ushāk (Turkey): use Turkish knot; 26; Bid Majnūn design in, 49, skill, 64; compared with Bijār, 124
Uzūn Hassān, Shah (1469–78): sumptuary carpets of, 3, 36; revived Tabrīz, 52

V

Veramin (near Tehrān), Mina Khanī design at, 42

X

Xenophon, references to carpets, 1 n.

Y

Yakūt (Arab geographer, 1225): mentions carpet-weaving in Azerbaijān, 3; mentions Sarāb, 67, and Sarūk, 140
Yaqūb-Khanī, Timūri sub-tribe (Khūrasān), 187
Yezd, 214–15, 189–90, 314; Herātī design in, 38; principal market for madder, 31; cotton mill, 25; imports wool from Kermān, 204
Yomūt (Turkoman tribe), 155–9; Turkish knot used, 26
"Yoraghān", misnomer for Georavān (*q.v.*), 61 n.

Z

Zabol or Nasratabād (Khūrasān), Balūchi tribes of, 187
Zarānd (Kermān), 203, Plates 90, 91
Zaveh (Khūrasān), Balūchi tribes of, 185
Zeman Khan (Kermān designer), 207, Plate 214
Zenjān, 67, 58; alum mine at, 32 n.; "Zenjān Mosūl" rugs of Khamseh (Hamadān), 93
Ziegler and Co., Messrs.: at Arāk, 135–6, 6 n.; sold "Ardebil" carpet, 8; example of their designs, Plate 137
Zūrabād (Khūrasān), Timūri tribal rugs, 187

GENERAL INDEX

A

Alamara-i-Abbasi (Chronicles of Shah Abbas), 200
Alizarine red, 31
Alum, see *Mordants*
"Anchor" design, Plates 124, 131
Arabesques: in Vienna floral carpet, 13, Plate 4; in borders, 36; in Harshang design, 49; Plates 213, 219, 233, 234, 237, 247, 349, 352–3, 389–90, 393–5, 398
Aubusson designs copied, 203, 208
"Audience" design, Bijār, 125

B

"Bakhtiari" design, Chahār Mahāl, 312, Plates 354–64
Banque Melli, Tehrān, Dept. of Economics of, 31 n.
Barberry, see *Dyestuffs, Natural*
Bibliographies, vi
Bid Majnūn design, 43, 49, Plates 32, 56, 125
Bird of Paradise motif, 51
"Bokhara" design, 186; adopted by Yomūt Turkomans, 159, and by Balūchis, 186
Boteh designs, 38, Plates 20–2; Boteh Mīrī version, origin of name of, 144–5; at Injilās, 95; Boteh Kharqaī version at Imamzadeh, 94, and Dorūksh, 171
Bureau of Design, proposal for, 363

C

"Carpet", defined, v
Carpet washing, 57, Plate 74
Cartouche border, 36; in "Ardebil" carpet, 10
"Chestnut" pattern, see *Gol Henaī*
Chronology of the Persian carpet, 369–72
Classic Period, in Kermān, 208, Plates 210–44
Cloud-band motifs: in "Arbebil" carpet, 10; in silk Hunting carpet, 11; in Vienna animal and floral carpet, 13; in Shah Abbasi designs, 43; in Meshed museum carpet, 169: not symbolic, 51; Plates 1, 2, 4, 213, 389
Cochineal Scale insect, 34 n., and see *Dyestuffs, Natural*
"Compartment" design, Plate 224
"Covered ground" designs, Kermān, 208, Plates 245–57
"Crab" design, see *Harshang*
Cracow Cathedral, fragment of carpet in, 18
Curvilinear weaving, 35–6; scale-paper drawings essential for, 28; ? began in fifteenth century, 3, and developed under Sefavi dynasty, 4; designs converted to rectilinear (*q.v.*) by rural weavers, 63–4

D

Dating antique carpets, technique of, 7–8
Dellal (broker), 91 n.
Design, 35–51; influence of early miniature painters on, 4, 8; of Kermān shawl designs on, 207, Plates 202–8, 252; permanent influence of Sefavi period, 18; use of scale-paper patterns, 28, 35; design in Tabrīz, 60; Herīz, 63–4; Hamadān, 95–6; Senneh, 122; Bijār, 125; Arāk and the Sarūk design, 141; Turkoman, 159; Kermān, 206–9; Isfahān, 308; Chahār Mahāl, 312; Jōshaqān, 312; Kashān, 336; interchange of designs among Balūchi, 186, Afshāri, 213–14, and Fārs tribes, 290; *wagireh* system (*q.v.*), 125; decline of standards in, 363–4

Main types of conventional design (indexed separately under first name): Herātī, Mahi or Fish; Boteh, Pine or Palm (includes Boteh Mīrī—or Seraband—Boteh Kharqaī, Boteh Termeī, Boteh Bademī, Boteh Jeqaī); Harshang or Crab; Gol Henaī, Garden Balsam or Henna Flower; Medallion-and-corner or Lechek Torūnj; Mina Khani; Shah Abbasi; Bid Majnūn or Weeping Willow; and Jōshaqānī. See also *Curvilinear Weaving*; and *Rectilinear Weaving*
Detached floral designs: introduced at Arāk, 141; spread to Kermān, 208; Plates 152, 259–60, 265, 267–8
Dianil, synthetic dye, 159; and see *Dyestuffs*
Dozar, a size of rug, 91 n., 94, 374
Dūghi, rose dye, 32, 142, 143
Dyeing methods, 29–34; Tabrīz, 60; Herīz, 65–6; Dergezin, 91; Kabūtarhāng, 92–3; Tuisarkhān, 93; Senneh, 122; Bijār, 32, 125; Mūshkabāds, 139; Arāk, 142; Seraband, 145; Turkoman tribes, 159, 163–4; Meshed, 168–9; Balūchi tribes, 186; Kermān, 209–10; Afshāri tribes, 213; Qashqaī, 287; Isfahān, 308–9; Chahār Mahāl, 311–12; Jōshaqān, 313; Kashān, 336; proposals for the future, 364–5; dyeing wool before spinning, 210, Plate 16; characteristic colours of various districts, 60. See also *Mordants*

Dyestuffs:
(a) *Natural*, 29–34; cochineal used in Meshed, 168; in Dorūkhsh, 171; pernicious use of lime with cochineal, 167, 210; lac and cochineal characteristic of Sefavi carpets of East Persia, 163; *kermes* insect dye, 159; *dūghi* rose of Arāk, 32, 60, painted back after fading, 142; ferruginous litharge (*mak*) used by Balūchi, 186; vine leaves, 122; pomegranate rind, 169; barberry, 34, 172; madder, 31–2; indigo, 32–3, 142
(b) "*Aniline*" (acid and basic) dyes, defined, 29, 29–34; at Tabrīz, 60; Zenjān, 67; Kabūtarhāng, 93; Bozchelū, 94; North-East Malayer, 100; Japalāk, 138; Armenian villages, 143; Seraband, 145; Dorūkhsh, 171; Turshīz, 173; Balūchi, 186; Timurī tribes, 187; Firdaus, 188; Chahār Mahāl, 312; Kashān, 336; should be totally prohibited, 364
(c) *Synthetic* ("*chrome*"), 29–34; used at Tabrīz, 60, 66; Khamseh (Hamadān), 94; Bijār, 125; Meshed, 168; Kermān, 209–10; Isfahān, 309; Chahār Mahāl, 312; Kashān, 336; *Rouge d'Orient* used by Turkomans, 155, 159; and *Dianil*, 159; less harm done if traditional mordants used, 31, 33, 98; synthetic indigo and madder, 142, 365; alizarine red, 31, 365

E

Economics of the industry: Western influences at Tabrīz, 56–7; Sarāb, 67; Hamadān, 90, 96; Malayer, 100;

Economics of the industry: *continued*
Senneh, 122; Kurdish tribes, 126; Arāk, 136; Kermān, 202–3, 206, 211; Fārs, 291–2; Isfahān, 307–8; boom conditions in internal market under Shah Riza, 203; proposals for the future, 362–8

Elliyeh design, Hamadān, 92
Encyclopaedia of Islam, The, vii
Export figures, 30 n., 373

F

Famous antique carpets: Garden carpet of Khosrō I, 2; "Ardebil", 7–11, 13, 17–18; all-silk Hunting carpet (Vienna), 11, 18, 25, Plate 214; "Chelsea" carpet, 11, 13, 17–18; Animal and Floral (Vienna), 13, 166; Rose-ground "Vase", 13–17, 36; Milan, 17–18; Inscribed Medallion (New York), 18; Medallion (Paris), 18; Kuzekenani (Meshed), 169, Plate 164; Sigismund Vasa's, 8

Farsibaff, type of Meshed carpet, 166–8, 172
"Fish" design, see *Herātī*
Floral Period, in Kermān, 208, Plates 258–69
"Flower and Bird" design, see *Gol-i-Bolbol*
Foreign influences: *Arab*: conquest, 2; on design, 4, 18, 51; racial, 87, 186–8, 287–8. *Turkish*: Seljūks introduced Turkish knot, 26–7; Persian carpet not of Turkish origin, 2; on *Harshang* design, 49; racial, 52, 87, 124, 144, 163. *Mongol*: dominated Persia, 1220–1449, 3; Persian carpet not of Mongol origin, 2; racial, 87. *Afghan*: conquest, 5, 53, 303, 307; designs copied, 188; racial, 163. *Kurdish*: on *Mina Khani* design, 42; on *Bid Majnūn* design, 43; racial, 119–26. *Chinese*: on design, 4, 11, 18, 51, Plate 55. *Armenian*: racial, 142–3. *Near East*: as market, 61, 140, 145, 308, 314, 363. *U.S.S.R.*: Russian shawl design copied, 312, Plate 363; political, 53–4, 57, 159, and see *Tudeh Party*. "Western": effect on size and colour, 56–7; Ziegler and other firms at Arāk, 135–6; at Kermān, 211; effect of decline of European demand, 57, 166, 169, 362–3. *U.S.A.*: non-Persian *Sarūk* design invented for American market, 141, 363; spreads to Hamadān villages, 92–3, and Kashān, 336; bad dyeing encouraged, 142; at Kermān, 207–9; also, 33, 56–7, 99, 136, 140–3, 169, 202, 204, 290. *British*: 53, 56. *French*: Watteau designs, 201; Aubusson, etc., 203, 207–8, 122, Plates 261–4, 286. *German and Swiss*: 33, 56, 60

G

"Garden Balsam" design, see *Gol Henaī*
Garden Carpet of Khosrō I, 2, 370–1
Ghiordes knot, misnomer for Turkish knot (*q.v.*), 26
Gilim: defined, 28; Turkoman, 159; Balūchi, 186–7
Gol Henaī design, 49, 36, 139, Plate 34
Gol-i-Bolbol design, Senneh, 122, Plate 118
Gol-i-Mirza Ali or *Gol-i-Frank* design, Senneh and Bijār, 122, Plate 121
Gol Mohammedi design, Senneh, 122
"Grape-vine" design, Plate 104
"Guard": defined, 36; twin guard, "Ardebil" carpet, 10

H

Harshang design, 49, 36, 139, Plate 33
"Hen" design, see *Morgi Design*
"Henna Flower" design, see *Gol Henaī*
Herātī design, 36–8, 62, 94–5, 122, 125, 139, 164, 171, 186, 214, Plates 17–19, 124
Holy Carpet of the Mosque at Ardebil, The (E. Stebbing), 6 n.
Hudūd-al-'Alam (*The Regions of the World*, A.D. 892), mentions Fārs rugs, 2, 3, 283
Hunting carpets, 164, Plates 61, 65, 185, 214; see also *Shikarga*, and under *Famous Carpets*

I

Indian rugs, 25, 28
Indigo, 32–3, 142, 186, 210, 312, 365
Insect Legion, The (Dr. Burr), 33–4, 159
"Isfahān" design, see *Shah Abbasi Design*
Islim motif, 164–6, 169, Plates 161, 170

J

Jadid carpet merchants, 163
Jahizi (dowry rug), 187
Jōshaqānī design, 49–50, 36, 139, 312, 314, Plate 35
Jūftī or *jūft ilmeh* knot, see under Knots

K

Kaveshk, Qashqāi name for weld, 287
Kellegi (head piece), defined, 55; 125, 164, 171, 188, 289, Plate 38
Kenareh (side piece), defined, 55, 374, Plate 38
Kermes insect dye, 159
Kharchāng design, see *Harshang*
Knots:
(a) *Persian* (*Farsī* or "Senneh"): described, 26–7, Plate 14; used in "Ardebil" carpet, 8, 10; Arāk, 139; Balūchi, 186; Timūrī, 187; Firdaus Arabs, 188; Kermān, 205; Afshārī, 213; Khamseh (Fārs), 287–9; Jōshaqān, 313; Kashān, 11, 335
(b) *Turkish* (*Turki* or "Ghiordes"): described, 26–7, Plate 14; used in Tabrīz, 58; Herīz, 61; Hamadān, 95–7; Malayer, 99; Senneh, 122; Seraband, 145; Afshārī, 213; Fārs, 286–8; Chahār Mahāl, 311; produces heavier fabric than the Persian knot, 97
(c) *Jūftī*: explained, 27, Plate 14; serviceable carpet *can* be made with it, 172, but greatest menace to the industry, 366–7, *et passim*; cannot be tied with Tabrīz hook, 59–60, and Tabrīz therefore immune; difficulty of introducing this hook elsewhere as remedy for, 367; knot used in Kabūtarhāng, 93; Meshed Farsibaffs, 167–8; Qaināt, 171–2; Turshīz, 173; Kermān, 210–11; Isfahān, 308; Jōshaqān, 314; Kashān, 336–7; Qūm, 339; almost unknown in Yezd, 214–15, and places listed at 366
Kuzekenani, modern Meshed carpet, 169, 203, Plate 164
Kuzem (lamb's wool), 58

L

Labour conditions: at Tabrīz, 60; Hamadān, 99; Kermān, 206 Kashān, 336
Landscape design, Plate 418
"Leaf" design, see *Boteh*
Lechek Torūnj design, see *Medallion-and-corner*

GENERAL INDEX

"Lightning" design at Kerdār, 94
Looms:
   (*a*) Ground or horizontal: described, 22–3, Plates 9, 156, 173, 198, 292; used by nomad and semi-nomadic tribes, 94, 157, 186, 188, 213, 287, 289 n., 311
   (*b*) Vertical: described, 23–4, Plates 10, 11, 39, 72, 112, 135; Isfahān and Shahr Kūrd type, 311; roller-type found in towns, in Kermān villages and Jōshaqān, 313

M

Madder, dyestuff, 31–2, 142, 164, 309; see also *Dyestuffs*
Mahi design, see *Herātī*
Mak, black dye, 186
Markets, external, see under *Foreign Influences*
Materials used:
   Wool: Makū wool compared with Kurdish, Kermānshāh and Khūrasān wools, 58; lambs' wool used in fine carpets, 58; skin-wool for cheap carpets, 58, 65; bazaar yarn always poor, 91; rise in price of wool, 96, *et passim*; cotton superior to wool for warps and wefts, 97, 213; all-wool carpets of Fārs would be improved by cotton backs, 290; Bijār woollen carpets, 124–5; Khūrasān wool, 166; faulty use of, in Meshed, 167, and Birjānd, 172; Kermān wool, 204; Australian wool used at Isfahān, 308, but abandoned in Kashān, 334–5; carding plants at Tabrīz, 58; Hamadān, 98; Kermān, 204; Kashān, 335; hand carding at Meshed, 167; Plates 73, 192–4, 373
   Cotton, 25–6; and see under *Wool* above
   Silk: in fifteenth-century carpet at Tabrīz, 2, 3; in sixteenth-century carpets, 4; in "Ardebil" carpet 8; in all-silk Hunting carpet, 11; in "Chelsea" carpet, 13; in Vienna animal carpet, 13; in Milan carpet, 17; in New York carpet, 18; rarely used today, 25; silk warps at Isfahān, 308; Plates 380, 383
   Goat-hair: used by Balūchi tribes, 25, 186
   Camel-hair: rarely used, 25, 98 n.; used in prayer rugs, 187
   Jute: used in India, not Persia, 25

Cowrie shells on selvedges, Balisht, 187
"Mecca Shirāz" rugs, see *Turkī Shirāz*
Medallion-and-corner designs, 41–2, 36; Tabrīz origin of, 60; Herīz rectilinear version of, 63–4, Plates 41–2; in "Ardebil", 10, and all-silk Hunting carpets, 11; at Bozchelū, 94; Kermān, 207–8; Kashān, 336; Plates 23, 24, 102, 106, 211, 233, 234, 270–2, 337, 345, 349, 384, 389, 392, 405
Mianfarsh (middle carpet), defined, 55, Plates 38, 76, 98
Mina Khanī design, 42–3, 36, 139, Plate 25
Miniature painters, influence on design of, 4
Mir carpets, 144–5, 38
Mordants: use of alum, 31–2; omitted altogether at Tabrīz, 66–7; alum preferable with alizarine red, 365; sodium hydrosulphite used with synthetic indigo, 33; potassium bichromate with other synthetics, 29; alum from melanterite, 186
Morgi design, 213, Plate 284
Museums, famous carpets in:
   London (Victoria and Albert), 7, 8, 11, 13, 17, Plates 25, 201, 312, 367
   Vienna (National), vi, 11, 13, 166
   Milan (Poldi Pezzoli), 7, 17–18
   Berlin (National), 13
   Munich (Residenz), 8
   New York (Metropolitan Museum of Art), 18
   Philadelphia, Pa. (Williams Collection), 62 n., 92
   Paris (Musée des Arts Décoratifs), 18
   Meshed Shrine Collection, 166, 169–70, 201, Plates 17, 91, 97, 181, 295, 361, 366
   Lamm Collection, 92
   McIlhenny Collection, 92
Mustōfi border (Kashān), 336

N

Nakhcheh nevis (design writer), 99

O

Oak bark, as dyestuff, 32; and see *Dyestuffs*
Old Oriental Carpets (Vienna), vi, 8, 10 n., 208
Orthography of Persian names, v–vi
Ostad (head weaver), 99

P

"Palm" design, see *Boteh*
Panel designs, Kermān, 208, Plates 222, 225, 227, 230–1, 239, 370
"Persia" preferred to "Iran", v, 281 n.
"Persian Garden" design, Plate 220
"Picture" carpets, 36 n.
Pile, length of, 140 n.
"Pine" design, see *Boteh*
Pomegranate rind, as dyestuff, 32; and see *Dyestuffs*
"Portico" design, Plates 347, 368
Potassium bichromate as a mordant, 29
Pushti, a size of rug, 91 n., 374

Q

Qajār dynasty (1796–1925); for chronology, see 371
Quality expressed in knots per square inch: "Ardebil" carpet, 8; all-silk Hunting carpet, 11; other Sefavi carpets, 13, 17, 18; Kuzekenani carpet, 169; Tabrīz carpets, 58 n.; Malayer, 100; Arāk, 136, 139–40; Kermān, 206; Isfahān, 308; Jōshaqān, 314; Kashān, 335–6; Qūm, 339; figures given are theoretical, 59, 206

R

Rectilinear weaving, 35, Plates 43–4, 51; rectilinear version of Herātī design, Plate 19, and of medallion-and-corner design, 41, 63–4, Plates 41–2; of Shah Abbasī design, 43; Bid Majnūn and Harshang designs rectilinear, 49; all tribal rugs rectilinear, 287; Bijār, 125; Afshāri, 213; Chahār Mahāl, 311; Jōshaqān, 17, 312; early forms of, 3. See also *Curvilinear Weaving*
Reseda lutuola, weld, 32; and see *Dyestuffs*
Rial, value of, 99 n.
Rouge d'Orient, synthetic dye, 155, 159; and see *Dyestuffs*
Rubia tinctorium, madder, 31–2; and see *Dyestuffs*
"Rug", defined, v

S

"Samovar" border, see *Tosbagheh*
Sarūk design: in Arāk, 141; Kashān, 336; Plate 152
Savonnerie designs copied, 203, 208

Sayyid, defined, 187 n.
School of Art, Tehrān, 43, 363
Sefavi dynasty; for chronology, see 371
Selvedges, how formed, 28
"Senneh" knot; see *Knots:* (a) *Persian*
"Seraband pine" design, see *Boteh Miri*
Shagird (apprentice), 99, 60
Shah Abbasi design, 43, 36, 139, 336, Plates 26–30
Shawl Period, in Kermān, 207–8, Plates 202–8
Shikarga (hunting carpet), 164
"Snake" motif, see *Islim*
Sodium hydrosulphite, used with synthetic indigo, 33
Survey of Persian Art, A, vi, 8 n., 17, 49 n., 210 n.
Symbolism in design, 51

T

Tachardia lacca, insect producing lac dye, 33
Talim (written pattern, India), 28
Torūnj, defined, 42
Tosbagheh border, 38, Plate 18

"Tree" design, 186–7, 207, 312, Plates 204, 338, 342, 383, 399
"Triclinium" design, Bijār, 125
Tūdeh Party, 57, 123, 170, 206
"Tulip" design, Plate 129
Turkibaff, type of Meshed carpet, 166–8
Turki Shirāz rugs of Qashqaī, 286
"Turtle" border, see *Tosbagheh*

V

"Vase" design, 13, 17, 36, 43, 199, Plates 5, 49, 101, 205, 243, 275, 347
Vekilli design (Senneh), 122, Plate 120
Vienna Book, The, see *Old Oriental Carpets*
Vine leaves as dyestuff, 32; and see *Dyestuffs*

W

Wagireh system: defined, 125; used by Ziegler, 136; 290
Walnut husks, as dyestuff, 32; and see *Dyestuffs*
Washing carpets, technique, 56–7, Plate 74

Weaving:
  Instruments used, 24, 25, Plates 13, 46, 133, 195, 198; Tabrīz hook, 24, 59, 168, 367, Plate 12
  Techniques, 27–8; Bijār, 124; Meshed Farsibaff, 168; Plates 112, 135, 156, 173, 195, 198. See also *Looms, Materials Used*, etc.
"Weeping Willow" design, see *Bid Majnūn*
Wefts: how to distinguish single and double weft, 95; single wefts at Karajā, 58, 62; Bilverdī, 63; Tuisarkhān, 93; in Hamadān villages, and tribal rugs, 95; North West Malayer, 100; Senneh, 122; Armenian villages, 143; Turkoman, 157; Balūchi tribes, 186; Arabs of Firdaus, 188; Afshāri, 213; Khamseh Confederation, 205; treble weft, Kermān, 205; Bijār, 124–5
Weld as dyestuff, 32; and see *Dyestuffs*
Wool, see under *Materials Used*

Z

Zar-o-cherek, a size of rug, 91 n., 374
Zar-o-nim, a size of rug, 91 n., 374
Zil-i-Soltan design, Plate 77